Religion and the Culture of Print
in Modern America

PRINT CULTURE HISTORY
IN MODERN AMERICA

Series Editors

James P. Danky, Wayne A. Wiegand, and Christine Pawley

Libraries as Agencies of Culture
Edited by Thomas Augst and Wayne Wiegand

*Purity in Print: Book Censorship in America from the Gilded Age
to the Computer Age, 2nd edition*
Paul S. Boyer

Religion and the Culture of Print in Modern America
Edited by Charles L. Cohen and Paul S. Boyer

*Women in Print: Essays on the Print Culture of American Women
from the Nineteenth and Twentieth Centuries*
Edited by James P. Danky and Wayne A. Wiegand

Bookwomen: Creating an Empire in Children's Book Publishing, 1919–1939
Jacalyn Eddy

Apostles of Culture: The Public Librarian and American Society, 1876–1920
Lora Dee Garrison

Religion and the Culture of Print in Modern America

Edited by
Charles L. Cohen
and
Paul S. Boyer

The University of Wisconsin Press

This book was published with the support of the **Anonymous Fund of the College of Letters and Science** and the **Lubar Institute for the Study of the Abrahamic Religions** at the University of Wisconsin–Madison.

Lubar Institute
for the Study of the Abrahamic Religions

The University of Wisconsin Press
1930 Monroe Street, 3rd Floor
Madison, Wisconsin 53711–2059

www.wisc.edu/wisconsinpress/

3 Henrietta Street
London WC2E 8LU, England

In collaboration with
Center for the History of Print Culture in Modern America
A joint project of the Wisconsin Historical Society and the University of Wisconsin–Madison
http://slisweb.lis.wisc.edu/~printcul/

1   3   5   4   2

Printed in the United States of America

Library of Congress Cataloging-in-Publication Data
Religion and the culture of print in modern America /
edited by Charles L. Cohen and Paul S. Boyer.
p.   cm. — (Print culture history in modern America)
Includes bibliographical references and index.
ISBN 0–299–22570–4 (cloth: alk. paper)
1. Religious literature — Publishing — United States.
2. Religious institutions — United States — Publishing.
3. Tract societies — United States.
I. Cohen, Charles Lloyd.   II. Boyer, Paul S.   III. Series.
Z286.R4R43   2008
200.973 — dc22   2007040160

To **Jim Danky**
—scholar, librarian, editor, and friend—
for his tireless dedication
to the Center for the History of Print Culture in Modern America
and, with Wayne Wiegand,
the book series Print Culture History in Modern America

Contents

Preface

Charles L. Cohen

The history of print culture in the United States has garnered growing scholarly attention over the past several decades, its coming of age signaled by the American Antiquarian Society's ongoing multivolume *A History of the Book in America*.[1] During the same span, religious history—legitimized intellectually by Sidney Ahlstrom's prize-winning *A Religious History of the American People*[2] and boosted professionally by religion's increasing prominence in public policy and discourse—has moved from a relatively narrow focus on denominational and institutional history to wide-ranging analyses of how spirituality permeates and affects social life. Given the interest in interdisciplinarity that now characterizes much historical research, it was perhaps inevitable that laborers in these two vineyards should start cultivating each other's vines. The collaboration thus far has produced some superior harvests, but for whatever reason, the vintages have clustered in the sixteenth through early nineteenth centuries.[3] Rectifying this chronological imbalance provides reason enough for the present volume, the first to survey the history of religious print culture in postbellum and modern America.

American religious history from the colonial period onward is, as Paul Boyer and I assert in part I, incomprehensible without reference to the centrality of print materials, and the progress of American print culture has owed much to the religious texts that have provided much of its intellectual substance and wares. Given the historical accidents of European settlement patterns, I maintain, a particularly Reformed Protestant bibliocentrism laid the foundation for a religious print culture that was anchored in the text of scripture, although it ranged, as Boyer details, across a variety of genres and formats. By the mid-nineteenth century, an informed observer might reasonably have assumed that Americans' robust religious print culture reflected—indeed, depended upon—Protestantism's continuing dominance and coherence. The future, however, disproved any such hypothesis. After the Civil War, an influx of non-Protestant populations and the rise of scientific naturalism reshaped the nation's religious landscape, and though the Bible's popularity never waned, Protestants feuded about its capacity for guiding the faithful through modern times. Yet even as Protestant unity fractured, the use of printed media to communicate religious messages ballooned. Although this collection provides no unifying explanation for that relationship, it does suggest that the increasing diversity of American spirituality has gone hand in hand with an ever-expanding supply of literary materials encouraging, explaining, and debating religion.

The essays that follow reveal much, albeit not all, of that diversity. They include pieces dedicated to Jewish, Mormon, and New Age print culture, but none devoted solely to Catholicism (though see Matthew Hedstrom's discussion of Thomas Merton in his piece on psychology and mysticism in the 1940s).[4] This lacuna reflects the prevailing underrepresentation of Catholicism within American religious history as a whole; notwithstanding the flourishing but relatively small group of historians working on the Church and the reception accorded recent work by the likes of Jay Dolan, John McGreevy, and Leslie Tentler,[5] scholars in general treat Catholicism like a wallflower while crowning Protestantism the belle of the ball. Frustratingly, not a single proposal among the dozens submitted for the conference from which this book has emerged dealt with the Roman Church, a sin of omission compounded by the editors' sin of (non-)commission in failing to solicit a possible addition while the book was in production. American Catholic print culture still awaits its full due.

Happily, that situation is improving. At the 2006 conference sponsored by the Center for the History of Print Culture in Modern America, Robert Orsi, the preeminent scholar of popular Catholicism in the United States, delivered a keynote address that illuminated the devotional world of Catholic youth while challenging critical assumptions on which the study of religion in print has rested.[6] Dispelling notions that the Church's traditional suspicion of the word made text minimized written language as a vehicle of faith, Orsi discovered a juvenile culture of print so populated by books, magazines, cards, certificates, scapulars, and guides that he organized them into no fewer than twenty-five different categories. Even more striking are the theoretical implications he has drawn from this evidentiary array.

Following the Jesuit scholar Walter Ong, Orsi characterizes Catholicism as a religion of incarnation, a faith in which the supernatural interpenetrates the natural and material objects can embody sacred presence. This perspective puts the Roman Church at odds with both Protestantism, which has historically denigrated such attitudes as "superstition," and Euro-American scholarship in religious studies, which, greatly informed by Protestant distrust of divine manifestations, has classified Catholic practice as premodern.[7] Divine immanence suffuses American Catholic print culture; rather than treating texts merely as objects whose meaning can be extracted by reading, the Church's young find the spirit literally within the letter and regard print as the instantiation of a Real Presence. Scholars, Orsi warns, should not dismiss such habits out of hand. To "treat printed things as devotional media" risks "historical disorientation," he acknowledges, but to refuse the dare hazards misconstruing Catholic devotionalism, in which the "use of printed idioms, the practices associated with them, and the functions and meanings of printed things in relationships between children and adults (both lay and religious adults) were all fundamentally shaped by the orientation of Catholic imaginations to presence."[8] Conceptualizing Catholic print culture in such fashion, Orsi alleges, questions received ideas about what constitutes both religious print culture and embedded constructions of "modernity." Future scholarship will have to work out the implications of his argument; meanwhile, this volume might be read as documenting those predominating strands of American religious print culture in which presence is absent.

Orsi's work provides a clue to the continuing robustness of American religious print culture — against expectation, that Catholicism rendered divinity immanent enhanced rather than sapped print's vitality as a spiritual technology — and suggests that a full analysis of the relationship between religion and print in modern America requires more knowledge of Catholic practices than we yet enjoy. Nevertheless, this volume does provide substantial material for sketching the larger story's contours. Events in the later nineteenth and early twentieth centuries forecast the capacity of American religious print culture to accommodate itself to wholesale economic, social, and cultural change. In one way or another, the essays in part 2 all touch on religious responses to modernity, understood here as a complex of developments including industrialization, increasing ethnic pluralism, urbanization, imperialism, greater federal authority over the states, and rising doubts about formerly unassailable pious verities. After noting that novels were major vehicles of nineteenth-century printed discourse and that they frequently carried religious images, James Ryan observes that midcentury novelists often deployed Quakers as exemplars of personal and public morality. Later authors, however, characterized Friends as ethical paragons who, precisely because they achieved levels of virtue unrealizable by others, were ineffectual anachronisms no longer able to engineer civic reform. By casting Quakers as both unrealizably virtuous and unable to meet modernity on its own terms, Ryan seems to say, writers were expressing lowered expectations for political, social, and religious improvement in fin-de-siècle America.

Authors working in a different genre advanced a more optimistic view of those values' abiding worth and the utility of advertising them both at home and abroad. Works of moral instruction aimed specifically at children had flourished in America at least since James Janeway's tales instructing colonial New England babes how to live (and die) well, but the medical missionaries who swarmed into Asia and Africa during the heyday of Western colonialism updated the mode by spicing their stories with exotic peoples and places. Casting their subjects as colorful "heathens," these tales, Rennie Schoepflin observes, provided American children with vivid images of human beings desperately in need of both Christ and health care, in the process emphasizing the superiority of American culture and the Protestant gospel. Such works inspired a goodly number of readers to take up the missionary's calling themselves, Schoepflin adds. Print could serve as an agent as well as a reflection of modernization. Facing an influx of "gentiles" and the federal government's aggressive intrusions into its legal and ecclesiastical affairs, the Church of Jesus Christ of Latter-day Saints transformed itself from a relatively inward-looking body dedicated to building the Kingdom of Zion unhindered by outside influences into a dynamic corporate religious institution. David Whittaker identifies Joseph Keeler, a leading Mormon civil and religious leader in turn-of-the-century Utah, as a pivotal figure in this transformation. Keeler's writings on such subjects as the bishop's court, the Church's bureaucracy, and the concept of the

Aaronic Priesthood helped precipitate what Whittaker calls Mormonism's "managerial revolution."

Print communication can foster a sense of common identity among readers both close to and distant from the actual center of distribution. Magazines helped create a transatlantic evangelical community during the mid-eighteenth-century awakenings in Britain and America, and part 3 presents two twentieth-century examples of periodicals establishing collective self-representations. Gari-Anne Patzwald introduces the Megiddo Church, a semi-communitarian, millennialist sect whose home congregation never numbered more than a few hundred adherents but whose publications, most notably the *Megiddo Message*, knit together isolated converts scattered across the United States. Patzwald makes an important point about how readers' responses can influence periodicals' content and point of view. As the circulation of the *Message* grew, correspondents began to provide more personal information and testimonies of their belief, which in turn led the magazine's staff increasingly to treat them as absent members of the congregation rather than simply as subscribers. This symbiosis intensified the Church's sense of itself as a distinct community. The *Hillel Review* exhibited a similar dynamic between editors and audiences at the University of Wisconsin during the 1920s. Attempting to cover multiple aspects of Jewish life rather than concentrating on a single feature, the paper's outlook changed, Jonathan Pollack relates, as its staff came to realize that controversy and tradition were critical features of identity for Jewish college students. Breaking with the ideals of Hillel's parent organization, B'nai B'rith, the *Review* advanced a broader version of what should constitute an American Jewish identity, one that emphasized religious participation, Zionist commitment, and an interest in Jewish affairs around the globe rather than concern with trying to fit into society.

Fascination with some of Fundamentalism's more sensational manifestations in American life during the 1920s, especially the Scopes trial, can obscure the primacy of print in inaugurating the movement (which coalesced, after all, around a pamphlet series), defending it and sustaining it during its long midcentury political quiescence. Part 4 indicates that some Fundamentalists were more intellectually and culturally sophisticated than the "gaping primates" caricatured by H. L. Mencken. Edward Davis draws attention first to the satiric quality of Ernest James Pace's cartoons, which skewered evolution as an unscientific hypothesis

with dangerous religious and social implications, and then to the seriousness with which leading scientists and liberal ministers sought to
refute Pace's and his colleagues' charges. Financed by the Rockefeller
Foundation, the American Institute of Sacred Literature countered Fundamentalist critics with its own pamphlet series. Written by some of the
era's most preeminent scientists, the tracts, published under the rubric
"Science and Religion," were designed to defend evolutionary theory
but not, as Davis makes clear, to contravene religious belief per se.
Rather, they sought to bring theologically sophisticated views of science
to popular audiences. The American Institute of Sacred Literature
pamphlets preview contemporary efforts by the Templeton Foundation, another agency funded by a wealthy financier, to harmonize the
intellectual projects of science and religion. In its day, Davis argues, the
"Science and Religion" series only further polarized American Christian opinion. Dissatisfied with their failure to overcome what they regarded as Americans' indifference to their position, Fundamentalists
voluntarily left mainstream public discourse by the end of the 1920s, but
their proselytizing efforts did not slacken. William Trollinger Jr. documents the role that the *Pilot* played in the labors of William Bell Riley, a
leading Fundamentalist preacher, to create a network of the devout.
Like Patzwald and Pollack, Trollinger is sensitive to the dynamic between a periodical's composers and consumers. The reports that the
journal printed from missionaries in the field were often quite candid in
noting failures to convert souls and in portraying the prominence of
women as missionaries even as Fundamentalist theology emphasized female submissiveness. Trollinger contends that such letters complicated
the *Pilot*'s message without, however, undermining orthodox doctrines.
Whatever the case, the *Pilot* manifestly succeeded in maintaining a vital,
large-scale community even as Fundamentalism faded from the commercial press.

Fundamentalists met modernism's challenge to traditional faith by
espousing a literalist reading of an inerrant text, a solution that many
Americans found neither intellectually satisfying nor spiritually comforting. Part 5 reveals how some of them found answers and solace in
books purchased through a national market buoyed by readers looking
for solutions to their spiritual quandaries. Such individuals, according
to Erin Smith, were less concerned with specific doctrines than with
whether a thinking denizen of modern society could reasonably enter-
tain any religious beliefs at all. Modeled on the already market-proven

Book-of-the-Month Club, the Religious Book Club catered to this audience's craving for a credible liberal religion and its taste for "middlebrow" fare, offering works that reflected rigorous scholarship without being overly academic, while simultaneously promising consumers a sense of authentic communion with authors and characters. Purveying selections that reconciled faith with modern science and that accepted religious pluralism alongside a sense of Protestantism's superiority, the Religious Book Club, Smith judges, intended not to pursue "Truth" but to meet its customers' spiritual needs—whatever they were. Matthew Hedstrom's research on three of middlebrow religious literature's best-selling authors during the 1940s—Joshua Liebman, Harry Emerson Fosdick, and Thomas Merton—complements this analysis. Where Smith emphasizes the market's willingness to provide readers with options to suit their preferences, Hedstrom discovers the sources of these particular authors' popularity in their ability to meld modern psychology with ancient mysticism and to soothe souls troubled by the Depression, World War II, and conflict with the Soviet Union. Like Smith, he sees the midcentury print culture of religious liberalism as fitting better with a consumer model of faith than with older models focused on salvation in another world. Its emergence, he insightfully suggests, forecast the psychological and mystical turns of mind that burst into prominence during the 1960s and have suffused American religiosity ever since.

Part 6 explores the contemporary scene, in which a market fully attuned to both niche interests and global demands provides literature for every religious persuasion, personal experience takes precedence for many self-styled believers over creedal niceties, eclecticism blurs theological boundaries, the preeminence of rationalist epistemology no longer seems assured, and the demands of packaging have so broken down old-fashioned consonances between format and subject matter that one cannot automatically determine a book's point of view—or even its genre—just by looking at its cover. Within such a cultural maelstrom, old controversies appear in new guises, while controversialists elicit cheers and jeers from unexpected quarters. Kathryn Kuhlman, a healing evangelist from a Pentecostal background, published three volumes of narratives asserting that her cures proceeded from supernatural rather than natural causes. But she did so, Candy Gunther Brown explains, in ways that angered erstwhile allies while confirming critics' suspicions of her as a charlatan. Seeking to substantiate the credibility of the Resurrection by exhibiting case after case of miraculous cures,

Kuhlman nevertheless angered some Christians by rejecting a dualist anthropology that cast the body as inferior to the spirit and insisting that her examples be accepted on the basis of independently verifiable medical evidence, not faith.

Karlyn Crowley's provocative dissection of second-wave feminism and New Age spirituality likewise finds some unexpected congruences. Feminists have excoriated New Age beliefs as at best irrelevant to empowering women and at worst politically retrograde, but Crowley argues that New Age culture actually grants women greater authority than they enjoy in many other venues and facilitates an alternate construction of female potency that, like feminism, offers a cogent critique of patriarchal institutions. Finally, Paul Gutjahr discloses how one publishing house dealt with a conundrum that Christian evangelists have pondered since at least Saint Jerome's day: how to conform the Book of Books to the sensibilities of readers in very different times and cultural milieus. Modern American presses have tried to bolster Bible sales by producing editions tailored expressly to niche markets, a trend that led Thomas Nelson Publishers to issue *Revolve*—scripture formatted to look like a magazine for adolescent girls. *Revolve*'s commercial success comes at too high a cost, Gutjahr opines, for in seeking to clothe the Good News in trendy gear, it and other editions that strive to be culturally relevant erode the sacred text's aura of timelessness and condemn it to obsolescence—as if it were an ordinary commodity.

How the intersections of religion and print culture may evolve beyond the already highly plastic expressions Brown, Crowley, and Gutjahr evoke is anyone's guess, though the Internet's impact will necessarily occupy future scholars. Historians are the world's worst prophets, but one might hazard two hypotheses: the Net will have fewer deleterious effects on modern print culture than some might suppose, and it will amplify the already intense and complex relationship between that culture and religion rather than alter or subvert it. Print culture's death has been exaggerated ever since the 1960s, when Marshall McLuhan prognosticated its demise. Moreover, though the Internet is in many obvious ways a visual and auditory medium, some of its most innovative means for exchanging data and fostering debate—instant messaging, chat rooms, blogs, and group-edited projects like Wikipedia—depend on writers inputting words via keyboards and should be understood as literary phenomena that extend print culture rather than comprising a new genre of communication. Too, the ways in which religion has seized upon new information technologies—from the codex to the printing press to the newspaper—provide good reason for thinking that it will take advantage of the Internet as well, though forecasting how religion and cyberspace will interact with any pretence of specificity would be futile at a time of such cultural turbulence and technological advance.

We might, nevertheless, heed the wisdom of the Preacher that "*there is* no new *thing* under the sun" (Ecclesiastes 1:9, KJV; emphasis in original) and predict one certainty. Gutjahr's depiction of the extremes to which publishers may go in order to hawk the world's all-time best seller ends the volume on the same observation with which it began: scripture's steadfast centrality to religious life in the United States. The Internet is not likely to change that situation a jot or a tittle. Searching for "Bible" and "America" through Google yields (in 0.27 seconds) "about 43,900,000" entries; someone surfing through them at the rate of 10 seconds/site would need nearly fourteen years to check out them all.[9] As long as American religious print culture endures, it would seem, the Bible we will always have with us.

Notes

1. Two of the projected five volumes of the series A History of the Book in America have appeared thus far: vol. 1, *The Colonial Book in the Atlantic World*, ed. Hugh Amory and David D. Hall (Worcester, MA: American Antiquarian Society, 2000); and vol. 3, *The Industrial Book, 1840–1880*, ed. Scott E. Casper, Jeffrey D. Groves, Stephen W. Nissenbaum, and Michael Winship (Chapel Hill: University of North Carolina Press, 2007). Vol. 4, *Print in Motion: The Expansion of Publishing and Reading in the United States, 1880–1940*, ed. Carl F. Kaestle and Janice A. Radway, is expected from the University of North Carolina Press in 2008.

2. Sidney Ahlstrom, *A Religious History of the American People* (New Haven, CT: Yale University Press, 1972).

3. The focus on the early modern period no doubt owes much to the pioneering work of Elizabeth Eisenstein, notably *The Printing Press as an Agent of Change: Communications and Cultural Transformations in Early Modern Europe* (New York: Cambridge University Press, 1979). For early American examples, see Amory and Hall, *Colonial Book in the Atlantic World;* David D. Hall, *Cultures of Print: Essays in the History of the Book* (Amherst: University of Massachusetts Press, 1996); and Frank Lambert, *"Pedlar in Divinity": George Whitefield and the Transatlantic Revivals, 1737–1770* (Princeton, NJ: Princeton University Press, 1994). For a representative work on the nineteenth century, see Paul C. Gutjahr, *An*

American Bible: A History of the Good Book in the United States, 1777–1880 (Stanford, CA: Stanford University Press, 1999).

4. Nor, for that matter, do any of them cover American Islamic, Hindu, or Buddhist print cultures, still-emergent phenomena the study of which has yet to develop.

5. Jay P. Dolan, *In Search of an American Catholicism: A History of Religion and Culture in Tension* (New York: Oxford University Press, 2002); John T. McGreevy, *Catholicism and American Freedom: A History* (New York: W. W. Norton, 2003); Leslie Woodcock Tentler, *Catholics and Contraception: An American History* (Ithaca, NY: Cornell University Press, 2004). For one of the few examples of work on Catholicism and print culture, see James Emmett Ryan, "Sentimental Catechism: Archbishop James Gibbons, Mass-Print Culture, and American Literary History," *Religion and American Culture* 7, no. 1 (1997): 81–119. *U.S. Catholic Historian* 25, no. 3 (2007) focuses on editors and their newspapers.

6. Robert A. Orsi, "Bleeding Saints, Troubled Angels and Dying Children: The Imaginative World of Catholic Periodicals for Young People in the 20th Century," address presented at the Conference on "Education and the Culture of Print in Modern America," Center for the History of Print Culture in Modern America, Madison, WI, 29 September 2006. For examples of Orsi's scholarship on lived Catholicism, see *The Madonna of 115th Street: Faith and Community in Italian Harlem, 1880–1950* (New Haven, CT: Yale University Press, 1985); *Thank You, St. Jude: Women's Devotion to the Patron Saint of Hopeless Causes* (New Haven, CT: Yale University Press, 1996); and *Between Heaven and Earth: The Religious Worlds People Make and the Scholars Who Study Them* (Princeton, NJ: Princeton University Press, 2005).

7. For the relationship between European scholars' concern with "modernity" and the emergence of religious studies as a field, see Hans G. Kippenberg, *Discovering Religious History in the Modern Age,* trans. Barbara Harshaw (Princeton, NJ: Princeton University Press, 2002).

8. Robert A. Orsi, "Printed Presence: 20th Century [*sic*] Catholic Print Culture for Youngsters in the United States," a version of "Bleeding Saints, Troubled Angels and Dying Children," submitted for future publication by the Center for Print Culture, 5, 6. My thanks to Professor Orsi for making this draft available.

9. http://www.google.com (accessed 14 August 2006). The calculation figures a year as 365.25 days.

Acknowledgments

This book owes its inception to Paul Boyer, who, during his years as Chair of the Center for the History of Print Culture in Modern America, deftly identified important opportunities and topics for our consideration. Founded in 1992 as a joint program of the Wisconsin Historical Society and the University of Wisconsin–Madison, the Center focuses on the diverse cultural forms that the historical sociology of print in America has comprehended from circa 1875 to the present. Boyer's suggestion that the Center explore print culture's role in the American religious experience both fit this mission perfectly and identified a field of inquiry that begged for scholarly engagement. Consequently, the Center dedicated a conference to the subject on 10–11 September 2004. The articles collected here enhance the investigation begun then. Elaborations of shorter papers, they represent only a select fraction of the original presentations, which sample in turn emerged from a much larger universe of proposals.

The Center's numerous projects (for more details, including our mission statement, see http://slisweb.lis.wisc.edu/~printcul/) enlist the wisdom and energy of many people. The list of conference panelists reflected the careful deliberations of Rima Apple, Ronald L. Numbers, Stephen L. Vaughn, Phyllis Weisbard, William J. Reese, and Charles Cohen, members of the Center's Advisory Board. The conference arrangements reflected the consummate professionalism of Jane Pearlmutter, assistant director, and Erin Meyer, the Center's research coordinator, both members of the School of Library and Information Studies, the Center's administrative home. Designing colloquia, the annual meeting, and biennial conferences always demands the good offices of the Advisory Board, who, in addition to those already cited, include: James L.

Baughman, Russ Castronovo, Greg Downey, Michael Edmonds, Kenneth Frazier, Michael Fultz, Peter Gottlieb, Tracy Honn, Madge H. Klais, Mary N. Layoun, Caroline Levine, Anne Lundin, Tony Michels, Adam Nelson, Louise S. Robbins, John L. Rudolph, Cherene Sherrard, Micaela Sullivan-Fowler, and David Zimmerman.

This volume, the sixth to be published by the University of Wisconsin Press as part of the series Print Culture History in Modern America, has benefited from the encouragement and support of Sheila Leary, interim director of the University of Wisconsin Press, and Gwen Walker, acquisitions editor. The editorial and production process was eased by the work of Paul Hedges, Matt Levin, Terry Emmrich, Carla Aspelmeier, and Sheila Moermond.

JAMES P. DANKY

Director, Center for the History of Print Culture in Modern America

1

Religion and Print Culture
in American History

Religion, Print Culture, and the Bible before 1876

CHARLES L. COHEN

The most vivid popular images of religious culture in the United States tend toward the hortatory (the firebrand preacher calling sinners to repent) and the architectural (a simple whitewashed church, more often than not, though the neo-Gothic splendor of the National Cathedral or the glassy futurism of the Crystal Cathedral have made their impressions too). Nevertheless, the contours of American religious life have always owed much to print and its vehicle and still do, even in an age that lasers rather than impresses words onto the page. As this volume and the conference from which it sprang make clear, the proliferation of media over the past hundred and twenty-five years means that Americans now have an unprecedented array of genres delivering the Word made print, and that they are as likely to turn to Bible-zines as scriptures, best sellers as sermons, and comics as prayer books. Modern American religious print culture owes its dizzying array of forms to such factors as new technologies, the power of nationally integrated markets, advances in advertising, and myriad sociointellectual changes: women's increasing public presence, science's challenge to orthodox cosmologies, and a spiritual diversity fostered by the intrusion of non-Christian traditions compounded by an upsurge of new movements. Yet its fundamental coupling of the spirit with the letter derives from habits laid down long before. To the degree that images like the evangelist and the clapboard meetinghouse still seem quintessentially "American," they recall a colonial and early national past in which "religion" intended "Protestantism" and "the Book" meant, not simply the Bible, but a very specific version thereof. To fully appreciate the universe of religion and print culture that this volume surveys, it might be useful to outline briefly what it replaced—a world not so much lost as engulfed.

To put the matter baldly, American religion before the Civil War was predominantly Protestant and the national religious culture of print bibliocentric, artifacts of how Europe's seventeenth-century imperial contests and religious geography played out in North America. Carried by its Spanish and Portuguese vectors, Catholicism established itself among the colonies of Mexico, Peru, and Brazil, but it lay more thinly on the ground in the borderlands to the north, where the Spanish struggled to maintain their grip.[1] Cast out from Florida in 1565, the French settled along the Saint Lawrence River Valley, far removed from Spanish menace; although Huguenots were active in early French colonizing activities, Cardinal Richelieu banned them from New France in 1627.[2] Into the thousand-mile gap between San Agustín and Québec, Protestantism inserted itself: tenuously at first in Dutch Nieuw Netherland, where after a quarter century only two *dominies* served a colony stretching from Fort Orange to the Delaware River; only slightly less tentatively in the Chesapeake, where too few ministers served too many parishes inhabited by a largely uninterested population; and robustly only in New England, where strenuous Puritan efforts to forge a godly society have caused many modern Christians (and some historians) to regard the seventeenth century as a golden age of American religion, when in fact a majority of the people south of the Hudson River lived beyond regular church governance. Even New England's vaunted Saints routinely practiced white magic to find objects unrecoverable by prayer or forestall things that went bump in the night, behavior that would appall their modern pious admirers.[3] A few Catholics participated in Lord Baltimore's radical experiment to provide refuge for his coreligionists, but they formed a minority from the outset.[4] Seventeenth-century Anglo-Americans were uniformly Protestant (some would say Christian) in neither belief nor practice.

But as Britain secured a firmer hold on its American territory in the eighteenth century, Protestants from northwest Europe poured in— Presbyterians from Ulster; a handful of Huguenots expelled from maritime France; Quakers from Wales, northern England, and the Continent; and hosts of Germans belonging to Lutheran, Reformed, and sectarian churches. The Church of England bestirred itself and dispatched some three hundred missionaries from 1701 to 1775.[5] Across the colonies denominations organized themselves, increasing the percentage of members and noncommunicating adherents. Anglo-Americans became more committed to their personal Protestantisms and to the empire as a bulwark of liberty against papist tyranny—and then, after the Revolution, to their new national state as a "Christian" (in other words, Protestant) republic. The percentage of Catholics increased during the mid-nineteenth century as the nation absorbed Irish immigrants along with Hispanics suddenly caught on the wrong side of the border when the Treaty of Guadalupe Hidalgo moved the line dividing Mexico from the United States hundreds of miles south. Some historians have argued that, in terms of members, the Roman Church was the single largest ecclesiastical institution in the United States as early as 1850. That claim is premature by several decades, but even if it were close to being fact, antebellum Catholics still comprised a minority of churchgoers awash in a sea of "by faith alone."

Majoritarian Protestantism meant a population versed in the principle of *sola scriptura*, which in turn contributed to the Bible's cultural preeminence. Anglo-American colonists always enjoyed varieties of religious literature, especially sermons. By the late seventeenth century, New Englanders had entered into the emerging transatlantic book trade, which provided them with manuals that spurred an upsurge in private devotionalism.[6] In the next century, the consumer revolution, flooding the colonies with luxury commodities trafficked over improved transportation networks, made possible transatlantic readerships for evangelical magazines generated by the Great Awakening.[7] Nineteenth-century technology—power presses, stereotyping, and the like—only further increased the kinds and volume of materials that readers could buy.[8] Still, the single most important book remained the Good One. Especially in the nineteenth century, scripture was marketed in an increasing array of formats, but virtually all the covers—most of which continued to be made of leather[9]—enfolded a single rendering of the text: the King

James Version (KJV), end product of the first great age of English Bible translation.

That era began with the publication of William Tyndale's first New Testament in February 1526. Several editions, all owing much to Tyndale's pioneering, appeared in subsequent decades, but by the late sixteenth century, two major versions—the Bishops' Bible, intended to be the house volume for the Church of England, and the Geneva Bible, beloved of Puritan nonconformists—more or less held the field. The Geneva Bible was more popular, in part because of its customer-friendly packaging: quarto rather than folio size for portability, Roman rather than black type for readability, chapters sectioned into numbered sentences for easier comprehension, plus an apparatus of twenty-six woodcuts, five maps, and marginalia. Perceiving some of the bordering notes to be seditious—he instanced the comment to Exodus 1:19 that declares the Hebrew midwives' "disobediēce" of Pharoah's extermination order to be "lawful"—King James I supported a new translation published in 1611, the same year that Shakespeare's *The Tempest*, a romance inspired by George Somers's unintended crack-up on Bermuda while trying to relieve the beleaguered settlement at Jamestown, was first played. The last Geneva Bible did not appear until 1644, but by then the Authorized Version (as the English called it) had infiltrated their hearts, minds, and language.[10] Catholics produced their own version, the Rheims-Douai, but its hyper-Latinate renderings—Matthew 6:11 comes out as "Giue vs to day our supersubstantial bread"—and the sometimes caustic anti-Protestant marginal comments added by Bishop Richard Challoner during his eighteenth-century revisions militated against its having any influence outside Catholic parishes.[11] For Protestants, meaning most Americans, KJV, as Paul Gutjahr has rightly remarked, remained "firmly entrenched as the monarch of American Protestant Bible versions" until virtually the end of the nineteenth century.[12]

Scholarship has not yet taken the full measure of what the authority that KJV enjoyed may have meant for American religious culture. Indeed, it might be easier to circumscribe its boundaries than to articulate its influence. For one thing, it was never the only game in town, if only because non-English editions carried by migrants attracted to Anglo-America by Britain's liberal naturalization policy or by missionaries to native peoples—John Eliot's Algonquian edition (full version 1663) was the first Bible in any tongue printed in Anglo-America—circulated alongside it, albeit within restricted circles.[13] Meanwhile, individuals like Charles Thomson, former secretary of the Continental Congress, whose 1808 translation included an Old Testament based on the Greek Septuagint, and Alexander Campbell, who produced a Bible anchored in the same primitivism that he imparted to the movement that became the Disciples of Christ, made English alternatives available.[14] Too, textual hegemony never meant interpretive uniformity; if *sola scriptura* is Protestantism's birthright, hermeneutic discord, even among members of the same ecclesiastical body, qualifies as its afterbirth. The primacy of KJV did not settle the disagreement between Puritans and Anglicans over whether one had to do what the Bible specifically enjoined or might do anything it did not explicitly forbid, preclude denominations from cementing disparate passages into hardening creeds, nor prevent exegetes from challenging long-standing Christian dogma, as the Unitarian Controversy proved. Factors like class, gender, and ethnicity further refracted interpretation, not to mention cultural inheritance and the power relationships between clergy and laity. Missionaries to Amerindians and African Americans ordinarily carried King James Bibles, but, to the extent that those peoples accepted Christianity, they did so on terms very different from those familiar to Anglo-American whites, who read the same words without parsing Jesus as a shaman or reworking Exodus into a liberation theology.[15] Finally, the very text itself could fuel controversy, as it did in the 1840s when Philadelphia Catholics, refusing to countenance schools forcing their children to read a Bible lacking the Church's sanction, requested the use of their own edition, precipitating deadly riots.[16] Merely to note KJV's predominance in itself says little about that version's actual cultural impact.

Moreover, after 1830, the Old and New Testaments, in whatever versions they existed, were not the only "Judeo-Christian" scriptures Americans could obtain. Protestants and Catholics might argue about the necessity of a version's basing itself on the Vulgate or about the canonicity of the apocalyptic/deuterocanonical books (translations of which the original KJV did include), but Joseph Smith brought into the world a completely new holy text. Latter-day Saints have, of course, lavished attention on the *Book of Mormon*, but non-Mormon scholars have essentially ignored its cultural impact as an American scripture, perhaps because they either did not consider it a legitimate addition to the Bible or, if they did (at least for courtesy's sake), thought it a matter of concern primarily for Temple Square. To be sure, rather than enriching the English language as had the King James Bible, the *Book of Mormon* replicated the former's cadences (not to mention large chunks of Isaiah), thereby appropriating to itself the reigning cultural standard for sacred diction even if (or perhaps because) the high Jacobean wordings sounded archaic in an age of democratically vernacular homespun.[17] Perhaps one needs to traverse the I-15 corridor's crazy quilt of lubricious greenery nestled amid the salt barrens, past places named Lehi and Nephi, to observe how the *Book of Mormon* has worked its will on a physical American landscape and to wonder where one might find a psychological analogue.[18] The extent to which it may have done so necessarily circumscribes the King James Bible's cultural "hegemony."

Yet for all the variant editions, doctrinal infighting, and competing canons, most nineteenth-century American Protestants identified what *they* considered scripture with all the certitude of Henry Fielding's Parson Thwackum: by Bible, they meant the Old and New Testaments; by Old and New Testaments, they meant KJV; and we should ponder what cultural impact such widespread loyalty may have had. For one thing, it provided Americans with, as an anonymous author put it in 1859, the "phrases with which their spiritual life and hope have been nurtured."[19] It may—as Bryan Bademan suggested during the conference—have in the late nineteenth century helped underwrite denominationalism and Protestant ecumenism.[20] It also helped fashion the national identity. Along with the Constitution, democratic institutions, and the perquisites of property holding, Americans venerated the Bible—and in an edition, ironically, authorized by a king, an association that, as perfervid republicans, they should have despised.

Finally, the use of a single edition grounded the nearly universal assumption that scripture's wisdom lay on the surface, not in arcane figures or encryptions. From the Revolution to the Civil War, commonsense philosophy guided theological exploration, assuring Americans that applying right reason to the literal words would bring the truth to light. Possessing the same text encouraged a widespread feeling that the Bible's meaning was essentially transparent—or, at least, should have been—for the irony is that a shared Bible helped render Jesus's maxim in Matthew 12:25 tragically prophetic: a text divided against itself could not stand. As Mark Noll has so poignantly observed, Americans' consensus that scripture said what it said and that it was a republican document led to hermeneutic fratricide. Pro-slavery advocates asserted, with substantial justification, that scripture sanctioned slavery; the proof was typographically clear. Abolitionists had either to argue that one must read the Bible's spirit against its letter or, like William Lloyd Garrison, deny its supreme authority altogether, an excruciating position for most.[21] KJV's ubiquity on both sides of the Mason-Dixon Line eliminated any possibility that polemicists might concede their opponents wrong on grounds that they used a faulty version; since everyone read from the same page, differences of opinion had to proceed from sin, bad faith, or worse.

War came, and at its end, assurance that the application of commonsense principles revealed in a Bible perfectly attuned to American republicanism had gone with the wind; but the popularity of KJV endured as the most popular edition of scripture well into the twentieth century, surviving the Revised Version's temporary ascendance in the 1880s and '90s. Yet straws in the breeze had long foretold the decline of its cultural authority; mid-nineteenth-century critics had increasingly questioned its accuracy, and the American Bible Society ventured a revision in 1851 only to withdraw it a few years later (at which point many of those responsible for the new translation quit).[22] Those gusts accelerated as the intellectual and demographic foundations of the Protestant hegemony crumbled, while the number of competing versions proliferated. By the late nineteenth century, the cultural supremacy of orthodox Protestantism was being hounded by the higher biblical criticism, scientific refutations that scripture spoke truly about the natural world, and an influx of Catholics, Eastern Orthodox Christians, and Jews yearning to breathe free.[23] The appearance of the Revised Version catalyzed a flurry of new translations, mainly by individuals, over the next four decades. Those trends have only accelerated since. Universities vie for Muslim scholars, Buddhists coach championship basketball teams and make blockbuster movies, while Wiccans run for political office. The complete Revised Standard Version appeared in 1952; within a generation, biblical scholar and historian F. F. Bruce could judge that "for the English-speaking world as a whole there is no modern version of the Bible which comes so near as the R.S.V. does to making the all-purpose provision which the [KJV] made for so many years."[24]

Nearly five centuries after Tyndale, we live in the second great age of English Bible translating.[25] New editions appear with dizzying frequency, their formats tuned to market proclivities with Scholastic subtlety, while their textual variations evince the confusion God unleashed at Babel. In the KJV, Paul's discourse on *agapē* in 1 Corinthians 13:1 begins with "Though I speak with the tongues of men and of angels." In the New Revised Standard Version and the Jerusalem Bible, however, the Apostle holds forth "in the tongues of mortals and of angels"; in the New American Bible he speaks "in human and angelic tongues"; and he employs even more imaginative locutions in paraphrases like the New Living Translation ("in any language in heaven or on earth") and *The Message* ("with human eloquence and angelic ecstasy").[26] The *New Oxford Annotated Bible with the Apocrypha* (which uses the New Revised Standard Version) bills itself as "An Ecumenical Study Bible" because it collects all of the documents deemed canonical by Catholics, Protestants, and/ or various Orthodox churches, but it cannot possibly aggregate all of the English versions of those works, nor does its comprehensiveness confer any special authority on its own language.[27] Since the Republic's centennial, an interplay between American religiosity and the culture of print far different from that characterized by Protestant bibliocentrism has emerged, one more doctrinally diverse and, even among Protestants, adhering to no universally definitive edition of scripture—a brave new world of spiritual and textual multiplicity revealed by the essays that follow.

Notes

1. For an introduction to the northern borderlands, see David J. Weber, *The Spanish Frontier in North America* (New Haven, CT: Yale University Press, 1992). For recent assessments of Spanish and Portuguese evangelism to the American Indians, see the essays by Daniel T. Reff, Barbara De Marco, Amy Bushnell Turner, Jaime Valenzuela Márquez, and Isabel dos Guimarães Sá, in *The Spiritual Conversion of the Americas*, ed. James Muldoon (Gainesville: University Press of Florida, 2004), and of Catholicism in one Spanish Borderlands colony, Robert L. Kapitzke, *Religion, Power, and Politics in Colonial St. Augustine* (Gainesville: University Press of Florida, 2001).

2. W. J. Eccles, *The French in North America*, rev. ed. (East Lansing: Michigan State University Press, 1998), 1–31 (for the Huguenots' banishment, 29), though Allan Greer, *The People of New France* (Toronto: University of Toronto Press, 1999 ed.), 76, 90–91, argues for a continuing if small Protestant presence. For a standard work on the Catholic Church in New France, see Cornelius J. Jaenen, *The Role of the Church in New France* (Toronto: McGraw-Hill Ryerson, 1976).

3. Jon Butler, *Awash in a Sea of Faith: Christianizing the American People* (New Haven, CT: Yale University Press, 1990), and Patricia Bonomi, *Under the Cope of Heaven: Religion, Society, and Politics in Colonial America* (New York: Oxford University Press, 1986), emphasize the tenuousness of seventeenth-century

ecclesiastical institutions in the Anglo-American colonies, though for a corrective regarding the strength of New England's church system, see Charles L. Cohen, "The Post-Puritan Paradigm in Early American Religious History," *William and Mary Quarterly*, 3rd ser., 54 (1997): 701–5. On the degree to which "alternative supernaturalisms" (i.e., "magic") suffused orthodox spirituality, see David D. Hall, *Worlds of Wonder, Days of Judgment* (New York: Alfred A. Knopf, 1989); Butler, *Awash in a Sea of Faith*, 67–97; Richard Godbeer, *The Devil's Dominion: Magic and Religion in Early New England* (New York: Cambridge University Press, 1992).

4. Thomas J. Curry, *The First Freedoms: Church and State in America to the Passage of the First Amendment* (New York: W. W. Norton, 1986), 29–53.

5. Jon Butler, "Protestant Pluralism," in *Encyclopedia of the North American Colonies*, ed. Jacob Ernest Cooke et al., 3 vols. (New York: Charles Scribners' Sons, 1993), 3:609–32.

6. Charles E. Hambrick-Stowe, *The Practice of Piety: Puritan Devotional Disciplines in Seventeenth-Century New England* (Chapel Hill: University of North Carolina Press, 1982). For the New England book trade, see Hugh Amory, "Printing and Bookselling in New England, 1638–1713," in *A History of the Book in America*, ed. David D. Hall and Hugh Amory, 5 vols. (Worcester, MA: American Antiquarian Society, 2000), 1: *The Colonial Book in the Atlantic World*, 83–116.

7. Frank Lambert, *Inventing the "Great Awakening"* (Princeton, NJ: Princeton University Press, 1999); Lambert, *Pedlar in Divinity: George Whitefield and the Transatlantic Revivals, 1737–1770* (Princeton, NJ: Princeton University Press, 1994). For the eighteenth-century colonial book trade, see Hall and Amory, *History of the Book in America*, vol. 1: James N. Green, "The Middle Colonies, 1680–1720," 199–223; Calhoun Winton, "The Southern Book Trade in the Eighteenth Century," 224–46; James N. Green, "The Middle Colonies, 1720–1790," Part 1: "English Books and Printing in the Age of Franklin," 247–97, A. Gregg Roeber, "The Middle Colonies, 1720–1790," Part 2: "German and Dutch Books and Printing," 298–313; and Hugh Amory, "The New England Book Trade, 1713–1790," 314–47.

8. Paul C. Gutjahr, *An American Bible: A History of the Good Book in the United States, 1777–1880* (Stanford, CA: Stanford University Press, 1999), 12–15.

9. Ibid., 42.

10. *The Geneva Bible: A Facsimile of the 1560 Edition* (Madison: University of Wisconsin Press, 1969 [1560]), 12 and Ex. 1:19; F. F. Bruce, *History of the Bible in English*, 3rd ed. (New York: Oxford University Press, 1978), 31, 86–95, 97.

11. *The Nevv Testament of Iesus Christ, Translated Faithfully into English . . .* (Rheims: John Fogny, 1582), Matt. 6:11; the Old Testament translated at Douai was published in 1609 (Bruce, *History of the Bible in English*, 114); Gutjahr, *American Bible*, 127. For Challoner's redactions, see *The New Testament of our Lord and Saviour Jesus Christ. Translated out of the Latin Vulgat* (Dublin?: n.p., 1749).

12. Gutjahr, *American Bible*, 91.

13. P. Marion Simms, *The Bible in America: Versions That Have Played Their Part in the Making of the Republic* (New York: Wilson-Erickson, 1936), 54–109; Richard W. Cogley, *John Eliot's Mission to the Indians Before King Philip's War* (Cambridge, MA: Harvard University Press, 1999), 120–21 and passim.

14. Gutjahr, *American Bible*, 93–95, 101–5.

15. On Amerindians, see Charles L. Cohen, "Conversion among Amerindians and Puritans: A Theological and Cultural Perspective," in *Puritanism: Transatlantic Perspectives on an Anglo-American Faith*, ed. Francis Bremer (Boston: Massachusetts Historical Society, 1993), 233–56; William G. McLoughlin, *Cherokees & Missionaries, 1789–1839* (Norman: University of Oklahoma Press, 1995 [orig. New Haven, CT: Yale University Press, 1984]), 197–212 and passim; Joel W. Martin, *The Land Looks After Us: A History of Native American Religion* (New York: Oxford University Press, 2001), 61–82. On African Americans: E. Brooks Holifield, *Theology in America: Christian Thought from the Age of the Puritans to the Civil War* (New Haven, CT: Yale University Press, 2003), 306–18; Mark A. Noll, *The Civil War as a Theological Crisis* (Chapel Hill: University of North Carolina Press, 2006), 64–72; Albert J. Raboteau, *A Fire in the Bones: Reflections on African-American Religious History* (Boston: Beacon Press, 1995), 17–36.

16. Lloyd P. Jorgensen, *The State and the Non-Public School, 1825–1925* (Columbia: University of Missouri Press, 1987), 76–83; Alexandra F. Griswold, "An Open Bible and Burning Churches: Authority, Truth, and Folk Belief in Protestant-Catholic Conflict, Philadelphia, 1844" (Ph.D. dissertation, University of Pennsylvania, 1997).

17. Terryl Givens, *By the Hand of Mormon: The American Scripture That Launched a New World Religion* (New York: Oxford University Press, 2002); Philip L. Barlow, *Mormons and the Bible: The Place of the Latter-day Saints in American Religion* (New York: Oxford University Press, 1991).

18. For a brief introduction to that discussion, see Charles L. Cohen, "The Construction of the Mormon People," *Journal of Mormon History* 32 (2006): 57–58.

19. "Revision of the English Bible," *The New Englander* 18 (1859): 144–63, quoted in Gutjahr, *American Bible*, 109.

20. Bryan Bademan, "'Perpetually in the Hands of the People': The King James Bible and Late Nineteenth-Century American Culture," paper delivered at the conference on "Religion and the Culture of Print in America: Authors, Publishers, Readers and More Since 1876," University of Wisconsin–Madison, 11 September 2004.

21. Mark A. Noll, *America's God: From Jonathan Edwards to Abraham Lincoln* (New York: Oxford University Press, 2002); Noll, *Civil War as a Theological Crisis*, passim.

22. Gutjahr, *American Bible*, 89.

23. James Turner, *Without God, Without Creed: The Origins of Unbelief in America* (Baltimore: Johns Hopkins University Press, 1985); Ronald L. Numbers, *Darwinism Comes to America* (Cambridge, MA: Harvard University Press, 1998); Grant Wacker, "The Demise of Biblical Civilization," in *The Bible in America*, ed. Nathan O. Hatch and Mark A. Noll (New York: Oxford University Press, 1982), 121–38.

24. Bruce, *History of the Bible in English*, 203.

25. In a more global treatment of the subject, Harry M. Orlinsky and Robert G. Bratcher, *A History of Bible Translation and the North American Contribution* (Atlanta: Scholars Press, 1991), identify four "great ages" of Bible translation — (1) 200 BCE–Fourth Century CE; (2) Fourth Century–1500; (3) 1500–1960; and (4) 1960–Present—and characterize the language of the latter two periods as "overwhelmingly English" (xi, xii). Although individual (and sometimes idiosyncratic) English Bibles appeared throughout their "third age," the most influential period of activity occurred between 1526 (Tyndale's New Testament) and 1611 (KJV), with the Revised Version of 1881–85 heralding renewed interest in translating.

26. One can compare readings by using *The Complete Parallel Bible: Containing the Old and New Testaments with the Apocryphal / Deuterocanonical Books: New Revised Standard Version, Revised English Bible, New American Bible, New Jerusalem Bible* (New York: Oxford University Press, 1993); and *The Contemporary Parallel New Testament: King James Version, New American Standard Bible, Updated Edition, New International Version, New Living Translation, New Century Version, Contemporary English Version, New King James Version, The Message*, ed. John R. Kohlenberger (New York: Oxford University Press, 1997). KJV famously translates *agapē* as "charity," hence the listing of gifts in 1 Cor. 13:13 as "faith, hope, charity," which has passed into popular culture through myriad avenues, including Don Cornell's standby, "The Bible Tells Me So." More recent versions prefer "love."

27. *The New Oxford Annotated Bible with the Apocryphal / Deuterocanonical Books*, rev. and enlgd., ed. Bruce M. Metzger and Roland E. Murphy (New York: Oxford University Press, 1991), notes twenty-six other translations and revisions in the "years following the publication of the Revised Standard Version" as well as twenty-five other translations and revisions of the New Testament alone (x).

From Tracts to Mass-Market Paperbacks

Spreading the Word via the Printed Page in America from the Early National Era to the Present

PAUL S. BOYER

I take my text from John 21:23, the last verse of the last of the four Gospels attributed to Matthew, Mark, Luke, and John that circulated among the early Christians: "And there are also many other things which Jesus did, the which, if they should be written every one, I suppose that even the world itself could not contain the books that could be written."

Dating from the dawn of Christianity, this text anticipates the importance of the written word in the Christian tradition. Indeed, as one contemplates the volume of printed material produced by American Christians from the early nineteenth century onward, one is struck by the prescience of whoever made that hyperbolic observation two thousand years ago. "The world itself" does, indeed, seem hardly able to contain that vast mountain of books, periodicals, tracts, and leaflets. And adherents of other faiths, not to mention successive generations of religious dissidents, scoffers, and critics, have made their own substantial contribution to this vast bibliography. One is reminded of another familiar text: "Furthermore, . . . my son, be admonished: of making many books, there is no end" (Ecclesiastes 12:12).

The history of religion in America is incomprehensible without close attention to the centrality of print materials in promoting, consolidating, defending, and sometimes attacking the cause of faith in its many manifestations. My examples in this overview essay come mainly from the Protestant tradition, the focus of my own work in American religious history. But an extensive literature documents the crucial role of print in other traditions as well.[1] Happily, too, many of the developments that I mention in passing are treated more fully in the essays that follow.

Christianity, like Judaism from which it sprang, is a religion of the Book, so the Bible, that all-time best seller, must be our beginning point. The Bible, itself a collection of books, is the Ur-source for the wide array of print materials discussed in *Religion and the Culture of Print in Modern America*. In the early national era, Philadelphia's Matthew Carey and Isaiah Thomas of Worcester, Massachusetts, pioneered in large-scale Bible printing and distribution. Carey's sales force included the Episcopal clergyman Mason Weems, best known for inventing and promulgating the legend of George Washington and the cherry tree. As Paul Gutjahr and others have documented, the American Bible Society (ABS), founded in 1816, centralized Bible production, distribution, and competitive pricing long before John D. Rockefeller or Andrew Carnegie—those titans of consolidated production and marketing—were even born.

Thanks to a corporate bureaucracy in New York City and a network of regional agents and outlets, the ABS soon dominated the market. The Society printed half a million Bibles in 1829–31 alone, charging six cents for New Testaments and forty-five cents for the entire Bible. When it opened in 1853, the ABS's new and expanded headquarters, the six-story Bible House, boasting the latest in steam-powered printing presses, was the largest publishing establishment in America.[2]

Thanks to the ABS and other publishers, Bibles pervaded nineteenth-century America, from inexpensive editions to lavishly produced family Bibles. My own bookshelves include a 1715 German Bible purchased by my father in the early 1920s; an 1819 ABS Bible from the library of my wife's Connecticut ancestors; the ABS Bible my great-grandfather took with him into war as a Union soldier in 1863; an 1870 family Bible acquired by my ancestors in southern Ohio containing birth, death, and marriage records going back to the eighteenth century; an ABS New Testament presented to my nine-year-old grandfather by his father in 1880 (and adorned by him with several drawings of fashionably dressed young ladies); a New Testament owned by my

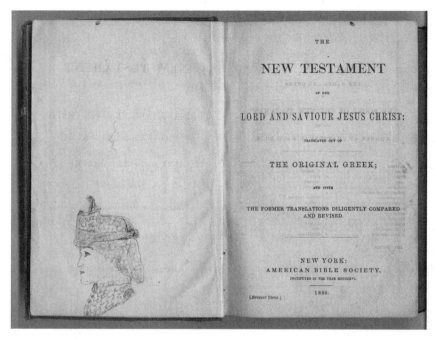

Figure 2.1. An American Bible Society New Testament presented to the author's grand-father in 1880, when he was nine years old, by his father. The blank pages provided sketching space for his artistic efforts. (New York: American Bible Society, 1880. Library of the Author.)

grandmother; a New Testament given to my father by his parents in 1913; a Greek New Testament acquired by my father around 1927; a New Testament presented to me by my grandparents in 1939; an illustrated Gospel of John I received as a Sunday school award on 26 July 1942 (a printed message on the inside front cover states: "In accepting this Gospel I agree to carry it in my pocket and to read it through at least once."); and a complete Bible, with the words of Jesus in red, presented as another Sunday school award in November 1943. Countless families, of course, have similar tangible reminders of the Bible's centrality in grassroots American religious history.[3]

The American Bible Society was eventually joined in its ministry by other Bible-distributing agencies, including the Gideons. The Gideons' beginning is the stuff of legend. On 24 September 1898, in the little town of Boscobel, Wisconsin, two traveling salesmen, John Nicholson and

Samuel Hill, both devout Christians, shared a room in the crowded Central Hotel, situated above a saloon. As they talked, they hatched the idea of placing Bibles in hotel rooms to reach the traveling public. The rest, as they say, is history. By 1920 over a million Gideon Bibles had been placed in hotel rooms nationwide. As with McDonald's hamburgers, the total must now be in the billions. Gideon Bibles nestle in the drawers of bedside stands in hotels and motels worldwide. On college and university campuses from Boston to Berkeley, volunteers from the Gideons and the Full Gospel Businessmen's Fellowship mark the beginning of each semester by passing out small green-bound Gideon New Testaments.[4]

Other faiths have picked up the idea. The Marriott motel chain, founded by the Mormon J. Willard Mariott, offers *The Book of Mormon* to its guests. Hotels owned by Japan's Nikko Corporation present Buddhist scriptures to the weary traveler.

The King James Bible of 1611 remains a mainstay of Protestant America's biblical culture, but a host of revisions and paraphrases have appeared over the years, including the Revised Version (1881–85), produced by a committee of mostly British scholars, and the Revised Standard Version (RSV) of 1952, prepared by U.S. scholars. (Many found these revisions distinctly inferior stylistically to the venerable King James Version. The critic Dwight Macdonald in a 1953 *New Yorker* essay excoriated the RSV team for having "mutilated or completely destroyed many of the phrases made precious by centuries of religious feeling and cultural tradition.")[5] Recent paraphrases include the American Bible Society's *Good News for Modern Man* (1966) and editions targeting young people, including *The Extreme Teen Bible*, hyped by Amazon.com in these words: "The *Extreme Teen Bible* dares teens to crack open its pages and live up to the cutting-edge standard found inside. The New King James translation (thoroughly explained in teen-friendly language) is clad in funky purple print and snowboard-type logos, appealing to the thrill seeker by promising a life of 'no fears, no regrets, just a future with a promise.' . . . Portraying Christ as the 'truest revolutionary of all time,' [the *Extreme Teen Bible* is] a survival guide to the world that teens live in."

❦

Surveying the role of print in the history of religion in the United States, one quickly realizes that the Bible is the merest tip of the iceberg. The

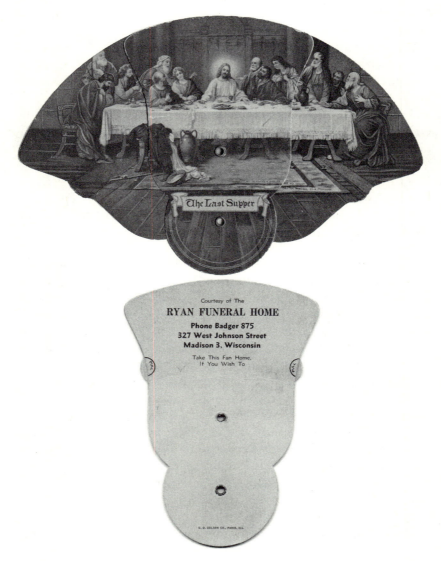

Figure 2.2. In the era before air conditioning, many churches during hot summers offered worshippers fans featuring biblical scenes, with ads from local undertakers on the back. (Produced for the Ryan Funeral Home, Madison, WI, ca. 1940s. Library of the Author.)

Puritan ministers of colonial New England regularly published their sermons, and this marriage of print and piety has persisted ever since.
From the outbreak of the Second Great Awakening in the West in the
1780s, culminating in the great revival at Cane Ridge, Kentucky, in
1801, American Protestantism has rolled forward on a vast tide of hymnals, denominational magazines, Sunday school quarterlies, children's
books, calendars, and even fans with a religious painting on one side
and the name of the local funeral home on the other—a little discreet
advertising as the faithful cooled themselves on hot summer Sundays. In
the same spirit, an 1886 Sunday school quarterly issued by the American Baptist Publication Society featured an advertisement for Hor-
ford's Acid Phosphate, good for "Dyspepsia, Mental and Physical Ex-
haustion, Nervousness, Diminished Vitality, etc."[6]

Revivalists have long used the printed word to extend and solidify
their ministries. In the late nineteenth century, Fleming H. Revell,
brother-in-law of the famed evangelist Dwight L. Moody, built a flourishing business publishing sermons, tracts, religious books, and Sunday
school papers. Moody himself in 1894 founded the Bible Institute Colportage Association to market religious works called the "Colportage
Library." It was named for the colporteurs, or book salesmen, who ped-
dled their wares, often on horseback, in remote parts of the country.
The Colportage Library offered cheap editions of Moody's sermons
and other religious works. In the 1930s it merged with Chicago's Moody
Bible Institute to become Moody Press, which remains a major pur-
veyor of evangelical publications and issues a popular religious magazine, *Moody Monthly*. Other evangelists built on Moody's example. The
post–World War II revivalist Billy Graham spread the word not only
through his citywide crusades and his "Hour of Decision" radio and
television programs, but also through a steady stream of books, beginning with *Peace with God* (1953) and *Decision* magazine, published by the
Billy Graham Evangelistic Association.[7]

ఎ

Religious children's books, hymnals, and tracts have all contributed
mightily to this Niagara of print material in American religious history.
The flow of religious literature for children began in 1656 with John
Cotton's wonderfully titled *Spiritual Milk for Boston Babes in either England,
Drawn Out of the Breasts of both Testaments for their Souls Nourishment.* Another

early work for the edification of the young, *A Token for Children* (1671), recounted the happy deaths of thirteen pious boys and girls. This long-
lived genre includes *The Child's Bible Stories* of 1865 and the popular
Egermeier's Bible Story Book by Elsie E. Egermeier, first published in 1922.
By 1955 sales had surpassed one million. I have warm boyhood memo-
ries of happy hours reading the adventures of the Sugar Creek Gang,
a series by Paul Hutchens launched by Moody Press in 1939 and beloved by thousands of boys growing up in evangelical households. A
graduate of Moody Bible Institute, Hutchens began as an evangelist
until he was sidelined by tuberculosis, when he turned to writing boys'
books.[8] The Sugar Creek Gang books remain in print in contemporary-
looking paperback editions, supplemented now by audiocassette and
CD versions.

A book of moral instruction for children that influenced me as a boy
was a little volume by Effie Mae Hency Williams called *A Hive of Busy
Bees*. It consisted of a series of short stories, told by a grandfather to his
grandchildren, illustrating various virtues: "Bee Obedient," "Bee Honest," and so forth. The "Bee Helpful" story made a particular impact:
young Alfred's mother, who is not feeling well, kindly asks him to help
wash the dishes before he goes off with his friends for a day of fishing.
But he can't be bothered and heedlessly goes off to the creek. At the end
of the day, writes Williams:

> Alfred was much pleased with their catch, and on the way home he said
> over and over, "Won't Mother be glad we went fishing today, when she
> sees our string of trout? She is so fond of trout." But even while he was
> saying it, he could not forget the tired look on his mother's face, or the
> hurt look in her eyes when he had refused to wash the dishes for her.
>
> When the boys reached the house, it seemed strangely quiet. They
> found the dishes cleared away, and the kitchen neatly swept. Alfred's
> mother was lying on the couch, and she seemed to be resting very
> comfortably.
>
> "See, Mother," said Alfred, "isn't this a nice string of trout?"
>
> But Mother did not answer. Alfred spoke to her again. Still no
> answer. He touched her hand then, and found it icy-cold.
>
> Then the awful truth dawned upon him—*his mother was dead!* She
> had died while he was fishing; but she had done the work that she had
> asked her boy to do.[9]

For days after reading that story, I made a special effort to help my
mother with the dishes.

The first book published in New England, *The Bay Psalm Book*, was a hymnal, and this genre, too, has enjoyed remarkable vitality. Of the thousands of Protestant hymnals published over the years, a few well-worn volumes in my library include *The Zion Songster* (1829), "a Collection of Hymns and Spiritual Songs Generally Sung at Camp and Prayer meetings and in Revivals of Religion"; *Hymns for Christian Melody*, published by "the Free-Will Baptist Connection" in 1841; *The Shawm* (1853), "A Library of Church Music; Embracing About One Thousand Pieces, Consisting of Psalm and Hymn Tunes Adapted to Every Meter in Use, Anthems, Chants, and Set Pieces"; *Hymns for the Use of the Methodist Episcopal Church* (1856); *Gospel Hymns No. 3* (1878), assembled by Ira D. Sankey, Dwight L. Moody's song leader; and *A Collection of Spiritual Hymns* (1902), published in Lancaster, Pennsylvania, "especially designed for the use of the Brethren in Christ, known as 'River Brethren.'"

My personal favorite among the hymnals I've accumulated from family sources or in used bookstores over the years is *The Charm* (1871), a collection of Sunday school music assembled by P. P. Bliss. The hymnal we used in the Brethren in Christ mission in Dayton, Ohio, that I attended as a boy contained many songs by P. P. Bliss—a name, I confess, that provoked irreverent mirth among myself and my friends.[10]

For sheer quantity and longevity, few genres outrank the lowly religious tract in the annals of American religious literature. Tracts as a vehicle of evangelism and religious exhortation were first championed by the English reformer Hannah More, founder of the Religious Tract Society in 1799. One of More's tracts of the 1790s, cautioning readers against "cunning women, fortune-tellers, conjurers, and interpretations of dreams," offers a revealing insight into English popular culture in the Age of the Enlightenment. It concludes solemnly: "The Bible will direct us what to do better than any conjurer, and there are no days unlucky but those which we make so by our own vanity, folly, and sin."[11]

The tract movement soon crossed the Atlantic, as Protestant leaders of the early Republic grappled with the dual challenges of urbanization and westward expansion. The presses of the American Tract Society, founded in New York City in 1825, produced millions of little missives that were shipped off to the growing cities and burgeoning settlements of the interior. Bulk shipments went to Sunday schools, poorhouses, prisons, orphanages, and immigration depots. Local tract societies conducted house-to-house distributions in poor districts of their cities. By 1831, six million tracts had been distributed in New York City alone.

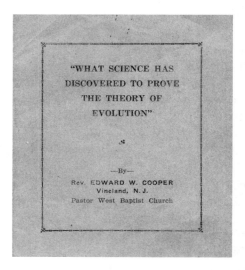

Figure 2.3. Since the eighteenth century, believers have used the unprepossessing religious tract to spread their message. This witty anti-evolution tract, probably from the 1920s, purporting to present all the scientific evidence for Darwin's theory, is totally blank. (Vineland, N.J., publisher not given. Library of the Author.)

Following a formula favored by Hannah More, many such tracts caught readers' attention by telling a cautionary story. A particularly popular narrative, offered in many variant forms, told of the young person from a pious rural home who comes to the big city, falls into sin, contracts a mysterious urban ailment, and returns home to die in the arms of his or her parents and family.[12]

♃♄

From the tract evolved Christian advice books and novels. An example of the former is the Reverend John Todd's *The Moral Influence, Dangers and Duties, Connected with Great Cities* (1841). This work, one of several in a similar vein by Todd, was directed at young people making the dangerous move from farm or village to the nation's burgeoning urban centers. The book luridly chronicles the perils of urban life, perhaps reflecting Todd's own experience. Born in Vermont in 1800, he became pastor of a Presbyterian church in Philadelphia. But financial reverses following the Panic of 1837 wrecked his church's building program and his personal finances, and in 1841 (the same year his cautionary book about cities was published) he left Philadelphia to take a pastorate in the small western Massachusetts town of Pittsfield.[13]

Sometimes these works of religious advice appeared in fictional form. After the success of *Uncle Tom's Cabin*, Harriet Beecher Stowe contributed to this genre with *The Minister's Wooing*, serialized in the *Atlantic Monthly* in 1858–59. The paradigmatic Christian novel is Charles M. Sheldon's *In His Steps*. In 1889 Sheldon, a graduate of Brown University and Andover Seminary, became pastor of a Congregational church in Topeka, Kansas. An advocate of the Social Gospel, which sought to involve Christians more fully in the problems of labor and the urban poor, he had earlier volunteered in a London settlement house. Upon arriving in Topeka, he had sought contact with the city's working class, even donning work clothes and taking a job as a common laborer. Soon Sheldon began to devote his Sunday evening services to "sermon stories": fictional narratives exploring Christianity's social implications in an urban-industrial age. The *Advance*, a Congregational magazine in Chicago, published several of these stories, and in 1896, as the nation grappled with a severe economic depression, Sheldon gathered them into a novel he called *In His Steps; or, What Would Jesus Do?* Owing to a defective copyright, sixteen different publishers soon had editions on the market.

A hundred thousand copies were sold the first year. In 1947 historian Frank L. Mott estimated total worldwide sales at six million, and millions more have certainly been sold in the sixty years since. In our own time, the phrase "What would Jesus do?" has become ubiquitous, leading to such spin-off books as Dr. Dan Colbert's *What Would Jesus Eat?* (Jesus, Colbert reports, would eat fish, cook with olive oil, and avoid McDonald's.)[14]

In His Steps begins on a Sunday morning in a comfortable church in the fictional Midwestern city of Raymond. A homeless man disrupts the service by telling of his rejection by the town's respectable citizens and, before collapsing, asks the question that has resonated down through the years: "What would Jesus do?" The minister, Reverend Maxwell, takes the man into his home, but he dies the following week. Shaken by this experience, the church members soon transform the town by their reformist energies: the newspaper editor features stories of social uplift rather than crime and corruption; a department-store owner introduces a profit-sharing plan with his employees; a choir member starts a music school in the slums; an heiress builds a home for wayward girls; saloons and brothels close as revival sweeps the town. As the "What would Jesus do?" campaign spreads to Chicago, converts start a settlement house and a cooking school for immigrant girls, and a slumlord has a change of heart. Sheldon's novel, in short, popularized the Social Gospel message of liberal Protestantism. Other Social Gospel ministers such as Josiah Strong, Washington Gladden, and Walter Rauschenbusch used the print medium to good effect, as did the British journalist William T. Stead in his muckraking exposé *If Christ Came to Chicago* (1894). Cumulatively, these works mark the years 1890–1910 as a transformative age when religious leaders employed the printed word to prick the conscience of a nation and played a seminal role in laying the groundwork for the Progressive reform movement.[15]

In His Steps also illustrates another aspect of the power of print in American religious history: its chameleon-like adaptability. Over the years, Sheldon's novel gave rise to a 1964 movie adaptation, now available in audiotape and DVD; a 1973 comic-book version; trendy contemporary paperback editions; and a tide of "WWJD" ("What would Jesus do?") bracelets, T-shirts, teddy bears, coffee mugs, and ballpoint pens.

In the process, Sheldon's message subtly evolved. In the 1973 comic-book version, for example, the homeless derelict is not the grizzled tramp of Sheldon's depression-era novel but a handsome, long-haired

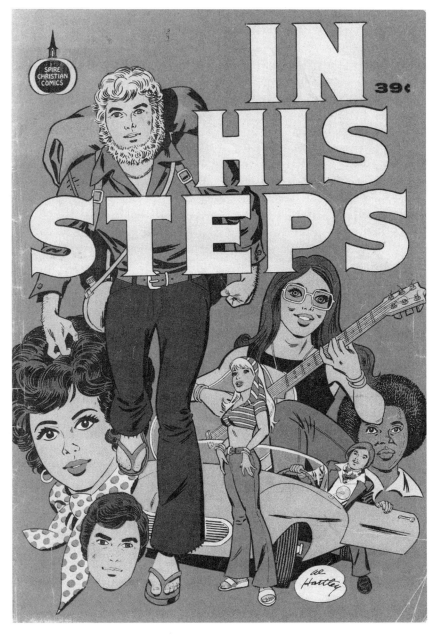

Figure 2.4. Charles M. Sheldon's 1896 novel *In His Steps*, featuring the question "What Would Jesus Do?" remains influential more than a century later. This 1973 comic-book version targeted contemporary youth. (© 1973 Spire Christian Comics. Reprinted by permission of Baker Publishing Group. Library of the Author.)

hippie hitchhiker. And the message is less one of social justice than of outraged morality. The newspaper editor stops advertising sexually suggestive movies and television producers ban risqué language and require female performers to dress more modestly. A teenage girl in a revealing two-piece outfit boasts "I'm hooked on *sex* and *drugs*," but renounces all this when she is born again. A college president proclaims, in a Frank Capra moment, "I'm going to get *involved* in politics and . . . clean things up."[16] In short, in its 1970s comic-book incarnation, *In His Steps* was transformed from a Social Gospel tract to a call for a post-1960s crusade against drugs, changing sexual mores, and the secular media—a striking corollary to Jerry Falwell's Moral Majority, founded in 1979.

The Christian comic book is, in fact, a very old genre. My own exposure to Bible stories in comic-book format in the 1940s was sometimes confusing. At age nine or ten, for example, I wondered why the beautiful young widow, Ruth the Moabite, spent the night in the bedroom of the wealthy landowner Boaz when she presumably had a perfectly good bed of her own. By the 1970s, the genre had evolved beyond Bible stories, with such titles as *Tom Landry and the Dallas Cowboys; The Cross and the Switchblade; Hello, I'm Johnny Cash; Up from Harlem;* and the intriguing *Hansi: The Girl Who Loved the Swastika.*[17]

One Christian comic-book series, launched in 1972, featured the popular teenage characters Archie, Veronica, and Jughead. The artist, Al Hartley, was the son of Congressman Fred Hartley, the New Jersey Republican whose name is best remembered as the second half of the 1947 Taft-Hartley Act, which trimmed the power of labor unions. Hartley was drawing a suggestive strip featuring a female character called "Pussy Cat" for a men's magazine when, in 1967, he found God. He persuaded Archie Comics to grant him use of the company's eponymous hero, and soon Archie and his friends began a new life as born-again Christians. Sales of Spire comics, the publisher of these religious titles, eventually topped forty million copies.[18]

Not only in comic books, but also throughout religious print culture, visual images have long augmented and in some cases supplanted the printed word. From the illustrated Bibles of Matthew Carey and Isaiah Thomas to *The Hieroglyphick Bible* featuring nearly 500 woodcuts of "emblematical figures, for the amusement of youth: designed chiefly to familiarize tender age, in a pleasing and diverting manner with early ideas of the Holy Scriptures" (1825) to children's Bible story books and Warner Sallman's ubiquitous "Head of Christ" painting, visual imagery has been central to American Christianity's use of the printing press.[19]

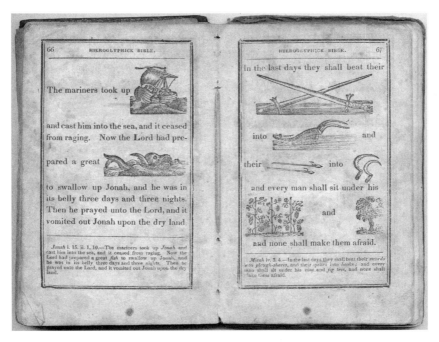

Figure 2.5. Illustrated Bible stories for children have a long history in American print culture. This example, *The Hieroglyphic Bible*, which uses rebuses to help children memorize Bible verses, was issued by Silas Andrus, a Hartford publisher, in 1825. (Library of the Author.)

A succession of new religious movements have relied on the printed word as well. Joseph Smith's *The Book of Mormon* (1830) became the foundational scripture of a religion that is today embraced by some twelve million members worldwide. In the 1830s and early 1840s the followers of William Miller of upstate New York, who calculated Christ's return in 1843 or 1844, used newspapers, posters, broadsides, and colorful charts to spread their message. Leading Millerites eventually pinned the date down precisely: 22 October 1844. The movement collapsed when the appointed day came and went, but out of the ashes arose the Seventh-day Adventist Church, inspired in part by the publications of Ellen G. White. Historian Ronald Numbers has shown that White plagiarized from various sources, but his revelation does not appear to have slowed the movement's growth. Like their Millerite ancestors, today's Adventists rely heavily on books, magazines, and brochures that vividly illustrate the horrors of the Last Days and the joys of Christ's millennial kingdom.[20] I once accepted an offer in an Adventist periodical for a free copy of an Adventist book on Bible prophecy. It duly arrived, delivered by the local Adventist minister and several of his flock. They reappeared at regular intervals for several months thereafter, before finally giving up on me. This underscored for me the importance of Janice Radway's point, made in another context, that one must approach print culture materials not in isolation, but embedded in their social and cultural milieu.[21]

Mary Baker Eddy's followers, too, built their Christian Science Church on the foundation of a book: Eddy's 1875 work *Science and Health*, to which she added *A Key to the Scriptures* in 1883. In keeping with their print-culture beginnings, Christian Scientists continue to propagate their faith through library-like "reading rooms" in cities across America, featuring Christian Science publications. The church's highly regarded newspaper, *The Christian Science Monitor*, devotes a page to church teachings, including liberal extracts from the writings of Mrs. Eddy.

So seriously has the Christian Science Church taken the printed word that in 1928, when the *Dictionary of American Biography* published a biography of Mary Baker Eddy by Arthur Schlesinger, Sr., that church leaders considered disrespectful, they offered to pay the cost of reprinting that entire volume of the reference work if they could have editorial control over the Eddy biography. The publisher, Charles Scribner's Sons, refused, and the *Nation* magazine publicized the episode in an article entitled "The Blight That Failed."[22]

The Jehovah's Witnesses, too, date their beginnings to a book: Charles Taze Russell's work of prophetic interpretation, *Millennial Dawn* (1886). With a boldness worthy of William Miller, Russell foresaw a major eschatological event in 1914. When war erupted in Europe in August 1914, the movement enjoyed a spurt of popularity. True to their print-culture roots, today's Witnesses distribute their *Watchtower* and *Awake* magazines on street corners and door-to-door. Indeed, the organization's official name is the Watchtower Bible and Tract Society.[23]

Herbert W. Armstrong's Worldwide Church of God, founded in 1933 to promote his belief that Anglo-Saxons are one of the lost tribes of Israel, won recruits not only through Armstrong's radio program, "The World Tomorrow," but also through the magazines *Plain Truth* and *Good News*, distributed free in airports and other public venues. At the church's peak in the 1970s and 1980s, before it was plagued by a succession crisis following Armstrong's death in 1986, eight million copies of *Plain Truth* and a million copies of *Good News* were distributed monthly.[24]

All these heterodox movements, from Mormonism on, spawned an outpouring of opposition polemic, as did the antebellum anti-Catholic crusade. The latter movement gave rise in 1836 to the mendacious but highly popular *Awful Disclosures of Maria Monk,* a sensational exposé of alleged sexual goings-on between priests and nuns in a Montreal convent, including the baptism, murder, and secret burial of nuns' newborn babies. Maria Monk and the ministers who promoted her story were soon exposed as frauds and bigots, but her book, like the later and equally fraudulent antisemitic *Protocols of the Elders of Zion,* took on a life of its own.[25]

Intramural battles within the Protestant fold, notably the epic struggle between "Modernists" and "Fundamentalists" that arose in the early twentieth century—and still continues today—generated their own torrent of polemical literature, beginning with *The Fundamentals* (1910-15), a twelve-volume paperback series of doctrinal statements funded by a wealthy California oilman, Lyman Stewart, and continued with a fusillade of books and articles from champions of liberal Protestantism like Harry Emerson Fosdick and Edward Mortimer Chapman.[26]

Closely linked to the rise of Fundamentalism was a highly idiosyncratic system of Bible prophecy interpretation called premillennial dispensationalism, based on an ingenious interpretation and collation of certain cryptic biblical texts. Formulated in the mid-nineteenth century by John Darby, a British churchman and founder of the Plymouth Brethren sect, premillennial dispensationalism quickly made its way to the United States, where, once again, the print-culture medium played a key role in its dissemination. The Reverend Cyrus Scofield's 1909 reference Bible offered Scofield's dispensationalist commentary on the same pages as the biblical text, so readers often could not recall whether they had read something in the biblical text itself or in Scofield's notes. As a bit of doggerel put it, parodying a familiar gospel song: "My hope is built on nothing less / Than Scofield's notes and Moody Press."

Published by Oxford University Press, and still in print today, having sold in excess of ten million copies, the *Scofield Reference Bible* remains a key source for prophecy beliefs that are widely held in contemporary America and continue to be promulgated by many paperback popularizers.[27]

ഖ

And what of the present? Certainly the technology has changed, from hand-set type and steam-powered printing presses to computerized composition and photo-offset printing. And the electronic media, from religious television broadcasts on cable and global communications satellites to the Internet and DVDs, offer potent alternatives to the printed page. But the print media, embedded within a larger web of communications technologies, remain central to contemporary American religious life. In the summer of 2004 Rick Warren's *The Purpose-Driven Life* topped *The New York Times'* "Advice, How-To, and Miscellaneous" category; in February 2006 Amazon.com still ranked Warren's book twenty-fifth in sales among its millions of hardback books.[28] Warren, a Southern Baptist minister, is the founding pastor of the fifteen-thousand-member Saddleback Church in Lake Forest, California. In contrast to Norman Vincent Peale, whose 1952 best seller *The Power of Positive Thinking* promised readers prosperity if they recited Bible verses such as "I can do all things through Christ, which strengtheneth me," or the more recent Robert Schuller of California's Crystal Cathedral, with his "possibility thinking" mantras, Rick Warren is firmly in the evangelical camp. The Bible is inerrant, his book insists, and one's duty is to discern God's will through prayer and daily devotional study. As the jacket copy puts it: "You are not an accident. Even before the universe was created, God had you in mind, and he planned you for his purposes. These purposes will extend far beyond the few years you will spend on earth. You were made to last forever." Reassuring words, indeed, in uncertain times gripped by fears of terrorism and of anonymity in a globalizing economy.

Dr. James Dobson (b. 1935), the conservative evangelical psychologist and founder of Focus on the Family in 1977 and of the political lobbying organization, the Family Research Council, spreads his message nationwide not only through a daily radio and television program, but also via some thirty books and *Focus on the Family Magazine,* which claims a readership in excess of one million. So powerful is Dobson and his media empire, including the print media, that he was regularly consulted by political operatives in the George W. Bush administration.[29]

ഖ

Bible prophecy interpretations, dating to the Millerites of the 1840s and the *Scofield Reference Bible* of the early twentieth century, continue to flourish in the print culture realm. Hal Lindsey's popularization of premillennial dispensationalism, *The Late Great Planet Earth,* published in 1970, became *the* nonfiction best seller of the decade, and continues to sell, together with a host of other works by the prolific Lindsey, including a 1996 prophecy novel, *Blood Moon.*[30] An erstwhile Mississippi River tugboat operator, Lindsey found God; attended Dallas Theological Seminary, the Harvard of dispensationalism; and joined a 1960s youth campaign, Bill Bright's Campus Crusade for Christ. He was preaching on the University of California, Los Angeles, campus in the late 1960s when his series of sermons on Bible prophecy drew packed audiences. With the aid of a ghostwriter, the underappreciated C. C. Carlson, he reworked his sermons into the manuscript that became *The Late Great Planet Earth.*

Lindsey is only one of many writers to exploit the current fascination with Bible prophecy. Pat Robertson's *The New World Order* (1991) found anticipations of the Antichrist in the emerging post–Cold War global system; Charles H. Dyer's *The Rise of Babylon: Sign of the End Times* (1991) saw Saddam Hussein as a likely Antichrist candidate; John Hagee, pastor of a 16,000-member church in San Antonio, saw Israel as the key to future apocalyptic events in *Final Dawn Over Jerusalem* (1998) and other books. Michael D. Evans's *The American Prophecies: Ancient Scriptures Reveal Our Nation's Future* made the *New York Times* best-seller lists in 2004.[31]

Outstripping all these authors were Tim LaHaye and Jerry B. Jenkins and their phenomenal best sellers, the *Left Behind* series, which began in 1995. This fourteen-volume series, with sales approaching seventy million as of 2006, is *The Late Great Planet Earth* on steroids. LaHaye's and Jenkins's fictionalization of John Darby's dispensationalist system of prophetic interpretation begins with the Rapture, when all true believers meet Jesus in the air, and continues on through the Tribulation, the rise of the Antichrist, Armageddon, and the Second Coming. Not only did the *Left Behind* books fly off the shelves, but they spawned an array of product tie-ins, including a movie, Internet Web sites, a video game, a series for kids, audio and CD versions, a dramatic version aired on Christian radio stations, and "Left Behind" T-shirts, jewelry, and mouse pads—all the marketing strategies associated with any contemporary mass-culture phenomenon.[32] Indeed, the line between "religious" and "secular" has become so hazy in contemporary U.S. mass culture as to be almost meaningless, and nowhere is this more evident than in the realm of print culture and its many ramifications.

With Americans' voracious appetite for Christian-themed books and other products producing billions in annual sales, global media conglomerates are paying attention. Scott, Foresman & Company acquired the venerable religious publisher Fleming H. Revell in 1978. In the same year, Zondervan Publishing Company of Grand Rapids, Michigan, founded in 1931 by the brothers Pat and Bernie Zondervan, was acquired by HarperCollins, a division of Rupert Murdoch's News Corporation. Zondervan, which published Hal Lindsey's *The Late Great Planet Earth* in 1970, is currently prospering as the publisher of Rick Warren's *The Purpose-Driven Life*. The TimeWarner Corporation has launched a conservative religious imprint, WarnerFaith, which publishes Michael Evans's *The American Prophecies* and other works targeting the evangelical market. Random House, too, has moved into the evangelical religious market with its WaterBrook Press imprint, publisher of Mary E. DeMuth's *Building the Christian Family You Never Had* (2006).

♃

Not only fundamentalists and popularizers of Bible prophecy are exploiting the print media. Liberal Protestantism, though weaker than in the days of the Social Gospel or even during the civil rights and anti–Vietnam War movements of the 1960s, remains alive, and its leaders continue to rely upon the printed word. Among the best known is Jim Wallis of the Sojourners movement of Washington, D.C., the author of *God's Politics* (2005) and other books and publisher of *Sojourners* magazine and *SoJoMail*, a free weekly e-zine.[33]

Indeed, religious publishing in the early twenty-first century is as dizzyingly diverse as the American religious scene itself. The "Religion" sections of today's bookstore chains overflow with works touting such old standbys as Nostradamus, astrology, and New Thought, along with Sufism, Buddhism, Gaia, feminist spirituality, the Kabbalah, and Native-American nature religion, not to mention Christian diet books, Ron Isaacs' *Ask the Rabbi*, and Jack Canfield's and Mark Victor Hansen's *Chicken Soup for the Soul* as well as its spin-off "chicken soup" books for teenagers, mothers, couples, and prisoners. Inevitably, of course, there is also *Christianity for Dummies*, by Richard J. Wagner, who, before he turned to writing for the "Dummy" series, honed his theological skills as vice president for product development of an Internet software company.[34]

♃

Having begun with a biblical text, I close with another one, from the Book of Revelation. It is sometimes forgotten that this apocalyptic work, dating from around AD 100, reveals hidden knowledge of the future that is contained *in a book*. At the outset, the author, John, is transported into the realm of the spirit and shown a book with seven seals. As each seal is broken, additional events that will unfold at the End of Time are revealed, each more fantastic than what came before.

Midway through Revelation, an angel appears bearing another small book, and John is commanded to eat it: "And I took the little book out of the angel's hand, and ate it up; and it was in my mouth sweet as honey, and as soon as I had eaten it, my belly was bitter." The Word, quite literally, becomes flesh.

As Revelation closes, we are reminded again of the book with seven seals that was given to John at the beginning of his vision. The book's seals now broken, John is commanded to keep it open, so its eschatological message will henceforth be accessible to all: "And [the angel] saith unto me, Seal not the sayings of the prophecy of this book: for the time is at hand."[35]

Books, in short, figure prominently both at the close of the Gospels and in Revelation, which concludes the biblical canon, as believers are instructed to spread truths revealed in books that must be open to all. For three centuries, religious writers and publishers in America have done their best to live up to that command. They continue to do so with undiminished zeal.

I can imagine no more appropriate and timely topic for the University of Wisconsin's Center for the History of Print Culture in Modern America than the subject of its 2004 conference: religion and the culture of print in America. That stimulating event, in turn, gave rise to the engrossing selection of essays that follow.

Notes

I would like to thank Paul Hass and Peter Johannes Thuesen for their helpful comments on this essay.

1. On American Catholicism and print culture, for example, Ann Taves, *The Household of Faith: Roman Catholic Devotions in Mid-Nineteenth Century America* (Notre Dame, IN: University of Notre Dame Press, 1986), examines the role of devotional literature in grassroots Catholicism; Colleen McDannell, *The*

Christian Home in Victorian America, 1840–1900 (Bloomington: Indiana University Press, 1986), examines Catholic as well as Protestant religious books and magazines; Robert S. Orsi, *Thank You, St. Jude: Women's Devotion to the Patron Saint of Hopeless Causes* (New Haven, CT: Yale University Press, 1996), discusses the key role of the publication *The Voice of Saint Jude* (later *St. Jude's Journal)* in sustaining this Chicago-based movement. A comprehensive history of American Catholic print culture remains to be written, however.

2. For a history stressing the ABS's innovative production and management strategies, see Peter J. Wosh, *Spreading the Word: The Bible Business in Nineteenth-Century America* (Ithaca, NY: Cornell University Press, 1994). Paul J. Gutjahr, *An American Bible: A History of the Good Book in the United States, 1777–1880* (Stanford, CA: Stanford University Press, 1999), is especially good on the role of Matthew Carey and Isaiah Thomas. See also Nathan O. Hatch and Mark A. Noll, eds., *The Bible in America: Essays in Cultural History* (New York: Oxford University Press, 1982), and Colleen McDannell, *Material Christianity: Religion and Popular Culture in America* (New Haven, CT: Yale University Press, 1998), chap. 3, "The Bible in Victorian America," 67–102. An excellent study bearing on the themes of this paper is R. Laurence Moore, *Selling God: American Religion in the Marketplace of Culture* (New York: Oxford University Press, 1994).

3. Gift Bibles and Testaments often provided an occasion for religious and moral exhortations. For example, the New Testament presented to my thirteen-year-old father in 1913 is inscribed: "May this little Testament be food to your soul, and a sure guide to your footsteps through this dark and sinful world, and lead you peacefully in through Heaven's gates is our prayer. Your Mama and Papa." In the New Testament my grandparents, William and Susie Boyer, presented to me at the age of three in 1939, they wrote: "We are glad you are a good boy in Sunday S[chool]. We hope you will grow up to be a good man and always love Jesus. We want you to meet us in Heaven. Grandpa and Grandma." The November 1943 Sunday school gift Bible bears a terser inscription: "Be a good boy, Paul."

4. M. A. Henderson, *Sowers of the Word: A 95-Year History of the Gideons International, 1899–1994* (n.p.: Gideons International, 1995); "Green Bibles Lead to Green Pastures: Members of Gideons International Come Out Faithfully Year After Year to Hand Out Bibles on Campuses," *The Daily Texan*, 28 August 2002, 12.

5. Dwight Macdonald, "Updating the Bible," *New Yorker* 29 (14 November 1953), reprinted in Macdonald, *Against the American Grain: Essays on the Effects of Mass Culture* (New York: Vintage Books, 1962), 262–84, quoted passage 272. Ironically, the RSV that Macdonald criticized so harshly was intended by its American editors to remedy the stylistic shortcomings of the 1881–85 British revision, a literalistic translation that privileged linguistic precision over stylistic

grace. Peter Johannes Thuesen, *In Discordance with the Scriptures: American Protestant Battles over Translating the Bible* (New York: Oxford University Press, 1999), tells the full story.

6. *Advanced Quarterly . . . Fourth Quarter,* ed. Edward G. Taylor, D.D. (Philadelphia: American Baptist Publication Society, 1886), inside front cover.

7. John Tebbel, *A History of Book Publishing in the United States,* vol. 2, *The Expansion of an Industry, 1865–1919* (New York: R. R. Bowker, 1975), 332–33 (Revell and Moody); Billy Graham, *Just As I Am: The Autobiography of Billy Graham* (San Francisco: HarperSanFrancisco, 1997); William C. Martin, *A Prophet with Honor: The Billy Graham Story* (New York: W.W. Morrow, 1991).

8. Elsie E. Egermeier, *Egermeier's Bible Story Book,* rev. ed. (Anderson, IN: The Warner Press, 1955 [orig. 1922]); on Paul Hutchens, see "About the Author of the Sugar Creek Gang," http://faith.edu/bookstore/scginfo.htm#Hutchens (accessed 27 August 2007).

9. Effie Mae Hency Williams, *A Hive of Busy Bees* (Anderson, IN: Gospel Trumpet Company, 1931), quoted passage, 31 (emphasis mine). The text of this book is available at the Project Gutenberg Online Book Catalog at http://www.gutenberg.org/etext/7027 (accessed 27 August 2007). A reprint has been issued by Grace & Truth Books of Sand Springs, OK. Various Web sites suggest that this reprint is popular with parents who home school their children.

10. Philip Paul Bliss (1838–76) was the author of such evangelical favorites as "Let the Lower Lights Be Burning" and "Almost Persuaded." He died with his wife in a railroad accident in Ashtabula, Ohio, in 1876. See also Stephen A. Marini, *Sacred Song in America: Religion, Music, and Public Culture* (Urbana: University of Illinois Press, 2003); Richard J. Mouw and Mark A. Noll, *Wonderful Words of Life: Hymns in American Protestant History and Theology* (Grand Rapids, MI: Wm. B. Eerdmans Publishing Co., 2004); Jon Michael Spencer, *Black Hymnody: A Hymnological History of the African-American Church* (Knoxville: University of Tennessee Press, 1992). For an interesting discussion of the role of hymnody in the evangelical tradition see Mark A. Noll, "Evangelicalism at Its Best," *Harvard Divinity Bulletin* 27, no. 2/3 (1998): 8–12.

11. Quoted in Michael Caines, "The Day I Dread," *Times Literary Supplement,* 13 August 2004, 13.

12. Paul Boyer, *Urban Masses and Moral Order in America, 1820–1920* (Cambridge, MA: Harvard University Press, 1978), chap. 2, "The Tract Societies: Transmitting a Traditional Morality by Untraditional Means," 22–33; David Morgan, *Protestants & Pictures: Religion, Visual Culture, and the Age of American Mass Production* (New York: Oxford University Press, 1999), chap. 2, "Evangelical Images and the American Tract Society," 43–74.

13. John Todd, *The Moral Influence, Dangers and Duties, Connected with Great Cities* (Northampton, MA: J. H. Butler, 1841); Boyer, *Urban Masses and Moral Order,* 72–73.

14. Paul S. Boyer, "*In His Steps:* A Reappraisal," *American Quarterly* 23, no. 1 (Spring 1971): 60–79; Don Colbert, *What Would Jesus Eat?* (Nashville: Nelson Books, 2002); Frank L. Mott, *Golden Multitudes: The Story of Best Sellers in the United States* (New York: Macmillan, 1947), 197.

15. Josiah Strong, *The Twentieth-Century City* (New York: Baker and Taylor, 1898) and *The Challenge of the City* (New York: Eaton and Mains, 1907); Washington Gladden, *Social Facts and Forces* (New York: G. P. Putnam's Sons, 1897); Walter Rauschenbusch, *Christianity and the Social Crisis* (New York: Macmillan, 1907); William T. Stead, *If Christ Came to Chicago* (Chicago, 1894); Boyer, *Urban Masses and Moral Order,* 220–60, passim.

16. "In His Steps," Spire Christian Comics (Old Tappan, NJ: Fleming H. Revell, 1977). Revell was also the publisher of the original edition of *In His Steps.*

17. "Hansi: The Girl Who Loved the Swastika," Spire Christian Comics (Fleming H. Revell), a comic-book version of the autobiography of Maria Anne Hirschmann (Wheaton, IL: Tyndale House Publishers, 1973), telling of her early life as an orphan in Czechoslovakia drawn into the Hitler Jugend movement, her conversion, and eventually her work as a youth missionary in California.

18. "Christian Comics Pioneers: Al Hartley," Christian Comics International Website: http://www.christiancomicsinternational.org/hartley_pioneer .html (accessed 27 August 2007). Hartley also drew the "In His Steps" comic book.

19. This is the organizing theme of David Morgan's valuable study *Protestants & Pictures,* cited above. See also McDannell, *Material Christianity;* David Morgan, *Icons of American Protestantism: The Art of Warner Sallman* (New Haven, CT: Yale University Press, 1996); and David Morgan and Sally M. Promey, eds., *The Visual Culture of American Religion* (Berkeley: University of California Press, 2001), a broad-ranging collection of essays discussing Jewish New Year cards, New Mexican *santos* images, and much else.

20. Boyer, *Urban Masses and Moral Order,* 81–84; Morgan, *Protestants & Pictures,* chaps. 4 and 5 ("Millerism and the Schematic Imagination" and "The Commerce of Images and Adventist Piety"), 123–200; Ronald L. Numbers, *Prophetess of Health: A Study of Ellen G. White* (New York: Harper & Row, 1976).

21. Janice A. Radway, *Reading the Romance: Women, Patriarchy, and Popular Literature* (Chapel Hill: University of North Carolina, Press, 1991).

22. Paul S. Boyer, *Purity in Print: Book Censorship in America from the Gilded Age to the Computer Age,* 2nd ed. (Madison: University of Wisconsin Press, 2002), 195.

23. M. James Penton, *Apocalypse Delayed: The Story of Jehovah's Witnesses* (Toronto: University of Toronto Press, 1985).

24. "The Worldwide Church of God" at http://truth.fateback.com/wcg .html (accessed 27 August 2007); for a skeptical view, see Joseph Martin Hopkins, *The Armstrong Empire: A Look at the Worldwide Church of God* (Grand Rapids, MI: Wm. B. Eerdmans Publishing Co., 1974).

25. Ray Allen Billington, "Monk, Maria," in Edward T. James, Janet W. James, and Paul S. Boyer, eds., *Notable American Women, 1607–1950* (Cambridge, MA: Harvard University Press, 1971), 2:560–61.

26. George Marsden, *Fundamentalism and American Culture: The Shaping of Twentieth-Century Evangelicalism, 1870–1925* (New York: Oxford University Press, 1980), 118–23; Harry Emerson Fosdick, *Challenges of the Present Crisis* (New York: Association Press, 1918) and "Shall the Fundamentalists Win?" *Christian Work* 102 (10 June 1922), 716–22, available online at http://historymatters.gmu.edu/ d/5070/ (accessed 27 August 2007); Edward Mortimer Chapman, *A Modernist and His Creed* (Boston: Houghton Mifflin Co., 1926).

27. Paul Boyer, *When Time Shall Be No More: Prophecy Belief in Modern American Culture* (Cambridge, MA: Harvard University Press, 1992), 97–99. See also Ernest R. Sandeen, *The Roots of Fundamentalism: British and American Millenarianism, 1800–1930* (Chicago: University of Chicago Press, 1970); and Timothy P. Weber, *Living in the Shadow of the Second Coming: American Premillennialism, 1875–1925* (New York: Oxford University Press, 1979).

28. Rick Warren, *The Purpose-Driven Life* (Grand Rapids, MI: Zondervan Publishing Co., 2002).

29. For an admiring treatment, see Dale Buss, *Family Man: The Biography of James Dobson* (Wheaton, IL: Tyndale House Publishers, 2005); more critical is Gil Alexander-Moegerle, *James Dobson's War on America* (Amherst, NY: Prometheus Books, 1997). For a quick biographical summary see http://www.answers .com/topic/james-dobson (accessed 27 August 2007).

30. Hal Lindsey, *The Late Great Planet Earth* (Grand Rapids, MI: Zondervan Publishing Co., 1970); Lindsey, *Blood Moon* (Palos Verdes, CA: Western Front Publishing Co., 1996).

31. Pat Robertson, *The New World Order* (Dallas: Word Publishing Co., 1991); Charles H. Dyer, *The Rise of Babylon: Sign of the End Times* (Wheaton, IL: Tyndale House Publishers, 1991); John Hagee, *Final Dawn Over Jerusalem* (Nashville, TN: Thomas Nelson Publishers, 1998); Michael D. Evans, *The American Prophecies: Ancient Scriptures Reveal Our Nation's Future* (New York: WarnerFaith, 2004).

32. Daisy Maryles, "Armageddon Has Arrived," *Publishers Weekly,* 21 April 2003; "'Left Behind' Video Game: Let us Prey," *Los Angeles Times,* 17 December 2006, A28.

33. Jim Wallis, *God's Politics: Why the Right Gets It Wrong and the Left Doesn't Get It* (San Francisco: HarperSanFrancisco, 2005). See also Jim Wallis, *Faith Works: How to Live Your Beliefs and Ignite Positive Social Change* (New York: Random House, 2005), with a foreword by Bill Moyers.

34. Ron Isaacs, *Ask the Rabbi: The Who, What, Where and Why of Being Jewish* (Hoboken, NJ: Jossey-Bass, 2003); Michael Berg, *The Way: Using the Wisdom of Kabbalah for Spiritual Transformation and Fulfillment* (Hoboken, NJ: John Wiley & Sons, 2002); Jack Canfield and Mark Victor Hansen, *Chicken Soup for the Soul*

(HCI, tenth anniversary ed., 2003); Richard J. Wagner, *Christianity for Dummies* (Hoboken, NJ: John Wiley & Sons, 2004). See also Wade Clark Roof, *Spiritual Marketplace: Baby Boomers and the Remaking of American Religion* (Princeton, NJ: Princeton University Press, 1999).

    35. Rev. 10:10, 22:10.

2

Printing Religious Fictions and Facts, 1800–1920

Quakers in American Print Culture, 1800–1950

JAMES EMMETT RYAN

One of the more memorable scenes from Harriet Beecher Stowe's *Uncle Tom's Cabin* (1852) occurs during Eliza Harris's flight from slavery, after she arrives at the safe domestic haven of Rachel and Simeon Halliday, members of a devout Quaker household who have offered her temporary lodging on behalf of the Underground Railroad. It is in this orderly place of cleanliness, courtesy, thrift, goodwill, and piety that the fugitive slave Eliza finally is enabled to sleep soundly, and subsequently to dream "of a beautiful country,—a land, it seemed to her, of rest,—green shores, pleasant islands, and beautifully glittering water; and there, in a house which kind voices told her was a home, she saw her boy playing, a free and happy child." And, indeed, upon waking the next morning, Eliza finds herself reunited with son and husband in the antebellum social oasis that is the Quaker settlement. If *Uncle Tom's Cabin* may be understood, in part, as promoting an idealized form of American family life, then surely the Quaker Halliday family is one of the preeminent examples of that domestic sphere.[1]

Temperate and serene, the men, women, and children in Stowe's Quaker settlement exude Christian virtue, moral gravity, robust health,[2] and personal strength; for them, social justice begins at home, and the Quaker doctrine of an "Inner Light" for each believer manifests itself in an environment of mutuality, candor, and dignity. Here, age is respected and venerated, especially among the women, whose beauty seems to ripen with the years rather than fade. No youthful beauty, the carefully coiffed and plainly dressed[3] Rachel Halliday possesses "one of those faces that time seems to touch only to brighten and adorn." Here, too, the authority of patriarchy largely gives way to the guiding genius of cheerful and industrious women. Simeon Halliday, "a tall, straight, muscular man," speaks few words and stands clear of the more-important kitchen labors of the household's women, who bustle about creating "an atmosphere of mutual confidence and good fellowship." A rare moral exemplar among Stowe's male characters in the novel, however, Simeon chastens his young son for hating the slaveholders who would have prevented George and Eliza from living in peace. Instead, the fictional Quaker patriarch serenely insists upon unconditional love and benevolence, and that he "would do even the same for the slave-holder as for the slave, if the Lord brought him to my door in affliction."[4]

However, despite all their admirable morality—which extended to the all-important notion of equality for women—Stowe's novel does not linger long among these Friends of the Quaker settlement. For all the optimism expressed about these believers in the "Inner Light" of Quak-erism, *Uncle Tom's Cabin* does not directly advocate a turn to Quakerism as a solution for the problem of American social ills. As one critic has noted, while highlighting the otherness of Quaker clothing and dialect, Stowe's novel also clearly indicates her admiration for the humanitar-ianism of Quakers. There are limits to her representations, however, for "No Quaker refers to the Inner Light, no Quaker discusses or even al-ludes to an inner awareness of spirituality, no Quaker refers to Christ."[5] Quakers in the novel are fashioned as exemplary figures of Christian virtue but do not dominate the narrative as a whole; they are presented as model Americans, but just as clearly their religious world seems to be little more than a fantasy, or an impossibility on the larger scale that interests Stowe. In this way, Stowe followed a formula that would be-come familiar over the course of the nineteenth century, as the Ameri-can popular novel increasingly displaced other printed genres like the sermon and the religious tract to become a leading print forum for moral and religious debates. Quakerism's representation in fiction as a set of exemplary American religious and social practices appears alongside its failure to attract large numbers of followers. Consistently in the socially progressive vanguard, and commonly used in fiction as one of the highest expressions of Christianity, Quakers in early American fiction are deployed for our admiration, but they also enlist our recognition of their broader failure to capture American religious enthusiasm in any significant way. Notable in early American fiction for their moral superiority, Quakers[6] are equally notable as angelic representations of an unrealizable social ideal: participants in a version of religious practice that inevitably will lie outside the popular reach.

Stowe's novel, with its immense and enduring popularity, was of great significance in the development of nineteenth-century American literature. And as a key artifact in the evolving national print culture, it illuminates a number of issues specifically relevant to Quaker religious life itself, that is, the actual history of this particular group of Christians in America. But *Uncle Tom's Cabin*, along with the many American novels that preceded and followed it in creating fictional characters who are Quakers, serves as important evidence of a shift that had already occurred with regard to how the values and practice of Quakerism were being represented within a complex and changing American print culture. Nineteenth-century writers of fiction were heir to a long tradition, dating from the 1650s, of Anglo-American writing about the Religious Society of Friends. By the time Harriet Beecher Stowe turned her attention to the Society of Friends, Quakers had been subject to both sympathetic and antagonistic representation in a wide range of printed materials for a full two centuries. *Uncle Tom's Cabin* is thus a case in point showing how Quakers were perceived within antebellum American culture, but in 1851 (the year in which it first appeared, in serialized form) it also figured as the latest—though by no means the last—in a long history of complex representations focused on a small fraction of the Protestant movement and enabled by a proliferating print culture to amplify those representations for a far larger community of readers.[7] Therefore, at its simplest level, the discussion that follows is meant, first, to suggest how frequently Quakers were used as moral exemplars in American fiction, especially that of the nineteenth and early twentieth century. Second, the evidence from many of these fictional narratives discloses a paradoxical reluctance to adopt wholeheartedly the religious views of these much-admired Quakers, whose model behavior, according to many of these writers, persistently lay just beyond the grasp of ordinary well-meaning Americans. Third, it will become clear from the shifting modes of fictional representation over more than a century that, although Quakers retained their utility as stock fictional characters for a very long time, the moral and cultural significance of Quakerism waxed and waned, as American novelists registered religious, demographic, and political changes in their fiction.

Finally, the representation of Quakers in American fiction, which began in earnest in the first decades of the nineteenth century and continued into the early years of the twentieth century, marks an important late phase in the development of the Quaker idea in Anglo-American print culture, of which the novel is one important component. As Ronald J. Zboray has argued convincingly, the evolution of American national culture has always been bound tightly to the history of the book, and the American novel came to maturity and began its most significant cultural work during the antebellum period, when "the printed word became the primary avenue of national enculturation." The vital center of printed discourse—which had earlier been located in theological debate, political argument, or personal letters—was by the middle of the nineteenth century centered in the world of fiction, which was proliferating in a booming marketplace of popular novels. As American fiction grew to a position of great power and influence among a nation of increasingly active readers, it became possible for a moralist like Stowe to have enormous influence on a national readership, and it became possible as well for her to propose Quaker values and identity as aspects of an extreme but perhaps unreachable type of American virtue. The widespread deployment of idealized Quakers into popular fiction of the nineteenth and twentieth century should be understood as an extension of an earlier period of American (and English) print culture (1650–1750) when Quakers and their orthodox adversaries were participants in ferocious theological debates. As the once-fraught theological controversies between Puritan and Quaker subsided and early eighteenth-century Quakers became much more quietistic in their religious expression (1750–1850), the debates surrounding American independence and the new Republic provided new opportunities for Quakers to be idealized as non-slave-holding members of harmonious and virtuous communities (the French enthusiasm for Americans is one example of this phenomenon, with late eighteenth-century writers like Voltaire and Crèvecoeur leading the way in expounding the virtues of Quakerism). This period also featured American writing with a decided focus on the Quaker-supported abolition of slavery, beginning with the late eighteenth-century antislavery journals of John Woolman and concluding with antislavery novels like *Uncle Tom's Cabin,* published in the years immediately preceding the Civil War.[8]

When the abolitionist movement intensified during the years before the Civil War, Quakers like Stowe's Halliday family demonstrated and embodied the ideals of domestic stability and racial benevolence that *Uncle Tom's Cabin* sponsors. Decades later and well into the twentieth century, when American regionalists and local colorists turned consistently to representations of the quaint, the picturesque, and the historically curious, Quakers were prominent among the stock figures that conjured up a sense of a uniquely admirable and yet uncannily repellent American tradition. Whereas early Puritan theology, as recalled acutely in novels like Nathaniel Hawthorne's *The Gentle Boy* (1839), had understood how the Religious Society of Friends could engender fanaticism and religious strife, by the late nineteenth and early twentieth century, Quakers came to be understood as rather ineffectual, indeed anachronistic figures: Americans who are morally correct and yet insufficiently equipped to wrestle with modernity.[9]

ℐℛ

One of the earliest American novels to depict Quakerism as an ideal form of American worship and moral practice, Elizabeth B. Lester's *The Quakers; A Tale* (1818) applied Quaker values to that most durable of all fictional themes: adultery. Kezia Brooks, the beautiful and wealthy young Friend at the center of *The Quakers,* speaks little of spirituality or the Inner Light, and instead harbors only the most diluted version of Quaker theology or religiosity; she "was mildly religious; a Christian in practice, rather than theory." Still, the novel makes clear that without her veneer of Quaker modesty and propriety, she would have been instantly subject to libertinism as well as her own vanity. The plot of *The Quakers,* which focuses on the courtship and married life of Kezia Brooks, shows her to be slightly vain, but otherwise good-hearted and loyal (largely because of her Quaker training). After she chooses unwisely to marry the rakish Robert Honour, however, the downward spiral begins. A brief period of wedded bliss is followed by Honour's descent into a profligate life of gambling, drinking, financial irresponsibility, and marital infidelity: all of which is tolerated and abetted because of Kezia's naive Quakerish "desire to please universally." When Honour's infidelity finally comes to

light, at the end of the novel, he impulsively agrees to a duel with one of
his enemies and is mortally wounded. At this point, Lester chooses to
end her novel with a turn to sincere Quaker faith. With a chastened and
newly devout Kezia by his side, the dying Honour undergoes a death-
bed conversion to Quakerism. The Quaker ideal, absent for most of the
novel, thus makes a critical appearance as the novel concludes—when
the incorrigible libertine discovers Quakerism to be salvific—but only
as his own demise becomes inevitable. Once again, as with Stowe's admirable and yet apparitional Quakers in *Uncle Tom's Cabin,* the literary
function of the Society of Friends and its members has much do with at-
testing to the values of Quaker morality versus other moral practices.
But Quakerism exists mostly outside the frame of the narrative itself:
for Harriet Beecher Stowe, the fleeting glimpses of the Halliday clan at
the Quaker settlement; for Elizabeth B. Lester, the suggestion that true
Quaker faith can exist only after an unseemly tale ends in tragedy.[10]

Harriet Beecher Stowe herself, initially through a youthful encounter with the Quaker Angelina Grimké in 1831, had long been fascinated
with the Society of Friends and its work on behalf of abolitionism and
women's rights. Well before the publication of *Uncle Tom's Cabin,* Stowe
had begun to use the device of the "good Quaker" in her fiction, as with
her 1845 sketch "Immediate Emancipation," in which a runaway slave
in Cincinnati is allowed to go free, thanks to the intervention of a Quaker
who convinces the slave's master of the evils of human bondage. However, like *Uncle Tom's Cabin,* this early sketch stops well short of advocating a turn to Quakerism among Stowe's enormous readership. In this
regard, Stowe turns to Quaker ideals in much the same way as her
contemporary, Margaret Fuller, whose magisterial proto-feminist tract
Woman in the Nineteenth Century (1845) appeared the same year as Stowe's
"Immediate Emancipation." For Fuller, Quakers—although mentioned
only briefly in *Woman in the Nineteenth Century*—provided a key model for
blending femininity with participation in the public sphere. Like the
great female stage performers of her day, writes Fuller, nineteenth-
century Quaker women had already made important advances on behalf of the feminist cause: "We should think those who had seen the
great actresses, and heard the Quaker preachers of modern times, would
not doubt, that women can express publicly the fullness of thought and
creation, without losing any of the peculiar beauty of her sex." Of
course, Margaret Fuller pointedly does not conclude that Quaker religiosity constituted anything resembling a sufficient feminist paradigm.

Like Stowe's Quakers, who are unmistakably feminine, Christian, and politically progressive, the Quaker women in Fuller's account suggest all of these traits, while nevertheless also appearing implicitly to be radically "other," and perhaps not entirely assimilable to the American political and social context.[11]

Assimilable or not, Quaker characters did appear with some regularity in nineteenth-century popular fiction, particularly in the later part of the century, and even as the plainly dressed Quaker became a less frequent sight in American communities. Generally speaking, however, the evidence from nineteenth-century American novels appears to support Henry Seidel Canby's comment that "the Quaker has been unfortunate in fiction and drama."[12] Fictional representations of American Quakers typically follow Stowe's narrative pattern of admiration for their piety and justice, while stopping well short of proselytizing on behalf of the Society of Friends, who usually appear to comprise a preternaturally gifted subset of humanity—ethereal savants of benevolence. And we see this ambivalence about Quakerism not only in Stowe's writings but in those of other writers as well. For example, in Rebecca Harding Davis's remarkable novella of the laboring classes, *Life in the Iron Mills* (1861), the nameless woman who, at the very last minute, rescues the lowly Deb Wolfe from dire impoverishment and criminality turns out to be a Quaker of nearly supernatural serenity and virtue. Just after her companion, the ill-fated working-class sculptor Hugh Wolfe, dies in jail of tuberculosis, his wife—the deformed and miserable Deb—finds comfort and recuperation at the hands of a Quaker woman, who appears miraculously at the moment of her gravest difficulty. It is the Quaker woman, "a homely body, coarsely dressed in gray and white," who attends to the wretched laborer in her hour of mourning and cares for the tragically dead sculptor's body. Eternally modest and yet teeming with Christian virtue, the homely Quaker woman serves here as an example of the sort of noble creature that Walt Whitman had in mind when speaking of laudable women in the Society of Friends, such as the abolitionist Lucretia Mott. "Do you know the Quaker women?" he once inquired of his companion Horace Traubel. "The women are the cream of the sect. It was not Lucretia Mott alone—I knew her just a little: she was a gracious, superb character, but she was not exceptional."[13]

Whether actual Quaker women were well-known or not, their plain way of dressing—a familiar marker for nineteenth-century readers who had observed Quakers—made it relatively easy to view them in theatrical terms, playing a social role for which "ordinary" Americans were not equipped. Whereas earlier generations of prosperous American Quakers exhibited considerable luxury in their clothing, nineteenth-century Friends actually adhered far more closely to the long-established doctrine of simple clothing. This is a key point, as the historian of clothing Leanna Lee-Whitman has noted, because "the quality of clothing worn by a person in the eighteenth and throughout most of the nineteenth century was the most common index of his or her social position in European and American society," and consequently dressing plainly allowed Quakers to distinguish themselves from more worldly Americans. The extreme alterity suggested by the Quaker woman's willfully drab attire, worn in a society of increasingly conspicuous consumption, however, also highlights the alterity of her benevolent actions in assisting the hapless Deb. Thus, the astonishing and gratifying scene of human rescue, when understood from the perspective of Davis's readers, creates a moral and logical impasse: rescuing the victims of brutal industrial labor becomes a desirable and necessary act, and yet the burden of rescue is borne by a phantomlike Quaker rather than by society as a whole.[14]

Consequently, although *Life in the Iron Mills* presents a devastating antebellum picture of the working poor of industrialized America, Davis offers very little in the way of practical remedy for the dire material circumstances of her impoverished mill workers. The upper-class characters in the story range from profoundly empathetic to coarsely indifferent, but none of them extends anything other than mere sympathy and prayers to the oppressed victims of subsistence wage slavery. In short, the novel's bold exposé stops well short of advocating broad social change or substantial intervention to alter the condition of the hapless workers. Instead, Davis allows her nameless Quaker woman to appear as a *deus ex machina*, appearing suddenly by the side of the bereaved woman to "solve" Deb's problematic life. The woman rescuer—angelic, pious, and serene like the Friends in Stowe's Quaker settlement— figures as both a superhero of benevolence and as a social impossibility: ordinary human beings find themselves incapable of aiding the poor, while the imaginary Quaker does what apparently only Quakers can do.

Even the Quakeress's description of her dwelling place partakes of this fantasy of altruistic perfection: "Thee sees the hills, friend, over the river? Thee sees how the light lies warm there, and the winds of God blow all the day? I live there,—where the blue smoke is, by the trees." The tranquility and moral steadfastness exuded by the Friends of Stowe's Quaker settlement in *Uncle Tom's Cabin* are reproduced by Davis's solitary Quaker woman in her pastoral abode, to which Deb retreats after her own three-year imprisonment for theft. Once again, what is striking about Davis's narrative strategy and commentary here is that she provides for a Quaker intervention precisely at the moment when things seem darkest for the oppressed laborer, a moment—it must be acknowledged—that coincides with the novella's clearest failure to propose a more thorough consideration of practical solutions for the plight of an American underclass. As Davis herself admits, "Three years after, the Quaker began her work. I end my story here." The work of the Quakeress, which amounts to a slow transformation of human neglect and criminality, then proceeds in a location that could not be more different from the bleak industrial landscapes of the iron mills: "There is no need to tire you with the long years of sunshine, and fresh air, and slow patient Christ-love, needed to make healthy and hopeful this impure body and soul. There is a homely pine house, on one of these hills, whose windows overlook broad, wooded slopes and clover-crimsoned meadows,—niched into the very place where the light is warmest, the air freest. It is the Friends' meeting house." Turning away from landscapes of urbanization, and evading any concerns for the vexed matter of industrialization and its attendant problem of the laboring classes, Davis effectively allows the Quaker woman's intervention—at once admirable and yet clearly a fantasy—to substitute for a broader conversation about such matters as social responsibility and workers' rights.[15]

In her subsequent reform novels, Rebecca Harding Davis would continue to rely heavily on the device of providing fictional Quaker interventions as an imaginary means of redress for the social problems of the day. Her praise of Friends was not limited to her fiction, however, and Davis often wrote admiringly of the influential Quaker abolitionists and activists whom she had befriended, such as Lucretia Mott and Wendell Phillips. But it is most notably her fiction that produces a form of Quakerism as benevolent fantasy. This fantasy appears prominently in Davis's *Waiting for the Verdict* (1867), a romance featuring two highly problematic courtships: one between a Northern woman (Rosslyn Burley) and a Southern man (Garrick Randolph), and the other between an affluent mulatto (Dr. John Broderip) and the white daughter of one of his patients (Margaret Conrad). Burley and Broderip—both bastard children of the same Alabama planter—eventually are taken into the

protective sphere of Quakers. For the orphan Rosslyn Burley, her transformation from crude, racist child to sophisticated and beautiful young
woman occurs largely at the hands of the wealthy Quaker woman who
befriends her and provides an education in liberalism and charity. As
for the mulatto John Broderick, his own childhood of abject poverty
and ignorance eventually gives way to an adult life of wealth and prominence (albeit a life lived as a black person "passing" for white), made
possible by yet another elderly Quaker woman, who purchases his freedom and makes possible his fine education in France. In each case, the
primary social adjustments are stimulated by Quakers: adoption of the
poor, education of the ignorant, tolerance of the racially "other," reconciliation of postbellum North and South.[16]

✒

Although she points to the dire need for social reform and especially
workers' rights in her fiction, Rebecca Harding Davis's rescuing Quaker
angel of *Life in the Iron Mills* demonstrates simultaneously the inability of
non-Quakers to seize the moral high ground of charitable intervention.
In this way, Davis shares with Stowe the implicit critique of an antebellum reformist movement that could never quite measure up to the
standards set by Quaker idealism. But Quakers in American fiction also
sharpened perspectives on the colonial past. For example, during the
antebellum years, Quakers were frequently used as stock characters, as
historical antitypes, for the purpose of expressing a certain amount of
regret about America's Puritan past. Decades after the Revolutionary
period, according to Lawrence Buell, American writers sometimes used
the time-honored habit of criticizing New England's Puritan past—a
habit that Nathaniel Hawthorne developed into high art in the creation
of such works as *The Gentle Boy* (1839) and *The Scarlet Letter* (1850)—to
create fiction in which "Quakerism is used as stick with which to beat
the Puritans." Buell points to the heroine of Eliza Buckminster Lee's
novel *Naomi* (1848) as one instance of this retrospective dichotomy of
colonial Puritans and Quakers. Naomi, a young English Puritan immigrant to colonial Massachusetts, becomes an exemplary figure for her
resistance to Puritan authority and her resolute adherence to the Quaker
doctrine of the Inner Light instead of mere biblical revelation. Jailed
briefly for her heresy, she triumphs eventually in Quaker marriage, set-
tling in New Jersey with a Harvard graduate who shares her Quaker

beliefs. Buell goes on to suggest, however, that the conclusion of *Naomi*, which depicts a newly founded and apparently blissful Quaker family, amounts to far less than a wholesale endorsement of the Society of Friends. Although Naomi adopts certain key aspects of Quakerism in the course of her resistance to the provinciality and repression of her Puritan elders, her own persistent characterization of Quakers as "ignorant," "vulgar" and "illiterate" signals a narrative tactic that elevates Quakerism as an abstract or didactic concept while disparaging Quakerism as a lived religion. In the end, remarks Buell, Lee's fictional heroine, although she adopts the apparent religious identity of Friends (and especially their religious individualism), nevertheless "finds most [Quakers] in appallingly bad taste."[17]

The development of Quakers as stock types in nineteenth- and early twentieth-century fiction should also be understood in the context of denominational growth and population change during these years. The shifting patterns of religious affiliation and regional demographics during the decades of slavery's abolition lessened the attention paid to the Quakers who had come so early to the fight against involuntary human servitude. Although by the mid-eighteenth century, English Quaker immigration—especially to the Delaware Valley region and its environs—had resulted in rapid growth to the point that Quakers had become the third-largest denomination in the colonies, the multifarious Christianization of America soon moved the Society of Friends to the margins of religious discourse and practice in the United States. In demonstrating this decline in the prominence of Quaker religion, whose primary contribution to American morals he views as the concept of "reciprocal freedom," the historian David Hackett Fischer notes that whereas "in early America, the Friends were not a small sect," after the mid-eighteenth century their numbers in British America "continued to rise in absolute terms, but began to fall relative to other religious groups. Among all American denominations, Quakers slipped to fifth place by 1775 (with 310 meetings); ninth place by 1820 (350 meetings); and sixty-sixth place by 1981 (532 meetings)." The relative marginalization of Quaker practice that these numbers suggest, however, seems not to correspond to a decline in imaginative engagement with fictional characters who exemplified various aspects of the mystical and proto-libertarian ethos associated with the Society of Friends.[18]

Enthusiasm for Quakers in fiction was not simply a matter of admiration for their abolitionist positions on slavery. Consequently, as the

nineteenth century unfolded, with its rapidly shifting religious demographics, the notion of American Quakerism as a quirky yet admirable
religious ideal lent itself persistently to the development of various stock
fictional characters, which both Stowe and Davis, and numerous other
writers, readily adopted for a range of purposes. Herman Melville, the
most prominent antebellum novelist to make significant use of Quaker
characters, does so most explicitly in *Moby-Dick* (1851), which features
the Quaker island of Nantucket as its early setting. Shrewd businessmen
and sailors, Quakers like Captain Peleg and Captain Bildad introduce
the youthful Ishmael to the business of whaling during the initial chapters of the novel. And Bildad's sister, Aunt Charity, embodies the charitable ideal of Quakerism that Stowe and Davis express in their own fiction. Attending to the needs of sailors in port, Aunt Charity, "a lean old
lady of a most determined and indefatigable spirit, but withal very kind-
hearted, . . . seemed resolved that, if *she* could help it, nothing should be
found wanting in the Pequod, after once fairly getting to sea."[19] Like the
unnamed Quakeress in Davis's *Life in the Iron Mills,* Aunt Charity conforms to the putative moral excellence of American Friends, providing
endless nurture and care for those within her domestic sphere (in this
case a ship rather than a cottage): "And like a sister of charity did this
charitable Aunt Charity bustle about hither and thither, ready to turn
her hand and heart to anything that promised to yield safety, comfort,
and consolation to all on board [the] ship."[20]

Melville's literary interest in the isolated island world of Massachusetts Quakers was far from unique during the nineteenth century. Nantucket's usefulness as a key site for the actual and imagined world of
American Quakerism can be seen in other fictional texts as well. Later
in the century, the novelist Mary Catherine Lee, in *A Quaker Girl of Nantucket* (1889), would return to the question of Quaker survival in America
by staging an encounter between two adolescent girls, one (Miriam
Swain) a rustic Quaker whose father serves as "overseer of the poor" on
Nantucket, the other a daughter of a wealthy Newport industrialist and
his chronically invalid wife. *A Quaker Girl of Nantucket*, written in a local-
color mode that highlights the "thee's" and "thou's" of Quaker language custom, reinforces the alterity that Quakerism stood for in the
masculine world of *Moby-Dick* and provides a contrast between the femi-
nized agenda of mainstream women's benevolent societies—Betty Vin-
ton, the young Newport girl, belongs to the Children's Charitable Guild
in New York—and dwindling numbers of pious Friends on Nantucket.

An exemplary young woman, Miriam Swain, embodies the familiar myth of Quaker charity and virtue; she is one "[in whose] blood was the calmness of generations of ancestors who had kept themselves in check and made serenity their religion. The first thing a Quaker child learns is self-command." In the eyes of many of these wealthy Newporters, the Quaker idea and way of life stands as both a much-needed remedy for modernity but also as a tradition that has been almost entirely erased: "Pity [the Quakers] are dying out, then,—that sect,—their influence is wanted in this country amazingly, to correct the national flurry."[21]

At the center of *Moby-Dick*, Captain Ahab of Nantucket stands as the one character most powerfully wrought from an amalgam of religious and philosophical discourses, among them the "Inner Light" of Quakerism. Like Peleg and Bildad, he "retain[s] in an uncommon measure the peculiarities of the Quaker, only variously and anomalously modified by things altogether alien and heterogeneous." The furthest thing from the pacifist tradition, Ahab and his fellow Quaker whaling captains are "fighting Quakers; they are Quakers with a vengeance." Bildad, not to mention Ahab, embodies the contradiction between Quaker pacifism and the bloody hunt for whales; it is he who "though a sworn foe to human bloodshed, yet had . . . in his straight-bodied coat, spilled tuns upon tuns of leviathan gore." With its biblical cadences, Ahab's soaring language owes a measure of its grandeur to "the thee and thou of the Quaker idiom," but Melville is careful to indicate that Ahab's personality and character, along with those of the other Nantucket captains, are aggressive mutations of Quakerism, whose peculiarities only result "from another phase of the Quaker, modified by individual circumstances."[22] In any case, Melville conforms to typical nineteenth-century attitudes about Quakerism by emphasizing their "peculiarity" or "queerness" (terms he uses frequently to describe the Nantucket Quaker whalemen), indicating their curious moral force while marginalizing them as decidedly quasi-American types.

The clearest precursor to Melville's use of Quakerism as an admirably pacifistic religious tradition—but one that nevertheless harbors and sometimes discloses extremely violent urges—appears in Robert Montgomery Bird's widely popular historical novel, *Nick of the Woods; or, The Jibbenainosay* (1837).[23] Sharing Captain Ahab's pathologically inverted Quakerism, with its enormous appetite for revenge and violence, the brutal Indian killer Nathan Slaughter figures the American Friend's impossibility in two separate ways. On the one hand, Bird represents

Nathan (a Quaker) in the early scenes of the book as a morally problematic person because of his extreme pacifism even in the face of imminent Indian attacks. He apparently does what no self-respecting American frontiersman may do during the troubling Kentucky border wars of the 1780s: he refuses to fight and kill Natives, even if his own life is in jeopardy. By turns fearful and genocidal, the purportedly noble young hero Roland Forrester describes their Native adversaries in bestial terms, as "yonder crawling reptiles,—reptiles in spirit as in movement" and urges Slaughter to fight. Slaughter concurs with Forrester's assessment of the Kentucky Indians, but nevertheless responds to a disbelieving Forrester in the pacifist mode: "Does thee think to have *me* do the wicked thing of shedding blood? Thee should remember, friend, that I am a follower of peaceful doctrines, a man of peace and amity." In the context of the novel (and in accord with his own opinion), Bird suggests that Quaker pacifism of this sort should be unthinkable for an American frontiersman confronting the perpetrators of murder, who, far from being heroic warriors, typically return from battle "laden with the scalps of miserable squaws and babes."[24]

On the other hand, and equally unthinkable, however, are Slaughter's acts of retribution against the Natives, for, as the novel eventually discloses, Nathan Slaughter's alter ego, Nick of the Woods, has been clandestinely performing horrific acts of vigilante murder, scalping, and mutilation against the encroaching Natives. It is here, then, that Bird discloses a second key aspect of the American Quaker's impossibility. Just as only a devout Quaker could have resisted the urge to combat and slay Indians during the conquest of the frontier, so, too, only a renegade Quaker—one like Nathan Slaughter, whose wife and children had been slaughtered by Natives—could muster the urge to kill Indians with such enthusiasm. A disturbed Quaker gone beyond the bloody logic of mere colonialism, Nick/Nathan exhibits a gluttony for murder, and a thrill for carnage, that places him well beyond the pale of "ordinary" frontier warfare. Having been revealed as the fervently willing executioner of Kentucky's Indian population, the violently warped Quakerism of Nathan Slaughter also suggests the radical fissures in his moral condition; "his appearance and demeanor were rather those of a truculent madman than of the simple-minded, inoffensive creature he had so long appeared to the eyes of all who knew him."[25] Insane or not, however, and in a pattern that would be rehearsed by the imaginary Quaker champions of wage laborers and slaves in Davis and Stowe's fiction, Bird's sinister and yet admirable Friend, Nick of the Woods, operates outside the conventional American moral compass, while serving to buffer conventional American morality from one of its most lamentable failures: the violent elimination of Native Americans.

Setting aside, for the moment, the dark and aggressive Quaker countertypes developed by Melville and Bird, American writers of the nineteenth century usually imagined Friends in a much more favorable and benevolent light. The nearly unanimous nineteenth-century literary admiration for Quakers would be marred only occasionally by criticism of this religious group, who of course had been the subject of intense and often-violent discrimination by the Puritans during the early American colonial period.[26] But ironically, one of the more prominent voices of criticism came from the poet and novelist Bayard Taylor, himself the product of a Kennett Square, Pennsylvania, Quaker family (though not a Quaker himself). The social world of Quaker Pennsylvania that is depicted in Taylor's novels, such as *Hannah Thurston: A Story of American Life* (1863) and *The Story of Kennett* (1866), reveals characters who are less notable for their charity and virtue than those depicted by novelists like Stowe and Davis. In Taylor's view, Quakerism had come to stand for excessive propriety and emotional restraint, which in turn led to Quaker families marked by a lack of intimacy and affection. When considering marriage, Hannah Thurston, the protagonist of the earlier novel, is admonished by her mother to choose a husband capable of expressing himself authentically, without the strictures of Quaker self-control. *The Story of Kennett,* which directly concerns an affluent Quaker family, even scrutinizes the religious practices emblematic of the Friends' meeting, with its apparently spontaneous expression of the "Inner Light." Suggesting a certain intellectual impoverishment in the sect, Taylor remarks of a Quaker speaker at a meeting that "a close connection of ideas, a logical derivation of argument from text, would have aroused their suspicions that the speaker depended rather upon his own active, conscious intellect than upon the moving of the spirit; but this aimless wandering of a half-awake soul through the cadences of a language which was neither song nor speech was, to their minds, the evidence of genuine inspiration."[27]

Despite his sometimes harsh assessment of bourgeois Quaker life and religious practice, Bayard Taylor also shares with other nineteenth-century fiction writers the tendency of assigning to Quakers certain stereotypical characteristics. As his modern literary biographer has suggested, Taylor's four novels share a number of stock characters, most notably, "the fatherless boy living with an older woman, usually his mother [or] an aunt, who is usually a Quaker" (in *Hannah Thurston*, the female character lives alone with a Quaker mother).[28] Along with Stowe and Davis, Taylor emphasizes the feminine practice of Quakerism and especially the idealized qualities of Quaker domesticity and ethical identity. It is true that Taylor finds fault with certain aspects of Quaker life, but he also retains a highly favorable view of them as virtuous citizens—exemplary (if possibly misguided) figures of Christian benevolence.[29] What is crucial in this regard is the way Taylor's Quaker legacies inevitably give way to more "up-to-date religious" and social alternatives. Quakerism in Taylor's fiction figures not only as goodness but as strangely anachronistic with relation to modern life. We can observe this contradiction in terms of narrative patterns: just as the fleeing Eliza in Stowe's novel pauses only briefly to linger among the comforts of the idealized Quaker settlement, so, too, does Bayard Taylor place his characters on a trajectory moving away from Quakerism, a religious spirit he associates with a no-longer-relevant American past.

This demotion of Quakerism to historical artifact[30] also gains force with the selection of unmarried, elderly, or widowed Quaker women as stock characters. Like the nameless and apparently unmarried Quaker woman who rescues Deborah Wolfe in Rebecca Harding Davis's *Life in the Iron Mills*, Taylor's Quaker women apparently combine moral excellence with infertility; they mark not the development of vital new currents of religious belief or the birth of a new generation of Friends, but instead signify a moribund religious tradition. With no pressing moral cause like abolitionism remaining in place to foster a mood of energy or vitality, Taylor's poem "The Quaker Widow" instead typifies an elegiac mood produced by the decline of an American religious tradition. Nearing her own death, the Quaker widow who narrates the poem describes the death of her husband and two of her close friends in terms both passive and elegiac: "It is not right to wish for death; the Lord disposes best. / His Spirit comes to quiet hearts, and fits them for His rest; / And that He halved our little flock was merciful, I see: / For Benjamin has two in heaven, and two are left with me." The widow's narrative of religious decline carries none of the energy of a jeremiad, and no enthusiasm for spiritual renewal, but only the somber recognition of a new generation's abandonment of the originary Quaker spirit in favor of materialism and modernity. As the poem concludes, she admits that "young people now-a-days / Have fallen sadly off, I think from all the good old ways"; thinking of her own daughter Ruth, the widow acknowledges that although Ruth adheres to some aspects of traditional Quaker life, she also has become too worldly: "It was brought upon my mind, remembering her, of late, / That we on dress and outward things perhaps lay too much weight."[31]

After the Civil War, as slavery receded and industrialization (with its continuing problems for the laboring classes) became an inescapable fact of American life, representation of Quakers in fiction came to signify once again an ethos weighted with concerns about women's rights, domestic thrift, pious behavior, and virtuous citizenship, but it is an ethos that no longer requires the commitments of abolitionism. This shift to the less overtly politicized Quaker domestic sphere can be seen in a number of post–Civil War novels. For example, yet another elderly Quaker woman plays a pivotal role in Louisa May Alcott's novel *Work* (1873), which, through the life of its young heroine Christie Devon, takes on the subject of "that large class of women who, moderately endowed with talents, earnest and true-hearted, are driven by necessity, temperament, or principle out into the world to find support, happiness, and homes for themselves." This novel, one of the first to include Quaker characters after the Emancipation Proclamation had freed American slaves and thus eliminated the unjust legal apparatus that had caused generations of Quakers to become activists in the antislavery movement, turns from slavery to the question of women's labor and women's rights. Though not a Quaker herself, the twenty-one-year-old Christie comes under the influence of Quaker culture at a critical point in her life. As its title suggests, *Work* considers the question of labor—especially women's labor—but the novel is distinctive for the way it blends Alcott's concerns for promoting a strong work ethic and for anatomizing the question of marriage for working class women. Eminently marriageable, and yet orphaned and financially insecure, Christie Devon shuttles from one humble job to the next: household servant, actress, governess, and laundress. And her life of menial labor appears to be inescapable until finally she accepts a service job in the household of old Mrs. Sterling, a widow and mother of thirty-one-year-old David Sterling, a kind but unambitious florist.

In *Work*, the Quaker household is represented in accord with nineteenth-century literary tradition: as a model of domestic tranquility. During her first meeting with the angelic Mrs. Sterling, for example,

Christie notices that her "kitchen was tidy with the immaculate order of which Shakers and Quakers alone seem to possess the secret."[32] Her loving son David, whom Christie eventually joins in wedded happiness, himself also retains certain Quaker traits and habits, although he maintains that "I wear drab because I like it, and say 'thee' to [Mother] because she likes it, and it is pleasant to have a little word all our own." The decline of Quakerism thus figures prominently as a theme in *Work*, but what links the novel most strikingly to the long tradition of Quakers in American fiction is its exposure of non-Quaker characters to the world of Quakers in order to educate them in certain avenues toward virtue. In Alcott's hands, as for so many other American novelists, Quakerism is administered homeopathically, temporarily, and often by Quaker women in scenes of domestic perfection. Almost always, though, Quaker life is described as illusory or untenable, but somehow necessary in small doses in order to create a virtuous citizenry. In the case of Christie Devon, marriage into a Quaker family stimulated her to a life of feminism and social activism after her husband's death in the Civil War. In *Work*, the influence of Quaker morality spawned by the elderly Mrs. Sterling, but not the practice of Quaker religion in any strict sense, produced two ideal types of liberal American. The first, David Sterling, whom Alcott presents as having served as a noble warrior for the antislavery North: "Spite of his Quaker ancestors, he was a good fighter, and, better still, a magnanimous enemy, hating slavery, but not the slave-holder, and often spared the master while he saved the chattel." Slavery having been vanquished, the second ideal type, Christie Devon, emerges in middle-aged widowhood as a community activist for women's rights, a woman transformed from a youthful life of menial labor to a Quaker-influenced adult who stands at the center of "a loving league of sisters, old and young, black and white, rich and poor, each ready to do her part to hasten the coming of the happy end."[33]

❧

As American print culture enlarged and diversified in the decades following the Civil War and the Emancipation Proclamation, with its extension of new rights to African Americans, Quakers were no longer necessary as stock fictional characters who favored the abolition of slavery. Nevertheless, the narrative device of using Quaker characters as angelic models of altruism and Christian virtue continued to be used regularly in popular magazines and books published during the late nineteenth century and well into the early years of the twentieth.[34] The Philadelphia physician and novelist S. Weir Mitchell based his most popular historical tale, *Hugh Wynne: Free Quaker* (1897), on the character of an adventurous young Quaker who eventually became involved in the Revolutionary War. A rather conventional sort of romance, constructed as a *Bildungsroman* in which a young Friend is expelled from the Philadelphia Quaker Meeting for youthful indiscretions such as drinking, carousing, gambling, and dueling, combined eventually with his desire to fight in the Revolutionary War (a moral impossibility for a devout Quaker), Mitchell's novel produces a relatively rare character in American fiction: a Quaker who stands as the central character in a novel. The fictional Hugh Wynne, who became one of the legendary Free Quakers (also known as "Fighting Quakers")[35] who set aside the Quaker code of nonviolence and willingly fought for American independence, has all the classic qualities typically associated with a romantic hero: wealthy, handsome, clever, and brave. But in nearly every important respect, he diverges from the qualities that had long been associated with Quakerism: piety, thrift, selfless benevolence, and refusal of worldly activities. As one critic has suggested, Hugh Wynne's demonstrated resistance to Quaker doctrine only reinforces the prevailing attitude toward this religious sect in America: "the non-Quaker writer seems to be interested in the Quaker hero only when he is at odds with the Society that produced him."[36] Inevitably, Hugh Wynne's actual Quakerism drains inexorably away, only to be replaced with a more generalized, nonsectarian virtue that places him in the service of the fight for American independence during the crucial years of the Revolution. His representation by Mitchell, then, uses the convenient vehicle of literary Quakerism: its substantial moral heft but not its profound spiritual content and deeper religious commitments. Hugh Wynne's adoption of the Free Quaker code, as narrated within Mitchell's historical novel, aligns him more squarely within an American political culture (and national memory) that prized violent resistance to colonial authority more highly than it did the inwardness and nonviolent ethos of traditional Quakerism.[37]

By World War I, however, and in part due to doctrinal changes and modernization within many branches of the Society of Friends itself, the stereotypical Quakers used by Stowe, Davis, Mitchell, and many other writers—Friends identifiable not only for their religious and moral fervency but also for their distinctive language, austere clothing, and rigid formality of manners—came to be used much less frequently in

American fiction. In fiction, if not in religious practice itself, Quakerism had apparently begun to outlive its usefulness as an exemplary counterpoint to "mainstream" values. As the charms of late nineteenth-century local color writing gave way to the new early-twentieth century seriousness of naturalist and then modernist fiction, literary portrayals of Quakerism as a primal (if always quaint, retrograde, and unrealizable) form of virtue began to disappear from American print culture. It comes as something of a surprise, then, to discover that Quakerism's literary epitaph would be written by Theodore Dreiser, one of America's most important and influential naturalist writers, and a novelist who had long been famous as a chronicler—in works such as *Sister Carrie* (1900), *Jennie Gerhardt* (1911), and *An American Tragedy* (1925)—of the human encounter with modernism, secularism, and materialism.

Dreiser's remarkable posthumous novel, *The Bulwark* (begun in 1914 but completed in 1945 and published in 1946), stands near the conclusion of a long tradition in American print culture, dating from the early decades of the nineteenth century, of using Quakers as exemplary characters. Because of its deeply sincere representation of an authentically devout Quaker, *The Bulwark* also reverses a good deal of the cynicism about the possibility of Quaker morality that Dreiser had demonstrated in *Sister Carrie*, published half a century before. In Dreiser's earlier and far more famous novel, the young Carrie Meeber—an amoral theatrical celebrity in the making—not only enacts the fakery of a new, more marketable name ("Carrie Madenda") but also finds her greatest stage success by enacting the role of a character who could be seen as her moral opposite: the "little Quakeress." When Dreiser finally turned to narrating a tale based upon Quaker virtue, his angle of view changed in favor of a radical sympathy for Quakerism. His protagonist, a banker named Solon Barnes, is the scion of a prosperous Maine farmer who moves to New Jersey to care for family members. Marking the shift in American life from the agrarian to the urban, Barnes is consequently a liminal character but, nevertheless, a sincere and devout Quaker who continues to embody all the traditional values endorsed by his religion: thrift, modesty, rigorous honesty, charity, and sobriety.[38] Always circumspect in financial matters, especially about his own financial success, Barnes is the sort of Quaker—like those constructed by nineteenth-century novelists—whose virtue seems unattainable by others. As one of his friends, herself a lapsed Quaker, remarks to one of Barnes's sons, Solon Barnes is "too religious. . . . All the Barnes . . . have been too set in the matter of religion and duty. They've hung onto their Quakerism until they're almost extinct as human beings—that is, all but the doctor and myself. Now, I haven't a thing against Quakers. I love them dearly. If I could live as they do, and keep my place in society, I'd do it. But it can't be done, Stewart. I can't do it. No one can."[39]

Set in the early decades of the twentieth century, *The Bulwark* chronicles the grim failure of Quakerism, in the person of the admirable Solon Barnes, to resist the forces of modernity. Refusing the tendency of certain earlier American novelists to view Quakers as unchanging pillars of virtue—as reliable but imaginary Friends existing at the margins of an unfriendly and morally debased nation—Dreiser's novel illustrates the tectonic power of modernity to overwhelm even the most virtuous individual and the most exemplary religious tradition. For all of his firm probity, the intensely virtuous Barnes is eventually shattered by the enormous moral failures that pervade the world around him: financial chicanery and criminality in his own bank, sexual promiscuity (including bisexuality) by his children, and, finally, a downward spiral of larceny, rape, murder, and suicide by his youngest son. Before his death from cancer at the end of the novel, Solon Barnes enjoys a minor reconciliation with some of his remaining children, but the elegiac tone pervading the book signals the wholesale failure of Quakerism—especially the austere version preferred by Solon Barnes—as a practical antidote to the troubles of modernity. Paradoxically, much of the difficulty in viewing the Quaker ideal as a helpful social and spiritual remedy, according to Dreiser, lay in its almost unimaginable virtuousness. Describing the placid Barnes homestead, for example, Dreiser seems to fault their tidy life for its failure to reflect the contingency and rough-cut difficulty of the actual world. In his view, "the atmosphere surrounding them seemed too fixed, too still. It was all too well ordered, too perfect for frail, restless, hungry human need."[40]

Failed or not as a religious tradition capable of salvaging modern morality, however, it is nevertheless clear that Quakerism had captured the imagination of yet another major American novelist, and this time one who had long been wary of organized religions. More specifically, *The Bulwark*'s religious thematics also disclose that, by the latter part of his career, Dreiser had immersed himself in the study of canonical Quaker writings. It is a novel that takes Quakerism with great seriousness, often using the stubbornly antimodern Solon Barnes to voice quotations from the Quaker *Book of Discipline* and from John Woolman's eighteenth-century *Journal*. Dreiser therefore appears on some levels to be overtly promoting the Quaker tradition, serving as evangelist for a faith that he construed as embodying a program of resistance to a range of moral quandaries, including materialism, sexual promiscuity, and market capitalism. But Dreiser himself, like the many other American novelists who found rich literary and moral resources within the Quaker tradition, never went so far as to adopt the Quaker faith himself, thereby following in the footsteps of his nineteenth-century predecessors, who similarly found in American Quakerism a religious practice that was at once both virtuous and impossible.[41] For many decades Dreiser had been wrestling in his fiction with a family legacy of puritanical German Catholicism inherited from his own father, but this secular urge was balanced against his own manifest desire to substitute some form of spiritual experience for the chaotic shallowness of twentieth-century life. However, and perhaps because of his deep commitment to realism—and to expressing the social world in its actuality—Dreiser found himself seeing, recognizing, and accepting the moral force of Quakerism, but without entirely adopting it wholeheartedly as his own religious, moral, or practical perspective.

The dovetailing of Dreiser's modernist sensibility with the after-images of Quaker values that his novel engages makes for a morally disconcerting narrative and a new view of Dreiser's place in the American tradition. F. O. Matthiesson, who, along with Lionel Trilling, was one of the few contemporary critics to examine *The Bulwark* in any detail, describes and defends this gradual (but never finalized) turn to Quaker religiosity in Dreiser's work, finding in it evidence of Dreiser's moral synthesis of politics (Marxist) and religion (generic Christian): "One might say that he was an old man, untroubled by inconsistencies that subsequent events would have made obvious. But . . . he had found—if more essentially in Woolman than in Marx—beliefs that he was convinced the world could no longer afford to ignore." As for Trilling, Dreiser's consideration of Quakerism was apparently complete but, nevertheless, deeply troubling. In the course of his full-scale attack on Dreiser's fiction in the opening pages of *The Liberal Imagination* (1950), Trilling insisted that the "blank pietism" of *The Bulwark* supplied proof that "Dreiser's religious affirmation was offensive; the offense lies in the vulgar ease of its formulation, as well as in the comfortable untroubled way in which Dreiser moved from nihilism to piety." Whatever the merits of Trilling's harsh assessment of Dreiser, what his criticism leaves out of consideration is Quakerism itself, not to mention its deployment in American fiction for more than a century. For in *The Bulwark* Dreiser had chosen not simply a turn toward generic Christianity or "blank pietism"; instead, he nominated Quakerism *specifically* for the religious paradigm in a novel that reversed many decades of secularism in his fiction.[42]

For writers of local color stories, historical fiction, and regionalist novels, there no doubt have been clear advantages (some of them commercial) to enlisting the stereotypical Quaker or Quakeress in the service of delineating norms and dominant values in American culture during a century and a half of the nation's most rapid growth and development. But Quakers in fiction also came to stand for the best people that most Americans never could become. The formulaic representation of Quakers in American print culture, which this essay has been surveying, produces characters with unimpeachably rigorous Christian faith, living domestic lives of order and harmony. These quaint figures appear to embody and to manifest the whole range of social virtues promoted by other evangelical Christian groups—charity without condescension, complete egalitarianism, unshakable pacifism, and flawless rectitude in business affairs—to an admirable degree. In popular American fiction, particularly for those genres operating in the didactic or reformist mode, such characters were used as a device for calibrating the moral urgency of the narrative. In essence, however, the American literary representation of what I have been calling "imaginary Friends" constructs two separate frameworks for understanding and evaluating human conduct. The first, inhabited by Quakers—but multiply indexed in terms of its alterity and practical impossibility—calls implacably for justice, peace, benevolence, restraint, equality, and a religious ethos motivated by the Inner Light resident in each believer. But the second framework, just as clearly suggested by the Quaker fiction under review here, implicitly concedes the higher moral and religious ground to Quakers, while nevertheless insisting upon the intrinsic goodness and virtue of its own radically more limited suggestions for American social, political, and religious improvement.

Notes

A previous form of this article appeared as "Imaginary Friends: Representing Quakers in Early American Fiction," *Studies in American Fiction* 31, no. 2 (Autumn 2003): 191–220.

1. Harriet Beecher Stowe, *Uncle Tom's Cabin, or, Life Among the Lowly*, ed. Ann Douglas (New York: Penguin Books, 1986 [orig. 1852]), 222.

2. Catherine E. Beecher also described Quakers as being healthier than other Americans. In a health manual published just before the Civil War, she reported most American women to be frail and unhealthy, but made an exception in the case of certain Quaker women: "The proportion of the sick and delicate to those who were strong and well was, in the majority of cases, a melancholy story. [But] . . . a lady from a country-town, not far from Philadelphia, gave an account showing eight out of ten perfectly healthy, and the other two were not much out of health. On inquiry, I found that this was a Quaker settlement, and most of the healthy ones were Quakers." Catherine E. Beecher, *Letters to the People on Health and Happiness* (New York: Arno Press & The New York Times, 1972 [orig. 1855]), 132.

3. For a detailed account of American Quaker dress, see Leanna Lee-Whitman, "Silks and Simplicity: A Study of Quaker Dress as Depicted in Portraits, 1718–1855" (Ph.D. dissertation, University of Pennsylvania, 1987). Lee-Whitman also traces the transformation in Quaker apparel from the eighteenth century, when "Quakers often wore stylish clothing in gay colors," to the nineteenth century, when Quakers typically adopted "the standard drab uniform" that has so often been associated with the "plain" sect. The wide-ranging essays in Emma Jones Lapsansky and Anne A. Verplanck, eds., *Quaker Aesthetics: Reflections on a Quaker Ethic in American Design and Consumption* (Philadelphia: University of Pennsylvania Press, 2003), explore in greater detail the considerable influence of Quaker design in American material culture.

4. Stowe, *Uncle Tom's Cabin*, 215, 223, 224.

5. Betty Jean Steele, "Quaker Characters in Selected American Novels, 1823–1899" (Ph.D. dissertation, Duke University, 1974), 123.

6. Although the popular writers described in this essay tended not to distinguish among the many theological variants of Quakerism in America, it is important to note that the movement was never entirely unified and was often divided by schisms over religious doctrine and practice. Nor was the Quaker ecclesiastical structure static over time. During the years 1750–70, for example, the Pennsylvania Quakers "tightened discipline, censured most transgressors, disowned others, and withdrew from politics in a colony they had once thoroughly dominated. This reformation deepened the introspection, pacifism, abolitionism, charity, and educational reforms for which nineteenth-century Quakerism became known." Jon Butler, *Awash in a Sea of Faith: Christianizing the American People* (Cambridge, MA: Harvard University Press, 1990), 127. For a helpful brief summary of the institutional development of the Quaker religion in America, see 118–20. On the orthodox Quaker movement of the nineteenth century, and its split from the Hicksite sect, see the thorough account provided in Thomas D. Hamm, *The Transformation of American Quakerism: Orthodox Friends,*

1800–1907 (Bloomington: Indiana University Press, 1988). For a narrower, but helpful, examination of Quaker schisms in Philadelphia since the Hicksite controversy, see E. Digby Baltzell, *Puritan Boston and Quaker Philadelphia: Two Protestant Ethics and the Spirit of Class Authority and Leadership* (New York: The Free Press, 1979), 433–51.

7. A lengthy bibliography of English and American publications in opposition to Quakerism may be found in Joseph Smith, *Bibliotecha Anti-Quakeriana; or, a Catalogue of Books Adverse to the Society of Friends* (London: Joseph Smith, 1873). English and American Quakers were also extremely prolific in their defense, especially during the first century of Quakerism (1650–1750), and Hugh Barbour estimates that by even so early a date as 1700, Quakers had already published at least 3,750 titles, along with another 2,000 extant letters and sundry documents that remain in manuscript form. Hugh Barbour, *Early Quaker Writings, 1650–1700* (Grand Rapids, MI: William B. Eerdmans, 1973), 5.

8. Catherine Maria Sedgwick, *A New England Tale; or, Sketches of New-England Character and Manners*, ed. Victoria Clements (New York: Oxford University Press, 1995 [orig. 1822]). Ronald J. Zboray, *A Fictive People: Antebellum Economic Development and the American Reading Public* (New York: Oxford University Press, 1993), xvi. For an extremely helpful and provocative discussion of the technological and economic underpinnings of antebellum print culture, see ibid., 1–82.

9. Nathaniel Hawthorne, *The Gentle Boy: A Thrice-Told Tale* (Boston: Weeks, Jordan and Co., 1839). In an excellent recent study of the radical Christian tradition in American writing, *Identifying the Image of God: Radical Christians and Nonviolent Power in the Antebellum United States* (New York: Oxford University Press, 2002), Dan McKanan writes of Quakers in nineteenth-century fiction as examples of "liberal interlopers" who "model a practice of liberal faith and devotion independent of violent social structures" (34; for a nuanced discussion of "the liberal encounter with Puritan violence" in liberal fiction of the nineteenth century, see 11–45).

10. Elizabeth B. Lester, *The Quakers; A Tale* (New York: James Eastburn & Company, 1818), 10, 147.

11. Stowe, "Immediate Emancipation: A Sketch," *New-York Evangelist*, 2 January 1845. For a discussion of the Stowe/Grimké encounter, see Joan E. Hedrick, *Harriet Beecher Stowe: A Life* (New York: Oxford University Press, 1994), 65–66. S. Margaret Fuller, *Woman in the Nineteenth Century*, facsimile edition with textual apparatus by Joel Myerson (Columbia: University of South Carolina Press, 1980 [orig. 1845]), 24. Fuller mentions Quakers again in *Woman in the Nineteenth Century* during her discussion of marriage as an occasion for intellectual companionship between husband and wife. In that context, she advances the example of "the pure and gentle Quaker poetess" Mary Hewitt, who along with her husband, William, had attained a level of literary accomplishment

that had earned her a place "among the constellation of distinguished English-women" (67). Fuller's untimely demise in 1850 prevented her from any commentary on Mary Hewitt's conversion to Roman Catholicism in 1882.

12. Henry Seidel Canby, *Classic Americans: A Study of Eminent American Writers from Irving to Whitman, with an Introductory Survey of the Colonial Background of Our National Literature* (New York: Harcourt, Brace & Company, 1931), 115. Canby, himself born into a Quaker family, nominates a possible exception to the unfortunate fate of Quakers in fiction by citing James Fenimore Cooper's Natty Bumppo, of the Leatherstocking Tales, as embodying the core of the Quaker ethos that Cooper had inherited from his own Quaker father: "It is Quaker morality, Quaker spirituality, and Natty is the best Quaker in American literature" (114). Henry Seidel Canby's contribution to Quaker fiction was *Our House* (New York: Macmillan, 1919), the story of an American Quaker family at the end of the nineteenth century, detailing the struggle of a son to become a successful writer.

13. Rebecca Harding Davis, *Life in the Iron Mills and Other Stories*, ed. Tillie Olson (New York: The Feminist Press at the City University of New York, 1972 [orig. 1861]). Whitman quoted in David S. Reynolds, *Walt Whitman: A Cultural Biography* (New York: Alfred A. Knopf, 1995), 219. Helpful accounts of Davis's life and writings are included in Jean Pfaelzer, *Parlor Radical: Rebecca Harding Davis and the Origins of American Social Realism* (Pittsburgh, PA: University of Pittsburgh Press, 1996); and Jane Attridge Rose, *Rebecca Harding Davis*, Twayne's United States Authors Series (New York: Twayne Publishers, 1993).

14. Lee-Whitman, *Silks and Simplicity*, 9. American Quakers, much like the Amish and Mennonites, were given explicit instructions about the plainness of their apparel, such as the following guidelines from the Philadelphia Yearly Meeting Book of Discipline (1762): "Advised, that all that profess the Truth, and their Children, whether Young or Grown up, keep to Plainness in Apparell As becomes the Truth and that none Wear long lapp'd Sleeves or Coates gathered at the Sides, or Superfluous Buttons, Or Broad Ribbons about their Hatts, or long curled Periwiggs and that no Women, their Children, or Servants Dress their Heads immodestly as is too common, nor use long scarves; and that all be careful about making, buying, or wearing . . . striped or flowered stuffs, or other useless and superfluous things" (quoted in Lee-Whitman, *Silks and Simplicity*, 10–11). The sketches in Sarah M. H. Gardner, *Quaker Idyls* (New York: Henry Holt and Company, 1894), also document the changes in Quaker clothing from the perspective of a late nineteenth-century Quaker woman.

15. Davis, *Life in the Iron Mills*, 63.

16. Rebecca Harding Davis, *Waiting for the Verdict* (Upper Saddle River, NJ: The Gregg Press, 1968 [orig. 1867]).

17. Lee's distaste for Quakerism comes as little surprise, when her link to

New England Puritanism is understood. A native of Portsmouth, New Hampshire, she was a descendant of seventeenth-century poet, and staunch Puritan, Anne Bradstreet (Steele, *Quaker Characters*, 55–56). Lawrence Buell, *New England Literary Culture: From Revolution through Renaissance* (Cambridge: Cambridge University Press, 1986), 249–50. In his superb account of nineteenth-century New England regionalism, Buell indicates the frequent intersection of Puritan and Quaker in antebellum New England fiction, but without observing the consistency with which American literary admiration for Quakerism only serves as a prelude to determining that Quakers are either dangerous or else an angelic impossibility. His comparison of Walter Scott and Nathaniel Hawthorne's views of national history, for example, makes a point about the symbolic value of Friends that corresponds to the argument made in this essay: "For Scott, the past stands for both the fascination and the horror of a more untrammeled expression of the passions that we moderns subdue. In Hawthorne and the New England romance generally, this symbolic relationship is reversed. It is the ancestors, like colonel Pyncheon and the Puritan elders in *The Scarlet Letter*, who ruin their adversaries by relentless application of law. The 'gules,' the spontaneous manifestations of impulse, are associated with the rebel protagonists, typically modern heroines in Quaker garb, who are projected back onto history as refreshing contrasts to the grayness of the Puritan establishment" (Buell, 244).

18. David Hackett Fischer, *Albion's Seed: Four British Folkways in America* (New York: Oxford University Press, 1989), 422–23. Fischer summarizes the social impact of Delaware Valley Quakerism in the following way: "Friends and neighbors alike embraced the idea of religious freedom and social pluralism. They favored a weak polity and strong communal groups. Most came to share the Quakers' concern for basic literacy and their contempt for higher learning. They also accepted Quaker ideas of the sanctity of property, equality of manners, simplicity of taste, as well as their ethic of work, their ideal of worldly asceticism, their belief in the importance of family and their habits of sexual prudery" (429). On the broader Quaker influence on the development of American social and political values, see the extended discussion in Fischer, 419–603. Butler, *Awash in a Sea of Faith*, provides additional perspectives on the complexity of American Christianity during the nineteenth century. For an illuminating discussion of tensions between Quakers and Puritans in colonial New England, see Philip F. Gura, *A Glimpse of Sion's Glory: Puritan Radicalism in New England, 1620–1660* (Middletown: Wesleyan University Press, 1984), 144–54.

19. Herman Melville, *Moby-Dick, or, The Whale* in *The Works of Herman Melville*, vol. 6, ed. Harrison Hayford et al. (Evanston: Northwestern University Press and Newberry Library, 1988 [orig. 1851]), 105.

20. Melville, *Moby-Dick*, 105.

21. Mary Catherine Lee, *A Quaker Girl of Nantucket* (Boston: Houghton, Mifflin and Company, 1889), 46, 50, 41.

22. Ibid., 82.

23. Robert Montgomery Bird, *Nick of the Woods; or The Jibbenainosay. A Tale of Kentucky*, ed. Mark Van Doren (New York: Macy-Masius, The Vanguard Press, 1928 [orig. 1837]). Perhaps fueled in part by the earlier success of James Fenimore Cooper's Leatherstocking Tales, as well as by the long tradition of American captivity narratives, *Nick of the Woods* was one of the more popular novels of the nineteenth century. After its publication in Philadelphia in 1837, it eventually appeared in at least twenty editions. A year before publishing *Nick of the Woods*, Bird had already satirized the Quaker call to benevolent social activism and philanthropy in *Sheppard Lee* (New York: Harper and Brothers, 1836).

24. Bird, *Nick of the Woods*, 131–32, 9.

25. Ibid., 386.

26. In the 1650s, for example, Quakers attempting to preach and evangelize in Boston found themselves facing violent resistance: "They met with fierce hostility, which ultimately resulted in the banishment from the Massachusetts Bay colony of twenty-two Quakers, the deaths of three or four, physical mutilation of several, and brutal beatings of more than thirty others." The situation remained unchanged decades later: "To do the will of God in Boston, if one were a Quaker during the [sixteen] fifties and early sixties, was a dangerous if not always fatal enterprise." Philip Greven, *The Protestant Temperament: Patterns of Child-Rearing, Religious Experience, and the Self in Early America* (Chicago: University of Chicago Press, 1988 ed.), 108. E. Digby Baltzell's history of cultural and political leadership, *Puritan Boston and Quaker Philadelphia: Two Protestant Ethics and the Spirit of Class Authority and Leadership* (New York: Free Press, 1979), provides a thorough account of American Quakerism's increasing marginality.

27. Bayard Taylor, *The Story of Kennett* (New York: G. P. Putnam, 1866), 79; *Hannah Thurston: A Story of American Life* (New York: G. P. Putnam's Sons, 1879 [orig. 1863]). As Betty Jean Steele has pointed out, in *The Gilded Age: A Tale of To-day* (Hartford, CT: American Publishing Co., 1873), Mark Twain and Charles Dudley Warner include a romantic subplot involving a young Quakeress named Ruth Bolton, and she too chafes at the strictures of "her tradition-bound life"; like S. Weir Mitchell's Hugh Wynne, Ruth's father had been expelled from the Quaker meeting for not following Quaker customs. See S. Weir Mitchell, *Hugh Wynne: Free Quaker* (Ridgewood, NJ: The Gregg Press, 1967 [orig. 1896]); Steele, *Quaker Characters*, 709; Twain and Warner, *Gilded Age*, 157.

28. Paul C. Wermuth, *Bayard Taylor*, Twayne United States Authors Series (New York: Twayne Publishers, 1973), 96.

29. Occasionally, practicing Quakers produced their own fictionalized accounts of their missionary work and social activism, as in Nellie Blessing-Eyster,

A Chinese Quaker: An Unfictitious Novel (New York: Fleming H. Revell Company, 1902), which details Quaker missionary work in San Francisco's Chinatown during the 1880s.

30. Quakers themselves also registered the increasing marginality of their religious movement, often relegating its importance to a lost era in American culture. See, for example, the historical sketches of New York, Philadelphia, and Boston Quakers in Sarah M. H. Gardner, *Quaker Idyls* (New York: Henry Holt & Co., 1894), which chart some examples of Quakers gradually adopting the more worldly customs of modernizing America; most of her sketches of American Quakers are retrospective, harking back to the antebellum era and in some cases the late eighteenth century. Similarly, Baltzell goes so far as to argue that Philadelphia Quakerism in particular came to embody "the metaphysical shallowness of antinomian enthusiasm or simple perfectionism," leading him to assert that "there has been no creative literature of the first rank by, or about, Philadelphia Quakers" (*Protestant Boston and Quaker Philadelphia*, 294).

31. Bayard Taylor, "The Quaker Widow," in *The Poems of Bayard Taylor* (Boston: Ticknor and Fields, 1865), 261–66. The concern over worldliness that Taylor's Quaker widow expresses corresponds to the "Hicksite separation" of 1827, during which a group of less affluent and more religiously intense Philadelphia Quakers—who were critical of the materialism and affluence of many Quakers—followed their leader, Elias Hicks, to found a new Quaker sect. The influence of Elias Hicks also spread well beyond the Delaware Valley of Pennsylvania. As an adult, the poet Walt Whitman, himself the son of a Quaker father, recalled the inspiration of hearing Hicks lecture on many occasions in New York City; see Howard W. Hintz, *The Quaker Influence in American Literature* (Port Washington, NY: Kennikat Press, 1965 [orig. 1940]), 60–61.

32. Louisa May Alcott, *Work* (Boston: Roberts Brothers, 1873), 11, 221.

33. Ibid., 266, 386, 442.

34. Anna Breiner Caulfield's annotated bibliography, *Quakers in Fiction: An Annotated Bibliography* (Northampton, MA: Pittenbruach Press, 1993), lists several hundred twentieth-century English and American novels with Quaker themes and characters, along with an equal number of juvenile novels concerned with Quaker life.

35. When state militias sent out their calls for help during the American Revolution, a number of Quakers—like the fictional Hugh Wynne—responded to their call to assist in the war against the British and were subsequently expelled from the main body of the Quaker religion. In Philadelphia, a group of approximately two hundred Free Quakers founded their own meetinghouse in Philadelphia, which operated until 1834, when the meetinghouse was closed by its last two members, one of whom was the flag maker Betsy Ross.

36. Steele, *Quaker Characters*, 50–51.

37. S. Weir Mitchell had already written extensively about the "problem" of Quakerism in an earlier novel, *Hephzibah Guinness; Thee and You; and A Draft on the Bank of Spain* (Philadelphia: J. B. Lippincott, 1880), in which he presented a forbiddingly austere woman, another grimly homely and infertile Quaker woman whose arrogance and rigidity as guardian of a beautiful sixteen-year-old girl cause the younger woman to seek for life beyond the Quaker meeting (see Steele, *Quaker Characters*, 103–5 for a more detailed discussion of this novel). N. P. Runyon's *The Quaker Scout* (New York: The Abbey Press, 1900), which centers on a heroic New York soldier during the Civil War, provides yet another fictional treatment of wartime valor by a fighting Quaker. Its hero, Ralph Dinsmore, had been inspired by a Quaker household's piety and virtue just before he had enlisted in the Northern army.

38. Dreiser's *The Bulwark: A Novel* (Garden City: Doubleday and Company, 1946) relied heavily on, and borrowed from, a series of religious memoirs written by a Philadelphia Quaker named Rufus M. Jones, who published these volumes between 1902 and 1934. Gerhard Friedrich has speculated that Dreiser may have read the first of these books, *A Boy's Religion from Memory* (1902), during 1902–3, the period after the publication of *Sister Carrie* when Dreiser was living in Philadelphia. See Gerhard Friedrich, "A Major Influence on Theodore Dreiser's *The Bulwark*," *American Literature* 29 (May 1957): 180–93. Friedrich also provides a list of the many books (a number of them heavily marked and annotated) related to Quakerism discovered in Dreiser's personal library, including several of the novels discussed in this essay.

39. Dreiser, *The Bulwark*, 253.

40. Ibid., 185.

41. Mark Twain and Charles Dudley Warner, for example, use a virtuous young Quaker girl as a primary character in *The Gilded Age*. In a novel otherwise brimming with bitter satire and criticism of American materialism and corruption, a Philadelphia Friend named Ruth Bolton is one of the novel's few subjects to emerge unscathed. She retains her virtue (even as her husband becomes a questionable financial speculator) and serves as an exemplary woman in her ambition to become a doctor and to form a truly loving family, but she pursues these ends only as she weakens her practice of Quakerism.

42. It is readily apparent that the turn to secularism that Dreiser resists, finally, in *The Bulwark* is a movement that Jenny Franchot has trenchantly described for religious belief in general: "Belief's transformation into pastness is, in fundamental respects, the narrative of Western culture's birth into the modern." See Jenny Franchot, "Unseemly Commemoration: Religion, Fragments, and the Icon," in Susan L. Mizruchi, ed., *Religion and Cultural Studies* (Princeton, NJ: Princeton University Press, 2001), 39. See also F. O. Matthiessen, *Theodore Dreiser* (New York: William Sloane Associates, 1951), 251. Matthiesson, himself

a Christian Socialist, researched *Theodore Dreiser* in the years following Dreiser's death in 1945; the study was published posthumously, after Matthiesson's suicide in 1951. Lionel Trilling, "Reality in America," in *The Liberal Imagination* (New York: Viking Press, 1950), 19, 20.

The Mythic Mission Lands

Medical Missionary Literature, American Children,
and Cultural Identity

RENNIE B. SCHOEPFLIN

In the middle of the nineteenth century the pathbreaking missionary work of Peter Parker, M.D. (1804–88), in China and Clara A. Swain, M.D. (1834–1910), in India ushered in an age of medical missions that made the missionary physician "the representative of all that was most admired in the later stages of the modern missionary movement."[1] By 1899 American missionary physicians holding regular medical diplomas numbered 338, over a third (127) of whom were women, and the world field comprised 348 hospitals, 774 dispensaries, and 45 medical schools.[2] Late nineteenth- and twentieth-century American missionaries took much with them to the "heathen of foreign lands"—Bibles and Christian literature, the physical trappings of their former lives, their families, and Western cultural values and social institutions—but scientific medicine often stood out for both missionaries and indigenous peoples.[3]

Native peoples often responded with curiosity, distrust, and fear when confronted by the strange ways of the mission doctors—they may even have thought that missionaries captured spirits in their black box cameras. However, they also soon recognized that although missionary medicine may have healed some diseases and could sometimes be used to their advantage in political and cultural power struggles, it also often proved to be incompatible with native healing, undermined cultural, social, and political authority, and arrived entangled with a Christian worldview not always friendly to indigenous religious sensibilities.[4]

Americans held generally positive views of medical missions, but early twentieth-century debates arose within and between liberal and evangelical Protestant missionaries over the extent to which such so-called humanitarian extensions of Western culture should play a role in fulfilling the Gospel commission. Was the healing attributed to medicine a sufficient justification in and of itself for Christian mission? Should it serve only as an entering wedge that would allow an explicit witness to the sacrifice of Jesus and a call to accept him as Lord and Savior? Or, should healed bodies and saved souls be understood as simply two sides of salvation's coin? For the authors of the sources I have examined for this study, the latter two answers predominated.[5] As one author put it, "I almost think that the medicine bottle in the hand of one [of] our Missionary doctors can open the doors of more heathen homes than any other key in the whole world!"[6]

My primary purpose here, however, is not to discuss what American medical missionaries took with them to foreign lands or how the receiving peoples understood them. Instead, I explicate the content of the stories the returning missionaries told to American children, examine the social contexts for their transmission, and reconstruct the stories' impact on their lives. I am less interested in recovering the facts of medical missions than I am in exploring the literary structures and the cultural content of medical missionary stories and the often highly gendered, racialized, and Westernized attitudes that they transmitted to American children.[7] My conclusions arise from a content analysis of scores of medical missionary stories read by and told to children and youth in the United States from about 1880 to 1980 and an examination of the historical sources that allow one to construct a social and cultural context for them. These stories appeared in a wide variety of Protestant denominational and interdenominational juvenile and children's literature—books, plays, Sunday school papers, story sermons, and teachers' missionary guides and study helps. And echoing religious historian Candy Gunther Brown's observation that the "unifying tendencies of evangelical print culture outran the most divisive intentions," the stories exhibited a surprisingly high level of continuity over time and across denomination.[8]

The nature of missionary literature followed the pattern established in the nineteenth century for the publication of materials devoted to the religious education of American young people. Spearheaded by the Sunday-school movement and the American Sunday-School Union, antebellum American religious educators called for a juvenile literature characterized by a clear moral and religious character, graded and adapted to children's development, of high literary quality, and written in American English about American people and places.[9] During the second half of the nineteenth century scores of books and weekly and monthly periodicals appeared, published by the Union, other interdenominational unions, and individual denominations for the purpose of covering the "whole field of education as related to religion," including domestic and foreign missions.[10] Given that American Sunday schools enrolled an estimated twenty-five million members in 1917, missionary stories reached a large audience with the potential for significant and widespread influence.[11]

The evidence makes clear that the authors and publishers of children's missionary literature borrowed extensively from each other, suggesting that neither denominational loyalty nor theological parochialism played a significant role in the content of the stories. And my content analysis of the stories bears this out. Even *Our Little Friend*, published by Seventh-day Adventists fiercely defensive of their sectarian theology and generally opposed to ecumenical mission practices, directly borrowed stories, with attribution, from the mission literature of nearly a dozen missionary publications representing several denominations, including the *Children's Missionary* (Presbyterian Church in the United States), the *Little Missionary* (Roman Catholic), the *Little Worker*, and the *Children's Missionary Friend* (Methodist Episcopal Church). Given that many of the stories emerged from an oral tradition associated with camp meetings, youth congresses, and Sabbath schools, stories took on a life of their own, merging and recycling from teller to teller and author to author, each adapting them to her own particular purpose. For example, key elements of an 1899 story about "How a Little Sick Boy was Cured" that appeared in *Our Little Friend*, reappeared in one of Margaret T. Applegarth's stories published in her 1917 junior series collection of *Missionary Stories for Little Folks*.[12] Despite this narrative ecumenicism, however, particular denominational concerns surfaced in the framing of the stories—for example, in identifying to which mission hospitals offerings should be sent, to which denomination the healed converted, or to which mission dispensary one should aspire for service.

Medical missionaries and their stories represented only one subset of the vast missionary literature created for informing and instructing the home front during the late nineteenth and twentieth centuries. And these medical stories shared many of the same characteristics of the missionary story genre—descriptions of foreign lands, the founding of mission stations and activities, the heroic missionaries confronting dangerous animals and often initially hostile natives, and lessons the reader could learn from the mission experience that would enhance their walk with God and move them to devote money, time, or career to mission service.[13]

The experiences of medical missionaries appeared in a variety of contexts and served several purposes. In some cases general missionary stories made passing references to Western or native medical practices or to the importance of medical missions. For example, W. A. Criswell, pastor of the First Baptist Church in Dallas, Texas, and Duke K. McCall, president of the Southern Baptist Theological Seminary, traveled around the world circa 1950, visiting, preaching, and baptizing under the auspices of the Foreign Mission Board of the Southern Baptist Convention. Their story of that trip, published as *Passport to the World*, described a Nigerian drugstore in which, instead of "shelves of neatly labeled bottles," they "saw displayed on the ends of sticks, dried bird heads, dead rats, and other small animals in various stages of decay. African natives boil such stuff and drink the liquid concoction. It is no wonder that the sick so often die. That kind of treatment would kill even a well man. The African cure for smallpox is to throw an old broom on top of the house and cast another old broom in the yard. The ineffectiveness of this treatment is proclaimed by entire villages which have been wiped out by smallpox epidemics." They also visited a hospital and leper colony in Ogbomosho, Nigeria, in which "there was so little equipment that, as Southern Baptists who sponsor the hospital, we were embarrassed." Nonetheless, "the important thing is that the sick are healed, the hopeless find hope, the unclean find friends. The Christ who cleansed lepers on the dusty roadside in Galilee long ago is still doing business through his followers today."[14]

Collections of short stories, anecdotes, and story sermons, such as *Children's Missionary Story-Sermons,* often included stories that featured medical missionaries.[15] These stories briefly related an incident in the life of a medical missionary to illustrate the importance of emulating the missionary's bravery, trust in God, and service to others. Pastors or Sunday school teachers appropriated them to capture the attention of children and youth and to focus their attention on the virtues of hard work, doing good, being a friend to Jesus, trusting God, and giving money to help the sick in foreign lands.

But how did the storytellers navigate their little listeners through the mission lands and introduce them to the people who needed medical assistance and the "true God"? Their longer narratives followed several main types: biography-autobiography, ethnography–cultural geography, and travelogue.[16] I have yet to discover stories in which the medical missionary "went native," that is, intentionally merged indigenous healing with Western medicine. Nonetheless, as historian Luise White has noted, for the natives the meaning of dispensed pills and ointments "was almost never the same as missionaries intended," and missionaries sometimes touted their own medicines as "superior magic."[17]

In the biography-autobiography the author presented both the external experiences and internal states of his characters. Although we cannot be certain from the texts themselves that these had been real children who experienced the events precisely as narrated, the author presented them as such. Typical of this form were the "Jungle Stories" of Eric B. Hare. A so-called medical evangelist, "Dr." Eric B. Hare had graduated from the nurse's training course at the Seventh-day Adventist sanitarium in Sydney, Australia, before embarking in 1915 with his new bride for mission service among the Karen people of Burma (see figure 4.1).[18] A gospel of healthful living, hydrotherapy, and an apocalyptic "end time" message had distinguished Adventist foreign missions since the 1880s. Adventists considered the medical missionary impulse to be the "right arm of the message." Their commitment to that belief led them to expand their 2 hospitals and sanitariums staffed by ten physicians in 1880 into 152 hospitals and sanitariums, 300 clinics and dispensaries, and thousands of physicians, dentists, nurses, and allied health professionals worldwide by the 1990s. In 1936 Hare published some of his Burma experiences in *Clever Queen: A Tale of the Jungle and of Devil Worshipers* and fascinated camp meeting audiences far and wide during the next decades with his energetic telling of "Mister Crooked Ears," "Silver and the Snake," "Chinese Lady and the Rats," and other missionary stories.[19] In the case of *Clever Queen* much authorial authority derived from the fact that Hare himself was a central participant in the story. Moreover, because he lived among the "natives" as a medical missionary, readers trusted his views to be more than superficial, and they were more likely to assume him to be a friendly outsider. One of

Dr. Rabbit examines patients in his dispensary at the Karen Mission Station.

Back row: Tha Myaing, Dr. Rabbit, Peter. *Front row:* Moo-gar; Nurse Mary Gibbs; Mrs. Hare; Peter's wife, Ma Keh; and dispensary assistant, Hla Kin.

The Karen Mission Station on the Salween River.

Figure 4.1. Eric Hare and assistants at his mission among the Karen people of Burma. (Hare, *Jungle Storyteller* [Washington, D.C.: Review and Herald Pub. Assn., 1967], 54.) In the book's original captions (above), Hare is identified by a nickname he adopted, "Dr. Rabbit."

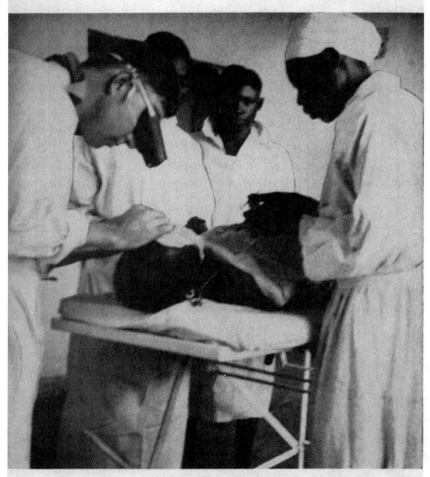

A Doctor and His Assistants

JUNGLE SURGERY

Cataract Operation in progress; Daudi assisting the author

Figure 4.2. Dr. Paul White and native assistant Daudi. (White, *Doctor of Tanganyika*, between pp. 30–31.)

the powers of such a narrative form lies in the way in which the listener can vicariously enter into the characters' experiences and sympathize with their circumstances, no matter how strange their beliefs or practices might seem.

Australian medical missionary Paul White also followed this literary form when he turned to write the internationally famous "Jungle Doctor" books after "his wife's health forced him to leave Africa."[20] (See figure 4.2.) Published throughout the United Kingdom and the United States, this series of nearly two dozen books traced White's adventures as a medical missionary serving at a Church Missionary Society (C.M.S., Anglican) hospital in central Tanganyika during the 1930s. Published into the 1960s with titles like *Jungle Doctor* (1942, first in the series), *Jungle Doctor Operates* (1944), and *Jungle Doctor Attacks Witchcraft* (1947), these books, reissued by Eerdmans in the 1950s and Moody Press in the 1970s, reached a wide-ranging, juvenile American audience with the adventures of medical missionary service. The Moody Press printings of the twenty-one titles in the *Jungle Doctor* series had widespread distribution, selling 407,809 copies between 1971 and 1979 alone.[21]

All of the key elements of medical missionary stories appeared in the "Jungle Doctor" series: the daily routines of mission life and the often quaint and naive customs of the natives; the dangers of weather, snakes, wild animals, and violent tribesmen; rampant but often needless disease and suffering; shortages of supplies and inadequate working conditions; continual struggles for authority with witch doctors; and the reward of seeing lives changed through the power of Jesus and Western medicine. However, the books stand out for their detailed descriptions of doctoring—the treatments and surgeries under the less than ideal conditions of the bush—and their comprehensive exploration of the integration of curing and converting. Readers discovered just how tough it could be to practice Western medicine without the institutional and technological infrastructures of the modern world. But they also could glimpse the sense of both personal accomplishment and thanks to God that came with having innovated, adapted, and prayed oneself to success.[22]

This sense of partnership with God became most apparent in the way White interwove spiritual and physical healing. A life-giving blood transfusion echoed Bwana Yesu Kristo's blood sacrifice, failure to follow instructions to keep a bandage over an ulcer got one into trouble just like "if we do not obey the words of God," and when parents demanded ointment for their child's serious burn that required a transfusion, Dr. White took his assistant aside and said

> My friend, this is not the way that the child should be treated. This is not the medicine that brings life. All we are doing is covering up the wound; we are not curing the root of the trouble. The child's relations are like those who would sit and cover their sins by putting on clean clothes, or a bright smile. This is not enough. Did not Jesus say, "No man comes to the Father, but by Me"?[23]

Clearly these stories not only taught about foreign lands and revealed the effectiveness "from the practical preaching angle, of a surgeon's knife," but they instructed their readers in moral principles and spiritual truths.[24]

A variation on biography-autobiography related the life stories of missionary heroes like David Livingstone (1813–73; Africa; see figure 4.3), Peter Parker (China), or Ida Scudder (1870–1959; India).[25] In *David and Susi*, for example, Lucy W. Peabody linked the heroism and cross-racial benevolence of the adult Livingstone with his early character development and childhood aspirations to become a missionary doctor. According to Peabody, when the young Livingstone "heard a doctor who had been in China tell about the sick children there who had no doctors Davie decided he would go to China and be a missionary. He knew he must study hard. He loved to play but he never forgot his plan. Davie was a good boy and good boys grow into good men."[26]

While primarily Anglo *male* physicians and *female* nurses or assistants populated the pantheons, there were exceptions. The "Our Girls" and "Our Circle Girls" sections of *Missionary Tidings* (Christian Woman's Board of Missions) often featured profiles of female medical mission-aries that not only described their current work in the mission fields but also outlined their spiritual and educational preparation as children and youth.[27] Writing to children in "Over the Teacups," Mrs. D. C. Brown noted that the "names of Olivia Baldwin, Annie Agnes Lackey, Ella Maddock, Dr. Mary Longdon [1869–1947; India], Dr. Jenny Crozier [1875–1959; India] and Zonetta Vance have become as familiar to us as our own." Such "women physicians, confronted with terrible diseases, operations that here the strongest men might shrink from—so little to work with, compared with our magnificent operating rooms and clini-cal wards. But they do it!" A "never-ending stream of suffer[er]s pass before" their eyes, but exhausted they continue working because "they

A snake bit this boy
"He healed the sick"

Figure 4.3. Dr. David Livingstone. (Peabody, *David and Susi: Black and White; Third Book of Stories for Little Children*, 27.)

know that with returning strength and gratitude comes the desire for spiritual healing, and thus the poor have the Gospel preached to them. Isn't it thrilling to think of it? Never say that the day of heroes is past."[28] Although authors and publishers often targeted books specifically for girls or boys, reading habits could not be so easily predicted. Who could say that girl readers did not enjoy and hope to emulate the heroic adventures of the predominantly male missionary doctors even though females typically appeared as nurses in the stories?[29]

In ethnography–cultural geography the author assumed the stance of an objective observer who took her readers on a bird's-eye tour of an exotic land. For example, consider the following visit to "Miss Rose M.

Kinney Girls' School at Ruk": "Dear Children: You have all heard of
the Pacific islands, and that some of them are high and very beau´ti-ful,
and some are low, hardly above the level of the sea. But all the larger
ones are in-hab´it-ed by a people who have a dark skin, black hair and
eyes. They live in little huts that are covered with leaves and have no
windows, with the ground for a floor. These children live on breadfruit,
co´co-nuts, and fish."[30]

One advantage of such an approach was that a lot of terrain could
be covered; but this advantage may have come at the cost of a deper-
sonalized listener response. Rarely did the narrative include the details
of personal encounter that allowed for the kind of reader identification
available in biography. In these stories, the medical missionary almost
always assumed the role of an explorer or sojourner, not an active participant in the people's lives or lands.

The travelogue combined elements of both narrative types. In *The
Congo Picture Book* and *With the Wild Men of Borneo*, typical of this style,
the authors took their readers on a trip from home base to mission
front.[31] The reader rode a steamer to the foreign land, disembarked,
and then toured the country on the way to the assigned mission post.
Then followed encounters with the native population that entailed healing, teaching, and preaching, but the authors gave detailed personal accounts of the persons involved in the encounters, thereby reducing the
abstraction so often present in the ethnographic form. (See figure 4.4.)

Although the medical missionary as active participant rather than
simply explorer, adventurer, or sojourner often seemed to allow a more
friendly view of native customs, nonetheless, the unconverted natives
usually tended to appear exotic, strange, evil, ignorant, and often help-
less no matter which literary approach the author adopted. Authors
often totalized the other's worldview and behavior as evil, while sympa-
thizing with their supposedly universalized experiences with pain, sickness, and sin and their need for physical and spiritual healing. And not
surprisingly, given the interweaving of physical and spiritual health in
most cultures, medical missionaries, eager to evaluate, judge, or even
deride both indigenous religion and health care, often combined a cari-
cature of both into their narratives.[32]

With no effort to contextualize, a missionary account of "A Heathen
Festival in India" described "a large ant-hill which in some way has become an object of worship. A temple has been built over it, and the

They learn to love the missionary as he heals their sicknesses and pains

Figure 4.4. Missionary doctor treating natives. (Boger, *The Congo Picture Book*, 90.)

word has gone abroad that dis-eas´es are cured there. So thousands of people visit the place." Near the temple, men and women repeatedly prostrated themselves on the ground and ritually pierced their children. The children had "a little flesh pinched up on their sides, wires put through the flesh, and, thus pierced, the children are carried in front of the idol, round the temple, and along the road to the other temple."[33] "All this," the author continued, "is being done to fulfil vows, or to obtain an answer to some prayer, or to get rid of sins, or to get help in some disease or sickness. And we, by your aid, are trying to lead them to the true Saviour; trying by our medical missions to give them health; and, above all, telling them of the love of the Father, and the true sal-va´tion from sin. Along the way our preachers were preaching, and amongst these people our Bible women are working."[34] Similarly, in "Pains and Pills, and a Cure that Kills!" Applegarth told her readers that if they were sick, a Chinese doctor "wouldn't do you a bit of good, because he would be a perfect old '*Ignoramus!'*" The Indians would "beat on drums to scare the spirits away" and in Africa the "Witch Doctor prances madly around, foaming at the mouth."[35]

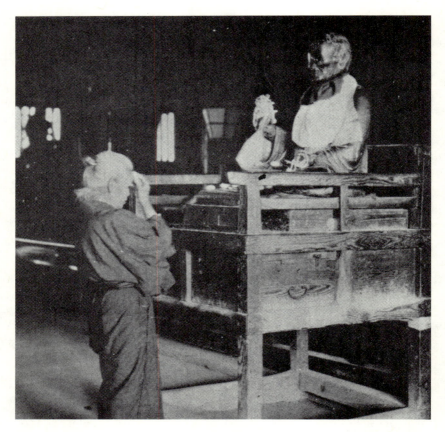

Figure 4.5. Japanese woman seeking health. (Applegarth, *The Honorable Japanese Fan*, between pp. 20–21.)

The caption that accompanied the photograph above (figure 4.5) further illustrates this tendency to deride rather than understand unfamiliar beliefs and practices:

> Every once in a while people rub the God-of-Healing so often in a certain spot that they actually wear away his nose or his jaws or his ears: for all the Boys-With-Mumps rub *his* jaws, then their own jaws, and all the deaf grannies rub *his* ears, then their own ears. This old lady, for instance, evidently has headaches, for you will notice how she rubs her brow, but a moment ago she undoubtedly rubbed the idol's forehead.
>
> Do you see the pathetic little offerings from sick patients—at least two aprons round his neck? A necklace in one hand and a bag in the

other? But, alas! alas! you and I cannot help but know that this unsani-
tary rubbing is an astonishingly easy way to *spread* disease and infection
instead of curing it.[36]

Only as natives slowly learned more about the white man's ways
did they "grow up" from their childlike selves, and missionary stories
formulized the transformation. Some sort of medical treatment usually
initiated the contact between native and missionary medicine. Then,
trained to read and understand the written word, the natives studied the
Bible, and prompted by the missionaries and previously converted natives, they learned about God, his only son Jesus, and their enemy the
devil. With this new cosmic vocabulary the converts could rename the
good spirits (God and his angels) and evil spirits (the devil and his angels)
of their former worldview and grow to understand the one, true, Christian God and the power of the devil that stood behind animism and
many of their native customs. The medical missionaries then linked a
Christian understanding of spirituality with Western customs regarding
the prevention and cure of disease. The really bright, promising men
and women then received practical training to assist the medical missionary and his staff in the operations of hospital, dispensary, and clinic.
Females primarily became nurses and males usually served as medical
assistants and dispensers.[37] (See figures 4.1, 4.2, and 4.6.)

The sketch that accompanied Applegarth's "Story of Two Hands"
(see figure 4.7) effectively summarizes the authors' striking contrast
between Western Christian and non-Western "heathen" ways of life.[38]
Ignorance, superstition, cruelty, and slavery to custom dominate the
backward "heathen" world, while community, medical education and
institutions, and spiritual liberation characterize the advanced world of
the Christian.

Ironically, however, the stories occasionally revealed that it was not
always clear who served the devil. Observing a Chinese child with an
unmistakably "large lump on her neck," a missionary woman asked the
girl's mother to "'Allow me to show you the way to the heal-sick house'"
for the "'doctor is there this moment. She will cure your child.'"[39] But
the mother "sprang to her feet with startled eyes" and retorted, "'Who
is sick? *You only* are sick. Get away! Get away! *We* here have no troubles.'"
A passerby explained to the confused Westerner that the mother feared
that her words would "attract the attention of evil spirits to her child,
and so she thinks they will gather around it and cause it to die. She loves

A SMILING GROUP OF TRAINED AFRICAN NURSES

Figure 4.6. Native nurses at Paul White's mission hospital. (White, *Doctor of Tanganyika*, between pp. 158–59.)

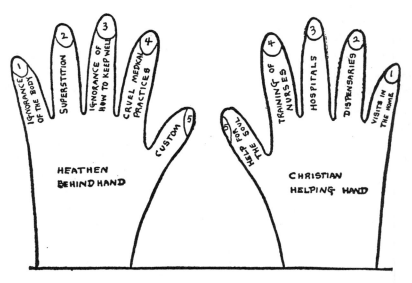

Figure 4.7. "The Story of the Two Hands." (Applegarth, *Missionary Stories for Little Folks; Second Series: Junior*, 275.)

her child. She called you the *sick one*, hoping the evil spirits may be deceived, and follow away after you."[40]

The preoccupation of the medical missionaries with Western modernity's concerns about "hygiene, efficiency, and progress effortlessly infiltrated" these stories as they did contemporary travel narratives.[41] When a new girl arrived at the Girls' School at Ruk, "they all gather around her and give her a welcome. These girls come to us with only a bit of cloth around the waist and perhaps another bit of cloth over their shoulders. One of the large girls will take the new one to the bath-tub and give her a bath, and then cut her hair, and we give her a new dress; then she is ready to take her place among the other girls. She is very shy at first, but the whole school set themselves to be her teacher, and one says, 'We do this;' and an-oth´er says, 'The teachers do not like to have us to do that;' so little by little she learns the new ways and begins the new life."[42]

And although "the Tibetans are kind, truthful, and honest, they are very ugly and dirty, and although they have so much snow and rushing rivers of clear, cold water, they seldom ever wash their bodies, not even their faces and hands, and *never* wash their clothes."[43] Any native resistance to such habits of cleanliness seemed strange to the narrators, since the missionaries "knew it was just plain, everyday *Common-sense*, the kind your mother and my mother had, because they lived in a Christian land."[44]

Clearly, an attitude of racial superiority underlies much of what I have been describing. Authors often depicted the so-called darker races as inferior, benighted, and degraded; they were not just dirty, they were ignorant and often stupid.[45] In 1917 Applegarth described the reaction of African children to the appearance of the missionary in the following terms: "She was the most astonishing person they had ever seen, for her skin was white like the clouds, and everybody else they knew had skin as black as coal! She had eyes as blue as the sky, and everybody else they knew had eyes as brown as the mud in the village streets. So it was no wonder they tagged around after her everywhere she went, exactly like 'Mary had a little lamb'—you know?"[46]

What strikes one in this passage is not the contrast between skin pigment of European and African, but the similes of comparison. The European is white and blue, like the sky above; the African is black and brown, like the earth beneath. But not just earth, rather coal and mud. Doubtless the comparisons registered only superficially with children;

nonetheless, the almost subliminal allusions to heaven and hell evoked by the upward and downward similes jolt today's adult reader.

But the sensibilities of many if not most authors to such implicitly racist language changed with the times.[47] For example, Applegarth's 1920 edition of *Lamplighters Across the Sea,* a collection of stories about the heroics of Bible translators, contained references to "petrified China-men," "The blackest little girl you ever saw," and "The wise(?) village witch-doctor," but these became "The terrified Chinese," "A little girl with dark brown skin," and "The village witch doctor" in the reissued 1947 edition.

Some authors even recognized faults with their own "white" race and noted the natives' good qualities, and they acknowledged the fact that missionaries, sometimes at least, brought corruption and illness as well as reforms and cures. W. E. Walston told "about the Kaffirs [of South Africa], who are gen´er-al-ly upright and honest before they learn the ways of the white men and Malays. Their as-so-ci-a´tion with Malays and other races has de-grad´ed them."[48] Describing the inhabi-tants of the Cook Islands, Adelaide D. Wellman asserted that: "In many respects these people are better off now than they were before any white people came among them. They do not fight so much, and are not in so much danger from one an-oth´er. They have better food, and those who are willing to work have learned to build for themselves better houses. Still, in some ways, they are not so well off as before. They have learned from white people a few bad habits. One of these injures their health and also spoils their teeth. They all used to have fine teeth. Can you think what the habit is that injures both health and teeth?"[49] And al-though the natives usually lacked a proper understanding of proper diet, hygiene, or disease, the stories made it clear that they loved their chil-dren, although Indians and Chinese preferred boys to girls. Paul White, noteworthy for his sensitivity to native ways, observed that he had "al-ways been struck with the way in which the Africans can handle a child. They have the knack of picking up and comforting a child, and, no mat-ter how fearsome their aspect, never seem to inspire fear in children."[50] And White's evenhandedness even extended to his evaluation of witch doctors, much of whose "work is sheer fraud, but over and over they produce cures because they produce a tangible cause for the trouble."[51]

Much of the impact of a good mission story lies in the context of the telling. An individual reader brings his/her own knowledge and experi-ence to the reading, and the author/editor presents a context for the printed text, including an intended audience, a religious milieu, photographs or sketches, and a relationship to Bible study lessons. And when shared orally in the intimacy of one's immediate family, a story's impact is mediated through the unique contexts of family history and experience. More could be said about the dynamics of each of these more private readings, but it is to the organizational and programmatic public contexts for medical missionary stories that I now turn. Sunday school and missionary association leaders not only repeated medical mission stories, they also created an instructional culture of missions for their children and youth.

Missionary Tidings (Disciples of Christ), published by the Christian Woman's Board of Missions (ca. 1874), argued that "the study of the lives of missionary heroes and heroines, and the association with the unselfish people who are carrying on this Christ-like work, will help the child to form higher and better and more unselfish ideals of life."[52] In the Board's "plan to disseminate missionary intelligence and create missionary zeal, naturally the children and young people were thought of as most hopeful soil in which to sow the seed for future harvesting" and so they organized mission bands and mission circles for the dissemination of mission stories, the creation of missionary activities, and the never-ignored necessity of raising missionary donations.[53] As a missionary program exercise for juniors related, "'I am the *hospital dime*. I send out missionary doctors and nurses and build hospitals and buy medicines. Wherever I go to work the people come flocking with the sick folks—the lame, the blind, and the crippled—just as they used to when Jesus was on earth. . . . They need more hospitals, and more doctors and nurses. If I had all of the other nine dimes in the missionary dollar I could use them every one in my work.'"[54]

Around 1877 under the auspices of the Christian Woman's Board, these Disciples of Christ women established Mission Bands or Mission Circles to stimulate the missionary spirit among young women and raise financial support for foreign missions.[55] Typical of both denominational and nondenominational organizations, their meetings centered on stories and participatory activities intended to make the needs in mission lands come alive.[56] For example, the program guide for February 1910 focused on *"Help and Healing in India—Sketches of Our Hospital Work."* After songs, scripture reading, prayer, and club business, the leaders were to "Appoint girls to represent our physicians. Let each girl introduce herself by displaying the picture of the medical missionary she represents, also any other pictures that have to do with her work. By referring to the annual report in the November *Missionary Tidings* and other numbers of the *Tidings* the girls will find material for a brief talk on their work." The closing prayer should remind the girls that "one of the greatest needs of the Christian Woman's Board of Missions is for the medical missionaries. Have a circle of prayer that some of the Circle girls may respond to this need."[57]

But what about the intended meanings of the authors? Why did they tell the stories, and what can we learn from an analysis of their content? Margaret T. Applegarth (1886–1976), author of dozens of widely distributed missionary stories and plays published under the auspices of denominational (including Baptist and Reformed Church in America), interdenominational (the Central Committee on the United Study of Foreign Missions),[58] and nondenominational presses, stated that she wrote her stories "not only to tell facts, but to create an *attitude of mind* towards missionary work around the world, which shall be unconsciously retained long after the details of the stories themselves are forgotten [and] so that we may raise a new generation with whom God's Kingdom shall be *one* vast enterprise, instead of *two!*" Clearly she hoped that children would come to see the world as populated by one people— God's children—and that children would be influenced to help those in moral and spiritual darkness find a better way. But she did not completely ignore denominational priorities. She encouraged children to plan each week for the Sabbath mission offering that would enable missionaries to continue their work in "*our* Hospital," "*our* missionary school," and "*our* orphanage."[59] And she undoubtedly shared the sentiments of those in Adventist publications who stated that often "the little folks who read this paper from week to week, have said that when they are grown, they will be foreign mis'sion-a-ries. Perhaps some of you are even thinking about the country you wish to go to. This is very good."[60] Just like the little Hebrew girl who helped Naaman, you too can be a "foreign mis'sion-a-ry, and a doctor, and a preacher" who helps people to learn to "worship the true God."[61]

After World War I many Americans came to believe that suspicions and misunderstandings of other peoples and their cultures had led to the devastation of the war. Due to the resultant internationalism and the influential missionary experiences of individuals like E. Stanley Jones and Daniel Fleming, missions in many Protestant churches shifted from an attitude of cultural superiority and judgment to an attitude of cultural sensitivity, openness, and friendship.[62] The International Council of Religious Education, representative of a broad range of Protestant denominations and nondenominational religious organizations, vigorously advocated this new mission emphasis. World friendship, according to Elizabeth Harris, secretary for elementary work at the Missionary Education Movement, meant "an emphasis upon the contributions of other peoples instead of the cultivation of a 'smug' satisfaction with ourselves."[63] Ralph E. Diffendorfer, corresponding secretary of the Board of Foreign Missions of the Methodist Episcopal Church, echoed Harris's sentiments; there had occurred "an awakening of races and peoples to a realization of their own worth," but he believed that the awakening, at least in Asia, was "very largely from the broadcasting . . . of the principles of Jesus Christ."[64] Clearly, world friendship did not include an embrace of cultural relativism; Christians had some things to offer to improve the beliefs and behaviors of the non-Westerner. And at the top of the list were Jesus, medicine, and Western health practices.

Mission stories and program plans seemed to reflect this prescriptive shift supported by mission advocates. For example, Emma T. Anderson's *A'Chu and Other Stories* "introduces the reader to the millions of China, the most populous, the most promising of all the mission fields of the world today." According to the publishers, "instead of abstract descriptions of manners and customs," Anderson has, "by a series of true stories, introduced the reader to the real home life of the common people" where the reader is "made to feel the vital power of a life changed by the religion of Jesus Christ." "If these stories shall serve to broaden the vision of those who read them; if they shall stir hearts to lay their best upon the altar of service, as the author of this little book has done; if the missionary spirit shall be strengthened in behalf of this great people, the hope entertained by author and publisher will have been realized."[65]

Countless Protestant children listened to thousands of missionary stories, but what did they make of such tales, what impact did they exert on their lives, and did the results bear any resemblance to what they were supposed to get out of the stories?[66] Adults tell stories and write children's literature, and they usually have clear intentions for what they relate. Not only do they want to communicate information, invoke emotional responses, change behavior, and instill values but, as Wendy Doniger O'Flaherty so aptly put it, they also want to create community—"to relive, together, the stories that they already know, stories about

Figure 4.8. Clever Queen's world. (Hare, *Clever Queen: A Tale of the Jungle and of Devil Worshipers*, book cover.)

themselves."[67] This impulse to link children to storytellers and to their pasts by transmitting a community's mythology may have been doubly imperative for the tellers of missionary stories for whom the universalizing character of Christianity should lead to the recognition, confrontation, and transformation of the non-Christian and his mythos. These stories were about what it meant to be a part of the Western, Christian community. Only superficially were they about the "other" and never about the transformation of the Christian healer into the "other." The storytellers rarely legitimized the exotic details of foreign lands by seating them firmly within their mythic otherness. Instead, in these stories natives sleepwalked through their existences, unaware of the universal struggle between good and evil of which they were a part, until awakened from their trance by the missionary preacher, teacher, or doctor.

A map of the Burmese world of the Karen peoples arrived on the covers of the 1957 edition of *Clever Queen*.[68] (See figure 4.8.) And what was Clever Queen's world like? Situated next to the Kawkeyet Pagoda on the Salween River, surrounded by jungle, tigers, snakes, and elephants, sat the Hares' Ohndaw Dispensary and School. The Karen cut bamboo and planted rice, used the rivers as roads, and lived in bamboo shelters roofed with grass. The map also identified the location of several key episodes in the story—Clever Queen's birthplace, the hideout on the mountainside, and Clever Queen's new home.

Readers learned of the beliefs and practices of the Karen from the text, where they were told that Karen believed that the odor of frying food "goes into their blood and produces boils and abscesses if they smell it while they have sores or pimples."[69] They discovered that the natives believed that the strength of Dr. Hare's medicine came from the picture of the rabbit he had attached to the bottles he dispensed, and they were instructed that one "can't help but feel sorry for the little children who are born among the devil worshipers."[70]

Such superstitious beliefs about the origin of disease and the magical influence of medicine bottle labels may have seemed odd and kind of quaint to readers, but devil worship was something else. Doubtless few Americans knew any devil worshippers, but their supernaturalist, often evangelical worldview made it clear to them that the devil existed and could entice boys and girls into his service. And many children had been told that Ouija boards foretold the future for the same devilish reasons that the chicken bones cast by the "heathen" did—odd and scary, perhaps, but real, not like the boogeyman under the bed. The authors of medical missionary stories not only steered their little listeners through exotic places like Burma. They also charted cosmological realms in which spiritual forces of good and evil struggled for the bodies and souls of little children both at home and in far-off lands.

In contrast to these and other Karen beliefs and practices, readers learned that the Hares, aided by converted Karen assistants, warned against the use of the disgusting betel nut, taught the importance of proper hygiene and diet, dispensed medicines, pulled teeth, and healed Clever Queen of her horrible boils. They operated a jungle school where Clever Queen gained freedom from "the devils" and learned to read and write like "the God worshippers." And, of course, the Hares preached the Gospel of Jesus, taught the doctrines of Adventism, and baptized many, including Clever Queen, into the Church. In short, medical missionary stories brought comfort to their listeners, legitimized Western cultural attitudes and values, and solidified a commitment to Western medicine.

Clearly a variety of factors influenced American men and women to sail across the seas, enter unfamiliar and often hostile lands, and bring the Gospel of salvation and the healing hand of Western medicine to native peoples. Some, like Ida Scudder, experienced firsthand as young people the need for female physicians in India where the people refused Western medical care rather than submit their women to examination by a male physician.[71] But what can be said about the impact of medical missionary stories on the career choices of their young audience? Aside from the occasional adult reminiscence, diary entry, or correspondence reference by adult missionaries, few records exist from which one might directly recover the impact of medical missionary stories on Protestant American children. But the evidence that does exist strongly suggests that the stories had a positive impact on later decisions to serve as medical missionaries. Margaret White Eggleston, author of many children's stories for religious education, was not alone in firmly believing that "many missionaries are on the field to-day as the result of a story of the life, work, or needs of some hero, or heroine, of the past."[72]

Thomas W. Ayers, a pioneer of Southern Baptist medical missions, resisted God's call to mission service for years, knew nothing of medical missions at the time he went to medical school, and only embarked for service to China in 1901 after his forty-first birthday when a sequence of events he could interpret only as God's insistence compelled his obedience. As a young man Ayers believed that "under the preaching of Dr. Charles A. Stakely, I had a very definite call from God to give myself as a foreign missionary" and only later came to believe that God "led me to study medicine in order to make of me a medical missionary." But as Ayers made clear to potential medical missionaries, both young and old, "the call of a need and the call of the crowd are both inspiring," but "the man or woman who goes to a non-Christian land as a medical missionary without the call of God will not be happy in the hardships incident to such a life, and the probability is that he or she will not remain." Clearly Stakely's stories of need had been important, but an inner conviction of God's call proved crucial.[73]

Mission stories reached their audiences through a variety of means with often unpredictable results. In the early 1900s the *Youth's Companion* reported that:

> A number of years ago the heart of a young girl was greatly moved by a letter from a missionary in India, describing the suffering which was caused by the absolute lack of all knowledge of the right way to treat the sick.
>
> To this young girl this feature of a missionary's work in India seemed at the same time the most trying and the most appealing.

The first response which she desired to make to this appeal was to go to India as a missionary herself. But when she began to prepare herself for that work, it was only to give it up almost immediately, because her health was evidently too weak to endure the strain of a missionary's life.

Nevertheless, she was not disheartened. She began at once to work for the accomplishment of an object which would seem to many but little better than an impossible dream. If she could not go to India herself, she would lay by her earnings for the founding of a modern, well-equipped hospital in the very midst of that country of ignorance, disease and suffering.[74]

Thwarted from her path to become a medical missionary, this young girl channeled her energies into fund-raising, and although she died before she could witness the realization of her goal, her parents and others saw the task to completion.

Gordon S. Seagrave (1897–1965), son of a long line of Baptist missionaries to the Karen of Lower Burma, sat at age five on the veranda of his home in Rangoon. As he listened to the "stories of wild jungles and great deeds" recounted by Robert Harper, an Irish medical missionary to northern Burma, his heart filled with childish enthusiasm for the romance of medical mission, and he announced to his mother that "when I grow up I'm going to be a medical missionary in the Shan States" of northern Burma.[75] Little did she know that her son would become the famed "Burma Surgeon" who for "20 years, as a young Baptist medical missionary . . . fought disease and filth, built a hospital, [and] taught native girls to be skilled nurses."[76]

Henry W. Frost, author of the foreword to *China Chats: Talks with Children About Things of China*, reported that on the basis of his personal experience "persons have received their first and deepest impressions in respect to foreign service in their early youth, indeed, in their childhood." "These bright and winsome tales, under the influence of the Spirit," he continued, "will undoubtedly perform a large work of grace and power, and, will lead many children to follow on to know the Lord, until as young men and women they are ready to follow the Lamb whithersoever He goeth."[77]

Whether by sermon, letter, oral presentation, or published story, medical mission stories drew American young people to health-care careers and foreign mission service, but their influence apparently declined as the century advanced. A 1968 global survey of medical missionaries conducted by the Medical Assistance Program documented the fact that missionary speakers and books on missions had a significant impact on influencing them to become medical missionaries. However, over time both of these influences had had a steadily diminishing impact. For example, those with thirteen to sixteen years of missionary service identified their most important influences as the missionary speaker (21.1 percent), parents (21.1 percent), books on missions (10.5 percent), and personal contact (5.3 percent). In contrast, those with four or fewer years of service ranked their most important influences as personal contact (26.9 percent), parents (19.2 percent), and the missionary speaker (15.4 percent), with books on missions just 5.8 percent. Undoubtedly, one's personal contact with a medical missionary always included the telling of some medical missionary experiences. Therefore, it is somewhat uncertain how to interpret this data. Possibly both the opportunity for personal contact with medical missionaries had increased, and the persuasiveness of the impersonal storyteller had declined. In either case it seems justified to conclude that missionary stories still carried some clout in the decision to become a medical missionary well into the late twentieth century.[78]

When medical missionaries returned "home" to America, they disembarked with a variety of foreign objects tucked away inside their baggage, but they also arrived with exotic and sometimes self-contradictory ideas hidden within their mission stories. This examination of mission stories corroborates the presence of the pervasive dualisms that Edward Said identified as integral to Orientalism and provides further evidence to support and extend Herb Swanson's assertion that, before 1920—and, we now see, thereafter as well—missionary literature often described the "non-Christian world as being immoral, benighted, idolatrous, pagan, barbaric, infidel, and so on down a long list of other terms that may be summarized best in that old-fashioned word 'heathenism.'"[79]

Medical missionary stories influenced a child's view of "mythic mission lands," contributed to the formation of her understanding of the gendered roles that medical doctors (male curers) and nurses (female caretakers) should play in bringing scientific medicine to "heathen lands," and may well have affected her career choices. As a missionary A-B-C exercise for primary children suggested, "D is for doctors, who for Jesus' sake / Make sick children well, curing many / an ache." But "N stands for nurses with caps clean and / white, / Filling the hearts of the sick with de- / light."[80] Moreover, the stories shaped children's views of the values, worldviews, and cultures of the peoples who "visited witch doctors and prayed to the devil." They may have also learned that "heathen" parents loved their children; but "heathen" ignorance of proper care often put those same children in jeopardy. As the *Mission Dayspring* (Congregational) reported, when a child in China "is sick, the doctor may puncture it with long needles, or give it horrid med´i-cines, which do no good and may do much harm. Perhaps the child gets well and seems to have a fair chance of living. But it will be allowed to chew green fruit, cu´cum-bers, and melons, eating rind and seeds; and the fact that any child can live in that way seems a miracle."[81]

Such stories portrayed to children the supposedly obvious advantages of the American ways of life, which were superior to the ways of the "heathen." But they also contained potentially confusing images of non-Western geography, culture, and technology as well. Such stories often possessed, like Malek Alloula's postcards of colonial Algerian harems, "a seductive appeal to the spirit of adventure and pioneering," but "their pseudoknowledge" often presented a "comic strip of colonial morality."[82] The transformations inside a child's mind upon hearing medical mission stories will forever remain somewhat mysterious. However, as these reconstructions suggest, medical missionary stories possessed a great potential to form within Protestant American children powerful mythic images of both the mission lands and the home front and to lead them to perpetuate their culture by remaking the world in Western Christian ways.

Notes

Thanks to James Danky, Fritz Guy, Ronald Numbers, Robert Schneider, Dana Robert, and this volume's anonymous reviewers for helpful comments; many thanks to Linn Tonstad and Joel McFadden for research assistance. The libraries and librarians at La Sierra University, Fuller Theological Seminary (especially William Kostlevy), Azusa Pacific University, Biola University, Claremont School of Theology, and Loma Linda University proved invaluable. Finally, I completed this essay while on the faculty of La Sierra University, Riverside, California; my thanks to the administration for its support. An earlier version of this article appeared as "Making Doctors and Nurses for Jesus: Medical Missionary Stories and American Children," *Church History* 74, 3 (September 2005): 557–90.

    1. Quotation from C. Peter Williams, "Healing and Evangelism: The

Place of Medicine in Later Victorian Protestant Missionary Thinking," in *The Church and Healing*, Studies in Church History, vol. 19, ed. W. J. Sheils for the Ecclesiastical History Society (Oxford: Basil Blackwell, 1982), 285. On Peter Parker, see Edward V. Gulick, *Peter Parker and the Opening of China* (Cambridge, MA: Harvard University Press, 1973). Daniel Wise briefly mentions Dr. Clara A. Swain, pioneer Methodist medical missionary, in *Our Missionary Heroes and Heroines; or, Heroic Deeds Done in Methodist Missionary Fields* (New York: Eaton & Mains, 1884), 242. For more on Swain and her experiences in India see Helen Barrett Montgomery, *Western Women in Eastern Lands: An Outline Study of Fifty Years of Woman's Work in Foreign Missions* (New York: Macmillan, 1910), 187–96, and Dana L. Robert, *American Women in Mission: A Social History of Their Thought and Practice* (Macon, GA: Mercer University Press, 1996), 162–65.

2. James S. Dennis, *Christian Missions and Social Progress*, 3 vols. (New York: Revell, 1897–1906), 2:402, 40n2.

3. On medical missions see Christoffer Grundmann, "Proclaiming the Gospel by Healing the Sick? Historical and Theological Annotations on Medical Mission," *International Bulletin of Missionary Research* 14 (July 1990): 120–26.

4. For recent work regarding postcolonialism and Western medicine, see Warwick Anderson, "Where Is the Postcolonial History of Medicine?" *Bulletin of the History of Medicine* 72 (1998): 522–30. For recent explorations of the complex interaction among medical missionaries, Western medicine, and indigenous peoples, see John M. Mackenzie, "Missionaries, Science, and the Environment in Nineteenth-Century Africa," in *The Imperial Horizons of British Protestant Missions, 1880–1914*, ed. Andrew Porter (Grand Rapids, MI: William B. Eerdmans Publishing Company, 2003), 106–30; Steven Feierman, "Explanation and Uncertainty in the Medical World of Ghaambo," *Bulletin of the History of Medicine* 74 (2000): 317–44; Luise White, "'They Could Make Their Victims Dull': Genders and Genres, Fantasies and Cures in Colonial Southern Uganda," *American Historical Review* 100 (1995): 1379–1402; Willem Berends, "African Traditional Healing Practices and the Christian Community," *Missiology: An International Review* 21 (July 1993): 275–88; Felix K. Ekechi, "The Medical Factor in Christian Conversion in Africa: Observations from Southeastern Nigeria," *Missiology: An International Review* 21 (July 1993): 289–309; Richard E. Elkins, "Blood Sacrifice and the Dynamics of Supernatural Power among the Manobo of Mindanao: Some Missiological Implications," *Missiology: An International Review* 21 (July 1993): 321–31; J. Paul Seale, "Christian Missionary Medicine and Traditional Healers: A Case Study in Collaboration from the Philippines," *Missiology: An International Review* 21 (July 1993): 311–20; and David Arnold, "Touching the Body: Perspectives on the Indian Plague, 1896–1900," in *Selected Subaltern Studies*, ed. Ranajit Guha and Gayatri Chakravorty Spivak (New York: Oxford University Press, 1988), 391–426.

5. An excellent historiographical overview of Christian mission studies recently appeared as Andrew Porter, "Church History, History of Christianity, Religious History: Some Reflections on British Missionary Enterprise Since the Late Eighteenth Century," *Church History* 71 (2002): 555–84. For a recent examination of the understudied cultural impact of missions on the home front, see Daniel H. Bays and Grant Wacker, eds., *The Foreign Missionary Enterprise at Home: Explorations in North American Cultural History* (Tuscaloosa: University of Alabama Press, 2003).

6. Margaret T. Applegarth, *Missionary Stories for Little Folks; Second Series: Junior* (New York: Harper and Brothers, 1917), 282.

7. In the parlance of historians of the book, I explore the "mediation," "appropriation," and "practice" of these texts, terms defined in Joan Shelley Rubin, "What Is the History of the History of Books?" *Journal of American History* 90 (2003): 555–75. For other helpful sources on the history of books, readers, and reading, see Hugh Amory and David D. Hall, eds., *A History of the Book in America*, vol. 1, *The Colonial Book in the Atlantic World* (New York: Cambridge University Press, 2000); Guglielmo Cavallo and Roger Chartier, eds., *A History of Reading in the West*, trans. Lydia G. Cochrane (Amherst: University of Massachusetts, 1999); and David D. Hall, *Cultures of Print: Essays in the History of the Book* (Amherst: University of Massachusetts Press, 1996).

8. Candy Gunther Brown, *Word in the World: Evangelical Writing, Publishing, and Reading in America, 1789–1880* (Chapel Hill: University of North Carolina Press, 2004), 40. The following denominations are represented in this study: Anglican, Baptist, Congregational, Disciples of Christ, Methodist, Presbyterian, Reformed, Seventh-day Adventist.

9. Edwin Wilbur Rice, *The Sunday-School Movement (1780–1917) and the American Sunday-School Union (1817–1917)* (Philadelphia: American Sunday-School Union, 1917; reprint, New York: Arno Press, 1971), 141–42. See also Anne M. Boylan, *Sunday School: The Formation of an American Institution, 1790–1880* (New Haven, CT: Yale University Press, 1988), and Robert W. Lynn and Elliott Wright, *The Big Little School: 200 Years of the Sunday School* (Birmingham, AL: Religious Education Press, 1980).

10. Rice, *Sunday-School Movement*, 159. For an insightful analysis of evangelical print culture, see Brown, *Word in the World*.

11. Ibid., 419.

12. "How a Little Sick Boy was Cured," *Our Little Friend* 10, no. 27 (29 December 1899): 214; Applegarth, *Missionary Stories; Second Series: Junior*, 286–91.

13. For example see Emma Anderson, *With Our Missionaries in China* (Mountain View, CA: Pacific Press Publishing Association, 1920) (Seventh-day Adventist), N. G. [Gust] Pearson, *With Christ in Congo: A Story of Twenty Years of Missionary Work in French Congo* (Chicago: Conference Press, n.d. [1942–1949?]) (Baptist).

14. W. A. Criswell and Duke K. McCall, *Passport to the World* (Nashville, TN: Broadman Press, 1951), 20–21, 23, 24.

15. For example see "'Jolly Good Fun'" and "When Livingstone Was Lost" in Hugh T. Kerr, *Children's Missionary Story-Sermons* (New York: Fleming H. Revell, 1915); "Should He Steal?" "One Girl's Dream," "Sona Mona Singh," "Liu Kwang Chao," and "An Indian Mother's Gift," in Margaret White Eggleston, *Seventy-Five Stories for the Worship Hour* (New York: Harper & Brothers, 1929); "A Woman Conquers Cannibals with Kindness" and "A Chinese Robber Has His Picture Taken (*A True Story*)," in Mary Kirkpatrick Berg, *Story Sermons for Junior Congregations* (New York: Harper & Brothers, 1930); "How One Doctor Works," "Sickness Packets or Joy Packets—Which?" and "The Monkey and the Medic," in G. B. F. Hallock, *Ninety-Nine New Sermons for Children* (New York: Harper & Brothers, 1937); and "David Livingstone, The Pathfinder of Africa," in Eugene Myers Harrison, *Giants of the Missionary Trail: The Life Stories of Eight Men Who Defied Death and Demons* (Chicago: Scripture Press, 1954).

16. I have greatly benefited from conversations with Jeffrey Dupée on these characterizations of narrative style. See also his *British Travel Writers in China—Writing Home to a British Public, 1890–1914* (Lewiston, NY: Edwin Mellen, 2004), 300–310.

17. Luise White, "'They Could Make Their Victims Dull,'" 1388, 1396.

18. Each of the photographs and drawings used in this article reflect the use of such illustrations to support the text's narrative and to provide a record of the events described. See Kathryn T. Long's exploration of the evolving role of photography in documenting missions in "'Cameras never lie': The Role of Photography in Telling the Story of American Evangelical Missions," *Church History* 72 (2003): 820–51.

19. Eric B. Hare, *Clever Queen: A Tale of the Jungle and of Devil Worshipers* (Mountain View, CA: Pacific Press Publishing Association, 1936). To hear Hare's distinctive storytelling, listen to *Eric B. Hare Stories*, vol. 1 (Nampa, ID: Chapel Records, 1980).

20. "December 3, 1926: Jungle Doctor Signed a Decision Card," http://chi.gospelcon.net/DAILYF/L001/12/daily-12-03-2001.shtml (accessed 6 September 2007).

21. Personal communication to author from Duane Koenig, Moody Press, 15 July 2005.

22. For examples among many of detailed descriptions of treatment and surgery, see Paul White, *Jungle Doctor Operates* (London: The Paternoster Press, 1950), 48–52, 106–12.

23. Paul White, *Jungle Doctor Meets a Lion* (Grand Rapids, MI: Wm. B. Eerdmans Publishing Company, 1951), 21, 53, 58.

24. White, *Jungle Doctor Operates*, 112.

25. See Andrew F. Walls, "The Legacy of David Livingstone," *International*

Bulletin of Missionary Research 11 (July 1987): 125–29; Gulick, *Peter Parker;* and Dorothy Clarke Wilson, *Dr. Ida: The Story of Dr. Ida Scudder of Vellore* (New York: McGraw-Hill, 1959).

26. Lucy W. Peabody, *David and Susi: Black and White; Third Book of Stories for Little Children* (Cambridge, MA: Central Committee on the United Study of Foreign Missions, 1928), 24.

27. See the profile of Jenny English Crozier, M.D., in "Our Girls," *Missionary Tidings* 22 (1904–5): 179–80.

28. Mrs. D. C. Brown, "Over the Teacups," *Missionary Tidings* 26 (1908–9): 170.

29. For a discussion of this and related issues, see Elizabeth Segel, "'As the Twig Is Bent . . . ': Gender and Childhood Reading," in *Gender and Reading: Essays on Readers, Texts, and Contexts,* ed. Elizabeth A. Flynn and Patrocinio P. Schweickart (Baltimore: Johns Hopkins University Press, 1986), 165–86.

30. "Miss Rose M. Kinney Girls' School at Ruk," *Our Little Friend* 10, no. 2 (7 July 1899): 9.

31. Bertha Spear Boger, *The Congo Picture Book* (Nashville, TN: Southern Publishing Association, 1925); Elizabeth Mershon, *With the Wild Men of Borneo* (Mountain View, CA: Pacific Press Publishing Association, 1922). See also Paul White, *Doctor of Tanganyika* (Grand Rapids, MI: Wm. B. Eerdmans Publishing, 1957).

32. For a helpful counterbalance to the totalizing and solipsistic tendencies of discourse theory on narratives about the "other," see Dupée, *British Travel Writers in China,* 1–24, and Dennis Porter, *Haunted Journeys: Desire and Transgression in European Travel Writing* (Princeton, NJ: Princeton University Press, 1992).

33. This appears to be a description of the Hindu ritual of thanksgiving and atonement, called Thaipusam, which continues in Malaysia but no longer in India.

34. "Heathen Festival in India," *Our Little Friend* 10, no. 19 (3 November 1899): 148.

35. Applegarth, *Missionary Stories; Second Series: Junior,* 268–74.

36. Margaret T. Applegarth, *The Honorable Japanese Fan* (West Medford, MA: The Central Committee on the United Study of Foreign Missions, 1923), between pages 20 and 21.

37. Paul White's "Jungle Doctor" stories are noteworthy for giving to the natives a clear and articulate voice in this process of cultural and social transformation.

38. Applegarth, *Missionary Stories; Second Series: Junior,* 275.

39. Note the pronoun "she" identifying a woman physician.

40. "Which One Was Sick?" in Emma T. Anderson, *A'Chu and Other Stories* (Takoma Park, MD: Review & Herald Publishing Assn., 1920), 253–54.

41. Dupée, *British Travel Writers in China,* 14.

42. Miss Rose M. Kinney Girls' School at Ruk," *Our Little Friend* 10, no. 2 (7 July 1899): 9–10.

43. "Country and People of Tibet," *Our Little Friend* 8, no. 32 (4 February 1898): 253. (From the *Children's Record*.)

44. Margaret T. Applegarth, "Monkey Tails and Other Tales," in *Missionary Stories for Little Folks; First Series: Primary* (New York: George H. Doran Company, 1917), 83.

45. See for example Applegarth, "What One Little Girl Became," in *Missionary Stories; Second Series: Junior*, 303.

46. Applegarth, "Banana Tree that was Dressed Up," in *Missionary Stories; Second Series: Junior*, 108.

47. For a helpful examination of race and missions in Africa, see Andrew C. Ross, "Christian Missions and the Mid-Nineteenth-Century Change in Attitudes to Race: The African Experience," in *The Imperial Horizons of British Protestant Missions, 1880–1914*, ed. Andrew Porter (Grand Rapids, MI: William B. Eerdmans Publishing Company, 2003), 85–105.

48. W. E. Walston, "About South Africa," *Our Little Friend* 10, no. 19 (3 November 1899): 148.

49. Adelaide D. Wellman, "The Cook Islands," *Our Little Friend* 11, no. 36 (1 March 1901): 286–87.

50. Paul White, *Doctor of Tanganyika*, 23.

51. Ibid., 115. For a good example of cross-cultural misunderstanding on both American and Chinese parts, see "In China and America" in Anita B. Ferris, *Missionary Program Material for Use with Boys and Girls* (New York: Missionary Education Movement of the United States and Canada, 1916), 40–41.

52. Annie E. Davidson, "The Educational Influence of the Christian Woman's Board of Missions on the Children," *Missionary Tidings* 23 (1905–6): 290.

53. "Circle Beginnings," *Missionary Tidings* 26 (1908–9): 36.

54. Ferris, *Missionary Program Material for Use with Boys and Girls*, 94.

55. "Circle Beginnings," *Missionary Tidings* 26 (1908–9): 36–37.

56. For missionary programs and activities for youth, see Christopher Coble, "The Role of Young People's Societies in the Training of Christian Womanhood (and Manhood), 1880–1910," in *Women and Twentieth-Century Protestantism*, ed. Margaret Lamberts Bendroth and Virginia Lieson Brereton (Urbana: University of Illinois Press, 2002), 74–92; Virginia Lieson Brereton, *Training God's Army: The American Bible School, 1880–1940* (Bloomington: Indiana University Press, 1990), 127–29. A good example of graded missionary program material for young people is Ferris, *Missionary Program Material for Use with Boys and Girls*.

57. "Circle Program for February," *Missionary Tidings* 27 (1909–10): 407.

58. The Central Committee on the United Study of Foreign Missions emerged from the New York Ecumenical Missionary Conference of 1900. Among other activities, the Committee annually published mission books for adults and children.

59. Applegarth, *Missionary Stories; Second Series: Junior*, viii (emphasis in original).

60. Mrs. A. W. Kuhl, "Foreign Missionaries," *Our Little Friend* 11, no. 18 (26 October 1900): 141.

61. Mrs. O. E. Cummings, "'The Maiden Missionary,'" *Our Little Friend* 12, no. 25 (20 December 1901): 198.

62. For a further exploration of the relationship between internationalization and the indigenization of Christian missions, see Dana L. Robert, "The First Globalization: The Internationalization of the Protestant Missionary Movement Between the World Wars," *International Bulletin of Missionary Research* 26 (April 2002): 50–66.

63. Elizabeth Harris, "The Missionary Education of Children," *The International Journal of Religious Education* 3 (1926–27): 14.

64. Ralph E. Diffendorfer, "The 'Disturbance of Growth' in Missionary Attitudes," *The International Journal of Religious Education* 4 (1927–28): 16.

65. Anderson, *A'Chu and Other Stories*, 7–8.

66. Although I reject the ahistorical tendencies of many who apply reception theory, I have found many of their sensibilities helpful in my reading of texts. See Norman H. Holland, "Reader-Response Criticism," in *The New Princeton Encyclopedia of Poetry and Poetics*, ed. Alex Preminger and T. V. F. Brogan (Princeton, NJ: Princeton University Press, 1993), 1014–16; James L. Machor, ed., *Readers in History: Nineteenth-Century American Literature and the Contexts of Response* (Baltimore: Johns Hopkins University Press, 1993); Robert C. Holub, *Reception Theory: A Critical Introduction* (New York: Methuen, 1984); Jane P. Tompkins, ed., *Reader-Response Criticism: From Formalism to Post-Structuralism* (Baltimore: Johns Hopkins University Press, 1980).

67. Wendy Doniger O'Flaherty, *Other Peoples' Myths: The Cave of Echoes* (New York: Macmillan, 1988), 148.

68. Eric B. Hare, *Clever Queen*.

69. Ibid., 32.

70. Ibid., 41, 6.

71. Mary Pauline Jeffery, *Ida S. Scudder of Vellore: The Life Story of Ida Sophia Scudder*, Jubilee ed. (Mysore City, India: Wesley Press, 1951), 26–27. For helpful insights into the motivations and experiences of female medical missionaries, see Leslie A. Flemming, ed., *Women's Work for Women: Missionaries and Social Change in Asia* (Boulder, CO: Westview Press, 1989); and Adrian A. Bennett, "Doing More Than They Intended," in *Historical Perspectives on the Wesleyan Tradition: Women in*

New Worlds, vol. 2, ed. Rosemary Skinner Keller, Louise L. Queen, and Hilah F. Thomas (Nashville, TN: Abingdon, 1982). For female motivations for missions in general see Dana L. Robert, *American Women in Mission: A Social History of Their Thought and Practice* (Macon, GA: Mercer University Press, 1997); and Lydia Huffman Hoyle, "Nineteenth-Century Single Women and Motivation for Mission," *International Bulletin of Missionary Research* 20 (April 1996): 58–64. For an early history of foreign mission work by women see Helen Barrett Montgomery, *Western Women in Eastern Lands: An Outline Study of Fifty Years of Woman's Work in Foreign Missions* (New York: Macmillan, 1910).

72. Margaret White Eggleston, *Seventy-Five Stories for the Worship Hour* (New York: Harper & Brothers, 1929), v.

73. T. W. Ayers, *Healing and Missions* (Richmond, VA: Educational Department, Foreign Mission Board, Southern Baptist Convention, 1930), 11, 12, 17.

74. Reproduced from the *Youth's Companion* as "A Failure That Bore Fruit," *Missionary Tidings* 26 (1908–9): 272.

75. Gordon S. Seagrave, *Burma Surgeon* (New York: W. W. Norton & Co., 1943), 11–12.

76. *Time* 45, no. 8 (19 February 1945): 53.

77. Frederic F. Helmer, *China Chats: Talks with Children About Things of China* (Philadelphia: The Sunday School Times Company, 1925), 7–8.

78. Edward R. Dayton, ed., *Medicine and Missions: A Survey of Medical Missions* (Wheaton, IL: Medical Assistance Program, Inc., 1969), 7–10. The Program surveyed over 1,000 medical missionaries and received 158 responses, of which 106 were from citizens of the United States.

79. Herb Swanson, "Said's *Orientalism* and the Study of Christian Missions," *International Bulletin of Missionary Research* 28 (July 2004): 109. This is not to say that these sources reveal all that can be said about the cultural imperialism of missionaries or to essentialize Said's definitions. See Andrew Porter's helpful correctives in "'Cultural Imperialism' and Protestant Missionary Enterprise, 1780–1914," *Journal of Imperial and Commonwealth History* 25 (1997): 367–91.

80. Emily Williston, "Missionary A-B-C's," in Ferris, *Missionary Program Material for Use with Boys and Girls,* 92–93.

81. James H. Roberts, "Child-Life in China," *Our Little Friend* 8, no. 34 (18 February 1898): 269 (from the *Mission Dayspring*).

82. Malek Alloula, *The Colonial Harem,* Theory and History of Literature, vol. 21, trans. Myrna Godzich and Wlad Godzich (Minneapolis: University of Minnesota Press, 1986), 4.

Joseph B. Keeler, Print Culture, and the Modernization of Mormonism, 1885–1918

DAVID J. WHITTAKER

The years flanking the start of the twentieth century comprised a time of transition for the Church of Jesus Christ of Latter-day Saints. Seventy years old in 1900, the Church and the larger Mormon society in which it resided still displayed much of their traditional character. Although some members congregated in urban densities that edged out along the Wasatch Front from Salt Lake City, Utah's capital and the Church's headquarters, most still lived in small, relatively self-contained agricultural communities in the Great Basin's interior; wherever they lived, however, they expected charismatic leaders to continue organizing the Church, directing devotional life, and keeping the federal government at arm's length. That formula had held sway during the Saints' half-century-long occupation of the intermountain West, allowing a unique intermixing of civil and ecclesiastical institutions to develop. Change was in the wind, however, and indeed had been for decades.

Increasing contacts with the gentile (non-Mormon) world had resulted in Utah's increasing implication in national economic and political networks. Brigham Young, who directed the migration to Utah in 1846–47 and led the Church until his death thirty years later, had steered the economy in the direction of Mormons' self-sufficiency, preferring short-haul exchange to national trade, stressing local, cooperative manufacturing over mining (which in California and Nevada had quickly attracted outside interests), and accepting commercial banking only grudgingly. Completion of the transcontinental railroad in 1869 had, however, begun Utah's integration into American capitalism, a process well along by the 1880s.[1] The long struggle to obtain Utah's statehood had culminated successfully in 1896, but only after Church of Jesus Christ of Latter-day Saints (LDS) leaders agreed to abandon their unique marriage system and extricate the Church from its long-standing embrace of the civil state. Latter-day Saints were once again full-fledged citizens of the United States, but any lingering sense they might have entertained that old gentile enmities had died and that they could continue to live without overmuch federal surveillance were dashed by the uproar over seating Reed Smoot, a Mormon Apostle, to the United States Senate. As Kathleen Flake has suggested, the public hearings that exercised the Upper House and many Americans between 1903 and 1907 gave the American people a fuller understanding of Mormonism and left no doubt among the faithful that the federal government would regulate and, if necessary, defang any religious group it deemed un-American.[2] All of these changes worked their influence on Temple Square. As Utah's gentile population increased, free markets took hold, and the government in Washington struck down Mormon legal and matrimonial arrangements, the Church moved to bring its internal workings in line with the new circumstances, developing a more rationalized bureaucracy, systematizing its internal workings (including its theology), and altering its relationship to the civil state. Joseph Keeler played an important role in these changes. Although virtually unknown to non-Mormon scholars, Keeler, whose life spanned the transitional era, helped transform the Church from a body bent on building the Kingdom of Zion in relative isolation to a dynamic, corporate religious institution that, by the end of the twentieth century, had established itself internationally. His writings, emblematic of a shift in Mormon print culture noteworthy in itself, facilitated the rationalization of the LDS Church.

Joseph B. Keeler (1855–1935): An Overview of His Life

Keeler's roots thrust deep into the soil of Mormon historical experience. His father, Daniel, a first-generation convert born in New Jersey, apprenticed as a stonemason in Philadelphia and worked in various places along the East Coast, including New York City, where he joined the Church in March 1840. That summer, he journeyed to western Illinois, joining those Saints building the city of Nauvoo. Daniel laid stone for a number of Mormon buildings, including the Nauvoo Temple, prior to the Mormon Exodus. Keeler's mother, Ann, joined the Church in New Jersey following her migration from Lancashire, England. Both Keeler's parents had married, raised children, and been widowed before finding each other.[3] Joseph, their first child, was born in Salt Lake City on 8 September 1855. His given names, Joseph Brigham, paid tribute to the Church's past and present prophets, Joseph Smith and Brigham Young. During the Utah War of 1857–58, when U.S. troops threatened Salt Lake City, the Keelers abandoned the capital, along with virtually its entire population, and relocated forty-five miles south to Provo. There, in the Utah Valley, Joseph Keeler and his wife, Martha Alice Fairbanks (29 June 1860–2 October 1938), whom he married in 1873 and with whom he raised ten children, spent most of their lives.

Keeler learned about hard physical labor at home, assisting his father in the construction business. During the 1860s he helped build the Church's first tabernacle (large meeting hall), in Provo, and from October 1874 to March 1875, served a building mission in southern Utah, helping to lay the stone foundation of the Saint George Temple, the first such structure that the Latter-day Saints completed in the Great Basin. But his family also encouraged reading, and, like so many nineteenth-century Americans, his introduction to print culture began with Scripture. His mother regularly read to her children from the family Bible that she had brought from England; young Keeler first learned his capital letters from its pages. In an early journal he recorded, "I was impressed with the thought that I was sent to earth to perform a mission— I began, therefore, to improve my mind by reading and studying good books."[4] These volumes were both secular and religious. Karl G. Maeser, the first principal of the Brigham Young Academy (BYA), established as a kind of high school in Provo in 1875, exercised a great influence over him.[5] Keeler enrolled in 1876 as one of BYA's initial students and the next year began as a reporter for the Provo *Territorial Enquirer*, gaining a good introduction to the printing business. After graduating in 1877, he served as the first president of the BYA Polysophical Society, a student group devoted to discussing books and ideas.[6]

Keeler's calling as a writer had manifested itself by the time he reached adulthood. He first gained a measure of literary notice and public visibility when the *Territorial Enquirer* published letters that he penned from Georgia during his service as a full-time proselytizer in the LDS Church's Southern States Mission between April 1880 and March 1882.[7] He also kept a personal journal of his mission and published his first pamphlet, *How to Get Salvation: The Faith and Teachings of the Latter-day Saints* (1880), a brief overview of Christian history from a Mormon perspective.[8] Following the organizational lead of forerunners like Orson Pratt and Orson Spencer, Keeler took his readers from the Church's beginnings through what Mormons considered the apostasy that spewed out the "great and abominable church" (1 Nephi 13.6), whose continued sway necessitated the restoration of lost authority and gospel truth that Joseph Smith, guided by heavenly visitations, made possible by revealing lost scripture.[9] Keeler published his ambitious pamphlet at a time when it was becoming less usual for missionaries to develop such aids for evangelization, since treatises written by Church leaders that explained Mormon history and doctrine were becoming more available and were widely considered throughout the community of Latter-day Saints to be more appropriate guides for spreading the faith than those penned by missionaries themselves.[10]

Keeler well exemplifies the pattern, common among nineteenth-century Mormons, of combining civic and educational work with Church callings. Following his mission, he began his long career as a faculty member and administrator at Brigham Young Academy (later, University). He joined BYA in 1884, the same year in which he was called as the first counselor to the president of the Utah State Young Men's Mutual Improvement Association (YMMIA), an organization for improving the religious knowledge, values, and morals of young Mormon men.[11] His ecclesiastical, educational, and civic prominence increased in concert. He was called as president of the Utah State YMMIA in 1893 and bishop of the Provo Fourth Ward two years later. He became in 1898 the first Church official to authorize single women to undertake full-time missions for the Church.[12] In 1892, having the previous year taken a Master of Accounts degree from Eastman Business College in Poughkeepsie, New York, he became a counselor (i.e., a vice president) to President Benjamin Cluff at BYA. He served as Provo city treasurer and, in 1897, gained election to the Provo City Council. Meanwhile he continued to write for the *Territorial Enquirer* and publish on both secular and religious topics. In 1891 he gathered his previously published essays on science and religion into a small book, *Foundation*

Stones of the Earth, and Other Essays, a typical rejection of Charles Darwin's theory of evolution on grounds that it transgressed a literal reading of Genesis. Keeler could not accept any account of life's origin that excluded either divine design or the Deity's active participation.[13] His rejection of evolution had an impact later at Brigham Young University. The next year he shared the technical knowledge gained at Eastman in his first textbook, *A Student's Guide for Book Keeping.*[14]

As part of a larger movement to decentralize local Church government, Church leaders in January 1901 met in Provo to divide the large Utah Stake into three smaller stakes: Utah, Nebo, and Alpine. David John, the new president of the Utah Stake, called Keeler as the president's first counselor. It was in this capacity and then as stake president in his own right (he was called in 1908) that Keeler made his most important contributions to Mormon print culture. Understanding his impact requires a brief sketch of how that culture had developed.

Early Mormon Print Culture

Nineteenth-century Saints were people of not just one book but of books in general, and periodicals too. The Church emerged at the same time that the young Republic experienced a proliferation of printing presses, technology that Church leaders seized upon to announce and spread the Latter-day truth. The paramount Mormon publication was, of course, the *Book of Mormon* (1830), whose appearance antedated the Church itself, but although most people then (and now) associate Mormons most strongly with that single text, Saints in fact immersed themselves in a wide variety of printed matter from the outset. Almost immediately following the Church's organization, leaders began newspapers to communicate with dispersed believers and inform the public. A compilation of Joseph Smith's revelations appeared first in 1833 and in revised format two years later; periodic editions inserted additional revelations regarding doctrine and practice that Smith, who insisted that prophecy did not end with the biblical age and that God still reveals His will in the present, continued to disclose. Pamphlets and books defending and explaining Church doctrine appeared as well.[15] From the pens of its most articulate converts, many of them Church leaders, came missionary pamphlets and books. Two brothers, Parley P. and Orson Pratt, proved especially productive and influential during the first generation.

Parley's death in 1857 helped bring the initial era of Mormon pamphleteering to an end, though other factors played a role too. Mormon publishers overestimated their markets, leaving large quantities of books unsold, and Brigham Young wanted to husband the Church's precious resources, sorely depleted by the move into a virtually uninhabited desert, for such projects as aiding even the poorest Latter-day Saints to gather in Zion and building the temple. He also thought that too much analysis of Mormon doctrine would kill the spirit of its central belief in continuing revelation and an open canon.[16]

The second phase of Mormon print culture, in which Keeler would so prominently figure, opened about a decade later in response to wholesale demographic, social, and economic changes that challenged Mormons' painfully constructed group cohesion and moral sensibilities. The transcontinental railroad made the intermountain West more accessible to gentile influence, ending Mormons' self-imposed isolation and threatening their self-sufficiency. Non-Mormons crowded into the territory, bringing with them such examples of gentile culture as the popular dime novel, whose consumption Church leaders considered a waste of time and money, not to mention inimical to Mormon industry and morals. To combat such influences, the Church, led by Brigham Young, took some institutional steps to improve religious education, creating mutual improvement associations for both adolescent women (the Young Women's Mutual Improvement Association, or YWMIA [1869]) and young men (YMMIA [1875]). Sunday schools, imported by English converts from Methodism, first appeared in the Salt Lake Valley as early as 1849, but not until 1872 did the Deseret Sunday School Union organize fully.[17] The Church's campaign to protect the next generation included creating periodicals such as the *Juvenile Instructor* (January 1866), *The Contributor* (October 1879), and *Improvement Era* (November 1897), all efforts to reach younger readers by providing them literature supporting LDS values and perspectives.

Although directing most of these efforts toward young adults, the Church also made sure to provide more systematic instruction for children. The Primary Association, an analog to the YMMIA and YWMIA, was founded in 1878 to instruct children ages three to twelve.[18] Some of Smith's early revelations had called for creating books to instruct juveniles, but the pressures of building Zion in an arid wilderness with minimal resources necessarily delayed these directives' implementation. Indeed, the first major breakthrough issued from a press overseas. In 1854 the Church released John Jaques' *Catechism for Children, Exhibiting the Prominent Doctrines of the Church of Jesus Christ of Latter-day Saints* in Liverpool, following its serialization in the *LDS Millennial Star,* an English Mormon newspaper, the previous year. Jaques' *Catechism* proved very popular among the Latter-day Saints, appearing in ever-larger English language printings up to its Salt Lake City edition of 1888, which brought the total to 35,000, not counting the printings in other languages. The need for Mormons to have such a basic instructional work is reflected in the fact that, notwithstanding its title, parents read it for themselves as avidly as to their offspring.[19]

The Church's primary printing operation outside the Liverpool mission publishing concern was the Deseret News Press, which has issued *The Deseret News* in Salt Lake City since 1850. George Q. Cannon, Brigham Young's counselor, provided another outlet for Mormon publications when he established his own business in the 1860s; it was soon printing periodicals, books, and other items.[20] He also operated a bookstore. The Church acquired Cannon's business enterprises before his death in 1901, combined them with other publishing and bookselling ventures, and in 1920 renamed the operation Deseret Book Company, the flagship of LDS publishing and distribution to the present. Deseret News Press constituted the Church's main publishing operation throughout the period under discussion, and it printed nearly all of Keeler's works.

Most of the Church's fundamental doctrines and practices had appeared in print by the 1870s, if not earlier, but regularly printed and systematically prepared guides for administration, handbooks for Church government, and lesson manuals for Latter-day Saints of all ages were still lacking. Keeler's greatest accomplishments in using print to help the Church accommodate to Utah's increasing integration into American life came in these areas. Three particular projects warrant attention here: his rationalization of the bishop's court, his calls to standardize the Church bureaucracy, and his innovative program for organizing the Aaronic Priesthood.

The Bishop's Court, Its History and Proceedings

In February 1901 Keeler delivered a lecture about the institution of the bishop's court to the Utah Stake High Council, a group of twelve men called to assist the stake presidency in administrating the unit's affairs.[21]

Prior to the talk, Keeler sent Anthon H. Lund, a member of the Church's First Presidency, an outline. Reviewing what he himself knew about LDS history, Lund complimented Keeler on his thorough study of the courts, noting that the variations in their judicial proceedings from ward to ward called for a more standardized approach to their operation.[22] If Lund read the lecture published the next year, as he undoubtedly did, he must have been quite pleased.

Keeler's twenty-two-page pamphlet addressed an important and complex issue, for during the course of the nineteenth century, Mormon bishops had accumulated civil powers far exceeding those of ecclesiastical officials in any other American religious body. Their authority had to be delimited both to clarify their role within the LDS hierarchy and to dispel any objections that their courts transgressed popular American notions about separating church and state.[23] From the office's inception, Mormon bishops had exercised control over temporal as well as religious affairs. During the Nauvoo, Illinois, period (1839–46), the Church assigned them responsibility for a geographical area called wards, so-called because of their concurrent use as voting districts. Once ensconced in the Great Basin, the Church formalized the ward system, assigning bishops and ordering the construction of chapels in every one.[24] Considered by the LDS hierarchy as "judges in Israel,"[25] bishops held authority to settle family arguments, adjudicate disputes among neighbors over property and water rights, receive tithes and free-will offerings on behalf of the Church, and care for widows and orphans. They also dealt with members' conduct and standing in the Church. As spelled out in Joseph Smith's early revelations, a bishop was technically the highest office in the Aaronic Priesthood—the lower of the two Mormon priestly orders that holds authority to, for instance, baptize individuals—but as ward structures evolved, two officers came to lead local congregations: the bishop, responsible for temporal affairs, and the presiding high priest, responsible for spiritual ones. During the 1850s Brigham Young merged these two positions into a single post that, despite its retaining the title "bishop," dealt with more than just mundane matters. The task of counseling the ward bishops and overseeing their work fell to the Church's presiding bishop, who reported to the First Presidency and the Quorum of the Twelve Apostles, the Church's highest governing authorities.

The judicial system of the early Mormon Church took shape in the interaction between scripture, Smith's revelations, and the Saints' experience. One of Smith's earliest revelations held that transgressors were to be "dealt with as the scriptures direct" (Doctrine and Covenants 20:80), which left a great deal of latitude about how to proceed. Absent clear instructions and precedents, Church courts initially decided cases on the basis of common sense, often putting them to congregational vote. The New Testament provided at least three practices for treating ecclesiastical malfeasances: (1) a mild form of exclusion that limited the wrongdoer's participation in the religious community for a short period; (2) a more formal ban, which deprived the person of all religious privileges for a longer or indefinite period; and (3) a complete banishment or excommunication from the religious community.[26] Soon a more formal judicial system superseded these decentralized practices. By 1835 the Church had constituted three main courts: the bishop's court (Doctrine and Covenants 42; 107:68, 72), the stake high council court (Doctrine and Covenants 102), and the council of the First Presidency (Doctrine and Covenants 102:78–81). Essentially, the bishop's courts served as units of judicial origin, with the other two acting as courts of appeal or, in more serious cases, courts of origination. Until the 1840s, bishops had regional as well as local responsibility, but by 1842, the Church had identified the Quorum of the Twelve Apostles with the quorum of twelve high priests identified in Doctrine and Covenants 107:78–84, thereafter granting it the highest judicial authority.

The priesthoods' judicial functions increased as the Church moved west.[27] In 1852, after two of the three judges federally appointed to the Utah Territorial Court "ran away" from their posts (for reasons including dislike of Mormonism, upset with the territory's political arrangements, and personal pique),[28] the Utah legislature transferred original jurisdiction for criminal matters from federal to local probate courts. Mormon bishops presided over most probate courts, which consequently took on far-ranging civil functions as well as ecclesiastical ones. Until 1874, when Congress passed the Poland Act, stripping the courts of their criminal jurisdiction, Mormon bishops heard both civil and criminal matters that, outside Utah, belonged to exclusively "secular" jurisdictions. The probate courts' extended authority was one of many problems facing Mormon leaders as they attempted to achieve Utah's statehood.[29] Bishops' extraordinary competence suggested to non-Mormons that little if any separation existed in Utah between church and state, a parlous constitutional situation. Aware of these public perceptions, Keeler in 1902 drew upon his own episcopal experience and his research into LDS history to author *The Bishop's Court*, which established more clearly than had any previous work the institution's proper organization and function under both LDS and federal law.

Following a short introduction, the pamphlet discussed the court's history and development. Keeler underlined the absence of systematic record keeping in the courts, the lack of procedural uniformity, and the need to establish a single method for governing wards.[30] The essay's remainder provided just such standard procedures, including the forms to be used for complaints and summonses. He also described the proper process for a trial and drew up sample forms for taking down testimony, reporting the court's decision, issuing a notice of appeal, and excommunicating the worst offenders. The two last pages summarized and reviewed the steps to be observed in such disciplinary matters.

This brief work, a first in Mormon print culture, provided the basis for regularizing the courts.[31] As late as 1939, a handbook of Church government compiled by a leading member of the Quorum of the Twelve Apostles recommended using several of Keeler's forms.[32] *The Bishop's Court* settled the jurisdiction of the courts, removing gentile doubts about their possibly usurping civil functions, and systematized the judicial process of Mormon ecclesiastical courts, a reform that helped preserve their popular legitimacy even as the locus of much LDS disciplinary activity moved away from rural villages, whose courts were adequately served by informal procedures, into urban areas where the volume of business, if nothing else, necessitated formal ones.

Theology Department Courses

Keeler's careful and systematic approach toward legal and organizational matters also manifested itself in his work as a teacher and director of the theological department at the Brigham Young Academy. In 1902–3 he prepared materials for four theology courses. Their subject matter addressed several of his ongoing interests in standardizing the Church's operations, such as systematizing the teaching of LDS administrative history to young Mormons and encouraging the Church bureaucracy's standardization.

The first two courses covered the Lesser (Aaronic) Priesthood in thirteen lessons; the second expatiated on Church government in nineteen.[33] In October 1903 BYA became Brigham Young University, and the next August, Deseret News Press published the course materials as *The Lesser Priesthood and Notes on Church Government*.[34] It quickly sold out, requiring a second edition in 1906. Issued with the strong approval of the First Presidency, the work won lauds from *The Deseret Evening News*, which published both a detailed article surveying the volume's content and a short editorial praising it.[35] Proud of its favorable reception, Keeler had a small broadside printed that quoted the coverage, publicizing the newspaper's recommendation that every Latter-day Saint library ought to have a copy.[36] He also called attention to part 4, "A Brief Concordance of the Doctrine and Covenants," highlighted in another issue of the *Deseret News*.[37]

Such publicity clearly boosted sales, and Keeler's own leaflets spread the word further. A letter from J. W. Paxman, president of the Juab, Utah, Stake, suggests the enthusiasm with which this volume was greeted:

> I have read your leaflets—every one of them—and enjoyed them very much. I placed the Leaflets, at my personal expense, in the Lesser Priesthood Quorums in this stake . . .
>
> I have recommended the work lately in the wards, as far as I have visited them and will speak of it in all the wards in the stake during the winter.
>
> [I] would like to see a copy of it in every home among the saints. It fills a long-felt need, and the Saints will have a much better understanding of the excellency of our church and its government by reading its pages.[38]

Joseph F. Smith, president of the Church, was hardly less complimentary: "You deserve great credit for your book and I commend your work. If there is an error in fact or doctrine in it I have not discovered it. It will be an excellent help to students of Church Organizations and Systems of Government and Discipline."[39]

In 1929 a third edition appeared, and it, too, was advertised by the publisher in specially printed bookmarks as a work that has "inestimable value for every member of the Church." *The Lesser Priesthood*'s influence extended well beyond Keeler's death. The work that succeeded it, John A. Widtsoe's *Priesthood and Church Government* (1939), owed much of its structure and contents to Keeler's work, as evidenced by Widtsoe's incorporating sixty-one excerpts into his own book.

First Steps in Church Government

During the winter of 1906 Keeler published *First Steps in Church Government; What Church Government Is and What It Does.*[40] Recommended and
then adopted as the lesson manual for the Lesser, or Aaronic, Priesthood, it was reprinted in 1912 and 1924. To fully appreciate what
Keeler was doing with these works, a brief overview of the nineteenth-
century Mormon concept of priesthood, especially the Aaronic, or
Lesser, Priesthood, is necessary. Today, young Mormon males enter
the Aaronic Priesthood at age twelve and advance through three callings: deacon (ages twelve to thirteen), teacher (fourteen to fifteen), and
priest (sixteen to eighteen). The ward bishop takes a major role in guiding these young men, reflected in the fact that his office is technically
the highest in the Lesser Priesthood. At age eighteen, all faithful, worthy
young men are given the Higher, or Melchizedek, Priesthood, and then
set apart to the office of an elder. The Aaronic Priesthood callings/as-
signments provide a series of mentoring experiences for young boys as
they mature. These callings school them in the basic duties and responsibilities of Church service and leadership. In addition to helping keep
them active in the Church, this training better prepares them to undertake full-time missions and to serve both the Church and society at
large.

Until the end of the nineteenth century, however, men, not boys,
generally held the Aaronic Priesthood.[41] Those called to serve in its
offices were usually designated "acting deacons" or "acting teachers."
Few boys were considered mature enough to enter the priesthood, and
those deemed acceptable were given the Melchizedek Priesthood. Keeler himself never received the Aaronic Priesthood in his youth, but while
working in the YMMIA, teaching at BYA, and serving as bishop, he
came to see the great value such callings could have for young men.

As a newly called bishop, Keeler found himself presiding over 150
young boys living in his ward. Church leaders since Brigham Young
had struggled with how to rein in such fellows, who did not always adhere to Mormon values and teachings.[42] The YMMIA was established
to be one of the solutions, and some of the larger wards formed literary
societies[43] for reading and debate, but these efforts attracted mostly those
who were already self-motivated, and even the most active ones failed to
provide their members with regular instruction. Passing the faith of the

pioneering parents to the next generation proved harder than anyone had supposed, especially since by the late nineteenth century young men were moving out of the hamlets and villages that had constituted the bedrock of Mormon Utah society. They still met weekly with other ward members and took on various obligations to their neighborhood or ward, but these tasks involved mainly manual labor like cutting wood or cleaning the chapel and did little to improve their spirituality or dedication to Mormon values. When adolescent males did meet to study, they might read adventure novels as readily as they did scriptures.[44]

Keeler's experience in both academic and ecclesiastical settings prepared him, as a new bishop, to organize and structure lessons for the young men in the Aaronic Priesthood.[45] Eventually, he expanded his handwritten notes and printed them, first as his theology lectures at the BYA, then as *The Lesser Priesthood and Church Government* in 1904. In 1906 his *First Steps in Church Government* systematized these lessons for the Aaronic Priesthood quorums.

The founding generation of Utah's Mormon leaders worried that young boys were not yet spiritually mature enough to handle official responsibilities. There is no evidence, for instance, that even Brigham Young's sons had been given the Aaronic Priesthood. Keeler, on the other hand, trusted them and established workable training regimens for them,[46] beginning with his own son, whom he ordained as a deacon at age twelve. Soon he was instructing other boys in his ward in their callings as well. His published works played so important a role in spiritually developing the Church's young men that they drew further notice to him. In 1908 Keeler was called to serve on the Church's General Priesthood Committee on Outlines, the same year he was called to the presidency of the Utah Stake.

Other contributions followed. In 1910 he introduced the Utah Stake to the Family Home Evening Program, which the entire Church would adopt in 1915. He was invited to write articles for *The Improvement Era*, the main English-language church periodical. In July 1913 he published "Organization and Government of the Church of Jesus Christ of Latter-day Saints," then, in June 1914, surveyed the contents of "A Typical Ward Service."[47] He addressed general conferences of the Church in 1902, 1911, and 1918, testimony to his stature as a stake president. His *Concordance* to the *Doctrine and Covenants* was officially sanctioned by its inclusion in the 1918 edition of those revelations issued by the Church.[48]

Summary and Conclusion

Joseph B. Keeler witnessed the passing of Mormonism's founding generation. With it went plural marriage, millennial expectations, and an emphasis on the immediate establishment of a political and economic Kingdom of God. Keeler's own generation experienced the shift from a rural, village community to an urban world in which the Church needed to help foster piety in the ward and nuclear family. His work proved central in several ways to standardizing and bureaucratizing the Church hierarchy, processes that themselves were part of a larger modernizing trend shaping not only the LDS Church but much of American life in the early twentieth century.[49]

Nineteenth-century Mormonism generally sought to maintain a stable society, often forced through circumstance into self-contained and isolated communities. Communication among members remained primarily oral, but supplemented by their printed newspapers. Face-to-face communication, centered in extended family and kin networks, was the norm. Such a traditional society was also reflected in its social structure and political organization, controlled as it was by an elite leadership class that seldom distinguished between the secular and the sacred. Plural marriage extended and reinforced this reality. The failure to separate church and state only added to the growing conflict with the larger society.

But by the end of the nineteenth century, modernization was making inroads and forcing a more dynamic challenge to Mormon group cohesion. Market forces and job patterns, the gradual movement from rural to urban settings, and the increasing melding of Utah politics with national power structures and national financial networks provided strong centrifugal forces on the Mormon Church and its members. These same forces, strongly at work in American society as reflected in the rise of the modern manufacturing system, the growth of transportation and communication networks, specialization in the job market, and a growing international outlook that was reflected in the Spanish-American War, were all part of the larger context of Joseph Keeler's life. While Mormons like Keeler did not produce novels that raised serious questions about what all these changes meant for Americans, their response certainly provides another window into the way Churches and religious people adjusted to the challenges that Theodore Dreiser, William Dean Howells, and Mark Twain raised in their novels. Mormons were not as innocent or as ignorant as the main character in *Sister Carrie*, but they could relate to Silas Lapham's need to keep the old values while confronting the amoral modern urban world. And Mormons could only partially identify with Twain's Connecticut Yankee Hank Morgan, who admired ingenuity and inventiveness but failed to see the costs of industrialization to society and its challenges to the core values of a traditional society. Mormonism came to feel at home in the modern world but has never lost the central core of the family-oriented values that had its roots in an earlier traditional society. Institutional shifts and adjustments encouraged by individuals like Keeler helped the Church step into a new century while keeping a solid foot in the old one.

For one thing, Keeler played a significant role in what might, following Alfred Chandler, be denominated Mormonism's "managerial revolution," the rationalization of its ecclesiastical structure into corporate-like forms staffed by "professional executives" (i.e., Church authorities) thoroughly prepped for their tasks. In the American economy, the managerial revolution realigned business organizations, enabling them to compete against national (and international) rivals, and created a steady supply of trained labor.[50] Out of deeply held religious conviction, Keeler saw that inducting the Church's young men into the Aaronic Priesthood earlier than had been conventional and educating them in their wards and schools developed a similar pool of leaders necessary to run a corporate religious headquarters or compete with missionaries from other faiths throughout the United States and abroad. This standardization of training would prove instrumental to the tremendous growth of the Mormon Church in the twentieth century. Keeler's printed works suggest that Mormon writing was moving away from its more polemical and freelance origins in the nineteenth century to a more standardized discourse that was carefully crafted and focused on institutional consumption. As the LDS entered the new century a recognized church in the newly created state of Utah, its partisans' rhetoric became less defensive and more geared to working out the Church's positions.

Keeler encouraged the Church's fiscal modernization as well. In 1897 he published a pamphlet on tithing.[51] At a time when the Church, intent on shoring up finances depleted by fending off the antipolygamy crusade, was coming to rely solely on cash contributions to fund its operations rather than accepting commodity donations-in-kind more typical of a frontier exchange economy, securing a regular flow of an instantly negotiable medium was crucial for maintaining the stability of an increasingly large-scale bureaucracy. That LDS leaders recognized this situation can be seen in the *Instructions to Presidents of Stakes*, which the Church began to issue in 1898 and that contained significant pronouncements on fiduciary as well as spiritual matters.[52] Keeler also worked hard to place BYU on a stronger financial footing.

Keeler's life reveals other dimensions of Mormon modernity. Church leaders had encouraged Mormons to abstain from tea, coffee, tobacco, and alcohol ever since Joseph Smith had revealed the "Word of Wisdom" (Doctrine and Covenants 89) in 1833, but nineteenth-century Saints, including Smith himself, sometimes observed it more in the breach than in the observance. Active in the national temperance movement that would lead to Prohibition, Keeler encouraged Mormons to obey Smith's injunctions to the letter. Church leaders, influenced by their own experiences, took the message to heart, making abstinence not just a voluntary act but prescribing it as a requirement for full church worthiness. Keeler's work with boys in the Aaronic Priesthood was a natural outgrowth of his concern for those most vulnerable to the temptations of demon rum and stimulants of all kinds.[53]

Finally, Keeler early caught the vision of promoting Mormon family life and family history, the latter a most characteristically Mormon engagement with print culture that inscribes not just a Saint's love for and interest in immediate, living kin, but that also situates the individual among people who, Mormons believe, will remain one's family for eternity. Pressured to end plural marriage and the sealing of nonbloodline relatives, the Church replaced these practices, which non-Mormons found particularly repellent, by facilitating individuals' research into their lineages and then doing temple work to seal direct family lines. In 1894, the year President Wilford Woodruff ended nonbloodline sealings, the Church organized the Utah Genealogical Society, forerunner of its Family History Library, the largest archives of genealogical records in the world.[54] Keeler wrote a manuscript genealogy of his family in 1891 and a larger, printed one in 1924.[55] Emphasis on such family ties evolved into the Church's regular Family Home Evening, which encouraged members to set aside one evening per week for developing family relationships and teaching the Gospel. Keeler introduced the practice into the Utah Stake in January 1910, the Church as a whole following suit in 1915. The Family Home Evening remains a central

Mormon domestic devotion, although the day itself has changed from Wednesday to Monday.

The manuals and handbooks that Keeler and his generation produced continue to appear in updated versions. His printed works made foundational contributions to the institutional coherence of the LDS Church and the growth of a major American religion, even though most Latter-day Saints, let alone gentiles, have forgotten them.

Notes

1. See Leonard J. Arrington, *Great Basin Kingdom: An Economic History of the Latter-day Saints, 1830–1900* (Cambridge, MA: Harvard University Press, 1958). A useful, one-volume chronological history of the Mormons is James B. Allen and Glen M. Leonard, *The Story of the Latter-day Saints*, revised and enlarged edition (Salt Lake City: Deseret Book, 1992). A good topical history is Leonard J. Arrington and Davis Bitton, *The Mormon Experience: A History of the Latter-day Saints* (New York: Alfred A. Knopf, 1979).

2. Thomas G. Alexander, *Mormonism in Transition: A History of the Latter-day Saints, 1890–1930* (Urbana: University of Illinois Press, 1986). For the coming of Utah statehood, see Edward Leo Lyman, *Political Deliverance: The Mormon Quest for Utah Statehood* (Urbana: University of Illinois Press, 1986). Kathleen Flake's study is *The Politics of American Religious Identity: The Seating of Senator Reed Smoot, Mormon Apostle* (Chapel Hill: University of North Carolina Press, 2004).

3. The main sources for Keeler's life are in the Joseph Brigham Keeler Collection (MSS 2016), L. Tom Perry Special Collections, Harold B. Lee Library, Brigham Young University, Provo, Utah (hereafter BYU Library), with additional material in the University Archives. Especially valuable biographical works in the Keeler Collection include Beulah McAllister, "A Treasured Heritage," an unpublished biography of Keeler by his daughter (266 pages, 1958); and Daniel M. Keeler, with Ellen Keeler Thompson and Daniel A. Keeler, *"Build Thee More Stately . . .": A History of Joseph Brigham Keeler and Martha Fairbanks Keeler and their Children* (Murray, Utah: Roylance Publishing, 1989). See also Clinton David Christensen, "Joseph Brigham Keeler: The Master's Builder" (Master's thesis, Brigham Young University, 1997).

4. Keeler Journal, BYU Library, 8.

5. On Karl Maeser, see Reinhard Maeser, *Karl G. Maeser: A Biography by His Son* (Provo, UT: Brigham Young University, 1928); Alma P. Burton, *Karl G. Maeser: Mormon Educator* (Salt Lake City: Deseret Book, 1953); and Douglas F. Tobler, "Karl G. Maeser's German Background, 1828–1856: The Making of Zion's Teacher," *BYU Studies* 17 (Winter 1977): 155–75.

6. The minutes of the first meetings of the Society are in Keeler's papers, BYU Library.

7. Photocopies of the published letters, as well as typescripts, are in the Keeler papers: Bx 1, fd. 14. The collection also contains his mission journal.

8. Published (dated 20 December 1880 at end) in White County, Georgia. The only known copy of the twenty-page work is in BYU Library.

9. Keeler cited Orson Pratt's earlier series, *The Kingdom of God* (1848–49), available to him in a volume entitled *Orson Pratt's Works*, first published in 1851 and reprinted several times thereafter. His mission journal suggests that he took with him copies of Orson Pratt's *Works*, Orson Spencer's *Letters* (published in various editions beginning in 1848), Parley P. Pratt's *Key to the Science of Theology* (first published in 1855), and John Taylor's *The Government of God* (1852). See also the discussion of Keeler's missionary pamphlet in Christensen, "Joseph Brigham Keeler," 47, 62–65.

10. See David J. Whittaker, "Early Mormon Pamphleteering" (Ph.D. dissertation, Brigham Young University, 1982), especially chapter 2, which traces the gradual centralization of official Mormon publishing into the hands of the Quorum of the Twelve Apostles and First Presidency. Such control was based on revelation and direction from Joseph Smith by 1842, and it was tightened after Smith's death in 1844 as Brigham Young and the Apostles consolidated their positions as leaders of the Mormon community. But pioneering in the American West, financial issues, growing conflicts with the federal government, and a lack of strong bureaucratic control meant that freelance publishing would continue sporadically until the twentieth century.

11. The Young Men's Mutual Improvement Association was organized in 1875 as an auxiliary organization to assist in the educational and cultural improvement of young men. For its early history, see Leon M. Strong, "A History of the YMMIA, 1875–1938" (Master's thesis, Brigham Young University, 1939).

12. While wives occasionally accompanied their missionary husbands before 1898, Keeler was the first to issue formal calls to women missionaries. He called two more single women on missions in 1901. All these calls were approved by Church leaders in Salt Lake City.

13. *Foundation Stones of the Earth, and Other Essays* (Provo: Enquirer Steam Print, 1891). This work gathered essays in the following order that he had published earlier in *The Contributor*: "Foundation Stones of the Earth," 11 (February 1890): 121–29; "Near [Nigh] the Throne of God," 10 (February 1889): 156–59; and "The Fallacy of Evolutionism," 9 (July 1888): 340–43.

14. *A Student's Guide to Book Keeping, double and single entry, for use in . . .* (n.p. [Provo]: n.p., 1892, copy in BYU library). Keeler's extensive and important roles in the early financial history of BYA and BYU or his community business involvement are ignored in this paper.

15. An excellent guide to the first century of Mormon publications is Chad J. Flake and Larry W. Draper, compilers, *A Mormon Bibliography, 1830–1930: Books, Pamphlets, Periodicals and Broadsides relating to the first century of Mormonism*, second edition, revised and enlarged, 2 vols. (Provo, UT: Religious Studies Center, Brigham Young University, 2004).

16. See David J. Whittaker, "Early Mormon Pamphleteering," *Journal of Mormon History* 4 (1977): 35–49.

17. See Deseret Sunday School Union, The Church of Jesus Christ of Latter-day Saints, *Jubilee History of the LDS Sunday Schools, 1849–1899* (Salt Lake City: Deseret Sunday Schools, 1900).

18. See Carol Cornwall Madsen and Susan Staker Oman, *Sisters and Little Saints, One Hundred Years of Primary* (Salt Lake City: Deseret Book, 1979).

19. For the larger story, see Davis Bitton, "Mormon Catechisms," in *Revelation, Reason, and Faith: Essays in Honor of Truman G. Madsen*, ed. Donald W. Parry, Daniel C. Peterson, and Stephen D. Ricks (Provo, UT: Foundation for Ancient Research and Mormon Studies, Brigham Young University, 2002), 407–32.

20. There is no full study of the history of George Q. Cannon as a writer and publisher. The best overall study is Davis Bitton, *George Q. Cannon, A Biography* (Salt Lake City: Deseret Book, 1999). A limited but important study is Lawrence R. Flake, "The Development of the *Juvenile Instructor* under George Q. Cannon and Its Function in Latter-day Saints Religious Education" (Master's thesis, BYU, 1969). A celebratory history of Deseret Book, with some information on the earlier Cannon publishing business, is Eleanor Knowles, *Deseret Book Company: 125 Years of Inspiration, Information and Ideas* (Salt Lake City: Deseret Book Company, 1991).

21. Bishops in the Church of Jesus Christ of Latter-day Saints are male laypersons who serve voluntarily for a number of years while also gainfully employed in their chosen occupation. Stake presidents, who usually serve a few years longer, are also male lay leaders. Unlike today, in the nineteenth century both bishops and stake presidents received financial allowances for their services.

22. McAllister, "Treasured Heritage," 176–78, reprints Lund's letter, dated 15 February 1901.

23. For a brief overview, see Dale Beecher, "The Office of Bishop," *Dialogue* 15 (Winter 1982): 103–15; see also D. Gene Pace, "Community Leadership on the Mormon Frontier: Mormon Bishops and the Political, Economic and Social Development of Utah before Statehood" (Ph.D. dissertation, Ohio State University, 1983).

24. A Mormon ward is essentially a parish; a stake is similar to a diocese. A stake is usually composed of about ten wards, although in the nineteenth century both wards and stakes were much larger units than is the case today.

25. *Doctrine and Covenants of the Church of Jesus Christ of Latter-day Saints, Containing Revelations Given to Joseph Smith, The Prophet* (Salt Lake City: Church of Jesus Christ of Latter-day Saints, 1981), 58:17. This volume of Mormon scripture (first published with this title in 1835) contains the revelations, epistles, and other directives given to/through founding prophet Joseph Smith, Jr. (1805–44).

26. Luke 6:22 seems to reflect these three gradations, as do several references in the Pauline epistles: 2 Thess. 3:10–15; 1 Cor. 5:13; Titus 3:10; 1 Tim. 1: 20, 6:3; Gal. 1:8.

27. For a brief summary, see David J. Whittaker, "The LDS Church Judicial System: A Selected Bibliography," Mormon History Association *Newsletter* 59 (October 1985): 8–10.

28. For the story of the "runaway" territorial officials, see Norman F. Furniss, *The Mormon Conflict, 1850–1859* (New Haven, CT: Yale University Press, 1960), 21–29.

29. On the history and function of early Mormon courts, with particular emphasis on the role of bishops, see Stephen J. Sorenson, "Civil and Criminal Jurisdiction of LDS Bishop's and High Council Courts, 1847–1852," *Task Papers in LDS History*, no. 17 (Salt Lake City: Historical Department of the Church of Jesus Christ of Latter-day Saints, 1977); James B. Allen, "The Unusual Jurisdiction of County Probate Courts in the Territory of Utah," *Utah Historical Quarterly* 36 (Spring 1968): 132–42; Jay E. Powell, "Fairness in the Salt Lake County Probate Court," *Utah Historical Quarterly* 38 (Summer 1970): 256–62; Elizabeth D. Gee, "Justice for All or for the 'Elect'?: The Utah County Probate Court, 1855–1872," *Utah Historical Quarterly* 48 (Spring 1980): 129–47; Raymond T. Swenson, "Resolution of Civil Disputes by Mormon Ecclesiastical Courts," *Utah Law Review* (1978): 573–95; C. Paul Dredge, "Dispute Settlement in the Mormon Community: The Operation of Ecclesiastical Courts in Utah," in Klaus-Friedrich Koch, ed., *The Anthropological Perspective*, Access to Justice, vol. 4 (Milan: A. Giuffrè, 1979), 191–215; R. Collin Mangrum, "Furthering the Cause of Zion: An Overview of the Mormon Ecclesiastical Court System in Early Utah," *Journal of Mormon History* 10 (1983): 79–90; and Edwin Brown Firmage and Richard Collin Mangrum, *Zion in the Courts: A Legal History of the Church of Jesus Christ of Latter-day Saints, 1830–1900* (Urbana: University of Illinois Press, 1988).

30. The 1877 Circular had also suggested that such records be kept. See James R. Clark, ed., *Messages of the First Presidency*, 6 vols. (Salt Lake City: Bookcraft, 1965–75), 2:287.

31. There are letters and discussions of Keeler's suggestions in the Letterbooks of the First Presidency, suggesting how influential his works were. Manuscripts in Church Library, The Church of Jesus Christ of Latter-day Saints, Salt Lake City. See also the talk of President Joseph F. Smith, 13 September 1917, to the Parowan Stake as published as "Principles of Government in the

Church," *The Improvement Era* 21 (November 1917): 3–11; and the discussion on Church courts in James E. Talmage, "Judiciary System of the Church," *The Improvement Era* 23 (April 1919): 498–500.

32. See John A. Widtsoe, compiler, *Priesthood and Church Government* (Salt Lake City: Deseret Book Co., 1939), 214–18.

33. Copies of these printed course materials are in BYU Library.

34. *The Lesser Priesthood and Notes on Church Government: Also a Concordance of the Doctrine and Covenants, for the Use of Church Schools and Priesthood Quorums* (Salt Lake City: Deseret News, 1904). The print run was 5,000 copies, suggesting an audience far larger than just students at BYU, "Preface," 2nd ed. (1906), iv.

35. "New Book for Church Workers," 10; and editorial, "A Valuable New Work," 4, *Deseret Evening News*, 16 July 1904. Keeler's *The Lesser Priesthood* was recommended for use as a textbook for Church classes in *Annual Instructions* 6 (1 December 1904): 19. The Church's First Presidency recommended in 1905, 1906, and 1908 in their *Annual Instructions* that Keeler's work "be used in all the Quorums of the Aaronic Priesthood throughout the Stakes of Zion." See, for instance, *Annual Instructions To Presidents of Stakes and Counselors, Bishops and Counselors, Stakes Clerks and General Authorities in Zion* 8 (1 December 1906): 19.

36. A copy of the broadside, *Lesser Priesthood, Church Government, and Concordance of the Doctrine and Covenants*, is in the L. Tom Perry Special Collections, BYU Library.

37. *Deseret Evening News*, 17 September 1904, 6.

38. J. W. Paxman to Joseph B. Keeler, 27 October 1904, as cited in Keeler, *"Build Thee More Stately . . . ,"* 387.

39. Letter of 7 January 1907, in ibid., 387.

40. *First Steps in Church Government; What Church Government Is and What It Does. A Book for Young Members of the Lesser Priesthood* (Salt Lake City: Deseret News, 1906). The Church's *Annual Instructions* 9 (1909): 31, recommended that both *Lesser Priesthood* and *First Steps* be used as textbooks for the Aaronic Priesthood classes throughout the Church. By 1909 there were 60 stakes in the Church, up from 22 in 1879. By 1930, the years of the Church's centennial, stakes numbered 104. As of 2006 there were 27,087 wards and branches (smaller wards) organized into 2,701 stakes.

41. See William G. Harley, "Ordained and Acting Teachers in the Lesser Priesthood, 1851–1883," *BYU Studies* 16 (Spring 1976): 375–98. Brigham Young, just before his death, had moved to reorganize the Priesthood Quorums churchwide, and in the important 11 July 1877 "Circular of the First Presidency," suggested that "it would be excellent training for the young men if they had the opportunity of acting in the offices of the lesser priesthood. They would thereby obtain very valuable experience, and when they obtain the Melchisedec priesthood they would be likely to place a higher value upon it." See Clark, *Messages of the First Presidency*, 2:287.

42. See Davis Bitton, "Zion's Rowdies: Growing Up on the Mormon Frontier," *Utah Historical Quarterly* 50 (Spring 1982): 182–95.

43. Ronald W. Walker, "Growing Up in Early Utah: The Wasatch Literary Association, 1874–1878," *Sunstone* 6 (November/December 1981): 44–51.

44. See the comments of William G. Hartley, "The Priesthood Reform Movement, 1908–1922," *BYU Studies* 13 (Winter 1973): 138.

45. Keeler's handwritten lessons for the Provo, Utah, Fourth Ward were really the first manuals for the Aaronic Priesthood in the Church.

46. For the larger picture, see William G. Hartley, "From Men to Boys: LDS Aaronic Priesthood Offices, 1829–1996," *Journal of Mormon History* 22 (Spring 1996): 80–136. As Hartley notes, other Church leaders at the same time were suggesting specific age rankings for the Aaronic Priesthood offices.

47. *The Improvement Era* 16 (July 1913): 918–27; 17 (June 1914): 738–50.

48. *Concordance to the Doctrine and Covenants*, which had been printed earlier in his work on the Lesser Priesthood. A committee had to choose between Keeler's and another prepared by John A. Widtsoe. Widtsoe's had been prepared earlier, and he gave a manuscript copy of it to the Church in April 1898. Widtsoe's work would be incorporated into the 1921 edition, but the committee chose Keeler's for the 1918 edition, perhaps because it was already in type from its earlier printings. See the discussion in the Letterbooks of the First Presidency, under the dates of 19 June and 11 July 1917. Here I benefit from notes from these volumes (which are now closed to research in the LDS Church Archives) in the Scott Kenney Papers, BYU Library. Keeler's *Concordance* appeared in *The Doctrine and Covenants* . . . (Salt Lake City: Deseret News, 1918), 504–49.

49. I am using the word in the sense suggested by Richard D. Brown, although I have applied it to the Latter-day Saints a few years after those on which Brown's arguments focused. See Brown, *Modernization: The Transformation of American Life, 1600–1865* (New York: Hill and Wang, 1976), especially chapter 1, 3–22. See also Douglas D. Alder's discussion of the changing nature of Mormon wards from the nineteenth to the twentieth century: "The Mormon Ward: Congregation or Community?" *Journal of Mormon History* 5 (1978): 61–78.

50. Alfred D. Chandler, Jr., *The Visible Hand: The Managerial Revolution in American Business* (Cambridge, MA: Belknap Press, 1977). More recently, see Jo Anne Yates, *Control through Communication: The Rise of System in American Management* (Baltimore: Johns Hopkins University Press, 1989).

51. *The Law of Tithing. As set forth in the Old Scriptures and in the Modern Revelation. . . . Compiled by Bishop Jos. B. Keeler* (Provo, UT: n.p., [1897]).

52. Copies of these *Annual Instructions* issued by the Church are in the BYU Library.

53. On Keeler's fight for prohibition (local option), see Christensen, "Joseph Brigham Keeler," 174–76. On the larger story, see Brent G. Thompson,

"Utah's Struggle for Prohibition, 1908–1917" (Master's thesis, University of Utah, 1979).

54. The best introduction to the early practices is Gordon Irving, "The Law of Adoption: One Phase of the Development of the Mormon Concept of Salvation, 1830–1900," *BYU Studies* 14 (Spring 1974): 291–314. See also Rex E. Cooper, *Promises Made to the Fathers: Mormon Covenant Organization* (Salt Lake City: University of Utah Press, 1990). For a summary of the changes made under the direction of Wilford Woodruff, see Thomas G. Alexander, *Things in Heaven and Earth: The Life and Times of Wilford Woodruff, a Mormon Prophet* (Salt Lake City: Signature Books, 1991), 321–22. For the Genealogical Society, see James B. Allen, Jessie L. Embry, and Kahlile Mehr, *Hearts Turned to the Fathers: A History of the Genealogical Society of Utah, 1894–1994* (Provo, UT: BYU Studies, 1994).

55. See *Genealogical Record of the Keeler Family* (14 pp.) (Provo, UT: Enquirer Steam Print, 1891); and Joseph Brigham Keeler, *Genealogical Record of the Keeler Family, 1726–1924* (79 pp.) (Provo, UT: Printed for the Author by the Post Publishing Company, 1924).

3

Print Culture and Religious Group Identity

The Select Few

The Megiddo Message *and the Building of a Community*

GARI-ANNE PATZWALD

Decades before Internet chatrooms and listservs, a small religious sect created an international community of loyal adherents through the effective use of publications sent through the mail. The Megiddo Church, a semi-communitarian[1] sect founded in Oregon in 1880 and located in Rochester, New York, since 1904, has never had more than about two hundred members in its home congregation.[2] However, through a ministry that focused on the creative use of its publications, particularly its magazine, the *Megiddo Message,* it developed a large constituency, many of whom considered themselves to be members of the Church even though they had little or no personal contact with the Rochester community.

The Megiddo Church's founder, Wisconsin Civil War veteran L. T. Nichols (1844–1912), began his ministry in Dodge County, Wisconsin. In 1873 he moved to Yamhill County, Oregon, where he established a small congregation affiliated with the Christadelphians,[3] a denomination associated with the Stone-Campbell movement.[4] He established an annual camp meeting, which often lasted as long as three weeks. He also acquired a printing press and began to distribute tracts and pamphlets.

In June 1883 Nichols was assaulted and wounded by an unknown assailant,[5] and as a result, he and some of his followers relocated to Dodge County, Minnesota. In Minnesota, Nichols separated from the Christadelphians, adopted the name "Christian Brethren" for his church, and established three congregations. At the same time, Maud Hembree, an Oregon convert, founded a congregation at Barry, Illinois, at the invitation of people who had become interested in Nichols's teachings through his tracts.[6]

With support from congregations he established, Nichols continued to publish pamphlets and tracts. Of particular interest to his followers was a Bible chronology in which Nichols predicted that the Second Coming of Christ would occur sometime between 1896 and 1901. As 1901 approached, Nichols felt compelled to carry the Brethren's message to a wider audience. Ordering the construction of a large steamboat, which he named the "Megiddo," he closed all his churches and gathered between eighty and ninety of his followers on the boat, which plied the Mississippi and Ohio River systems during the navigation seasons of 1901 through 1903, stopping at ports along the way where the Brethren held meetings. While on the rivers, Nichols continued to publish tracts, as well as flyers for distribution to announce meetings.[7]

Evangelization has always been critical to the growth of the Megiddo Mission (as the group came to be called in Rochester) because its sense of the imminence of the return of Christ has led it to discourage marriage and promote celibacy. Consequently, almost all new members have been converts and have included families with children.

Having determined that all areas reachable via the river systems had been evangelized, in January 1904 the Brethren relocated to Rochester, New York. From there they sent out missionaries to sell Nichols's publications. The missionaries traveled to major cities in the Northeast and adjacent areas of Ontario, Canada, visiting smaller communities along the way.

The period from the middle of the nineteenth century through World War II, during which the Megiddo Mission developed, was one of great growth in religious publishing. For example, periodicals related to the Holiness Movement grew in number from fewer than ten at the time of the Civil War to over fifty by 1900.[8] Several groups were organized around their periodicals, most notably the antidenominational Church of God movement, whose members were known by the name of their publication, *The Gospel Trumpet*.[9]

In this environment, one would expect an avid publisher of tracts such as L. T. Nichols to have been at the forefront in developing a periodical; but for reasons that are not clear, he was not. The development of a periodical for the Christian Brethren was left to his successors.

When Nichols died in February 1912, he was quickly succeeded by his able assistant, Maud Hembree, who continued to send missionaries out to sell Nichols's publications, the most popular of which remained his *Bible Chronology*, now updated to predict Christ's return sometime between 1941 and 1952, and a pamphlet titled *What Must We Do to Be Saved?* The publications were usually sold in sets, and people were encouraged to read them repeatedly since there were no new words forthcoming from the founder.[10]

In 1914 two ambitious young boys from a Mission family, Clyde and Carroll Branham, decided to produce a local newsletter for the church. Each copy of the *Megiddo News* was laboriously typed by hand; the papers were sold and subscriptions solicited after Sunday morning services. The paper consisted of a summary of the previous Sunday's sermon, local news of members, and a weather report.

The members of the Mission were so enthusiastic about the paper that they soon provided the boys with a small press on which to print the paper. The weather report was soon dropped and other features gradually began to appear, but the local focus remained a constant. The subscription price was listed as "50 cts. per year (Postage Extra.),"[11] suggesting that subscriptions sent outside of the home church were the exception. Those few who received the *News* via mail were probably members on mission away from Rochester, along with a few people who had been associated with the Mission in the past and who remained in contact.

By April 1915 the Mission leadership apparently began to see the paper's potential as part of its outreach. They changed the name of the periodical from *Megiddo News* to *Megiddo Message* and produced an issue devoted to one of the several beliefs that are unique to the Megiddos— that Christmas should be celebrated in the spring[12]—which contained elements that suggest they were targeting a larger audience. The issue presented the rationale for the springtime celebration of Christmas, and referred to Maud Hembree "our lady minister," apparently for the benefit of those who did not know that the Church had female leadership. It also included a list of available Megiddo publications with their prices.

Having preserved a large collection of L. T. Nichols's sermons, in 1915 the Megiddos began to publish them in installments in the *Message*. By 14 November 1915 Nichols's sermons were being published in their entirety, replacing the summary of Hembree's sermons on the front page. The problem of providing interested parties with new material by Nichols had been solved.

In 1915 Maud Hembree assumed editorship of the *Message* and under her direction the magazine gradually developed into a more professional operation, probably shaped by her own interests in edifying popular magazines such as *Literary Digest*, which she often quoted. The *Message* also came to reflect her views and interests. Of particular note is the gradual deemphasis on specific dates for the Second Coming of Christ in favor of a more general sense that all were living in the end times.

The issue of Sunday, 21 November 1915, featured the first of what would become a staple of the *Message*, a question from a reader on a religious topic with the answer provided by a member of the Mission. The questions, most of which would be published anonymously, provided readers with an opportunity to gain clarification on issues for which they could not readily find answers in Megiddo literature. It also gave the Mission the opportunity to address issues that the editor or pastor considered important. Questions on issues of particular significance to the Megiddos, such as the role of women in the church, would appear repeatedly. Thus, the *Message* became a teaching tool.

Despite the apparent shift toward using the *Message* to promote the Mission's outreach program, it still retained its local flavor. For example, missionaries often went on trips during which they would locate in a city for several weeks and canvass the city and surrounding areas. When this occurred, the *Message* sometimes published addresses at which people could write the missionaries. The 14 May 1916 issue reported that a group of missionaries had arrived in Youngstown, Ohio, and gave their addresses. In keeping with the Megiddo emphasis on decorum, the women were located on Ridge Avenue, while the lone male in the party was staying at another location, on Mahoning Avenue.

The readership grew quickly. The 11 June 1916 issue reported that "the circulation of our little paper is steadily increasing and its biweekly arrival is looked forward to with pleasure and interest, which we greatly desire may deepen and intensify as it is sent out on its silent mission, to arouse and enlighten a world in slumber and darkness."

Initially, *Message* subscriptions were sold by missionaries to people who purchased literature. However, about 1920, the Mission began what became known as the "Elijah campaign." Based on Nichols's teaching that the prophet Elijah is waiting on another planet to return to Earth to herald the coming of Christ, the Mission began to place advertisements in national magazines offering a free or fairly inexpensive (ten cents) pamphlet on the coming of Elijah. Those who responded received, along with the pamphlet, advertisements for other Megiddo literature and the offer of a free six-month subscription to the *Message.* The campaign focused on magazines read primarily by people in "the small towns and R. F. D.s" (e.g., *Capper's Weekly, Farm News, Pathfinder*), and while much of the previously limited readership had been urban, a new audience developed among people in rural America. The number of subscriptions burgeoned. The "Summary of the Year's Work" in the 1922 Christmas issue reported that "in 1920 we printed 650 papers at an issue, of which our mailing list claimed 323, at the present time we print 1,200 and the mailing list has grown to 875; an increase of 96 per cent. in the number printed, and 170 per cent. in the number mailed. Approximately 31,000 copies of the *Message* were printed during the year."[13]

By 1923 the Mission was placing advertisements in publications in parts of the English-speaking world beyond the United States: Canada, England, Ireland, Scotland, Wales, Australia, New Zealand, Africa, and India. As a result, letters to the editor began to appear from other countries, primarily from Canada, where the *Message* was read by many people in small communities in Ontario, the Prairie Provinces, and the Maritimes, as indicated by the places from which letters were received.[14]

As the number of subscribers and correspondents grew, the magazine increasingly demonstrated a tendency of the Mission to treat subscribers as merely absent members of the congregation. While early letters to the editor were mainly paeans of praise for the magazine, later correspondents began to provide more personal information and testimonies.

Targeting a rural audience proved to be a stroke of genius, for people in isolated circumstances had special reasons to welcome the biweekly arrival of the magazine. However, they received more than a magazine for their subscriptions. What made the *Message* unique for its subscribers was the fact that members of the Mission who could not travel began a mission of developing and maintaining contact with *Message* subscribers. Monthly form letters written by female members of the

Mission called "Maranatha" letters and letters written by men called
"Progressive" letters were sent to subscribers. These letters contained
edifying messages that encouraged readers to persevere in their attempts
to live according to biblical principles. Readers were encouraged, if not
expected, to respond to the letters, and many responses were printed in
the *Message*.[15] A recipient of the letters in Milton, Iowa, described them
as "a wonderful bond that holds together those of us that are seeking
eternal life with all its blessings: a threefold cord and very strong," while
a Pennsylvania reader wrote that "it would be a cold world if we who
live so far away from the fountain head could not receive letters or little
epistles like those we receive from the brethren at home."[16]

By the 1930s, particularly after Maud Hembree's death in 1935, the
activities of the Maranatha sisters and Progressive brothers became increasingly prominent in the *Message*. Ella Skeels, L. T. Nichols's sister,
who succeeded Hembree as pastor, was not the prolific writer that her
predecessor had been, and as a consequence, the sermons published in
the magazine were those of Nichols and Hembree.[17] Maranatha and
Progressive "papers," edifying articles written by members, appeared in
the *Message,* often several in a single issue. At the same time, letters from
readers responding to the monthly Maranatha and Progressive letters
came to dominate the "From Our Mailbag" page of the magazine.[18]
These letters assumed that the magazine's readers had received and
read the Maranatha and Progressive letters, much as if they had all attended the same religious service and heard the same sermon. This
probably contributed to the sense that all were part of a single congregation. As one reader of the Maranatha letters wrote: "You Maranatha
Sisters are surely doing a grand work, and we scattered abroad truly appreciate this, as we long to be more nearly connected to the fountainhead of Truth."[19]

Readers responded in kind to the Mission's apparent inclusion of
them in the congregation. By the mid-1930s the Mission and the *Message*
readership had begun to communicate using terms that had special
meaning to the correspondents. The community at Rochester was the
"fountainhead." Both Maud Hembree and Ella Skeels were referred to
as "our Mother in Israel," a reference to the prophetess Deborah in the
Book of Judges, while Ella Skeels was also called "our spiritual mother."
The contents of Megiddo publications and letters were "spiritual food"
or "the loaf of bread and bottle of water." Faults were the "the old
man," a concept drawn from the Apostle Paul, and the goal of readers

(both female and male) was to replace him with "the new man." If one were successful in doing that, one might gain "the prize"—salvation or eternal life.

The sense of belonging to the Mission even though living at a distance was expressed by a reader from Lowville in northern New York State. "It is indeed a privilege to belong to this royal family," she wrote in 1957. "I often think, how can it be that we are selected from earth's millions to be part of this holy family? What a privilege!"[20]

In addition to the Maranatha and Progressive letters, members also wrote personal letters to distant subscribers. Often these letters answered readers' personal religious questions. Members also sent mimeographed copies of sermons that were not printed in the magazine. By 1930 the Mission had also developed weekly Sunday school lessons for both adults and children that were sent to subscribers on request. In the 1950s and 1960s the Mission produced *Children's Doings*, a magazine for children.

Some *Message* readers maintained correspondence with several members of the Mission at once. A woman from central New York wrote: "I cannot tell you how very glad I am always to get your letters, in fact, letters from any of the sisters. Today I received two—one from Sister V—— and one from Sister A. N——. These letters give me courage and spur me on to greater efforts. . . . Received a list of words with their meanings from Sis. S——. Please thank her for me, and say to her that I will write as soon as I can find time . . . Am enclosing two pink cards for the last dollar I sent to Sis. McD——. Did she get it? I must write to Sister O—— next. Enjoyed her letter so much."[21]

Readers who appear to have been inundated with publications and correspondence from the Mission indicated that they would welcome even more material. A brother and sister from Florida wrote: "We always enjoy reading your letters. . . . I think it was Sister Bryant who sent us a 4th of July program, also clippings from the paper. . . . We are more thankful each day that we came in contact with the Megiddo Mission. . . . What grand sermons we receive from time to time! and we read and re-read them, and also the S. S. [Sunday school] lessons . . . ; we love to read or hear anything from the Mission."[22]

The fact that many readers felt they were part of the community is demonstrated by the frequent use of the word "our" to refer especially to the leadership of the church. For example, in the wake of Maud Hembree's death in 1935, the *Message* printed a number of letters referring to her in such terms as "our beloved leader" and "our dearly beloved sister and teacher."[23]

In what was probably an attempt to unite readers in a common practice, the *Message* printed a tool to help adherents develop more righteous lifestyles. At the heart of Megiddo doctrine is the belief that salvation is not based on faith, but on doing everything commanded by the Bible.[24] Consequently, "right living" is a focus of the ministry. To this end, in 1931 a "Daily Record Chart" was printed in the *Message* to assist subscribers in overcoming bad habits and wrong thinking. The top line of the chart listed "the most familiar evils which beset the pathway of the average human being," such as jealousy, anger, impatience, "puffed up," and "self-justification." There were blank spaces in which to record personal faults. Each day, the user was supposed to record an average for each deficiency. The goal was to defeat all of the evils within two years. Each form covered one month and supplies were available on request. Since no letters to the editor expressed appreciation for the form or testified to its usefulness and no further offers were made to send the form to subscribers, it appears that this initiative was not a great success. However, this does not mean that the message of the need for right living was lost on the group's adherents; over the years the *Message* included hundreds of letters from readers reporting on their efforts to overcome faults and live in a way that would earn them eternal life.[25]

The emphasis on doing good works to earn salvation also manifested itself in the tendency of readers to read the same Megiddo publications repeatedly. Typical was the experience of a reader from Minneapolis who wrote, "three copies has [*sic*] come to me, and I thank God from the depths of my heart for this Divine Messenger. . . . I have read the last one through twice and am now reading it for the third time and writing out the references." Bible memorization was also a common practice among both members of the Mission in Rochester and distant adherents.[26]

Articles dealing with the end times frequently appeared in the *Message,* and as a result, readers often wrote about the need to put extra efforts into perfecting themselves so that they would be among those acceptable to Christ when he returned. Some older readers bemoaned the possibility that they might not have enough time to make the changes necessary to earn salvation.

The most ambitious publication of the Mission was a two-volume compilation of edited sermons and articles by Maud Hembree, which appeared in 1933 and 1934 under the title *The Known Bible and Its Defense.* Each volume was approximately four hundred pages in length, and the books were eagerly purchased by readers of the *Message.* Missionaries also sold copies of the book and donated copies to libraries of all kinds throughout the United States. The book was well received, one *Message* reader even designating it "the Book of the Century" and "a death blow to the arguments of atheism, infidelity, and false theology."[27]

In addition to printed materials, subscribers occasionally received visits from Megiddo missionaries. Sometimes these were the missionaries who had sold them their subscriptions to the *Message;* often they were missionaries who had simply targeted subscribers for visits when they were in an area. Some subscribers even wrote requesting visits. Missionaries often reduced the cost of going on mission by accepting the hospitality of *Message* subscribers.

A visit to the "fountainhead" became a goal for many subscribers. Even some who lived at great distances were so inspired by the magazine and the attention they received from the members that they visited the Mission, especially at times of holiday celebrations, which were held at Christmas, Easter, Independence Day, the Founder's Birthday (October 1), and Thanksgiving. These visits were viewed as a privilege by some, and they often strengthened the visitor's attachment to the Mission.

A reader from Lytle, Texas, wrote: "I cannot begin to tell you how much I enjoyed the visit from Brothers Flowerday and Thayer, and Sisters Thatcher and Hughes. . . . I am so grateful I have been permitted to see them and behold the light that shines in them. . . . Is it any wonder Sister ——— said she was hungering and thirsting for that peace, and that she intended to return for another visit to the Mission? And I do hope she can make the visit. She said if the Lord willed, she would go in the spring. I pray Him to help me to grow worthy enough to make that visit some day, also, if it is His will."[28]

A woman from Brownsville, Texas, where a small group of Megiddo followers resided, even adopted the conservative dress style of the Megiddo women following a visit in 1948. After returning to Texas, she wrote that she was "getting quite used to my dress" and that she, her mother, and another woman were working to make dresses for themselves based on a pattern provided by one of the women at the Mission.[29]

One subscriber who lived in sparsely populated rural Wyoming, but who had managed to pay a visit to the Mission, wrote: "Maranatha! I will not only try to answer your Maranatha letter, but also your good letter received this noon. I just can't wait for the mail man these days, and usually begin to watch for him about 11:30. As his truck comes into view to the top of our Sunny Divide, the next quarter mile to our mail box is an anxious one. For I begin to wonder then, which of the Sisters of mine are paying me a visit this morning. And when I finally get the letter I always look at the signature. It is easy now to picture you as I read your words of comfort and help, and I feel very close to you. Do please keep up writing and I know that answering is helping me to keep my 'eyes on the prize.'"[30] Another visitor felt so at home at the Mission that upon returning home to Whitehouse, Ohio, she wrote that she was "homesick for the Megiddo Mission."[31]

People are often attracted to sects with unusual beliefs because the prospect of having special knowledge to which others are not privy is appealing to them or because they believe that by being one of the select few to know the truth, they will have special opportunities for salvation or for exalted positions in an afterlife. L. T. Nichols had maintained that the Megiddos would have a special role when Elijah returned, either in proclaiming the return or in raising the dead. Having the knowledge imparted by Megiddo literature even gave some a certain sense of superiority. As one reader wrote, "I am sorry that the truth is too plain for the general public to understand, but I am thankful to God that he so wonderfully blessed me with an understanding of his blessed word."[32]

The celebration of True Christmas, which L. T. Nichols determined also included the beginning of the New Year and which he named after the Hebrew month of Abib, was of particular significance to many readers of the *Message*. The magazine printed several letters expressing appreciation for the knowledge of the true date of Christmas—the first new moon after the vernal equinox—and promising never to celebrate Christmas in December again.

Letters described home celebrations of the Abib holiday. In response, the *Message* often published the order of service for the celebration at Rochester and an account of the service with lists of out-of-town visitors attending. Beginning about 1925 the *Message* printed special programs for readers to use for home services.[33] Readers were also offered placards to put in their windows to announce the true date of Christmas,[34] and eventually there were even Abib greeting cards that were distributed free to readers.

The 26 April and 9 May 1925 issues of the *Message* noted that Abib celebrations had been held in over twenty cities, including Phoenix,

Arizona, where twenty-six people gathered to celebrate; Portland, Oregon; Oklahoma City; Plant City, Florida; Sparta, Kentucky; and three cities in Canada.

A typical home celebration was described in a letter to the *Message* from two young sisters from Groton, New York: "For Christmas eve we are going to have a prayer, hymns, recording of 'Silent Night' while mother reads of the birth of Jesus, and then gifts. After our Christmas dinner our program will include music, readings, questions made out by Father on Acts, with a prize for the one who answers the most correctly. Each one is to do something individually, which is to be a surprise to the rest."[35]

One reader from Rock Island, Illinois, who could not attend the 1963 Abib services attempted to unite with the members of the Rochester congregation in spirit: "We had a nice program today. We sang some Christmas songs and read a piece out of the *Message* on True Christmas. . . . We had our lunch about 11:30 so we would be eating the same time that you would be."[36]

The Mission received a poignant letter from F. J. P. of Chicago, who wrote: "As I sat this evening reading the *Message,* I tried with the aid of the article in the new Christmas number to visualize and imagine the scene in Rochester. I had bought flowers and the house looked lovely, and the placard was conspicuously placed—but I was alone, by myself in the belief, and, consequently, subject to ridicule and banter."[37] A reader in Charlestown, Mississippi, closed his store for the day to celebrate Abib and "an old acquaintance came to visit" and "laughed" at him.[38] Adhering to Megiddo teachings was not without its sacrifices.

In contrast to the lone celebrants was a group in Swansea, Wales, where Nichols had preached in the 1890s, who were regular correspondents with the Mission and who had great expectations for their Christmas celebration. In 1925 they sent for four hundred copies of Nichols's publication "True Christmas and New Year," "a copy of which they propose to hand to each individual attending their Christmas exercises."[39]

In order to emphasize that Abib was actually Christmas, the Megiddos sent Christmas gifts to many of their regular correspondents, particularly families with children. In contrast to the toys that most children received, the gifts from Megiddo were useful or educational items. A reader from Glendale, Arizona, wrote: "The box from the Mission arrived in time, and the children enjoyed their presents. They were all delighted with their 'Abib' spoons, and the boys like their bookmarks.

W—— was pleased with her pretty dress material and collar. We want to thank all those at the Mission who had a part in sending the gifts."[40]

Several Canadian families had what might be described as an anti-Christmas celebration on 25 December 1937, "not to commemorate the day in any way, but being a holiday from regular work it provided time for those who work to take part in the exercises." They met in a basement room to discuss the signs of the times and read a Megiddo sermon. Then they went upstairs where other members of the family had prepared a program that included music, drama, and a memorial tribute to Maud Hembree.[41]

True Christmas celebrations were frequently a major focus of small groups of adherents, often members of a single family, who gathered either weekly or periodically in many parts of the English-speaking world to read Megiddo literature and reinforce each other's faith. These groups were often referred to as "ecclesias" in the *Message,* a term used by Christadelphians and Megiddos to denote congregations. Prior to 1958, when the Megiddo Mission established guidelines for membership, it is likely that members of the ecclesias, as well as other regular correspondents, were considered to have the status of members of the church.[42]

As Philip Jenkins states, "New religions flourish by providing believers with what they cannot obtain in the mainstream organizations of the day: sects and cults live on the unpaid bills of the churches."[43] Indeed, many subscribers reported being seekers who had tried several denominations only to find all of them lacking. As Mrs. A. J. R. of San Antonio, Texas, wrote: "I received the free literature. . . . I found it all in perfect harmony with Bible teaching. Have studied the Bible for twenty-five years, but have not been able to unite with any denomination: seemed there was something wrong with all of them. This sounds good to me. Will investigate further." Another reader wrote, "I have roamed the creeds, sects, ists and isms through and through to find the truth, to find that which is beyond the reproach of critics, and since finding the works of our great leader [L. T. Nichols] (for I recognize him as such) I have gone no further."[44]

Ruth A. Tucker notes that new religions often have an "ability to reach out and meet the needs of people who are suffering and dejected."[45] This seems to be the case with the Megiddos, since they built a large readership among the frail elderly and chronically ill. This is somewhat ironic because the period in which the *Message* attracted its most devoted readership was one in which faith healing ministries flourished, while the Megiddos, like other dispensationalist sects, do not believe in faith healing. Instead they believe that "the power Jesus gave his disciples was for them alone, and not for Christians today. . . . We cannot heal the sick, we cannot raise the dead . . . [or] open blind eyes." Instead, these things "will be restored when the prophet Elijah comes as Christ's forerunner."[46] For the elderly and infirm, the *Message* and the letters and visits from members provided stimulating relief from the monotony of isolation. As one reader wrote, "No one knows what those sermons mean to me, especially when I can't go out at all. . . . Sometimes people ask me if I do not get lonesome, and I tell them no, not when I have these papers and my Bible."[47] Some invalids may also have been reassured because some faith healers claimed that those who prayed and were not healed lacked sufficient faith to receive healing.[48]

Interest in Megiddo literature was not limited to adults. Occasionally the Mission received letters from children such as James A. D., whose letter appeared in the 23 January 1927 issue of the *Message:* "I am a boy nine years old. A year ago my mother . . . sent for your books and we think they are wonderful. . . . I do errands nights and mornings for a neighbor and have earned one dollar ($1.00) which I am sending to you, to help tell other boys and girls about God. . . . I wish we lived in Rochester so we could come to your meetings. It is hard to live where you are the only boy that believes in the true religion."

An eight-year-old reader from Fort Plain, New York, even got into a bit of trouble in school because of his adherence to Megiddo teachings. As he wrote:

> Early in December our teacher gave us a few words to write in sentences, one of them being Santa Claus. I wrote, "Santa Claus is a myth." My teacher marked it wrong and corrected by writing, "Santa Claus comes in the night."
>
> She returned our lessons for us to copy in our composition books, and I wrote it down "Santa Claus is a myth." I knew if I wrote it her way I would be writing a lie.[49]

Some readers were so enthusiastic about the *Message* that they subscribed at great personal sacrifice. A Texas farmer wrote: "Will you please send my paper and I will send the money the first of March. That is as soon as we can borrow money at our banks. Our crop was destroyed by hail last June and it put us in a hard place. I will send you as much as $2.00. We can't do without the paper; it is the only light we have ever received on the Bible."[50]

Many people had difficulty renewing their subscriptions during the Great Depression. In 1933 a woman wrote to say that times were "so dull here, no work to do, and one can hardly get by. . . . I can't ask you to send the *Message* any longer till I can pay for it, but I don't see what I will do without it." She asked if the Mission had "any left-overs of any kind—it doesn't matter if they are fifteen years old—please send them to me."[51] Those who could not pay need not have worried about being deprived of their spiritual food. According to the 18 March 1939 issue, "The *Message* is sent to any one who appreciates it, the matter of finances not being considered. If one is able to pay for his or her subscription, it helps to spread the Truth; if not, the *Message* may be had for the asking."

Over the years, the letters to the *Message* reflect a small core of devoted correspondents whose letters appear frequently, interspersed with letters from new subscribers and occasional writers. Since the letters that were published were designed to encourage others, they were often effusive in their praise of the Mission, its doctrines, and the *Message*. As a young man from Wausau, Wisconsin, wrote, "I do not want to be without this wonderful paper. To me life would not be worth living without this message of cheer and comfort. I have enjoyed it so much these last two years and can not tell you in words how much help I have received from it. I absolutely couldn't get along without it."[52] Occasionally, however, the Mission published letters in which the praise seemed faint at best. While praising Megiddo publications, a reader from Fort Wayne, Indiana, stated: "It is strange we never heard of you people till last spring, not even from the pulpit where one can hear them denouncing Russell, Christian Science, New Thought, Unity, Mr. Fosdick, and many others. But we never heard about you people."[53] One would think that the Megiddos would not have desired or expected to be included in a list of people and movements of which they too were highly critical.

In 1924, at the behest of member David M. Sweeting, the Mission began an active campaign to enlist readers as salespeople for the magazine. Sweeting was ill and could not go on mission that year so he drafted a letter to be sent to subscribers "urging each to tell their friends of this life-giving little magazine." The letter asked each person to attempt to secure at least ten new subscribers. This campaign resulted in an immediate increase in the number of subscribers, and encouraging readers to recruit new subscribers became an integral part of the marketing strategy for the magazine.[54] Over the next decade, readers convinced others to subscribe, gave gift subscriptions to friends and neighbors, placed advertisements for Megiddo literature in local newspapers, and sent lists of names for free six-month subscriptions. Many readers felt so obligated to gain new subscribers that they wrote apologetic letters to the Mission when they failed at the task.

Readers found creative ways to interest people in the *Message*. A reader near Auckland, New Zealand, took issues of the magazine to the city with him and put them in boxes that were used to collect reading material to be sent to people in remote areas surrounding the city. A woman from Winnipeg, Manitoba, took copies of the *Message* with her on a visit to friends, but her friends were not interested. Undaunted, she distributed copies to people she met on the train on her return trip home. In 1932 a reader from Missiouri sent money for nine subscriptions and reported that he had "distributed about ninety copies of the *Message*, sending them into fifty different towns."[55]

For the Megiddos and many *Message* subscribers, the advent of World War II intensified the sense of urgency to achieve salvation as they interpreted the war and related world events as sure signs that they were living in the last days before the return of Elijah. In 1942 the Mission produced a pamphlet from the contents of a *Message* article titled "What Can One Man Do?"[56] The pamphlet noted that while "the crumbling edge of the abyss is still a little distant from favored America," the signs from Europe, Asia, or Africa were not encouraging. The pamphlet went on to call its readers to become part of Christ, "a *multitudinous man* . . . composed of ordinary men and women who refused to remain ordinary; they became extraordinary by overcoming." This pamphlet received an enthusiastic reception from one *Message* reader from Savannah, Missouri, who wrote, "Thank you for your many kindnesses to me, especially the last supply of 'What Can One Man Do?' I need more of them and I would greatly like it if you could send me several hundred more of them for distribution. They are so good I get a thrill from giving them to those who will be able to get good from them. My prayer is that God will continue to bless and support such distribution of Christian literature."[57]

Although there was still some missionary travel, direct outreach by members of the Rochester congregation was curtailed by fuel rationing during the war. The Mission became more dependent on readers' sending lists of names (often accompanied by donations) to help increase the number of subscribers to the *Message*. "Items from Our Mail Bag" frequently noted that letters that were printed had included lists of names for trial subscriptions. Mission travel resumed after World War II, partially fueled by an influx of distant adherents who relocated to Rochester during the ten-year period following the War.

In 1957, in response to a series of *Message* articles titled "Pressing On," some adherents in Rome, Georgia, began a missionary campaign. Signing their letter "The Travelers," they wrote: "We are pressing on, holding meetings at homes in the evenings and visiting homes in our missionary work during the day. I must say that we have enjoyed every minute of our journey together, meeting and talking with people in restaurants, at motels, and on the street."[58]

Children even got involved in the mission work. A mother from Peoria, Arizona, wrote:

> The children left for school as usual. Wynona got out some more pamphlets to take with her to school today, as she finds opportunity to give them out every once in a while when someone asks her a question.
>
> She keeps them handy in her zip binder, or locker. . . . It takes plenty of courage to dare to be different and that is what we must have in this evil generation.[59]

A woman from Cheyenne, Wyoming, wrote that she had found a "Jesus Saves" booklet in one of the rest rooms of the filling station that she and her husband operated and that gave her an idea. "I left an 'Elijah' book in each of the rooms after that. About four times a day I visit the rooms and replenish any that are gone. . . . So far eight have disappeared; five in the men's room and three from the ladies'. I gather from this that men are more interested."[60]

In addition to recruiting new subscribers, many correspondents also contributed financially to the Mission, some sending small gifts with their subscription renewals. Tithing was practiced at the Mission in Rochester and there are a few letters that suggest that some adherents in distant places also sent tithes to the Mission.[61] There is no indication that this practice was widespread among *Message* readers or that it was specifically encouraged by the Mission, but it is further evidence that some distant readers of Megiddo materials considered the Mission to be their home church.

The *Message* regularly publishes obituaries of members of the Rochester congregation, frequent visitors, and regular correspondents to the *Message,* which in the past have sometimes included detailed descriptions of their funerals.[62] The Megiddos offered to officiate at funerals for deceased followers, even if it meant traveling great distances. In October 1943 an elderly member of a small group of Megiddo adherents who had "been a frequent and consistent [correspondent] with the fountainhead" died in Santa Monica, California. The funeral was held two days after the death, but burial was delayed until the arrival of E. C. Branham of the Rochester congregation, who conducted a graveside service. In January 1933 the Mission received a telegram requesting a funeral for a reader in West Leyden, New York, and the assistant pastor and the men's "Double Quartet" journeyed from Rochester to conduct the funeral.[63] In 1939, when one "of our subscribers and correspondents" died in Cambridge, Iowa, the Mission sent a funeral sermon to the family, which was read by a friend of the deceased's son.[64] Messages from relatives of readers announcing the death of a loved one who had been a longtime subscriber were often acknowledged in the pages of the magazine.

Some *Message* readers became such devoted followers that they moved to Rochester to participate in the life of the Church. Typical of these was Mora W. Kelly (1881–1940), an Arkansas native who had a career as a schoolteacher and principal. In 1930 he became interested in the Mission and became a regular correspondent with members in Rochester. In 1938 he and his family moved to Rochester.[65]

In spite of efforts to create a sense of community among readers and correspondents, the Mission was not forthcoming in the pages of the *Message* about many events that affected it from the 1930s through the 1950s. The Mission was involved in several legal cases related to such matters as tax exemptions for members the Mission claimed were missionaries and the estate of Maud Hembree, which was claimed by the children she had left behind in Oregon when she moved east with the Brethren. The case that garnered the most publicity was a child custody case in which an invalid mother claimed that Megiddo teachings to which her husband adhered were detrimental to their daughter's development. In spite of widespread coverage in western New York newspapers, nothing about any of these cases appeared in the *Message,* although the principals in the custody case had been mentioned as visitors in past issues and the father had been reported as going on occasional mission trips. The failure to mention these events in the *Message* may have contributed to the fact that a number of people who moved to the Rochester area to fellowship with the congregation left within a short time.

Beginning in the 1950s the Church experienced difficulty keeping its young members. It is likely that as the neighborhood surrounding the Mission became increasingly commercial, including the addition of an ice cream parlor, a variety store, and a motion picture theater, it became more difficult to shield children from the larger society when they were regularly exposed to opportunities outside the Mission. Today, the membership is largely comprised of older adults, with few younger attendees, most of whom are related to the older members.

The most significant event that was not described in the *Message* was a serious split that the Mission suffered in 1958, which cost the Mission some of its most active members, both old and new, and substantially reduced the size of the membership in Rochester. Ironically, the group that left the Mission was led by Clyde Branham, who as a young boy had been one of the founders of the *Megiddo News*.[66]

Throughout the 1950s, letters to the Mission became a less and less prominent feature of the *Message*. The reason for this is not clear, but may be due to the need to focus efforts either on integrating several new families who joined the Mission in the period after World War II or on inner conflicts that eventually resulted in the split. Following the split, letters from many longtime correspondents no longer appeared, suggesting that the people with whom those who had left had built relationships no longer wrote to the Mission. Letters from other readers began to appear, but, with a few exceptions, the new writers conveyed less of a sense of belonging to the Mission than had earlier correspondents.[67] At the same time, the letters published increasingly reflected a greater sense of the imminence of the coming of Elijah. In January 1967 a subscriber from Fort Worth, Texas, renewed his subscription and asked the Mission to "keep me on the list until Judgment Day."[68]

The *Message* changed very little in content and focus from its founding to the 1970s. This was probably due to the fact that the leadership of the Mission was drawn exclusively from people who had known L. T. Nichols personally and were devoted to his ideas. In the 1970s the magazine, which had ignored most current events, suddenly began to address such topics as popular music and the pardon of Richard Nixon by President Gerald Ford. The reasons for the change are a matter for conjecture. It is likely that the Church's loss of membership at the time of the split and the resulting loss of contact with members of its subscription base caused the leadership, headed by the last pastor to have known

Nichols, the aging Kenneth E. Flowerday, to attempt to catch the attention of a new audience that might be more interested in current events.[69]

The *Megiddo Message* is still published in Rochester by the faithful remnant of about thirty-five members, most of whom live in a complex of Church-owned buildings or on adjacent streets. The current editor owns a graphic design business and, as a result, the *Message* is colorful and esthetically pleasing. There is little news of the local church, with the exception of announcements of holiday celebrations and obituaries. Obituaries of longtime correspondents still appear. In 2004, for the first time, photographs of some of the distant adherents were published with the obituaries. There are rarely any letters to the editor, and articles, rather than sermons, are the magazine's main features. The *Message* is now published ten times a year, and about 14,000 copies are sent out, a large number being free subscriptions sent to libraries.[70]

One of the members still uses his vacations from work to visit subscribers to the *Message,* sometimes taking other members with him. The Mission's pastor also still responds to occasional requests to perform funerals for distant *Message* correspondents and occasional visitors when their families request it.

The Church still sells pamphlets and tracts, many of them scaled-down versions of those produced by their founder, and a pseudonymously authored book, *Millennium Superworld,* which anticipates the world as it will become after the return of Elijah, whose arrival it still eagerly anticipates.

The Church is suspicious of the influence of broadcast media and rejects the use of television as a means of spreading its message. Consequently, it is ironic that, as the energy needed to produce the *Message* declines with the aging of the membership, the Megiddo Church has turned to the Internet to attempt to reach new audiences. They have developed a Web site and an online Bible study, and one can link to information about them from the Web site of the local daily newspaper. This form of evangelization requires that rather than the Megiddos seeking out potential converts, interested parties must find them on the World Wide Web. This is a reversal of previous practice and would seem to be a haphazard method of reaching people.

The future of the Church is tenuous at best, but given its strong financial base and the willingness of the leadership to hire people from outside for work the members can no longer do, it may well be able to maintain its Web site, and even produce the *Message,* for many years to come. However, one must ask if the Megiddo Church is likely to appeal to users of the Web, who are more likely to search for diet, sex, and shopping-related sites than the site of a small religious sect with unusual beliefs.

Notes

1. The Church has many of the characteristics of a communal society but does not believe in community of goods. It is, however, characterized by a high degree of economic cooperation. Throughout most of its existence, the Church has been supported by tithes of members who were either employed by local industries or had their own businesses. Because celibacy is encouraged, the Church has benefited from its inheritance of property from deceased members.

2. The term "member" is used here to designate anyone who regularly participated in the activities of the Megiddo community. The sect did not have actual membership requirements until it suffered a split in 1958, at which time it became important to determine who was, and who was not, a member.

3. On the Christadelphians, see Charles H. Lippy, *The Christadelphians in North America* (Lewiston, NY: Edwin Mellen Press, 1989), and Bryan R. Wilson, *Sects and Society: A Sociological Study of Elim Tabernacle, Christian Science, and Christadelphians* (Berkeley: University of California Press, 1961).

4. The movement, also known as the Restorationist movement, which emerged in the United States in the first half of the nineteenth century, sought to revitalize Christianity by restoring practices of the church described in the New Testament. The most prominent denominations that grew out of the movement are the Churches of Christ and the Christian Church (Disciples of Christ).

5. Local newspapers at the time suggested that the shooter was the son of a Nichols follower who believed that his mother was being financially exploited by Nichols. No one was ever arrested for the crime.

6. A congregation established at Davenport, Iowa, was short lived.

7. Without extant Megiddo writings from the period, it is impossible to know how the members responded to the failure of Nichols's predictions to be realized. However, since few members left during and immediately after the boat ministry, perhaps J. Gordon Melton is correct in stating that contrary to popular belief, "nonfulfillment provides a test for the system and for the personal ties built within the group. Times of testing tend to strengthen, not destroy, religious groups." See J. Gordon Melton, "Spiritualization and Reaffirmation: What Really Happens When Prophecy Fails," *American Studies* 26 (Fall 1985): 19–20.

8. Norman K. Dann, "Spatial Diffusion of a Religious Movement," *Journal for the Scientific Study of Religion* 15 (1976): 353. A similar increase is evident in the number of religious periodicals published in Victorian England, which rose from 223 in 1860 to 551 in 1900. Patrick Scott, "Victorian Religious Periodicals: Fragments That Remain," in *The Materials, Sources and Methods of Ecclesiastical History,* ed. Derek Baker (Oxford, UK: Basil Blackwell for the Ecclesiastical History Society, 1975), 339.

9. The Church of God movement later evolved into the Church of God (Anderson, Indiana).

10. The Megiddo missionaries distributed large numbers of the pamphlets, which they called "books," some of which were over fifty pages in length. In 1915, for example, canvassers sold over ten thousand books in a four-week period on a trip to Detroit, Michigan. *Megiddo News,* 14 November 1915.

11. *Megiddo News,* 3 January 1915, first page. Note: early issues of the Megiddo magazine did not include page numbers.

12. For centuries scholars have debated the time of year in which Christ was born and many have determined that he was probably born in the spring because it is unlikely that the shepherds, who are so prominent in the Christmas story, would have been in the fields in December. The Megiddos are the only group of which I am aware that believes that Christmas should actually be *celebrated* in the spring.

13. *Megiddo Message,* 29 March 1922, 17.

14. *Megiddo Message,* 15 April 1923, 8. There were surprising numbers of subscribers in Newfoundland given the area's small population.

15. "Maranatha," which means "Christ is coming," and "Progressive" were the names of groups formed at the Mission for various activities. In the 1930s a third group, the Young Gleaners, composed of male youth, was created, and this group sent letters to younger readers of the *Message.* In the 31 May 1947 issue, a letter from a brother from Stewiacke, Nova Scotia, states that he has received the Progressive letter and is "answering inside the 7-day limit," suggesting that readers were asked to reply within a week of receiving the letter.

16. *Megiddo Message,* 10 May 1952, 9; 14 February 1953, 9.

17. Skeels's ministry was devoted to promoting her late brother's ideas and emphasizing his importance to the Mission. She was in frail health when she succeeded Hembree, and she delegated most of her pastoral responsibilities to Percy J. Thatcher, who would succeed her as pastor. However, she took an active role in editing the *Message,* corresponded with readers, and held morning study programs for the women of the Mission.

18. Responses to the Maranatha letters appeared more frequently than did responses to the Progressive letters. It is likely that the male members of the Mission, most of whom were employed outside the Mission, had less time to write, and male subscribers, who were also working, had less time to reply.

While both men and women subscribed to the *Message*, it is also likely that more women than men subscribed, although there is no statistical evidence to support this.

19. *Megiddo Message*, 1 December 1945, 9.

20. *Megiddo Message*, 1 June 1957, 2.

21. *Megiddo Message*, 8 November 1931, 9.

22. *Megiddo Message*, 25 October 1931, 9.

23. *Megiddo Message*, 29 December 1935, 9. At the time of Hembree's death, the Mission sent a photograph of the late leader to subscribers, an action that elicited expressions of gratitude from readers. One wrote, "Oh, I am so pleased to have her picture and so large and beautiful a one it is! I set it on the buffet, and anywhere I may be in the dining room her lovely eyes seem to be looking in that direction." *Megiddo Message*, 17 May 1936, 9.

24. The Megiddos believe that this is the great discovery that L. T. Nichols made in 1880, which determines the date of the founding of the church.

25. "The Daily Record Chart," *Megiddo Message*, 12 April 1931, 7–8. Few of the letters refer to the specific sins that the reader is attempting to overcome. However, they often refer to the sins of society, such as "pleasure-seeking" and "immoral dress," and a reader from Texas reported having "overcome 65 years of smoking, drinking, and cussing" (*Megiddo Message*, 26 June 1927, 8; April 1967, 2). The few concrete examples suggest that the sins are the same ones identified by the major Jewish, Protestant, and Roman Catholic periodicals of the period that were examined by Sister Mary Patrice Thaman for her study *Manners and Morals of the 1920s: A Survey of the Religious Press* (Westport, CT: Greenwood Press, 1977 [orig. 1954]).

26. *Megiddo Message*, 3 May 1936, 8. Bible memorization is still emphasized among the Megiddos. Somewhat problematic is the fact that the Church recognizes many translations of scripture and not all members memorize from the same version of the Bible.

27. *Megiddo Message*, 10 September 1933, 9. Individual *Message* subscribers also donated copies of the books to public libraries (*Megiddo Message*, 14 November 1937, 7). According to the OCLC WorldCat database, sixty-six participating libraries own at least one volume of the set. Several of the libraries have it in historical collections.

28. *Megiddo Message*, 25 January 1947. Kenneth Flowerday would become president of the Church upon the death of Percy Thatcher in 1958.

29. *Megiddo Message*, 26 September 1946. In 1948 all of the women of the Mission would have dressed in a style not unlike that of the Megiddo women who arrived in Rochester in 1904. Some of the women still dress in that style, although the younger women tend to wear somewhat more contemporary clothes that retain the characteristic ankle-length skirts, long sleeves, and high necklines.

30. *Megiddo Message*, 27 March 1943, 9.

31. *Megiddo Message*, 26 May 1951, 9.

32. *Megiddo Message*, 30 October 1927, 8.

33. "A Christmas Service at Home," *Megiddo Message*, 25 March 1926, 22. From an early date, the Megiddos sold copies of their hymnals, which were often used for the home celebrations.

34. The 15 February 1925 issue of the *Message* (7) described the placard as being "18 x 16 in., suitable for hanging in window, bearing the words 'Abib 1st True Christmas and New Year March 25, Roman Time 1925.'"

35. *Megiddo Message*, 22 April 1944, 9.

36. *Megiddo Message*, 13 April 1963, 2.

37. *Megiddo Message*, 25 April 1926, 8.

38. *Megiddo Message*, 23 May 1926, 8.

39. *Megiddo Message*, 25 March 1925, 23. *Message* readers also often celebrated other Megiddo holidays. In 1939, in an attempt to feel united with the Rochester congregation, a reader in Chatfield, Minnesota, held a solitary celebration of the founder's birthday. She "set an extra vase of flowers on the living room table with the Bible and picture of our leader beside them, and at the time I believed the services were being held at Megiddo, I read a *Message* dated Sept. 23, 1934, *As Others Saw Him*." *Megiddo Message*, 25 November 1939, 9.

40. *Megiddo Message*, 12 May 1951. Fruit, nuts, writing materials, and grooming items were also among the items sent in Abib packages.

41. *Megiddo Message*, 5 February 1937, 9.

42. Among the cities where these groups met were places as diverse as Phoenix, Arizona, and Hornbeck, Louisiana.

43. Philip Jenkins, *Mystics and Messiahs: Cults and New Religions in American History* (Oxford, UK: Oxford University Press, 2000), 21.

44. *Megiddo Message*, 16 April 1922, 8; 29 June 1924, 8. One reader was quite specific regarding the eclectic group of religions she had considered: Seventh-day Adventism, Methodism, "the Christian or Campbellite Church," Mormonism, and Christian Science. *Megiddo Message*, 13 May 1928, 9.

45. Ruth A. Tucker, *Another Gospel: Alternative Religions and the New Age Movement* (Grand Rapids, MI: Academic Books, 1989), 30.

46. "Miracles Today?" *Megiddo Message*, May/June 2004, 24.

47. *Megiddo Message*, 29 February 1920, 8.

48. On the reasons that were given for people's failure to receive healing, see Nancy A. Hardesty, *Faith Cure: Divine Healing in the Pentecostal and Healing Movements* (Peabody, MA: Hendrickson Publishers, 2003), 129–47. For a criticism of faith healing that is contemporary with the early years of the *Message*, see Arno Clemens Gaebelein, *The Healing Question: An Examination of the Claims of Faith-Healing and Divine Healing Systems in the Light of the Scriptures and History* (New York: Publication Office of "Our Hope," 1925).

49. *Megiddo Message*, 5 April 1925, 8. The boy who wrote the letter and his family were regular correspondents with the *Message* and frequent visitors to Rochester. The boy grew up to operate the family farm with his brother. When his brother died in 1980, he moved to Rochester at the invitation of the Megiddo Church. He died 1 March 2004. (Obituary, *Megiddo Message*, May/June 2004, 13.)

50. *Megiddo Message*, 16 March 1930, 9.

51. *Megiddo Message*, 22 October 1933, 9.

52. *Megiddo Message*, 9 December 1928, 9.

53. *Megiddo Message*, 12 July 1936, 9. "Russell" refers to Charles Taze Russell, one of the founders of Jehovah's Witnesses; Harry Emerson Fosdick was a popular liberal preacher and radio personality who is probably best remembered as the author of the popular hymn, "God of Grace and God of Glory."

54. *Megiddo Message*, 14 June 1925, 7. The following issue reported that 127 names had been added to the list of subscribers.

55. *Megiddo Message*, 15 April 1928, 9; 25 November 1928; 6 November 1932, 9.

56. *Megiddo Message*, 5 October 1941, 5–6.

57. *Megiddo Message*, 9 October 1943, 9. This pamphlet apparently had some enduring value. In 1951 a woman from Manatee, Florida, wrote that she had found a copy of it "on the roadside" and requested a dozen copies of the tract "to send to some of the well-intentioned 'blind leaders of the blind.'" *Megiddo Message*, 7 July 1951, 9.

58. *Megiddo Message*, 30 November 1957, 2.

59. *Megiddo Message*, 12 November 1960, 2.

60. *Megiddo Message*, 22 November 1941, 9.

61. For example, in a letter to the *Message* that was published in the 29 October 1922 issue, a reader from Sedan, Kansas, wrote, "We are enclosing [a] money order for $11.50, which is our tithes for September, we expect to send them each month if the Lord permits." Other letters from readers who sent tithes to the Mission appear in 24 May 1931, 15 January 1944, and 26 August 1944 issues of the *Message*.

62. The obituary and funeral description for Anna Mary Martin, who had died in Missouri, occupied nearly an entire page of the 12 August 1917 issue.

63. *Megiddo Message*, 12 February 1933, 9. On the same page is an obituary for a reader from Louisiana.

64. Kate Scott (obituary), *Megiddo Message*, 13 May 1939, 8.

65. Mora W. Kelly (obituary), *Megiddo Message*, 14 September 1940, 9. A family of sixteen moved from Canada to the Mission shortly after World War II. Another Canadian family moved to Rochester in 1956. Others moved in family groups from Iowa, New Jersey, and Oregon.

66. The causes of the split are unclear. Current members tend to attribute it to lifestyle issues, such as whether or not to allow males and females to swim together. This may well have been a factor since several new families had joined the Church just prior to the split and many of those families, along with several longtime members, left at the time. However, a power struggle in the face of the declining health of Pastor Percy Thatcher, who died later that year, cannot be ruled out as a cause. Many of the few families with young children left the Church at the time of the split. A small student population and the expenditure required to bring the Megiddo's school up to state standards led to the closing of the school shortly after the split. This may have been a factor in discouraging additional families from joining the community. For information about the split and legal matters in which the Megiddos were involved, see Gari-Anne Patzwald, *Waiting for Elijah* (Knoxville: University of Tennessee Press, 2002), 143–63.

67. However, as late as the July 1965 issue, a writer from Russellville, Arkansas, identified himself as a "new member of the Megiddo Progressives."

68. *Megiddo Message,* January 1967, 2.

69. The Megiddos do not watch television and listen only to what they consider to be edifying radio programs (e.g., classical music). They do not read fiction and they read newspapers and magazines highly selectively. However, they are aware of the influence of the broadcast and print media on the general public and since the 1970s have often addressed the negative aspects of this influence in the pages of the *Message.*

70. In an online union list of serials, 169 libraries are listed as having the magazine, but of those that report holdings, 3 no longer receive it, and 47 keep issues for a year or less. WorldCat Union List of Serials (accessed 30 August 2007).

"Is This We Have among Us Here a Jew?"

The Hillel Review *and Jewish Identity at the University of Wisconsin, 1925–31*

JONATHAN Z. S. POLLACK

In March 1925 a new student-produced periodical appeared at the University of Wisconsin, designed to "awaken a greater interest, a more active participation, a more sincere and determined effort on the part of the student community to further all things Jewish." The *Hillel Review*,[1] which would publish for the next thirty-six years, defined "all things Jewish" as "cultural Judaism" at Wisconsin. Examples of this "cultural Judaism" in this first year included lectures by visiting rabbis and Wisconsin professors, purely social functions like dances and teas, a non-credit course in early Jewish history and philosophy, discussion groups on current events, and student-produced plays. *Hillel Review*'s main function, initially, was to publicize these events.[2]

Over the next six years, the *Hillel Review*'s definition of "Jewish culture" expanded to include religious life and Zionism, two other major components of what contemporary scholars, and even 1920s Jewish leaders, considered the main building blocks of Jewish identity. The concept of Jewishness as a culture appealed to Jews around the world who had come to question orthodox Judaism but bristled at the anti-semitic[3] idea that Jews were a distinct race.[4]

Most forms of Jewish print culture during this time focused on one of these aspects of Jewish identity. The Reform, Conservative, and Orthodox branches of Judaism published materials on religious practice, directed at rabbis as well as the broader Jewish public. By the 1920s most major cities had at least one English-language Jewish weekly, devoted to the social whirl of the communities they covered, along with publicity for fund-raising drives and coverage of the Zionist movement. The Yiddish-language press included a variety of periodicals, from socialist and communist newspapers to religious writings. Like other foreign-language newspapers, Yiddish papers served as agents for "Americanization," helping first-generation Americans make sense of their surroundings in a familiar language. Publications of Jewish lodges and mutual-aid societies, especially the International Order of B'nai B'rith,[5] sought to present Jewish ideas in a consciously American context, stressing the Jewish roots of American ideas as well as individual Jews' contributions to American society.

The *Hillel Review*, though, attempted to cover Judaism, Zionism, Jewish life abroad, and local Jewish social life in one periodical. Although there were still some Jewish students coming to Wisconsin who had been born abroad, after the mid-1920s the vast majority of Jewish students at Wisconsin had been born in the United States and attended American schools, so they were immersed in American culture. Too young for membership in any but the "junior" branches of Jewish mutual-aid and charitable societies, Jewish college students nonetheless craved the same kinds of social news that their parents read about in the Anglo-Jewish press. During the first five years of the *Hillel Review*'s publication, which coincided with the years that the chapter was led by Reform rabbi Solomon Landman, *Hillel Review* editors sought to reclaim traditional Jewish practice for college students, even when these ideas contradicted the ideals of B'nai B'rith, the Hillel Foundation's parent organization, or the Reform movement. As a result, the first five years of *Hillel Review* display a transition from a purely social Jewish identity to an identity more closely tied to religious, Zionist, and global Jewish concerns.

Inspirations for the Hillel Foundation

B'nai B'rith, the Menorah Society (a national Jewish debating society, explained in detail below), and the watchful eyes of college students' parents provided three guiding forces for the development of a Jewish student group that would address the social, intellectual, and religious meanings of Jewish culture at Wisconsin. These three forces came together in Wisconsin's Hillel Foundation, which gave its name to the *Hillel Review*. Wisconsin's was the second such foundation created by B'nai B'rith. B'nai B'rith's approach to Jewish identity was the base of Hillel's philosophy in the early years of the organization.

B'nai B'rith dates back to the 1840s, when German Jews had begun to settle in the United States in some numbers. The Jewish settlers who had fanned out across the country ranged from Orthodox Jews to nonbelievers. The founders of B'nai B'rith wanted to create a mutual-aid society in which Jewish men could associate with their fellow Jews free from conflicts about religiosity, language, or social class. To ensure this fellowship, B'nai B'rith published materials stressing its broad-ranging vision of Jewish solidarity, which would be accomplished by avoiding controversial topics like religious philosophies and Zionism. Controversy from the outside, in the form of a mob's lynching of pencil-factory owner Leo Frank in 1914, led to the formation of the Anti-Defamation League of B'nai B'rith.

The ADL took B'nai B'rith's version of a nondenominational, American Jewish identity and broadcast it to the general public. Although antisemitism was still overt and popular across America in the 1920s, many American Jews felt that the graver problem for the future of American Jewish communities was that the open nature of American society threatened to absorb all but the most superficial forms of Jewish identity. American Jews shunned the idea of returning to the ghettos of central Europe, but to traditionally minded Jews, at least those closed communities forced Jews together and made assimilation impossible. Assimilation seemed all too easy in 1920s America, despite overt acts of antisemitism that occasionally surfaced. To counter these dual threats, B'nai B'rith set up a college-student organization, using the B'nai B'rith model, at the University of Illinois in 1923 and the University of Wisconsin a year later.[6]

Before Wisconsin had its Hillel chapter, the Menorah Society had functioned as a multipurpose Jewish student organization on the campus. Jewish students who otherwise held various interests, ranging from debating and literary societies to athletics and journalism, joined Menorah to discuss issues in Jewish culture.[7]

Wisconsin's Menorah chapter had a direct link with the initial chapter, which had been founded at Harvard in 1906. Horace Kallen, one of those founders, came to Wisconsin to teach philosophy in 1911. That same fall, Wisconsin's Menorah Society began meeting, drawing an average of forty students per year. Although Menorah at Wisconsin, as elsewhere, tried to be a place where students might figure out for themselves the nature of "Jewish culture," many students did not seem to have an interest in that degree of intellectual work on top of their required course loads.[8]

Absorbed into Hillel as a committee by 1926, the Menorah Society made a last-ditch effort to attract students. Sending a mimeographed copy of a Leo Tolstoy essay on Jews in Russia earned the committee mild rebuke in the *Hillel Review,* where the editorial committee claimed that "it is doubtful that [students] will wade through a page or two of closely written, unappetizing mimeographed sheets," and in any case: "Most of us are quite fed up with opinions of ourselves; we have heard of our glorious history and our fine traits; we appreciate both our possibilities and our limitations. We are tired of being told what we are. Perhaps that is why we have not come to Menorah to Menorah's satisfaction."[9] Although on some level, Jewish students were anxious about their identities as Jews in the Protestant world of academia, they were not inclined to tackle those ideas in a particularly rigorous, systematic way. American-born, the sons and daughters of junk dealers, entrepreneurs, and professionals, the Jewish students who came to Wisconsin held the pragmatic belief that "Jewish culture" had to be broader and more inclusive than discussions of what it meant to be a Jew.

Left to their own devices, Jewish college students sought connections to other Jews in social fraternities and sororities. However, observers in advisory and parental roles worried about fraternities' effects on Jewish students' identification with tradition.

Louis B. Wolfenson, a professor of ancient Hebrew and Greek, also served as the faculty advisor for the short-lived Jewish Students' Association at Wisconsin, which was a student congregation of the Reform Union of American Hebrew Congregations. Addressing the Sholom Aleichem Circle, a Milwaukee Jewish literary society, Wolfenson worried that fraternities exacerbated class distinctions among Jewish students, which then compromised efforts at Jewish unity.[10]

Beyond the social stratification that fraternity life encouraged, observant Jewish parents had other reasons to worry about their children's religious observance and physical safety in the Greek world. As if to demonstrate that there was nothing particularly Jewish about Wisconsin's Zeta Beta Tau chapter,[11] the fraternity served shrimp cocktail, the definitive unkosher dish, as the appetizer for its first initiation banquet. More alarmingly to the campus community and Jews across the state, ZBT received unwelcome publicity in the spring of 1924 when a first-year Wisconsin student died from a previously undiagnosed heart condition after a night of drinking bootleg liquor at the ZBT house. The combination of students' disrespect for dietary laws (*kashrut*), Prohibition law, and basic safety made students' social activities seem dangerous to Jewish observers.[12]

Jewish parents' worries about what would happen to their children at college were not limited to violations of *kashrut* and the dangers of bootleg liquor. Jewish print media were full of cautionary tales of the ways that going off to college would imperil their students' ties to Jewish culture. In particular, the editors of the *B'nai B'rith Magazine* gave extensive coverage to these issues, in part to publicize their effort to create a national network of Hillel Foundations on college campuses. In a 1927 article, Los Angeles rabbi Edgar F. Magnin praised the achievements of Jewish culture but disparaged the way that Jews in universities had either become alienated from their culture or superdefensive of it. Magnin dismissed Orthodox Jewish students' upbringing in homes run by "exponents of a religion which is of the Ghetto type" and saw students claiming to be from Reform backgrounds as coming from homes where "the fire of the spirit had become so extinguished that the building had become a veritable refrigerator." In a short story in a humor column, a Jewish girl turned down by a sorority at a small Eastern college begged her father to "get rid of our outlandish name," so he obliged, changing the obviously Jewish "Levy" to the Welsh "Llewellyn." In another short story, two competitive Jewish mothers, trying to impress each other with their daughters' accomplishments in college, react with alarm when their daughters inform them of their upcoming double wedding—to two department-store clerks, who to them represented the opposite of the upwardly mobile law and medical students they had hoped their daughters would marry.[13]

Although these pieces all appeared in a journal designed to inspire pride in Jewish identity, *B'nai B'rith Magazine* defined this term in a rather narrow fashion. It was important for Jews to identify themselves with being "American," but that term was never clarified. Jews who ran from tradition altogether were derided as viciously as those who tried to preserve European Orthodoxy in the United States. Immigrant Jews' pretensions to wealth and status were mocked, along with the fitful attempts by other Jews to hide their backgrounds (one story features a subplot involving the protagonist's nose job, performed by a Dr. Nasalheimer), and traditional approaches to Judaism were disdained as well. Jewish peoplehood, if defined as simply being around other Jews, is taken as a given, and Zionism is simply absent.[14] These contradictory concerns, first expressed in the official magazine of Hillel's parent organization, became the guiding principles of Wisconsin Hillel's newspaper.

Hillel Foundation and *Hillel Review* under Solomon Landman: B'nai B'rith for College Students

UW's Hillel Foundation followed the B'nai B'rith model of Jewish identity most closely when it began in 1924. The organization downplayed religious observance and Zionism but stressed wholesome social activities with other Jews as the focal point of Jewish identity. Directed by Solomon Landman, a Reform rabbi who had previously served a congregation in Easton, Pennsylvania, the Wisconsin Hillel would function as the Illinois foundation had—as a place where Jewish students could participate in a broad range of activities in a Jewish setting. The *Hillel Review,* beginning in the second semester of Hillel's existence, followed this model as well, at least for its first few years. After not publishing for all of calendar year 1928, when Hillel members instead put out a literary magazine entitled *Hillel Quarterly, Hillel Review* emerged in 1929 as a publication reoriented toward a broader, yet more contentious, idea of Jewish identity.

In its initial issue, the *Hillel Review* editors proclaimed that Hillel was: "bound by no set philosophy of Jewish life. It is limited by no 'ism.' It does not seek to force any interpretation of Judaism upon anybody. It seeks merely to serve—to serve the Jewish student as an agency to express himself or herself as a Jew or a Jewess along whatever line that appeals to him or her."[15]

This ecumenical statement of purpose, though seeming to include all possible aspects of Jewish life, made it difficult for Jewish students with strong commitments to religious or Zionist movements to enter the Hillel mainstream. In 1925 Orthodox services received little mention in the paper, and the Palestine Builders, the university's student Zionist society, also received little notice. Students who identified with a specific "ism" when they arrived on campus saw their interests marginalized in favor of a broader conception of Jewishness.

The *Hillel Review* promoted visiting lecturers, charitable works, and social activities. A parade of visiting rabbis and university professors gave sermons at Hillel, as part of the Sunday morning services that Landman conducted.[16] The 12 January 1926 issue of the *Review* is devoted almost entirely to the Loan Fund Drive, a fund-raiser for Jewish students who were unable to get loans from the University. The Loan Fund Drive was one of Hillel's largest undertakings; under the leadership of one medical student were five captains, together overseeing a total of sixty solicitors, who had the goal of canvassing several hundred Jewish students at Wisconsin that year. Like similar loan programs in Jewish communities across the country, the Hillel loan program would lend small amounts of money to other Jews, interest free, in order to keep Jews from falling into poverty.[17]

Social activities were the primary focus of Hillel during this period, however. Students could come to Hillel for informal mixers twice per week, and students joined Hillel dramatic companies and debate societies. Fitting the then-popular stereotype, Hillel's basketball teams consistently dominated Wisconsin's "church league," a predecessor of intramural sports in which campus religious organizations fielded teams. Study groups, which met in the week leading up to final exams, were also popular activities in an academic arena where Jewish students felt pressure from their parents to excel, even though the general campus atmosphere was often hostile to intellectuals.[18]

Religious life in the pages of *Hillel Review* presumed that Jewish college students had come to find traditional Judaism irrelevant, and the *Review* promoted Hillel as a place for students to encounter a more modern brand of Judaism. For example, Hillel's weekly Shabbat services, following the practice in the more radical Reform temples, took place on Sunday, presumably to allow students to use the traditional Friday to Saturday night Shabbat to pursue the same social activities as other students. The focus of the Sunday service was generally a speaker, sometimes Jewish, sometimes not, lecturing on issues of national or Jewish importance. Although a few students wrote glowing praises in the *Review* for Rabbi Landman's services, other editorials point out that fewer than a hundred students, out of more than five hundred Jewish students enrolled at the university, attended Hillel services. Hillel also followed the Reform practice of ignoring traditional Jewish prohibitions against mixing meat and dairy dishes at the same meal. Hillel "cafeteria suppers" served corned beef sandwiches alongside cheese sandwiches as a way for students to socialize during exam week.[19]

In a development that must have surprised a Reform rabbi like Landman, Jewish students began to demand more orthodox options for observance. During the spring of 1926 the same Social Welfare committee that organized the loan drive began making arrangements for Jewish students to attend Passover seders and to receive kosher-for-Passover food for the whole eight-day holiday, if desired, from Madison Jewish families. That fall, Foster Schlutz, a transfer student from the University of Illinois, began leading Orthodox services on Friday nights.[20]

In 1927 *Hillel Review* associate editor Sol Tax wrote a poem that outlined the themes that the *Review* would eventually tackle under his editorship in 1929 and 1930:

> Is this we have among us here
> A Jew?
> This man—where is his hawklike beak I've
> Heard so much about?
> And he is poor:
> Can Jews be poor?
> And I was in the precincts of his home last night.
> The blood of Christian children—
> Where was it?
> On the table all that I could see
> Was pig's meat
> And milk to drink down with it.
> Have I erred, I thought,
> The Jew can surely not dwell here?
> But there he was, the man they call
> A Jew
> I walked into the temple
> On Friday night last week
> To see my Jew. I found him not.
> I asked him, and he said
> His father's God was foolish;
> Their faith, he said, was shopworn.
> Is this we have among us here
> A Jew?[21]

As editor of the *Review* in 1929 and 1930, Tax moved the *Review* away from being such an official organ of Hillel, its Rabbi, and the B'nai

B'rith and toward a more independent paper that welcomed controversies on religion, Jewish identity, and Zionism. As demonstrated in this poem, Tax took antisemitism as a constant obstacle that could not be overcome, so he sought to urge Jews to look inward and see how far they had strayed from traditions. To Tax and his colleagues, the idea of Jewish culture needed to understand the diversity of the Jewish experience. Even though he was often skeptical of Jewish leaders, Tax believed that religious practice was central to being Jewish.

The Reconstruction of the *Hillel Review:*
1929–31

After an experiment publishing a quarterly literary magazine and a short, irregular bulletin of Hillel functions called *Hillel-O-Grams,* Hillel resumed publishing the *Hillel Review* with the 12 October 1929 issue. In the interim, student interfraternity organizations that excluded Jews had received notoriety in Madison papers, and the fact that many Madison landlords refused to rent to Jewish students had made national news.[22] Responding to these events, editors Sol Tax, Leonard Einstein, and Ben Salinsky injected a harder-hitting perspective into the *Hillel Review* during the next two years. These years mark a clear departure from the nonconfrontational B'nai B'rith approach that characterized the *Review*'s first few years of publication. Although prompted largely by tense conditions for Jews on campus, the *Review*'s perspective also seemed to embody the definition of "Jewish culture" promoted by Mordecai M. Kaplan, a former professor at the Conservative Jewish Theological Seminary. While teaching there, Kaplan became disenchanted with Conservative ideology and in 1922 began the Society for the Advancement of Judaism, which became known as Reconstructionist Judaism.

Briefly stated, Kaplan's concept of "Judaism as a civilization" envisioned Judaism as something deeper than just a religion. Although Kaplan believed that Judaism could flourish around the world, he found the United States, as a country that stressed individual citizenship as opposed to citizenship partially defined by membership in another religious or cultural group (as was the case in the then-new democracies of eastern Europe), a difficult place for Judaism to survive as a civilization. Palestine, or even European countries where Jews enjoyed official minority-group status, seemed to Kaplan areas where the Jewish civilization could be reestablished more easily.[23]

Despite its new commitment to a broader conception of "Jewish culture," the *Review* in the 1929–30 and 1930–31 academic years continued some of the same ideas that it had from the start. Demonstrations of Jewish excellence, whether academic or athletic, at Wisconsin or elsewhere, received coverage, as did the activities of the Jewish sororities and fraternities. Like other Anglo-Jewish newspapers of the period, the *Review* covered visits by alumni and friends to Jewish students' homes at Wisconsin, as well as Jewish students' vacations and trips home. For a Wisconsin "fathers' day" event, for which students' fathers were invited to Wisconsin to attend classes and social activities, the *Review* stressed the virtues of Hillel and advised Jewish students to bring their fathers to the variety of programs that Hillel offered: social-welfare activities, drama practice, Friday night services, the Hillel talent show, and Rabbi Landman's Sunday morning service.[24]

The usual Jewish activities of the early to mid-1920s acquired a streak of introspection, prompted by the antisemitic incidents in the campus area. In the fall of 1928 a group calling itself the Apex Club held interfraternity dances off campus, so as to avoid what they considered the "obnoxious" Jewish students at the student union. One year later, after mailing in a signed lease for a room in a private dormitory, a Jewish student was told that she could not actually move in when she showed up with her parents before the start of the semester, since the dorm feared that too many Jewish residents would prompt Christian women to leave. These incidents, and the Wisconsin administration's lackluster response to them, sparked discussions among Jewish students about the dim possibilities of assimilation in a gentile world. These arguments then appeared in the *Hillel Review*.[25]

In stark contrast to the boosterish and publicity-based roots of the *Hillel Review* in its early years, weekly editorials from 1929 to 1931 grapple with the constraints on Jews during that time, and how Jews could best go about negotiating them. The idea of Jewish "identity," "peoplehood," or "culture" had an increasingly defensive sense to it. Constant reminders from *Hillel Review* writers that Jews should not be defensive or ashamed of their background tend to convey the opposite effect. In addition to the aspects of life that bound Jews together, concepts of "Jewishness" also implied aspects of life that separated Jews from gentiles. *Review* editorials encourage readers to be open with and proud of their Jewishness, but they caution against being defiant or defensive. Clearly, this would be a difficult road to follow; what strikes one person as "pride" could be seen by someone else as "obnoxiousness."[26]

The older concept that all Jews on a college campus would have a common set of needs that would draw them together also came under siege in these years. Due to the growing number of Jewish fraternities and sororities, class differences within the campus Jewish community became more sharply articulated than had been the case in the 1920s, much to the dismay of the *Hillel Review* staff. Fraternity rush week seemed like a microcosm of the snobbery that existed at Jewish country clubs.[27]

Harsh appraisals of Jewish women along lines of social class and status on campus emerged as well. The *Review* saw fit to print the views of a student who classified Jewish women on campus into four unflattering groups:

1. The conspicuous New York type of free-thinking girl who is supposed to be original in dress and manner. She smokes enough cigarettes to blow a smoke screen around her short, fat—not stout—and dark complexioned body.
2. The sophisticated, as she believes, presumably independent, sorority girl type, who knows nothing, and does nothing else except to try to impress others with her own self importance. She considers the alleged number of her father's money-bags sufficient reason to make her desirable for anyone.
3. The somewhat fine and fair non-sorority girl type, who appreciates the advantages of being independent but who is so conscious of her own fair beauty and few qualities that by attempting to make others realize them, she herself becomes despicable.
4. The non-sorority type of girl who is so ugly and void of personality that it is needless to describe her.[28]

On top of Jewish students' conflicted identities about how to express their Jewishness in public, Jewish women on campus also had to navigate standards of acceptable female behavior and appearance. To the writer, and with the consent of the editors who ran the insulting letter, Jewish women who were politically outspoken did not fit American ideas about desirability. Jewish women were expected to be well-off and attractive but to downplay both qualities. The *Review* received many rebuttals, especially from women who questioned if the letter writer had ever had an actual date. However, even though the original provocation ran under the alias "Eros II," Ben Salinsky, the *Review*'s executive editor, claimed that he could not run unsigned rebuttals. After a few weeks, Salinsky weighed in to end the controversy, and while he admitted that Eros II's letter was "too harsh," he also believed that "the four types were a fair analysis." Salinsky's main disagreements were that not all women on campus fit these unflattering portraits and that the letter writer overlooked the faults of Jewish men on campus. In the same issue, the *Review* also ran an anonymous rebuttal from members of a predominantly Jewish women's rooming house, which assailed the masculinity and attractiveness of "Eros II."[29]

These intramural arguments represent some cracks in the ideal of universal Jewish peoplehood. At the same time, though, the fact that this whole debate was published indicates a commitment on the part of the *Hillel Review* to encourage vigorous debate about what it meant to be Jewish on a college campus circa 1930.

Departing from the B'nai B'rith model of avoiding controversial subjects like Zionism, the *Hillel Review* from 1929 to 1931 discussed the issue in the widest possible way. *Hillel Review* contributors and editors discussed the Soviet Jewish "homeland" of Birobidjian, located on the Siberian-Manchurian border, thousands of miles from the traditional centers of Jewish settlement in the old Pale of Settlement. During this time, Madison's chapter of Avukah, a national student Zionist organization, became Hillel's Hebrew Literature and Culture group as opposed to functioning as a separate organization. Zionism was taken for granted enough among Hillel members that the *Review* published debates about Zionism in Palestine versus the idea of a Jewish homeland in the Soviet Union as well as conflicting reactions to the massacre of Zionists in 1929. Although Zionist issues received fewer column inches than athletics or social events, their presence in any form signals students' use of the *Review* to explore this aspect of Jewish identity.[30]

Contrary to the Reform vision of Jewish leaders like Solomon Landman, Jewish students at Wisconsin actually demanded more traditional forms of religious observance, and they used the *Hillel Review* to work out ways that traditional Judaism could fit with the modern world. Although traditional Orthodoxy held little appeal for the increasingly American-born student population, Jewish students wrote nostalgically about Shabbat observances at home, and many sought to make Hillel a center to carry on those traditions. In the fall of 1929 the *Review* published a series of flip commentaries on biblical stories entitled "First Impressions of

the Bible." Examining trends in Judaism elsewhere, the editors of the
"Jewish World" column praised rabbis who called for a more modern
approach to Judaism. In equal measure, the column criticized Jewish
community centers that focused on athletics and "Jewish culture" while
neglecting traditional Jewish education and religious practice. In March
1930 members of Hillel's liturgy committee managed to put these ideas
into action by abolishing the Sunday morning service in favor of a
student-led service on Friday night, which combined the Orthodox service with a choir, in the Reform style. Students also built an ark to contain the Torah and built a raised platform (*bimah*) from which to conduct the services. Hillel's small multipurpose auditorium would more
clearly be designed for religious services.[31]

Jewish students' attraction to the antiwar movement of the time
prompted *Hillel Review* editors to take a broader view of Judaism's role in
world affairs. Building on the role of peacemaking in Judaism, the *Hillel
Review* successfully campaigned for Landman to sign the Percentage
Peace Plan, in which people in countries around the world would sign
agreements with each other, as individuals, not to wage war on each
other. Landman answered the challenge by pledging Hillel's support for
the plan, beginning an uneasy relationship between Hillel and liberal
causes on the Wisconsin campus.[32]

The Transformation of *Hillel Review*

In the six years from its founding to 1931, *Hillel Review* changed from a
publicity sheet to a serious forum for discussing the nature of Jewish identity on a college campus in the Midwest. Ironically, the paper's recurring
focus on questions of Jewish identity came to resemble much of the writing in the *Menorah Journal*, the official publication of the less popular debating society that Hillel absorbed early in its presence at Wisconsin.

Although the definitions of desirable and undesirable characteristics
of Jews, and the question if all Jews shared any identifiable characteristics, remained constant, there is no question that the students who produced the *Review* brought a more traditional brand of Judaism to the
campus. The *Review* also broke with B'nai B'rith practice in its spirited
defense of Zionism and through the space it provided to writers who
took firm stands on other controversial subjects.

Perhaps persuaded by the *Review*'s love of controversy, and its less-than-enthusiastic treatment of Reform Judaism, Solomon Landman stepped down as Wisconsin Hillel director in 1931. His replacement, Max Kadushin, had received his rabbinical training at the Jewish Theological Seminary. There Kadushin studied with Mordecai Kaplan and became one of his early admirers. While at Wisconsin, Kadushin built on Kaplan's works and published his idea of "organic Judaism," which sees Zionism and traditional Judaism at the core of any concept of a more general "Jewish culture." Although Kadushin's ideas were popular at Wisconsin, measured in student demands for classes in Hebrew language, Talmud, and Kabbalah, students on the *Review* had already laid the groundwork for this conception of Judaism in the years before Kadushin became the Hillel director. By 1931 students had come to realize that controversy and tradition were critical aspects of Jewish identity for college students, and they shaped their newspaper to reflect that reality.

Notes

1. Named for the great sage of ancient Israel.
2. *Hillel Review* 1, no. 1 (12 March 1925): 2.
3. Although often rendered "anti-Semitic," the earlier usage implies that there is such thing as a "Semitic race."
4. On the evolving concept of Jewish identity during this period, see Seth Korelitz, "The Menorah Idea: From Religion to Culture, From Race to Ethnicity," *American Jewish History* 85, no. 1 (March 1997): 75–100; Mitchell B. Hart, *Social Science and the Politics of Modern Jewish Identity* (Stanford, CA: Stanford University Press, 2000), 139–68; William Toll, "Horace M. Kallen: Pluralism and American Jewish Identity," *American Jewish History* 85, no. 1 (March 1997): 57–74.
5. Hebrew for "Sons of the Covenant."
6. For a good history of the B'nai B'rith, see Deborah Dash Moore, *B'nai B'rith and the Challenge of Ethnic Leadership* (Albany: SUNY Press, 1982), esp. 135–51 for information on the early relationship between B'nai B'rith and Hillel. Popular Jewish fiction dealt with the rock-and-a-hard-place nature of anti-semitism and openness; for an example set in a city based on Madison, see Elias Tobenkin, *God of Might* (New York: Minton, Balch, 1925). For the roots of the Illinois Hillel, see Winton U. Solberg, "The Early Years of the Jewish Presence at the University of Illinois," *Religion and American Culture* 2, no. 2 (1992): 215–45.

7. Information on the other activities of Menorah members came from the Wisconsin *Badger* yearbooks, 1912–27, University of Wisconsin Archives (hereafter, UW Archives).

8. For more on Kallen's role in founding Menorah, see Lauren B. Strauss, "Staying Afloat in the Melting Pot," *American Jewish History* 84, no. 4 (December 1996): 315–31; Korelitz, "Menorah Idea"; and Jenna Weissman Joselit, "Against Ghettoism: A History of the Intercollegiate Menorah Association, 1906–1930," *American Jewish Archives* 30 (November 1978): 133–54.

9. Both quotes are from *Hillel Review* 3, no. 7 (20 January 1927): 2. For another example of Menorah's lukewarm reception once a Hillel Foundation appeared, see Solberg, "Early Years of the Jewish Presence," 228–32.

10. "Prof. Wolfenson Describes Jewish Student Life at University of Wisconsin," *Wisconsin Jewish Chronicle*, 8 September 1922, 1, 4.

11. Zeta Beta Tau (ZBT) is the oldest historically Jewish fraternity, founded in 1898.

12. The menu for Alpha Kappa of Zeta Beta Tau Initiation Banquet, 24 March 1923, appears in Jacob E. Altschuler scrapbooks, vol. 4, UW Archives; a full report on the death of Stanley W. Rosenthal, including the subsequent ZBT-imposed suspension of the chapter members involved, appears in Division of Student Affairs, Office of Dean of Student Affairs, General Correspondence Files, 1920–1945 (Scott H. Goodnight), series 19/2/1–3, box 10, Zeta Beta Tau folder, UW Archives.

13. Edgar F. Magnin, "The Problem of the Jewish University Student," *B'nai B'rith Magazine* 41, no. 4 (January 1927): 159; Urva Porah, "Thinking Aloud," *B'nai B'rith Magazine* 42, no. 4 (January 1928): 91; Esther Morris, "The Best Laid Plans," *B'nai B'rith Magazine* 44, no. 5 (February 1930): 184–85, 194.

14. Porah, "Thinking Aloud," 91.

15. *Hillel Review* 1, no. 1 (12 March 1925): 2.

16. Holding Shabbat services on Sunday in order to boost attendance, especially among young people, was common in Reform congregations in the nineteenth century. By the 1920s, however, only the most radical Reform temples held such services. See Kerry M. Olitzky, "The Sunday-Sabbath Movement in American Reform Judaism: Strategy or Evolution?" *American Jewish Archives* 34, no. 1 (April 1982): 75–88.

17. *Hillel Review* 2, no. 6 (12 January 1926), 3.

18. For a national perspective on the Jewish nature of basketball at this time, see Peter Levine, *Ellis Island to Ebbets Field: Sport and the American Jewish Experience* (New York: Oxford University Press, 1992), 26–51. For examples of Wisconsin coverage, see *Hillel Review* 2, no. 13 (29 May 1926): 2, 3; *Hillel Review* no. 1 (9 October 1926): 1, 4; *Hillel Review* 3, no. 7 (20 January 1927): 4.

19. *Hillel Review* 2, no. 13 (29 May 1926): 2; Leslie G. Keller, Max Kossoris, and H. A. Kovenock, "Is Hillel Accomplishing its Purpose?" *Hillel Review* 2, no. 13 (29 May 1926): 7; *Hillel Review* 3, no. 2 (26 October 1926): 2.

20. *Hillel Review* 2, no. 13 (29 May 1926): 7; *Hillel Review* 3, no. 2 (9 October 1926): 4.

21. S. T. [Sol Tax], "Is This A Jew?" *Hillel Review* 3, no. 12 (16 April 1927): 2.

22. For more detail on antisemitic incidents at Wisconsin during this time, see Jonathan Z. S. Pollack, "Jewish Problems: Eastern and Western Jewish Identities in Conflict at the University of Wisconsin, 1919–1941," *American Jewish History* 89, no. 2 (June 2001): 161–80, and E. David Cronon and John W. Jenkins, *The University of Wisconsin: A History*, vol. 3, *1925–1945* (Madison: University of Wisconsin Press, 1994), 119, 675–76.

23. Marc Lee Raphael, *Profiles in American Judaism* (San Francisco: Harper & Row, 1984), 179–94; Mordecai M. Kaplan, *Judaism as a Civilization: Toward a Reconstruction of American-Jewish Life* (New York: Macmillan, 1934).

24. Every issue of the *Hillel Review* for these academic years contains reportage on Jewish students' social activities. Fathers' day events appear in Ben E. Salinsky, "Editorial," *Hillel Review* 6, no. 2 (10 October 1930): 2.

25. A clip file in the B'nai B'rith Hillel Foundation papers, box 1, folder 2, documents the coverage of these events in the Madison and university newspapers. For a more detailed discussion of these two incidents, see Pollack, "Jewish Problems."

26. Luby Bragarnick, "Professor Perlman Considered National Economics Authority," *Hillel Review* 5, no. 2 (12 October 1929): 2, 4. Every page 2 editorial in *Hillel Review* from 19 October 1929 to 18 January 1930 (5, nos. 3–12) dealt at least in part with this same theme.

27. Leonard R. Einstein editorials, *Hillel Review* 5, no. 19 (29 March 1930): 2; *Hillel Review* 5, no. 21 (26 April 1930): 2; Ben E. Salinsky editorial, *Hillel Review* 6, no. 5 (24 October 1930): 2.

28. Eros II, "What Say You?" *Hillel Review* 6, no. 18 (20 March 1931): 2.

29. Ben E. Salinsky, "The Controversy," plus unsigned articles "Some of the Girls from 2 Langdon" and "What Say You?" *Hillel Review* 6, no. 19 (27 March 1931): 2–3.

30. Sam Rabinowitz, "Jews of Russia Are Suffering Great Hardship," *Hillel Review* 5, no. 2 (12 October 1929): 3–4; unsigned articles on editorial page, *Hillel Review* 5, no. 8 (24 November 1929): 2; *Hillel Review* 5, no. 11 (14 December 1929): 2; *Hillel Review* 5, no. 26 (31 May 1930): 2; *Hillel Review* 6, no. 4 (17 October 1930): 2; Julius C. Edelstein, "I'm Telling You," *Hillel Review* 6, no. 19 (27 March 1931): 2, 4.

31. "First Impressions of the Bible" ran in *Hillel Review* 5, nos. 2–5 (12 October–2 November 1929), always on page 2. See the "Jewish World"

columns, *Hillel Review* 5, no. 8 (23 November 1929): 2; and 5 no. 21 (26 April 1930): 2. For the switch to a Friday night service, see *Hillel Review* 5, no. 18 (22 March 1930): 1; and 6, no. 4 (17 October 1930): 1.

   32. *Hillel Review* 5, no. 6 (9 November 1929): 2; and 5, no. 7 (16 November 1929): 1–2.

4

The Print Culture
of Fundamentalism

Fundamentalist Cartoons, Modernist Pamphlets, and the Religious Image of Science in the Scopes Era

EDWARD B. DAVIS

The trial of John Scopes for teaching evolution in Dayton, Tennessee, has attracted much attention from historians in the eight decades since Judge John Raulston gaveled the proceedings to a close at midday on Tuesday, 21 July 1925. Edward J. Larson's Pulitzer Prize–winning book, *Summer for the Gods*, one of the more recent studies, is undoubtedly the most heavily researched and wide-ranging. As Larson shows, the trial was originally intended to showcase the liberal religious views of several carefully selected Protestant scientists and theologians, before an atheist attorney from Chicago (Clarence Darrow) effectively destroyed any effort to project a positive religious message from the Rhea County courthouse. Another recent similarly titled book, Paul K. Conkin's *When All the Gods Trembled,* offers insightful analysis of the lively religious conversation about evolution among the self-styled "fundamentalists" and "modernists" who roiled American intellectual life in the 1920s.[1] Yet we still know surprisingly little about important aspects of the ways in which fundamentalists and modernists used religious publishers to disseminate their competing images of modern scientific knowledge. This essay begins to fill this gap in our knowledge, drawing on hitherto overlooked sources. First I illustrate (both literally and figuratively) how fundamentalists used cartoons in the *Sunday School Times* to demonize evolution. Then I describe how modernist scientists and clergy defended evolution and advanced their own theological interpretations of science in a widely distributed series of pamphlets on "Science and Religion," published by the Divinity School at the University of Chicago.

In order to understand fundamentalist cartoons, we must first understand what fundamentalism was about. Some of the ideas associated with the movement have their roots in the nineteenth century, but the word "fundamentalist" itself was not used in print until 1 July 1920, when it was defined by Curtis Lee Laws, editor of *The Watchman-Examiner*, a national Baptist weekly. As Laws used the word, "fundamentalists" were those "who cling to the great fundamentals and who mean to do battle royal" in their defense, implicitly but clearly in opposition to those liberal Protestants who sought to reformulate traditional Christian beliefs to make them more consistent with modern secular thought and culture.[2] As this definition suggests, "fundamentalism" is best understood as an attitude—the militant rejection of modernity in the name of religion—rather than as a specific set of doctrines to be defended, although doctrinal differences obviously motivated fundamentalists to take action.[3] This attitude was ubiquitous in fundamentalist publications of the 1920s and is literally illustrated best by the cartoon reproduced in figure 8.1. Drawn by an unidentified artist and published in December 1927 by *The King's Business*, the official organ of the Bible Institute of Los Angeles, it aptly depicts how fundamentalists saw the Bible coming under fierce attack by multiple forces of modernity. *The King's Business* often published cartoons—they used the work of at least three different artists between 1919 and 1925—thus using a medium that was rapidly growing in popularity.[4]

Religious cartoons of this type were probably invented by Frank Beard, the originator of the "Chalk Talks" at the first summer Chautauqua program in 1874. A cartoon he had drawn at the age of eighteen was published by Currier & Ives and used in the Republican campaign in 1860. Poor hearing kept him out of uniform during the Civil War, but he covered the Army of the Potomac as a cartoonist for *Frank Leslie's Illustrated News* and *Harper's Weekly*. After the war, with Thomas Nast and others, he helped to create the modern political cartoon and was known especially for the illustrations he made for Fletcher G. Welch's book about the Democratic convention of 1872, *That Convention; or, Five Days a*

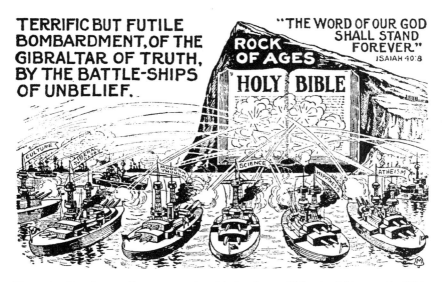

Figure 8.1. Fundamentalists, prepared to "do battle royal" for the faith, saw the Bible (here shown as the Rock of Gibraltar) as under attack by the battleships of modernity, including "hypothesis" and "science," both references to evolution. (*The King's Business*, December 1927, 800. The identity of the cartoonist is not known. Courtesy of Biola University.)

Politician (1872). Around the middle of the next decade, Beard began to draw cartoons and write poetry advancing religious reform, and his contributions started to appear in a Methodist weekly from Chicago, the *Ram's Horn*. He edited that magazine from 1890 until his death in 1905, and his temperance cartoons drew wide attention. Many of his images were collected and published in several books, including *Fifty Great Cartoons* (1895).[5] Beard's work represents a further example of a phenomenon noted by R. Laurence Moore, whose book *Selling God* documents many ways in which American religious promoters have adapted the "worldly" techniques of secular culture to their own purposes.[6]

Clearly Beard had struck a chord, for a new generation of religious cartoonists following in his footsteps appeared during and after the First World War. Among them were Urban Sereno Abell, Frederick William Alden (whose work includes the illustrations for Bertram Henry Shadduck's antievolution booklets), John Morton Espey, and Percy H. Kadey.[7] Probably the most widely published fundamentalist cartoonist of this period, however, was Ernest James Pace (1879–1946), whose career somewhat mirrored Beard's own experience. Born in Columbus, Ohio, the young Pace wanted a military career but failed to receive an appointment to West Point. Turning instead to art, he joined the staff of the Chicago *Journal* as a political cartoonist. In Chicago, he met a Danish man whose strong Christian example resulted in Pace's conversion, "like stepping out of a deep dark cellar into the blazing light of the noonday. Naturally," he added, as if it were the obvious result, "I lost all interest in politics, and lost my job. At once I set about preparing for Christian work, and offered some drawings for Frank Beard, famous cartoonist of the *Ram's Horn*." Beard liked one, added color, and used it on the cover of an issue, but Pace would not become known as a religious cartoonist for many years yet.[8]

Pace was licensed as a minister by the United Brethren in Christ Church on the first day of the twentieth century and married later that year. He enrolled at Otterbein College in Westerville, Ohio, affiliated with his denomination, and was ordained after graduating in 1905. Pace and his wife Cornelia served ten years as missionaries in the Philippines, where in February 1914 he experienced a crisis of faith after reading a review of a "rankly Modernist book fresh from the press of Chicago University" (which book he did not say). "I had not realized until then," he recalled twenty years later, "what an insidious peril lurks in this dreadful thing of Modernism, and how almost unconsciously it eats like a cancer into the vitals of one's faith." The ensuing spiritual struggle lasted several days and resulted in a profound experience of regeneration, in which "every nook and cranny of my being was every whit made clean," and "springs of water made glad the desolate desert of my soul." Ever since, Pace emphasized, "Modernism has had no more influence over me than to awaken a burning hatred of it." Within a year, Pace fell ill with an unidentified ailment that his doctors called "tropical sprue" and returned to America, where he soon recovered and for a short time studied Hebrew at Princeton Seminary.

Late in 1916 Pace was invited by another recent convert to fundamentalism, Charles Gallaudet Trumbull, to assume the role of cartoonist for *The Sunday School Times*, a weekly magazine Trumbull edited for nearly one hundred thousand readers in more than one hundred nations. Aimed at Sunday school teachers and superintendents, the *Times* provided detailed lesson plans two weeks in advance and feature articles on a wide variety of subjects related to, or impinging upon, fundamentalist Christians throughout the world. In about a quarter century, more than fifteen hundred Pace cartoons appeared in the *Times,* bombarding readers with simple, powerful images of salvation and other aspects of fundamentalism, including all the important parts of the antievolutionist message that William Jennings Bryan, William Bell Riley, and other fundamentalist leaders were beginning to preach.[9] Although most of Pace's cartoons appeared in the *Sunday School Times,* some also appeared in several other religious magazines, including (among others) *The King's Business, The Religious Telescope, The Christian Worker's Magazine* and its successor, the *Moody Bible Institute Monthly* (Pace directed the missionary course at Moody from 1917 to 1922). Hundreds of Pace's cartoons were converted into colored lantern slides for lectures he gave at Bible conferences; they were also rented or sold for use in churches. By 1932, twenty sets of thirty to forty slides each were available, including several containing images attacking evolution.[10] As a further way of disseminating Pace's art years after his death, the Faithful Words Publishing Company of St. Louis sold calendars featuring his images in the 1950s and early 1960s. Selected cartoons were published in at least six anthologies[11] and used to illustrate William Jennings Bryan's book *Seven Questions in Dispute* (1924), itself reprinted from a series of articles in the *Sunday School Times.*[12] Bryan himself suggested the idea for the cartoon that serves as the frontispiece (figure 8.2).[13]

Pace began to draw cartoons about evolution at least as early as October 1920, but it was not until mid-1922 that he picked up the pace, publishing five cartoons about science in twelve months. The first of these (figure 8.3) summarizes the standard objection that evolution is only a speculative hypothesis, a "science falsely so-called" that is headed for a collision with the facts. Another cartoon (figure 8.4) employs Pace's stock image of the college professor as bogeyman, stealing the faith of students—or as in this case, driving the ship of "popular education" toward the rocks of "infidelity," while a student is told to throw the Bible overboard. Several more evolution cartoons appeared in the years leading up to the Scopes trial, and following Bryan's death shortly after the trial, Pace kept the issues in the fundamentalists' mailboxes, continuing to hammer away at evolution on Bryan's behalf. His cartoon (figure 8.5) of a professor denying design and purpose in the universe, citing an address by Philadelphia neurologist Francis X. Dercum, makes one of Bryan's fundamental points about higher education: public education fails the test of religious neutrality, yet private religious colleges cannot receive public funds.[14] Perhaps his most striking image (figure 8.6)

Figure 8.2. "The Descent of the Modernists," Ernest James Pace. William Jennings Bryan suggested the content of this cartoon to Charles Trumbull, editor of the *Sunday School Times*, in January 1924. (Bryan, *Seven Questions in Dispute*, frontispiece. Library of the Author.)

Figure 8.3. "Leaking Badly and Headed for the Earth," Ernest James Pace. (*Sunday School Times*, 3 June 1922, 334. Courtesy of Speer Library, Princeton Theological Seminary.)

Figure 8.4. "Give Us All the Sail You've Got, and Heave the Ballast Overboard," Ernest James Pace. (Colored slide in the set "The Home," number 16, Billy Graham Center Museum, accession #81.1074. Courtesy of the Billy Graham Center Museum, Wheaton, Illinois.) The same image was published in the *Sunday School Times*, 19 January 1929, 39. When churches showed the slide, an accompanying mimeographed text was read: "It is not slander to say that popular education today has as its particular dogma the god-denying theory of evolution. There is no use for the Bible. It is thrown overboard and the boat is sailing straight to the rock of infidelity. Many young people come home from colleges and universities honeycombed with deadly doctrines that destroy the soul. And the home is responsible; the home must consider; the home cannot ignore the fact that God holds it accountable for these terrible conditions." (Billy Graham Center Museum, accession #81.1828. Courtesy of the Billy Graham Center Museum, Wheaton, Illinois.)

Figure 8.5. "Professing Themselves to Be Wise, They Became Fools," Ernest James Pace. (Colored slide in the set "Up to Date But Deadly," number 24, Billy Graham Center Museum, accession #81.1070. Courtesy of the Billy Graham Center Museum, Wheaton, Illinois.) The same image was published in the *Sunday School Times*, 11 June 1927, 367. When churches showed the slide, an accompanying mimeographed text was read: "Modernism is building the great institutions, giving millions for endowment, in order to teach the people the untruth which we read here. 'There was no such thing as design in the coming into being in the first place of living matter, and neither purpose nor design in the steps by which living creatures became more and more complex, highly organized and intelligent. In short there never was, as regards living matter, special intervention of the Deity.' Some of us know that is untrue, by experience as well as by observations. 'Isn't it a shame to endow pagan universities with millions to teach this, while Bible institutions and schools go begging?'" (Billy Graham Center Museum, accession #84.475. Courtesy of the Billy Graham Center Museum, Wheaton, Illinois.)

Figure 8.6. "Writing on the Sand," Ernest James Pace. (*Sunday School Times*, 27 March 1926, 192. Courtesy of Speer Library, Princeton Theological Seminary.)

shows another professor, this time tracing the ultimate materialistic claim ("All is explained by evolution") on the shore, suggesting just the opposite of William Paley's famous metaphor of a watch found on the heath as a clear instance of design.

Some of Pace's most powerful cartoons have obvious links with the anti-German propaganda of the First World War. A cartoon from 1922 (figure 8.7), the year in which Bryan began to call for laws banning the teaching of evolution in public institutions, shows Bryan as the hero of Verdun, refusing to let the German "enemies of the Bible" pass. Another cartoon (figure 8.8) skillfully employs the image of the *Lusitania* to alert fundamentalists to the dangers of higher biblical criticism—"made in Germany" by Christian scholars who, like Judas, had betrayed their Lord. In cartoons such as these, Pace was simply making visible the connection that most fundamentalists already perceived between German ideas, evolution, and biblical criticism. German intellectuals had used evolution to justify militarism, as documented in works such as *Headquarters Nights* (1917) by Stanford University biologist Vernon Kellogg, who was appalled by what he had learned from dinner conversations with German officers in Belgium before the United States entered the war. It was especially this virulent type of social Darwinism that led Bryan to come out publicly against the teaching of evolution in the early 1920s.[15] Furthermore, German scholars had created "higher" biblical criticism over the past two centuries, and the German model of higher

Figure 8.7. "Verdun," Ernest James Pace. (*Sunday School Times*, 19 August 1922, 495. Courtesy of Speer Library, Princeton Theological Seminary.)

Figure 8.8. "The Judas-2," Ernest James Pace. (Colored slide in the set "The Meaning and Menace of Modernism," number 10, Billy Graham Center Museum, accession #81.1071. Courtesy of the Billy Graham Center Museum, Wheaton, Illinois.) When churches showed the slide, an accompanying mimeographed text was read: "In this slide, a cartoon drawn during the late war, when it was common for German U-Boats to send to the bottom defenseless merchantmen. Prompted by the thought that modernism originated in Germany, we have labeled the submarine J-2 the J standing for Judas. Little cares he that many of God's little ones are on board the ship." (Billy Graham Center Museum, accession #81.1837. Courtesy of the Billy Graham Center Museum, Wheaton, Illinois.)

education had transformed American higher education since the 1870s. These facts only added fuel to the fire of Wagnerian proportions that was raging against "German" ideas among fundamentalists, who rallied around Bryan as their champion.

The role of visual images in helping to shape the figurative image of science is important and often overlooked. As Constance Areson Clark has recently argued, "we cannot understand the complex relationship of science and its larger public if we look at words alone," and her splendid study of the pictures used to popularize evolution in works by professional scientists helpfully illuminates the themes of this essay.[16] Pace's cartoons and lectures, no less than Bryan's books and speeches, bombarded Americans with verbal and visual images aimed at undermining the credibility and legitimacy of evolution. Lampooned in word and art as an unproved hypothesis that was actually unscientific, as an unfounded guess with dangerous religious and social implications, evolution was completely rejected by fundamentalists. The larger public was so sufficiently sympathetic to much of this rhetoric that their elected representatives banned the teaching of evolution in one state and nearly did so in others. How was the scientific community to respond?

In such a climate of controversy, it is easy to see why many scientists felt that some sort of *religious* response to this rhetoric was necessary, that political and scientific responses alone were insufficient. Many liberal Protestant clergy had similar feelings, so when the opportunity to enlist support from the scientists for their "modernist" religious views presented itself, they took full advantage of it. The occasion came in February 1922, when the *New York Times* published a Sunday editorial by Bryan.[17] Repeating objections he had been making in stump speeches across the nation for several months, Bryan argued that evolution was "only a guess and was never anything more," though scientists might dress it up as a "hypothesis." Furthermore, evolution was religiously dangerous, since it denied miracles and the supernatural, ultimately "leaving the Bible a story book without binding authority on the conscience of man." Those who tried to combine evolution with belief in God, Bryan claimed, would suffer Charles Darwin's fate and become agnostics. Since evolution was neither a proven fact nor religiously neutral, it should not be taught in public schools. These were serious charges, made by a well-known if aging politician who retained a loyal following in large parts of the nation, and they called for an answer. The

Times invited two prominent local scientists to respond the following Sunday, Princeton biologist Edwin Grant Conklin and paleontologist Henry Fairfield Osborn, president of the American Museum of Natural History. A third editorial, by popular Manhattan pastor Harry Emerson Fosdick, appeared the next week, followed two days later by Bryan's reply to Conklin and Osborn.[18]

At that point, Conklin and Osborn were already serving on a committee of the American Association for the Advancement of Science (AAAS) to counter the antievolution campaign. They began to think about how best to disseminate their ideas further, and they realized that clergy would be important allies in any such venture. For his part, Fosdick thought that the scientists needed to explain their ideas more clearly to the public. As he told Syracuse University geologist Harry N. Eaton, "If we are going to break the inflated bubble of verbose gentlemen like Mr. Bryan, I think that some scientists will have to get busy on popular propaganda distinctly distasteful though it will be to them." The opportunity for the scientists and the clergy to collaborate on this soon materialized, when Conklin learned that the American Institute of Sacred Literature (AISL) was hoping to publish some essays, including his own, as pamphlets for wide distribution.[19]

Founded in December 1880 by William Rainey Harper at the old Morgan Park Theological Seminary in Chicago, the AISL was originally called the Correspondence School for Hebrew. Over the next decade, as Harper moved first to Yale and then back to Chicago to become the first president of the University of Chicago in 1891, the school steadily broadened its focus to include not only the other biblical languages and their cognates, but also biblical literature, history, and theology; the AISL name, adopted in 1889, reflected these changes. Harper's role in directing the organization diminished owing to his responsibilities to the university, but the Institute's place within the university was strengthened and it flourished for four decades before the Depression brought about its decline and eventual demise in 1944.[20] The AISL produced course materials to provide continuing education to Protestant ministers and Sunday school teachers, emphasizing the conclusions of modern biblical scholarship and (in some cases) the very liberal theology of the Divinity School faculty. However, they did not publish any pamphlets until 1917, when they printed Shailer Mathews's famous attack on premillennialism, "Will Christ Come Again?"[21]

Even before Bryan's editorial was printed in the *New York Times,* the AISL had been thinking about how best to respond to the antievolutionists, but no specific strategy had been adopted. By early June 1922, however, they decided to invite Fosdick and Conklin to submit their editorials for publication in September as the first two pamphlets in a series of "Popular Religious Leaflets" on "Science and Religion." The series, which would eventually include ten titles, was edited by Shailer Mathews, dean of the Divinity School. Mathews himself wrote one pamphlet and Fosdick wrote two. The rest were written by seven scientists, five of whom served at some point as presidents of the AAAS. In addition to Conklin, these include Nobel laureates for physics Robert A. Millikan of the California Institute of Technology and Arthur Holly Compton of the University of Chicago, geologist Kirtley Mather of Harvard, physicist and inventor Michael Pupin of Columbia, astronomer Edwin Frost of Chicago, and naturalist Samuel Christian Schmucker of West Chester (Pennsylvania) State Normal School. Compton's pamphlet, "Life After Death" (1930), also included contributions from Mathews and Charles Gilkey, dean of the Rockefeller Chapel at the University of Chicago and former pastor of the Hyde Park Baptist Church, where Mathews and Compton were members and where Mather had attended while a graduate student.[22]

Despite the eminence of the authors, the pamphlets themselves today are rare and virtually unknown to historians. Small enough to fit into a shirt pocket, they have been easily lost or discarded in the eighty years since they were printed, and research libraries do not usually collect and catalog religious tracts. I discovered them while researching a debate about evolution in which Schmucker participated, when a copy of his pamphlet turned up at the Gettysburg College library (Schmucker's grandfather, Samuel Simon Schmucker, one of the most influential American theologians of the nineteenth century, founded the college and the Lutheran seminary nearby).[23] Inside the front cover was a list of some other titles in the series.

Forgotten today, the pamphlets were anything but rare in the years surrounding the Scopes trial. Printed by the tens of thousands, they were widely circulated, especially to people who played important roles in the national debate about evolution and the schools. Every public high school principal in the United States received copies of at least some of the pamphlets in the series, as did every legislator at every level of government,[24] numerous university chaplains, some thirty thousand

Protestant ministers, and more than one thousand scientists, carefully chosen to represent the elite of the American scientific establishment. At many research universities, scientists made them required course reading or distributed them individually to students; pastors and university chaplains made them available in their churches and chapels. At Dartmouth College, they were used in the first required course on evolution at an American college, taught by the prominent biologist William Patten.[25] In 1930, a full five years after the Scopes trial, religious organizations on forty-one campuses, including Columbia University, Cornell University, and the University of Pennsylvania, ordered AISL pamphlets in bulk.

Such a massive campaign of public dissemination was made possible by contributions from hundreds of people, including more than one hundred top scientists—men (nearly all of them were male) who were "starred" in *American Men of Science*, as the biographical dictionary of the AAAS was then called. Beginning with the first edition of that work in 1906, editor James McKeen Cattell placed asterisks next to one thousand names, identifying them as the "most eminent" people in their fields, according to a complicated system he had concocted to select them. This practice continued through the 1943 edition, with some new stars being added each time.[26] Those who managed to attain this sign of eminence were specifically targeted by the AISL to receive sample pamphlets with a letter soliciting contributions. In each of the annual fund lists for a twelve-year period overlapping with the publication dates of the pamphlets, the names of "starred" scientists are omnipresent.[27]

Shailer Mathews, the key figure in the project, undoubtedly knew that substantial support from leading scientists would impress the Rockefeller Foundation, a crucially important benefactor of science at the time, while leading to further links with the scientific community that might advance the modernist cause in religion. John D. Rockefeller had started the University of Chicago as well as its Divinity School, and his son John D. Rockefeller Jr. ensured that the Rockefeller Foundation underwrote AISL activities. The "Science and Religion" pamphlets were particularly important to John Jr., who agreed to match a percentage of all other contributions. They were also important to the AAAS, which contributed five times to the annual AISL fund. In 1924–25 and 1925–26, the two fiscal years overlapping with the Scopes trial, more than one hundred individual scientists donated to the pamphlet fund, including Compton, Millikan, Kellogg, eugenicist Charles Davenport, astronomers George Ellery Hale and Henry Norris Russell (AAAS president in 1933), surgeon William W. Keen, and paleontologist Charles Doolittle Walcott (AAAS president in 1923).

The significance of a publication project of this nature and magnitude should not be overlooked. Religious pamphlets have been printed for hundreds of years, and at times they have proved very effective—the important role of pamphlets for spreading controversial ideas during the Reformation, for example, is well documented.[28] Evangelical tracts had been ubiquitous in America since the early nineteenth century,[29] and in the early twentieth century conservative Protestants continued to favor them as a means to convey their criticisms of modernism to American Christians. The very word "fundamentalist" clearly referred implicitly to *The Fundamentals* (1910–15), a transatlantic collection of ninety articles in twelve paper-bound volumes, printed by the millions, paid for by California oil magnates Lyman and Milton Stewart, and mailed free to Protestant pastors, Sunday school superintendents, and other religious workers across the nation. Although evolution was not a principal target of the authors of *The Fundamentals*—just two of the ninety articles can be described as antievolutionary, and several prominent theistic evolutionists were among the contributors—modernist theology was in the center of the crosshairs, so it is not surprising that Mathews and the AISL would also use oil money to respond in kind, starting with Mathews's pamphlet on the second coming.[30] When they entered the fray over evolution a few years later, however, they realized that they could expand the audience for their message well beyond the existing list of AISL subscribers, mainly consisting of Protestant pastors in the United States and Canada, to include legislators, scientists, and the university students whom the scientists taught.

If the pamphlets were a central part of modernist efforts to combat the antievolution movement, they also brought theologically sophisticated views of science before large numbers of average Americans, views quite similar to those of some leading scientists and theologians today. Although two of America's best-known theologians contributed to the series, the most sophisticated theological position was articulated by one of the scientists, Samuel Schmucker. His 1926 pamphlet, entitled "Through Science to God," represents an attempt to construct a post-Darwinian natural theology—in itself an interesting feature—using facts from ornithology to argue for a type of theism. Having once studied sexual selection in beetles, Schmucker used hummingbirds to illustrate how evolution works by sexual selection. Then he derived a moral lesson from the fact that the males have only attractive coloration to draw the female, not protective coloration to hide from predators: "Here at last, in the bird-world as in the human world at its highest, perfect love has cast out fear," an allusion to 1 John 4:18. He went on to ask why beauty seems to increase with time in evolutionary history, and why the overall trend of evolution has been "steadily upward, through long, succeeding ages?" The answer, he suggested, is that the laws of nature that produced this trend are "not the fiat of almighty God," but "the manifestation in nature of the presence of the indwelling God," so that they are "eternal even as God is eternal." Apparently unaware that he was contradicting Isaac Newton's conception of gravitation, Schmucker concluded that gravity "is inherent in the nature of the bodies. It was not 'put there' by a higher power."[31]

Clearly, Schmucker's concept of God was not traditional. Casting aside all vestiges of a transcendent Creator, he constructed an evolutionary theism that made the world coeternal with a wholly immanent God. Ultimately, he made God indistinguishable from the laws of nature and the evolutionary progress they had produced. Thus he placed religious hope in the evolutionary process that had given rise to humankind. This process would, he argued elsewhere, lead inevitably to human moral perfection as we slowly but surely cast off our animal nature. Schmucker was therefore an outspoken advocate of eugenics, which he saw as the best means by which humans could carry out God's desire to eliminate sinful behaviors—even sexual promiscuity, the exploitation of workers, and undemocratic systems of government.[32]

Schmucker was hardly alone in this. Liberal Protestant scientists and clergy of the 1920s took to eugenics like bees to pollen—despite the fact that Francis Galton, who coined the word in 1883, had seen eugenics as a form of scientific religion that would supplant traditional religion. The liberals understood their own faith more in terms of social action, not orthodox belief, and they saw many eugenic reforms as morally appropriate means to spread the kingdom of God on earth. Liberal clergy were especially keen to cooperate with scientists—and to be seen as doing so—at a time when their conservative religious opponents were fighting tooth and nail against evolution. Fosdick, Gilkey, and dozens of other pastors served formally as advisors to the American Eugenics Society, while Schmucker and many other Protestant scientists offered explicit religious justification for their efforts to promote eugenics.[33]

In a fascinating book about modern American religion and science, historian James Gilbert notes that "neither science nor religion has had a stable and permanent definition in American culture. They continually shift in meaning and in their relation to each other."[34] It is precisely this phenomenon, in his opinion, that has made possible the persistence of religion in the highly scientific society of contemporary America. Shifting—and highly contested—definitions of both "science" and "religion" are most evident when their "relationship" is being negotiated. At such times the conversation between religion and science becomes particularly intense, and scientists themselves have been among the most outspoken voices in this conversation. Millikan's AISL pamphlet shows this very clearly. Its title, "A Scientist Confesses His Faith," neatly sums up the contents: a litany of testimonies from religious scientists past and present, to the individual and cumulative effect "that there is actually no conflict whatever between science and religion when each is correctly understood." Embedded within the litany are implicit, purely functional definitions of the key terms underlying his claim. "The purpose of science," he wrote, "is to develop without prejudice or preconception of any kind a knowledge of the facts, the laws, and the processes of nature. The even more important task of religion, on the other hand, is to develop the consciences, the ideals, and the aspirations of mankind."[35] Precisely the same words had appeared in the *New York Times* just a few months earlier, in a short statement about science and religion that Millikan had drafted with substantial input and encouragement from his brother-in-law Robert Brown, a liberal Congregationalist minister from Connecticut.[36] Forty-five leading scientists, theologians, and public servants signed the statement, including Millikan, Conklin, and Pupin. This statement was yet another way in which the modernists sought to influence public opinion about evolution.

In his pamphlet, Millikan admitted that his "definition of religion is in essence that embodied in the teachings of Jesus, who, unlike many of his followers of narrower vision, did not concern himself at all with creeds, but centered his whole teaching about a life of service and the spread of the spirit of love."[37] In earlier years, when they were both teaching at Chicago, Millikan (or possibly someone else in his presence) had asked Mathews whether he believed in God, only to get the reply, "That, my friend, is a question which requires an education rather than an answer."[38] One does wonder at times whether Mathews was even capable of answering this question directly; certainly he could not answer it simply. He wanted a new Christian faith to replace the old, the religion of Jesus without the Jesus of religion, and he counted Millikan and many other scientists among his allies in this manifestly religious cause. Harvard geologist Kirtley Mather, who had taken a Bible course from Mathews as an undergraduate at Chicago, was likewise attracted to Mathews's understanding of Christian faith. For more than thirty years, he taught a large adult Sunday school class (known as "The Mather Class") for the Newton Centre Baptist Church near Boston, introducing perhaps thousands of parishioners to a God who does not perform miracles, cannot act in nature to answer prayers, and does not provide clear hope of personal immortality to creatures.[39] When Princeton biologist Edwin Grant Conklin presented a similar view of religion to Philadelphians in the mid-1920s, he called his lecture "The Religion of Science," and the term does seem to fit.[40]

The modernist view of religion, as expressed by these leading scientists of the 1920s, contrasts sharply with that of the first American Darwinian, Harvard botanist Asa Gray. Like Millikan, Gray was also an outspoken defender of the "compatibility"—the word he chose—of evolution and religion. Unlike Millikan, however, the type of religion he meant was orthodox Christianity. Addressing the student body of Yale Divinity School in 1880, he identified "the essential contents of that Christianity which is in my view as compatible with my evolutionary conceptions as with former scientific beliefs," as being "briefly summed up" in the Apostles' and Nicene Creeds, two statements of faith used as touchstones of Christian orthodoxy since the fourth century.[41] Gray was not the only orthodox Christian of his generation who embraced modern science, but with the rise of fundamentalism in the 1920s people like Gray became almost invisible. For the most part, among American Protestants of the 1920s, the fundamentalists accepted orthodox theology while rejecting the "hypothesis" of evolution, while the modernists found harmony with modern science only by rejecting the orthodox view of a transcendent God.

The very liberal religious views espoused by the authors of the AISL pamphlets, such as Schmucker, Conklin, Mather, and Millikan, clearly contributed further to the polarization of opinion among American Christians at the time. As polemical tracts intended to discredit fundamentalism and to promote liberal religious ideas, the AISL pamphlets reinforced fundamentalist fears that evolution contradicts traditional Christian faith. A pastor's widow from Pennsylvania described the pamphlets as "poison," thought that Fosdick was "doing more harm than Tom Paine or [Robert] Ingersoll ever did," and saw Mathews as "making more infidels & causing our young people to depart from the faith." A representative of the Presbyterian Board of Foreign Missions, itself rent by theological disputes at that time, tellingly addressed his letter to "The American Institute against Sacred Literature." Although he appreciated Mathews, he saw Conklin and Fosdick as "not fit for young people." Professing "the greatest respect for all scientists as such," he denounced "such higher critics & half baked scientists who pronounced guessing hypotheses as real truth as if they knew everything. Real scientists are very humble but these so called evolutionists are proud in their apishness & perverseness."[42] Millikan's pamphlet provoked one recipient to return it with a comment scrawled on the front cover, amounting to what is probably the rawest response any pamphlet received: Millikan had "the wrong kind of faith," and the leaflet, nominally priced at three cents apiece, was "not worth 3¢ a carload, except for kindling or the toilet."[43] Letters from Tennessee pastors, responding to an AISL mailing from the end of May 1925, just as Bryan and Darrow were posturing for reporters in Dayton a few weeks before the trial, are no less pointed. "When 'Evolution' has 'saved' your own damned, hell-bound Chicago and Illinois," wrote a Methodist minister from Madisonville, "then come and save Christian Tennessee! I challenge you to publish *this* to Illinois, and Chicago." A slightly more sympathetic minister from Nashville noted that the type of evolution described in AISL literature "is most devoutly believed by all of our ministers, teachers, and Legislatures." The type of evolution that had been banned "is that which excludes God from the universe," such as the version found in *Compton's Pictured Encyclopedia*—published in Chicago, he did not hesitate to point out—which "accounts for the evolution of all material things from one original piece of protoplasm that was forever here, and this theory excludes God from the universe. Such books can no longer be taught in our public schools. Do you not think we are right?" Baptist evangelist J. E. Skinner saw the kind of religious interpretation provided by the AISL as providing "the best possible means" for the "utter defeat" of evolution. As long as evolution had stayed "in the realm of science there was no war upon it, and perhaps never would have been; but when it assumed a relationship in the religious realm and began its attack on Revealed religion, the war was on, and will be on till its folly is corrected." Another Baptist minister informed the AISL "that my state never did a more noble thing in her history." Tennessee "has only taken the lead in a great movement which will never stop until this damnable theory has been banished from our land." He reproached the AISL for "spreading a *theory* that is daming [*sic*] the lives and wrecking the faith of boys and girls. Your organization is a wolf in sheep's clothing."[44]

All told, the Pace cartoons and the AISL pamphlets provide new insights into the intense debate about the meaning of science and the nature of religion that took place among American Protestants in the 1920s. From popular publications such as these, we see just how the fundamentalists and the modernists both attempted to influence public opinion about the religious image of science in the decade of the Scopes trial.

Notes

I gratefully acknowledge support from the National Science Foundation (SES-9818198) and the John Templeton Foundation (ID#2047) for the larger project on which this article is based. Comments from Paul Conkin, James P. Danky, David Hollinger, George Murphy, Ronald L. Numbers, and two anonymous reviewers have been helpful. The opinions expressed in this article and the responsibility for any errors are, however, entirely my own.

This is a longer version of my essay "Science and Religious Fundamentalism in the 1920s: Religious Pamphlets by Leading Scientists of the Scopes Era Provide Insight into Public Debates about Science and Religion," *American Scientist* 93 (May–June 2005): 254–60. I am grateful to Rosalind Reid and Sigma Xi for permission to reprint portions of that article here. Earlier versions were presented at conferences sponsored by the American Association for the Advancement of Science, the American Scientific Affiliation, and the History of Science Society.

1. Edward J. Larson, *Summer for the Gods: The Scopes Trial and America's Continuing Debate over Science and Religion* (New York: Basic Books, 1997), and Paul K. Conkin, *When All the Gods Trembled: Darwinism, Scopes, and American Intellectuals* (Lanham, MD: Rowman & Littlefield, 1998).

2. "Convention Side Lights," *Watchman-Examiner*, 1 July 1920, 834.

3. Here I follow the persuasive interpretation of George Marsden, *Fundamentalism and American Culture: The Shaping of Twentieth-Century Evangelicalism, 1870–1925* (New York: Oxford University Press, 1980).

4. Six cartoons from *The King's Business* are reproduced in Marsden, *Fundamentalism and American Culture*. These are by at least three different artists, including G. F. Barbour, Grover Martin, and E. J. Pace. The monogram "M" in the lower right-hand corner of the image in figure 8.1 suggests that Martin may

have drawn that image also. Although Marsden briefly mentions one of Pace's articles on 217–18, the cartoons as such are not discussed in the book.

5. On Beard, see *American National Biography;* on his work for the *Ram's Horn,* including many images, see http://ehistory.osu.edu/osu/mmh/Rams_Horn/default.cfm (accessed 30 October 2007). Fletcher G. Welch, *That Convention; or, Five Days a Politician* (New York: F. G. Welch, 1872); Beard, *Fifty Great Cartoons* (Chicago: Ram's Horn Press, 1895). Our ignorance of the history of this genre is considerable.

6. R. Laurence Moore, *Selling God: American Religion in the Marketplace of Culture* (Oxford: Oxford University Press, 1994).

7. For information about Beard, Pace, and several early religious cartoonists, see http://www.christiancomicsinternational.org/pioneers_index.html (accessed 30 October 2007).

8. E. J. Pace, "The Christian Cartoonist," *Sunday School Times,* 18 February 1933, 114. I also quote from an obituary, "E. J. Pace—Christian Cartoonist," *Sunday School Times,* 6 July 1946, 610–12, which includes part of the letter Pace wrote to a fellow missionary, giving his testimony. Small folders on Pace are found in the Moody Bible Institute Archives and in the Office of Archives and Special Collections, Princeton Theological Seminary. I am grateful to Joseph Cataio and the late William O. Harris for locating these. A Web site devoted to Pace, http://www.christiancomicsinternational.org/pace_pioneer.html (accessed 30 October 2007), is generally reliable and reproduces cartoons from many of the publications to which he contributed. Alec Stevens, *E. J. Pace: Christian Cartoonist* (Dover, NJ: Calvary Comics, 2006) came to hand too late for inclusion.

9. According to the *N.W. Ayer & Son's American Newspaper Annual and Directory* (Philadelphia: N.W. Ayer & Son, 1920–29), circulation during the 1920s averaged 96,000. On Trumbull (1872–1941), see *Who Was Who in America,* and Joel A. Carpenter, *Revive Us Again: The Reawakening of American Fundamentalism* (New York: Oxford University Press, 1997), 25–26.

10. In the early 1920s these were rented and sold by The George W. Bond Slide Company of Chicago; see Pace, *Christian Cartoons* (Philadelphia: The Sunday School Times Company, 1922), 3. By 1932 this was handled by The McIntosh Stereopticon Company, also of Chicago; see the caption to the cartoon in the *Sunday School Times,* 1 October 1932, 517. The museum of the Billy Graham Center, Wheaton, Illinois, has a large collection of Pace slides in its archives.

11. *Christian Cartoons; Talking Object Lessons* (Grand Rapids, MI: Zondervan, 1942); *Life Begins at . . . ?* 2nd ed. (Findlay, Ohio: Fundamental Truth Publishers, 1936); *From Death Unto Life* (St. Louis: Faithful Words Publishing Company, 1943); and *Pictures That Talk,* series 1 and 2 (Chicago: Bible Institute Colportage Association, ca. 1931), mentioned in "The Lesson Cartoons in Booklet Form," *Sunday School Times,* 31 October 1931, 612.

12. William Jennings Bryan, *Seven Questions in Dispute* (New York: Revell, 1924).

13. For more information about this particular cartoon, see James R. Moore, *The Future of Science and Religious Belief: Theological Views in the Twentieth Century* (Milton Keynes: The Open University Press, 1981), 40.

14. Pace quotes not Dercum's address itself but a reporter's account, "The Realm of Faith," *New York Times,* 1 May 1927, E8. The address was published as Dercum, "The Origin and Activities of the American Philosophical Society and an Address on the Dynamic Factor in Evolution," *Proceedings of the American Philosophical Society* 66 (1927): 19–45, esp. 30–32. On Dercum, the physician who succeeded Charles Doolittle Walcott as president of the American Philosophical Society, see Albert P. Brubaker, "Francis X. Dercum," *Proceedings of the American Philosophical Society* 71 (1932): 39–48.

15. Stephen Jay Gould, "William Jennings Bryan's Last Campaign," *Natural History* 96 (1987): 16–26.

16. Constance Areson Clark, "Evolution for John Doe: Pictures, the Public, and the Scopes Trial Debate," *Journal of American History* 87 (2000): 1275–1303. Her point (1278) about our knowledge of the larger issues is worth quoting: "Historians have not yet explored the reciprocal influences of science and larger cultural issues in this [Scopes] debate."

17. William Jennings Bryan, "God and Evolution," *New York Times,* 26 February 1922, 84.

18. Edwin Grant Conklin, "God and Evolution," *New York Times,* 5 March 1922, 103; Henry Fairfield Osborn, "Evolution and Religion," *New York Times,* 5 March 1922, 91; and Harry Emerson Fosdick, "Evolution and Mr. Bryan," *New York Times,* 12 March 1922, 91.

19. Fosdick to Eaton, 11 April 1922, Harry Emerson Fosdick Collection, Union Theological Seminary, New York, Series 3C, Box 1, Folder 6. I lack space here to provide more details about how the collaboration came about; the larger story is part of a work in progress.

20. I rely here on the only history of the AISL, Kenneth N. Beck, "The American Institute of Sacred Literature: A Historical Analysis of an Adult Education Institution" (Ph.D. dissertation, University of Chicago, 1968), and on the information accompanying the finding list for the American Institute of Sacred Literature Records, Special Collections, University of Chicago Library.

21. Mathews, "Will Christ Come Again?" (Chicago: American Institute of Sacred Literature, 1917).

22. Actually, Compton's pamphlet was not officially included in the series on "Science and Religion," but it was originally intended to be part of the series and its content warrants that I treat it as if it were. I should also point out that Pupin was neither a Protestant nor a modernist; he was a Serbian Orthodox believer and thus a very interesting inclusion with this group. For a short

spiritual biography of Pupin, see Edward B. Davis, "Michael Idvorsky Pupin: Cosmic Beauty, Created Order, and the Divine Word," in *Eminent Lives in Twentieth-Century Science and Religion*, ed. N. A. Rupke (Frankfurt am Main: Peter Lang, 2007), 197–217.

23. I wrote about this debate in Edward B. Davis, "Fundamentalism and Folk Science Between the Wars," *Religion and American Culture* 5 (1995): 217–48. Schmucker's pamphlet is called "Through Science to God, The Humming Bird's Story, An Evolutionary Interpretation" (Chicago: American Institute of Sacred Literature, 1926).

24. For the claim about legislators, see the AISL report to the president of the University of Chicago for 1923–24, American Institute of Sacred Literature Records, Special Collections, University of Chicago Library, Box 12, Folder 2. Extensive information on other recipients is found elsewhere in the same archive. I will provide full documentation in the book I am writing.

25. See the letters from Patten to Ernest D. Burton, 8 April 1923, and to Shailer Mathews, 7 January 1924, American Institute of Sacred Literature Records, Special Collections, University of Chicago Library, Box 11, Folder 7 (Burton) and Box 12, Folder 3 (Mathews). For more on Patten's course, see Gregg Mitman, "Evolution as Gospel: William Patten, the Language of Democracy, and the Great War," *Isis* 81 (September 1990): 446–63.

26. For more on this antiquated form of assigning prestige, see Michael M. Sokal, "Stargazing: James McKeen Cattell, *American Men of Science*, and the Reward Structure of the American Scientific Community, 1906–1944," in *Psychology, Science, and Human Affairs: Essays in Honor of William Bevan*, ed. F. Kessel (Boulder, CO: Westview Press, 1995), 64–86.

27. Information about contributions to the pamphlet fund in this paragraph and the following paragraph has been distilled from many manuscripts in the American Institute of Sacred Literature Records, Special Collections, University of Chicago Library; a complete list will be provided in the book I am now writing.

28. See, for example, Elizabeth L. Eisenstein, *The Printing Revolution in Early Modern Europe* (Cambridge: Cambridge University Press, 1993); Lucian Febvre and Henri-Jean Martin, *The Coming of the Book: The Impact of Printing, 1450–1800* (London: Verso, 1976); and Steven Ozment, *The Age of Reform, 1250–1550* (New Haven, CT: Yale University Press, 1980), 199–203, including the extensive references there.

29. See David Paul Nord, *Faith in Reading: Religious Publishing and the Birth of Mass Media in America* (Oxford: Oxford University Press, 2004); and Candy Gunther Brown, *Word in the World: Evangelical Writing, Publishing, and Reading in America, 1789–1880* (Chapel Hill: University of North Carolina Press, 2004).

30. As Marsden observes, "One of the conspicuous absences in the series is of sharp polemics against biological evolution," quoting the introduction to *The*

Fundamentals: A Testimony to Truth, ed. George M. Marsden (New York: Garland Publications, 1988), 4 vols., no page.

31. Schmucker, "Through Science to God," 21–22.

32. For more on this aspect of his thought, see my essay "Fundamentalism and Folk Science Between the Wars."

33. Christine Rosen, *Preaching Eugenics: Religious Leaders and the American Eugenics Movement* (New York: Oxford University Press, 2004).

34. James Gilbert, *Redeeming Culture: American Religion in an Age of Science* (Chicago: University of Chicago Press, 1997), 9.

35. Robert A. Millikan, *A Scientist Confesses His Faith* (Chicago: American Institute of Sacred Literature, 1923), 8 and 16.

36. "Deny Science Wars Against Religion, Forty Scientists, Clergymen and Prominent Educators Attack 'Two Erroneous Views,'" *New York Times,* 27 May 1923, 1.

37. Millikan, "A Scientist Confesses His Faith," 16.

38. Robert Millikan, *The Autobiography of Robert A. Millikan* (New York: Prentice-Hall, 1950), 287. It is not fully clear in context whether Millikan or someone else actually asked Mathews this question.

39. On Mather's class, see Kennard Baker Bork, *Cracking Rocks and Defending Democracy: Kirtley Fletcher Mather, 1888–1978* (San Francisco: Pacific Division, American Association for the Advancement of Science, 1994), 78–81. For a statement of his views, see Kirtley F. Mather, *Science in Search of God* (New York: Henry Holt, 1928).

40. "Religion of Science very different from religion of tradition & Revelation," Edwin Grant Conklin Papers, Manuscripts Division, Department of Rare Books and Special Collections, Princeton University Library, carton 14, folder on "Religion and Science." To the best of my knowledge, the term "religion of science" was first used in the United States in 1860, and several books were printed between 1860 and 1925 with that very title. I plan to give a short history of the term elsewhere.

41. Asa Gray, *Natural Science and Religion* (New York: Charles Scribner's Sons, 1880), 108–9.

42. Mrs. J. Horner Kerr to AISL, 18 September 1922; John Lohriller to AISL, 23 September 1922, American Institute of Sacred Literature Records, Special Collections, University of Chicago Library, Box 11, Folder 4.

43. The defaced pamphlet is found in American Institute of Sacred Literature Records, Special Collections, University of Chicago Library, Box 11, Folder 8.

44. A. S. Ulm to AISL, 8 June 1925; M. R. Cooper to AISL, 4 June 1925; Skinner to AISL, 6 June 1925; H. McCormick Lintz to AISL, 17 June 1925, American Institute of Sacred Literature Records, Special Collections, University of Chicago Library, Box 12, Folder 7. See Guy Stanton Ford, ed., *Compton's*

Pictured Encyclopedia: to Inspire Ambition, to Stimulate the Imagination, to Provide the Inquiring Mind with Accurate Information Told in an Interesting Style, and Thus Lead into Broader Fields of Knowledge, Such Is the Purpose of this Work, 8 vols. (Chicago: F.E. Compton & Company, 1922), 3:1208–11.

Reports from the Front Lines of Fundamentalism

William Bell Riley's The Pilot *and Its Correspondents, 1920–47*

WILLIAM VANCE TROLLINGER JR.

From the very first English settlement, American Protestants have demonstrated great faith in the written word to convert sinners, inspire spiritual growth, induce moral conduct, create community, and transform society. The result of this confidence in the Word and in words has been that, for four centuries, Protestants have inundated America with a mind-boggling number of hymnals, pamphlets, books, Sunday school lessons, sermon aids, magazines, commentaries, and, of course, Bibles.

When it comes to the first half of the twentieth century, one could make a very good case that the most important publishing endeavor was periodicals. In fact, given all the Protestant magazines to be read, one wonders how any faithful Protestant had time to hold a job, much less go to church. It seems that almost every Protestant denomination published a periodical, sometimes multiple periodicals. In 1945, for example, the Federal Council of Churches' *Yearbook of American Churches* listed 431 denominational periodicals published by 136 denominations. While this list of periodicals is clearly incomplete—eighty-eight denominations failed to provide the *Yearbook* with information about their publications—the numbers are overwhelming.[1]

While the established mainline denominations had the largest publishing enterprises, small, recently established denominations accounted
for many of these periodicals. According to the *Yearbook*, the Missionary
Church Association, which was founded in 1898 and which had 5,000
members, managed to publish a periodical, as did the General Association of Regular Baptists, which was larger (22,000 members), but which
had been in existence only since 1932. And then there was the Pillar of
Fire, a holiness group that, under the leadership of Alma White, broke
off from the Methodists in 1901; it managed to produce five separate
magazines, despite having only 4,044 members.[2]

That these groups all published periodicals suggests the importance that even the smallest sectarian groups placed on producing and
distributing their own periodicals. In fact, and as I have argued elsewhere, the farther one proceeds to the margins of American Protestantism, the more important the publishing enterprise, and the more fren-
zied the publishing activity. Driven by a desire to convert others to their
understanding of the truth, determined to create and maintain community in the face of mainstream indifference and/or opposition, small denominations and new movements used print to survive and thrive in the
American religious landscape.[3]

One powerful example of the importance of periodicals for groups
outside the American Protestant mainstream can be found in the fundamentalist network centered around Baptist minister William Bell
Riley. Born in Kentucky in 1861, and trained at Louisville's Southern
Seminary, Riley—having served a number of churches in Indiana and
Illinois—assumed the pastorate of Minneapolis's First Baptist Church
in 1897. Within a few years he had transformed it into a "soulwinning
machine" (by the 1940s the church had over thirty-five hundred members). In 1919 Riley moved onto the national stage, founding the World's
Christian Fundamentals Association; during the next decade he spearheaded the campaign to eliminate the teaching of evolution in the public schools and to remove liberals from positions of leadership in the
major Protestant denominations.[4]

But by the mid-1920s the fundamentalist crusade had collapsed.
Riley responded by turning his attention to building a powerful grassroots network of churches, ministers, and missionaries centered around
his church and, particularly, his Northwestern Bible School (which had
been established in Minneapolis in 1902). Crucial to sustaining Riley's
fundamentalist empire was his periodical, *The Pilot*. Started as a

mimeographed student newspaper in 1920, the magazine had within a few years become a standardized, typeset monthly magazine, with Northwestern faculty members writing many of the articles. By the 1930s the magazine—now edited by the dean of women (who happened to be Riley's wife)—featured articles by Riley and other national fundamentalist leaders; with a readership in the thousands, *The Pilot* had been transformed into one of fundamentalism's flagship periodicals.

For conservative Protestants in the Northwestern orbit, *The Pilot* was an invaluable resource, providing clergy and laypersons with biblical expositions, devotional aids, sermon outlines, inspirational stories, and Sunday school lessons, as well as articles on politics, culture, theology, the state of American Protestant denominations, the fundamentalist movement, and, of course, the work of Northwestern Bible School. In all of this *The Pilot* was creating and sustaining a sense of fundamentalist community. Nowhere was this community more evident than in the reports and letters to *The Pilot* from Northwestern graduates engaged in "full-time Christian service." Ministers and evangelists in the United States, primarily in the upper Midwest, along with missionaries across the globe, wrote *The Pilot,* testifying to "their work for the Lord," and, in a sense, their work for W. B. Riley and Northwestern. As we shall see, these reports both confirmed and complicated the message that Riley and his editors sought to convey to their readers.

℘

From the thousands of reports made by ministers and missionaries to *The Pilot* between 1920 and 1947 (the year of William Bell Riley's death),[5] one very clear and consistent message came through: to serve the Lord meant a life of almost frenetic activity. The contemplative tradition in Christianity was nowhere to be found in updates from folks like Harry Westberg, who in November 1933 informed readers that, as a missionary to the rural reaches of northern Minnesota, he regularly "preaches in three conservation camps, has four regular preaching stations, conducts three Sunday-schools, and substitutes for other missionaries occasionally," for an average of "twelve services [every] two weeks." The idea of a forty-hour work week was alien to men like Leonard Marquardt, who in 1943 proudly reported from Blackduck, Minnesota, that he served as the pastor for "four Presbyterian churches"—leading "six [worship] services each Sunday," not to mention youth group meetings—while at the same time having charge of funeral services in "three other communities" and "correspond[ing] with eighty young men who are in the armed forces." Westberg and Marquardt were not unusual in their conviction that this activity on behalf of the Lord could be quantified, sometimes in quite specific terms. Describing his work in northern Minnesota in a 1936 report, Gordon Hansen observed that in a "field that extends over an area of about 2500 square miles," "regular Bible study services" were being conducted "in twenty different communities," 500 families were being reached by home visitation, and "sixteen Daily Vacation Bible Schools were conducted last summer with an enrollment of about 300 children." Traveling preachers accumulated particularly impressive statistics. For example, Albert Fuller reported in April 1939 that in the past five months he had "traveled 4,209 miles, distributed 425 Scripture portions and Testaments, [and] organized 2 Sunday schools" in rural Oregon. Two years earlier Frank McQuoid happily announced that he had just completed "an encouraging year" in northwestern Wisconsin, in which he "preached 155 services, made 209 calls, held 58 prayer meetings, and drove 9,169 miles in the interest of the Gospel."[6]

There must have been occasions when *Pilot* subscribers found these accounts—with preachers racing hither and yon, and with the daunting strings of numbers—to be exhausting reading. Still, most would have shared the assumption that all this activity was pleasing to God, and the hope that it would eventually mean success in new converts and revived churches. And in fact, many of the reports (particularly those from the United States) were indeed tales of success, in which the fundamentalist pastor—through a combination of hard work, correct theology, and God's assistance—had brought to life a "spiritually dead" church or region. Despite the passage of decades, many of these success stories were eerily similar. In April 1924 Walter Bridge reported that while "the field [West Concord, Minnesota] was in a run down condition" prior to his arrival, his "preaching of the old time Gospel" had resulted in a threefold increase in attendance; twenty-three years later Von Elbert informed *Pilot* readers that while his Knoxville, Iowa, Baptist church "was in deplorable condition when [he] first arrived on the field, . . . now the Sunday school has increased from four classes with an attendance of thirty-five to twelve classes with an attendance of 127." But sometimes correspondents (perhaps with flourishes added by *Pilot* editors) presented more elaborate versions of the standard tale of success: "When the present pastor [Allan Williams] came to the field . . . there was very little activity for Christ. No church in the entire county sponsored either a prayer-meeting or a Sunday evening preaching service. Very few people were even concerned about spiritual things. The preaching of the pre-millennial, imminent, and personal return of Christ was unknown. Today the Baptist Church has a well-attended Sunday evening service and mid-week prayer service, and the past year the church had two-thirds of the baptisms of the Southwestern Association of Minnesota Baptists."[7]

While reports from missionaries outside the States often contained the same sense of constant activity, they diverged from the home-based reports in that there was much less emphasis on success in numbers of souls converted and churches "planted." As we shall see, the explanation may have been a simple one; in other words, fundamentalists abroad often did not succeed in the way that fundamentalists at home did. But these standard accounts of fundamentalists overseas made up for their apparent lack of soul-winning success with an emphasis on the faithfulness, steadfastness, and courage displayed by missionaries. The most dramatic reports—and there were quite a few of these—had to do with the heroism of missionaries in the face of war. The most dramatic accounts came out of the Sino-Japanese War and World War II. For example, Clara Nelson wrote from Shanghai in 1938 that, although her mission was only a few blocks inside Chinese lines, and she and her charges "heard the noise of the guns and artillery day and night . . . [and] watched the [Japanese] airplanes drop their bombs," it was "impossible to move, as we have one hundred fifty homeless Chinese girls to care for," and "so we trusted the Lord to protect us." This 1942 report on the heroism of Mary Laughlin, missionary in Burma, struck a similar note: "When fifty civilians were killed in the railroad yards . . . [in a raid] 170 miles north of Rangoon, with cool nerve [she] gathered up the wounded from the platform slippery with blood[,] calmed 69 children whose school principal . . . had been killed beside a railroad coach, wrapped bandages on the injured, and held flashlights while a surgeon amputated limbs and sewed up wounds in a tiny emergency hospital all the following night."[8]

Of course, the opportunity to display personal heroism was *not* the primary purpose of fundamentalist foreign missions, and when World War II was over the editors of the *Pilot* deliberately sought to refocus readers' attention on the primary task of saving souls: while "many . . . missionaries were killed and many were victims of the concentration

camps . . . , [the] *challenge* to the rest of us [is] to push out into these va-
cated fields" as soon as possible and "not wait till the enemy has planted
his tares."[9] In this instance, the enemy referred to was Satan. But correspondents to the *Pilot* made more frequent and combative reference to
specific earthly enemies, in the process reinforcing the notion—central
to the fundamentalist movement—that they and their readers were the
community of the saved at war with forces of the damned. Interestingly,
ministers and evangelists working in the United States and missionaries
overseas focused much of their attention on two enemies frequently attacked elsewhere in the *Pilot:* Catholicism and Communism. Regarding
the former, foreign missionaries angrily attacked, to quote from the January 1927 issue of the *Pilot*, the "Romanized paganism with its idolatry,
immorality and superstition" that, in places like Venezuela, had created
a populace "diseased in body and soul." While missionaries were striving mightily to bring the Word of God to these "lost souls," the Catholic
Church had responded by pulling out all the stops to make sure that the
people remained "in darkness": Garnet Campsall reported from Ecuador in 1931 that "an unscrupulous priest" had forced him to abandon
his "work among the Quichua Indians," while in 1935 Helen Brown
Carder told *Pilot* readers that she and her husband (missionaries in the
Canary Islands) were battling a propaganda campaign mounted "by
Roman fanatics and priests, who are destroying all the Gospel literature
they can find."[10]

Fundamentalist workers in northern Minnesota and elsewhere likewise lamented the Catholic Church's efforts to keep Slavic and other
immigrants in its thrall.[11] But they complained at much greater length
about the influence of Communism in these troublesome mining communities. As Bertha Needham reported in 1925, not only did the immigrants "boast of their infidelity and Bolshevism," but they also in-
culcated their children with "Bolshevistic ideas and we [missionaries]
bear the awful consequences of this propaganda"; put more pointedly
in a later issue of the *Pilot*, "the children are taught to ridicule the existence of God." But workers in the States not only encountered Communism in Eastern European immigrant communities: one fundamentalist
worker reported from Kansas City in 1941 that "Negroes in the United
States" had such little "knowledge of God's Word" that "thousands" of
them had been converted to Communism by agitators "who [had] received special training in Moscow" and who were "now engaged in our
country organizing atheistic societies." Still, it was foreign missionaries

who had the most to say about this great enemy, particularly those missionaries who were in China in the 1930s. As Gladys Lindholm saw it, the Chinese revolution was clearly a war against the Gospel: Wherever Mao's forces go, their cry is "'Down with Christianity,' 'Down with the foreigner,' and 'Down with the wealthy.'" For fundamentalists reporting from China, it was a struggle to explain to readers how Communism could be "triumphing in some parts of the [mission] field," even in places where churches had been established. Irma Day's cosmic explication was representative of how missionaries dealt with this issue in the *Pilot:* the "direct attack[s] of the enemy against our [Christianity's] forward move into untouched regions" has made clear to us that we are "wrestl[ing] not against flesh and blood, but against the hosts of wicked spirits in the heavenlies."[12]

Besides Catholicism and Communism, foreign missionaries— particularly those located in Africa and the Middle East—also focused on a third great enemy: Islam. In contrast with the *Pilot*'s attention to (sometimes obsession with) Catholicism and Communism, the magazine (and W. B. Riley himself) had very little to say about Islam in these years. In keeping with this lack of attention in the magazine, foreign missionaries portrayed Islam less as an active opponent of true Christianity (in contrast with what they had to say about Catholicism and Communism) than as a set of superstitious beliefs that held its followers in servile ignorance. Still, the result was the same, in other words, a host of people who simply were not responsive to the Gospel. As Clifford and Ruth Kencke reported from Nigeria in February 1941, "surely there is more hope for the raw pagan" than for the African who has "had his spirit deadened by the spirit of Mohammedanism." Fellow missionary Albert Teichroew elaborated on the point a few months later: While pagans of Nigeria "sit in . . . dark heathenism, there are far more results among them from the preaching of the Gospel, than among the Mohammedans who have adopted so many Arabic customs."[13]

A number of missionaries made much of the fact that Muslim women were particularly oppressed. To quote Maynard Caneday from the May 1928 issue of the *Pilot,* "the women here in Morocco" suffer greatly "under the crushing, cruel treatment of the Mohammedan religion," which regards them "as nothing better than beasts of burden."[14] This concern for the oppression of Muslim women was striking, in light of the patriarchal nature of fundamentalism. In fact, the *Pilot* itself was filled with pronouncements admonishing their female readers to accept their subordinate role, especially within the church. As Northwestern Bible School professor and *Pilot* columnist C. W. Foley said in 1931 in response to a question from two readers: "It is as plain as anything could be, that a woman is not to take the oversight of the church, or publicly teach or preach in the man's appointed place." Foley and other *Pilot* contributors pointed to the fact that there was no "Scripture authorizing a woman to take full charge of an assembly, and occupy the position plainly assigned to man throughout the Word of Inspiration."[15] There was practical reason for this divinely sanctioned hierarchy, given that women—Eve was but the first case in point—were "more easily deceived" than men, and thus much more likely to concoct and perpetrate "false doctrines." While fundamentalist preacher Mark Matthews made the case in unusually vituperative language in 1940, the general point was one frequently reiterated in the pages of the *Pilot:* the "female 'pulpiteeress' is an unscriptural monstrosity and belongs to the zone of ecclesiastical freaks."[16]

Somewhat paradoxically, at the same time that they were being taught that women ministers were unbiblical monstrosities, *Pilot* subscribers were also reading reports from women ministers and missionaries about their work on behalf of the Lord. As regards women working in the States, these reports were more frequent in the 1920s and 1930s, perhaps indicating that, by the 1940s, Northwestern had successfully trained an "adequate supply" of men willing to serve as rural ministers and evangelists. But throughout this entire period *Pilot* subscribers were treated to the accounts of the labors of evangelist Alma Reiber and song leader Irene Murray. Through these fifty-odd reports, *Pilot* readers followed Reiber and Murray on their travels from fundamentalist church to fundamentalist church in Minnesota, Wisconsin, Iowa, Illinois, Michigan, Nebraska, and the Dakotas. As Reiber reported in 1928, "our work has taken us to the little country churches, the city missions, and the larger city churches, but wherever we have gone we have found the need of the human heart to be the same." Sometimes the news included reference to their soul-winning success, even among adult males: "at Maynard [Minnesota] blessings were again showered upon the people and many found the Lord, among them heads of families."[17] Perhaps some fundamentalist readers found a way to square the articles on female submission with the existence of successful fundamentalist evangelists who happened to be women on the grounds that these women worked in churches for relatively brief periods of time, and thus did not have time or opportunity to "usurp authority" from men. But this argument was never made in the *Pilot*. Moreover, and as Reiber and Murray frequently reported, much of their work involved supplying pulpits for months at a time. For example, in the January 1943 *Pilot* subscribers read that Reiber and Murray "will be supplying the church [in Peru, Nebraska] for some months" while also "engaged in evangelistic meetings . . . in that vicinity."[18]

Not to put too fine a point on it, the editors of the *Pilot* made no effort to adapt the magazine's fundamentalist theology to the realities of women in the pulpit. Perhaps Riley and his fundamentalist compatriots were, at the end of the day, more interested in spreading the Gospel than in maintaining the doctrinal line on female submission. This certainly seems to have been the case with overseas workers. Although women other than Reiber and Murray reported to the *Pilot* from stations in the United States,[19] accounts of women missionaries preaching and teaching the Gospel in Asia and Africa appeared in virtually every issue of the periodical, offering what could be seen as an ever-present counter to the "male headship" message relentlessly preached elsewhere in the *Pilot*. In fact, and in an interesting contrast to their adamant refusal to publicly countenance women ministers, the editors of the *Pilot* never articulated a policy flatly opposing the notion of women serving as missionaries outside the United States. The failure to do so was probably due to the stark reality—evinced by the ubiquity of these reports from women missionaries—that, without women, fundamentalist missions boards would never have been able to fill their international openings.

Still, the *Pilot* editors did betray an obvious discomfort with the gendered realities of foreign mission work, best seen in the articles that employed appeals to biblical authority and male pride to induce men to become missionaries. The April 1930 article "Wanted—Some Real Men" was typical: "To whom was Jesus speaking when He said, 'Go ye into all the world?' Not to women. . . . Does it not make you [men] ashamed to think that women must go out and do the work that you have been asked to do?" Only slightly more subtle was George Brown's 1934 article, "Missions—A Man's Job," in which the author noted that "the missionary ministry of the Church . . . continues to rest largely upon the over-burdened shoulders" of women, despite the fact that Jesus "chose twelve *men*" as his disciples, thus clearly indicating who bore responsibility for "the evangelization of the world."[20]

More pointedly, there were admonitions from missionaries them-selves to men back in the States—that is, male readers of the *Pilot*—to fulfill their God-given responsibilities. Garnet Campsall's January 1931 letter from Ecuador included a straightforward appeal to manliness that was reminiscent of early twentieth-century liberal Protestant appeals to "muscular" Christianity: "If you can't stand the dirt, the fleas, the lice, the persecution, stay home. But if you want a real man's job with glad knowledge that Christ is backing you up with every move just get down on your knees and tell Him you are ready [to go]." But the most direct challenges came from women missionaries. Correspondents such as Signe Johnson (writing in 1940) were not subtle in their complaints: "on this stretch of territory [in Morocco] with its two hundred thousand natives there are five foreign women working at present, while many strong Christian men at home are cultivating their garden patches! Is it any wonder that this part of God's field (the world) is under cultivated, and the crops are poor?" Equally unsubtle were the two unnamed women who wrote to the *Pilot* in June 1935 from somewhere in Africa, lamenting that, while "our mission is crying for men, men, men, . . . they are not answering," which meant that the "gospel would never reach these people unless we . . . two weak women . . . preach it."[21]

There is a sense in which it is difficult to know how to read these complaints and admonitions. Did these women missionaries really want men to take over the work of foreign missions? Were they trying—by lamenting the lack of men on the mission field—to defend themselves against attacks by fundamentalist critics that they were violating biblical rules against female authority? Or—perhaps most likely—were they simply expressing frustration with the fact that despite all the verbiage about male leadership, women were the ones bearing the exhausting burdens of mission work in an alien land? However one reads these com-plaints from women missionaries—and it seems plausible that women readers responded to these complaints and admonitions differently from men readers—the salient point here is that the *Pilot* conveyed a real sense of lament about the numbers of women who were serving as for-eign missionaries (a reality ironically reinforced by their innumerable reports in the magazine) and about the lack of full-time Christian work-ers in general. These laments were not subtle: they were directed at the *Pilot* readers, that is, at the fundamentalist community itself. Most dra-matic were challenges from the missionaries themselves to fundamental-ists to give up their lives of comfort to go into foreign missions, including this striking example from Helen Brown, writing from Venezuela in October 1925: "I say shame, shame on the followers of Christ who care more for their stomachs, outward appearance, and luxury of pleasure than for the carrying out of His command and the salvaging of immortal souls." In addition to these laments about the lack of fundamentalist workers overseas, there were also occasional complaints about the failure of ministers to accept pulpits in rural America: "We see many small churches with closed doors, in communities where hundreds of children are without any religious instruction. What is the trouble? Are we preparing for the ministry men who are afraid of hardship," or have they been led "to believe that God always provides salaries that will provide luxuries?"[22]

We can certainly read these complaints about too few male missionaries and too few Christian workers in general as reflecting a sense on the part of ministers and missionaries that the fundamentalist community was failing to live up to its responsibilities to the movement. But it is striking how often these fundamentalist workers made reference to *their own* failures in their correspondence with the *Pilot*. While the periodical's editors worked overtime to present an upbeat, "fundamentalism on the march" narrative, the reports from ministers and missionaries exposed readers to some remarkably honest, occasionally painful, stories about the realities of life in the field.

While placing great emphasis on foreign missionaries' faithfulness and courage in the face of difficult, even terrifying, challenges, the *Pilot* carried surprisingly few reports about soul-winning successes. Sometimes missionaries were quite explicit about the fact that their work often had not resulted in many (or any) conversions. One wonders how faithful *Pilot* readers responded to Signe Johnson's candid 1929 admission that, while "I wish I could tell you about great results from the work done in Morocco," the reality is that "the stubborn walls of these Moslems" remain in place and "hence the harvest has not yet come"; or to Albert Teichroew's aforementioned 1942 report from Nigeria lamenting the lack of converts "among the Mohammedans who have adopted so many Arabic customs"; or Alice Schleuter's observation in 1940 from the Amazon rain forest of Ecuador: "[W]hen one looks at these Jivaros [Indians] it seems like a hopeless task to teach them very much, or to expect them to understand the way of salvation."[23]

But candor about difficulties and failures appears as well in some of the reports from fundamentalists working in North America. Sometimes these accounts concluded with the missionary bravely asserting that God "will work it out in the end," or that—to quote the aforementioned Signe Johnson—"the Lord will soon answer our prayers"; sometimes the reports lacked even a pro forma statement of confidence in God's providence. Not surprisingly, accounts of difficulties and failures on the domestic mission field spiked in the bleakest years of the Great Depression. All of the following appeared in the pages of the *Pilot* between 1930 and 1936: Reporting from Saskatchewan, Jalmar and Ruth Erickson sadly observed that while we "have put forth our greatest efforts," it has "apparently [been] without results. . . . Discouragement would inevitably follow were we dependent for encouragement on that which is humanly visible; but we have the assurance from the Word that it . . . 'shall not return void.'" Margaret Hendrickson used the same phrase to console herself: "Our work here at Orr [Minnesota] is chiefly among the Finnish people, a people noted for their unbelief and rebellion. It is very difficult and discouraging at times to bring them the Gospel when we see how they mock it and ridicule the idea of a God . . . but we have God's wonderful promise that 'His Word shall not return unto Him void.'" The Finns in Canada were just as unresponsive, as Rexford Smart discovered: "As far as I know, no one else has ever been in [this atheistic] community except a short-term missionary. . . . I do not feel equal to [this challenge], and it seems all others so far, though more talented than I, feel similarly." William Shillingsburg had a similar experience with the Chippewas on Minnesota's Red Lake Reservation: this "band of Chippewas definitely reject the Gospel, and, had their leaders power to do so, they would drive out the missionaries." Three years later Ralph Hill was there, and he confirmed Shillingsburg's sense of rejection: "After years of effort in this field, there is now only one convert." And Walter Radke had his own troubles in Missouri: "The work here at Logan [Missouri] seems to be progressing very slowly. . . . A Sunday School has been started several times but for lack of leadership it has failed."[24]

୬୦

For William Bell Riley the *Pilot* was a wonderful medium whereby the great leader and his associates could communicate with the fundamentalist network centered around his Northwestern Bible School of Minneapolis. For this community of believers—centered in the upper Midwest, but national in scope—the *Pilot* provided a plethora of written material. Most of the material contained in its pages—which included biblical expositions, sermon outlines, and Sunday school lessons as well as articles (often written by Riley) on the advance of fundamentalism in a oft-hostile religious and cultural climate—was written or closely vetted by the periodical's editors and was, almost without exception, "on message." But in the midst of all this information and exhortations from headquarters came reports from Christian workers in the field. The *Pilot*'s editors gave much space to news from Northwestern graduates engaged in "full-time Christian service." And these ministers and missionaries were clearly eager to inform their fellow fundamentalists where they were, what they were doing, and how God was working through them.

As we have seen, many of the reports "from the field" did reinforce the *Pilot*'s central themes: the model Christian engaged in constant activity on behalf of the Lord; fundamentalists faced formidable earthly and spiritual enemies; hard work and correct theology equal great soul-winning success. Yet, as we have also seen, some of these reports—especially those dealing with women missionaries and ministers and those (generally from missionaries working overseas or in particularly unreceptive communities in the United States) describing the failure to win souls—were at odds with the *Pilot*'s message. Sometimes the contrast could be quite jarring.

There is no question that the letters from ministers and missionaries published in the *Pilot* complicated what William Bell Riley and his associates were attempting to communicate to their fundamentalist subscribers. In keeping with the fundamentalist proclivity for military metaphors, one might think of these letters as missives from foot soldiers on the frontlines, missives that sometimes contained information that did not jive with what the generals were saying. But while these letters *complicated* the *Pilot*'s message, they did not, I would argue, *undermine* it. Yes, the reports from women ministers and missionaries suggested the possibility that they could preach the Gospel, inside or outside the States, as well as men; but in telling their stories, and in decrying the paucity of men in Christian service, they never directly challenged—and sometimes reiterated—the idea that men were the ones who should be preaching the Gospel. Likewise, while ministers and missionaries were surprisingly forthright in delineating their failures, suggesting a counter-narrative to the "fundamentalism on the march" motif, the fact is that they lamented not the failure of the fundamentalist message or God's failure to provide for them, but *their own* personal failure.

Some readers might have understood these "complications" to the fundamentalist message as discrediting the message itself. For example, some readers (particularly women readers) might very well have understood the reports from Alma Reiber and Irene Murray as giving the lie to the patriarchal conceit that God wanted men and not women to serve as ministers of the Gospel. But while this is a reasonable speculation, we cannot assume that readers, even women readers, made this interpretive leap. What we do know is that the letters and reports contained in the *Pilot* sometimes challenged, but almost always remained within, the confines of acceptable fundamentalist discourse.

Of course, it is possible that *Pilot* editors received but refused to print letters that explicitly undermined and not just complicated the fundamentalist message. For example, there may have been correspondence that called for equality in the church between men and women, or that blamed the failure to secure converts on the mission field on fundamentalism and its painfully narrow approach to the Gospel. This said, to make too much of alleged unpublished letters could distract us from what we learn from the letters that *were* published in the *Pilot*. These reports allow us a penetrating look into the hearts and minds of real live fundamentalist workers, in all their inconsistencies and discomforts and failures, in all their dogged determination to live up to what they understood as God's truth and God's calling. What these reports offer is a glimpse into fundamentalism at the grassroots level, beyond the rhetorical pronouncements of the movement's leaders.

Notes

I would like to thank Peter Thuesen and the anonymous readers of an earlier draft for their very helpful insights.

1. William Vance Trollinger Jr., "An Outpouring of 'Faithful' Words: Protestant Publishing in the United States, 1880–1945," in *A History of the Book in America*, vol. 4, *Print in Motion: The Expansion of Publishing and Reading in the United States, 1880–1945*, ed. Carl F. Kaestle and Janice A. Radway (Chapel Hill: University of North Carolina Press, forthcoming).

2. *Yearbook of American Churches*, ed. Benson Y. Landis (Lebanon, PA: Sowers Printing Co., 1945), 5–86. It should be noted that the denominational

membership numbers in this *Yearbook* were not always terribly up-to-date; the Pillar of Fire numbers, for example, came from a 1936 report, and may understate the membership by a few thousand. Of course, membership statistics for church groups on the margins of American religion are almost always inexact.

3. Trollinger, "Outpouring of 'Faithful' Words."

4. William Vance Trollinger Jr., *God's Empire: William Bell Riley and Midwestern Fundamentalism* (Madison: University of Wisconsin Press, 1990), 10–61.

5. Within a few years of Riley's death the fundamentalist empire centered around his Northwestern Bible School fragmented and collapsed, and by 1956 the *Pilot* had gone out of existence. For the purposes of this study, then, the year of Riley's death (1947) makes a logical endpoint.

6. *The Pilot* 14 (November 1933): 51 (Harry Westberg); *Pilot* 23 (1943): 219 (Leonard Marquardt); *Pilot* 16 (1936): 146 (Gordon Hansen); *Pilot* 19 (1939): 214 (Albert Fuller); *Pilot* 17 (1937): 247 (Frank McQuoid). For other examples see: *Pilot* 17 (1937): 115 (Peter MacFarlane); *Pilot* 23 (1943): 327 (Donald Haight); *Pilot* 26 (1946): 239 (Elizabeth Mills).

7. *Pilot* 4 (1924): 52 (Walter Bridge); *Pilot* 27 (1947): 146 (Von Elbert); *Pilot* 23 (1943): 239 (Allan Williams). For other examples see W. B. Riley, "Rebuilding a Baptist Association," *Pilot* 22 (1942): 311–12 (George Siemens); *Pilot* 24 (1944): 264 (Lois Thom and Cecile Clevenger).

8. *Pilot* 18 (1938): 276–77 (Clara Nelson); *Pilot* 22 (1942): 220 (Mary Laughlin). For other examples see *Pilot* 10 (1930): 317 (Jennie Wedison); *Pilot* 19 (1941): 242 (Mathilda Anderson).

9. *Pilot* 27 (1946): 47. This challenge was written in the context of a report from missionary Sylvia Cushing Sivag, who was "recuperating from [her] Concentration Camp experience in Borneo."

10. Helen Brown, "A Vision of a Lost Land," *Pilot* 7 (1927): 7; *Pilot* 11 (1931): 183 (Garnet Campsall); *Pilot* 16 (1935): 50 (Helen Brown Carder).

11. For references to the challenges of converting Catholic immigrants, see Bertha Needham, "The Harvest Fields of Minnesota," *Pilot* 10 (1930): 119; "Northern Minnesota—A True Mission Field," *Pilot* 11 (1930): 86. It should be noted in these latter two reports there was much more concern about Communism than Catholicism.

12. Needham, "Harvest Fields of Minnesota," 119; "Northern Minnesota," 86; *Pilot* 21 (1941): 210–11 (Eva Jantz Blevens); *Pilot* 10 (1930): 318 (Gladys Lindholm); *Pilot* 15 (1935): 233 (Irma Day). For other examples, see Esther Hokanson, "Communism in China," *Pilot* 11 (1930): 79; "The Japanese-Chinese War," *Pilot* 18 (1938): 294. The latter article includes an argument that, because of Communism, missionaries in China were at much greater risk than missionaries in Japan.

13. *Pilot* 21 (1941): 147 (Clifford and Ruth Nelson Kencke); *Pilot* 22 (1942): 355 (Albert Teichroew). For other examples see *Pilot* 15 (1934): 63 (Frank Shortridge); *Pilot* 9 (1929): 21 (Signe Johnson).

14. *Pilot* 8 (1928): 13. Josephine Bulifant reported from Nigeria that one of the tasks of the Sudan Interior Mission was "to rescue . . . Christian girls from marriage to pagan and Moslem men who would have made their lives one long misery." *Pilot* 15 (1935): 170.

15. C. W. Foley, "Have You a Question?" *Pilot* 11 (1931): 335; C. W. Foley, "Perplexing Questions," *Pilot* 10 (1930): 319.

16. W. F. McMillan, "Have You a Question?" *Pilot* 15 (1935): 143; W. F. McMillan, "The Question Box," ibid. 18 (1938): 255; C. W. Foley, "Have You a Question?" *Pilot* 13 (1933): 127; Mark Matthews, "Should Women Preach?" *Pilot* 20 (1940): 319.

17. *Pilot* 8 (1928): 13; *Pilot* 6 (1926): 12; *Pilot* 16 (1936): 246.

18. *Pilot* 23 (1943): 121. One year later Reiber and Murray were still at the church in Peru. *Pilot* 24 (1944): 117.

19. For examples of other women ministers and evangelists working in the United States who sent information to the *Pilot*, see *Pilot* 9 (1928): 17 (Myrtle Gage); *Pilot* 10 (1930): 183 (Sadie Busse and Henriette Rodgers); *Pilot* 15 (1935): 204 (Sadie Busse and Elsie Parks); *Pilot* 17 (1937): 153 (Merle Bunker); *Pilot* 19 (1939): 214 (Vivian Ditlefson and Harriett Gleason).

20. "Wanted—Some Real Men," *Pilot* 10 (1930): 196; George Brown, "Missions—A Man's Job," *Pilot* 15 (1934): 234 (emphasis in original). See also George Brown, "How to Interest Men in Missions," *Pilot* 17 (1937): 137.

21. *Pilot* 11 (1931): 110 (Garnet Campsall); *Pilot* 20 (1940): 275 (Signe Johnson); "Women's Position in the Church," *Pilot* 15 (1935): 271. For other examples see Margaret Reynolds, "India Calls," *Pilot* 11 (1931): 180; Mildred Dunbar, "The Russian Department," *Pilot* 27 (194): 278, 283.

22. *Pilot* 6 (1925): 9 (Helen Brown); "Workers Needed," *Pilot* 17 (1937): 291. In a particularly melodramatic example an anonymous author chastised readers for their unwillingness to become missionaries: "Is it nothing to you? Through what special merit on your part is it that you were born in America, and not in darkened, sorrowing Africa; that the body of that Chinese baby floating down the river or cast into the refuse-cart was not yours; that you are not committing suicide in veiled Thibet as a remedy for despair[?]" "Is It Nothing to You?" *Pilot* 4 (1924): 62.

23. For examples, see *Pilot* 9 (1929): 21 (Signe Johnson); *Pilot* 15 (1934): 63 (Frank Shortridge); *Pilot* 20 (1940): 117 (Alice Schleuter).

24. Ruth Genung Erickson, "Part of the Canadian Frontier," *Pilot* 10 (1930): 240; *Pilot* 10 (1930): 183 (Margaret Hendrickson); *Pilot* 13 (1933): 243 (Rexford Smart); *Pilot* 11 (1930): 86 (William Shillingsburg); *Pilot* 13 (1933): 316 (Ralph Hill); *Pilot* 16 (1936): 147 (Walter Radke).

5

Popular Print Culture and Consumerism, 1920–50

The Religious Book Club

Print Culture, Consumerism, and the Spiritual Life
of American Protestants between the Wars

ERIN A. SMITH

"Matters of the spirit are common subjects of conversation," asserted
Publishers' Weekly in 1924. "People may be heard discussing them in
crowded elevators, in restaurants, in subway trains or between the
acts."[1] The sentiment was widely held. Most cultural critics of the 1920s
agreed that Americans were undergoing a "religious renaissance" that
profoundly influenced the print culture of the age.[2] A new translation of
the New Testament was running in newspaper syndication. The front
pages were filled with the Scopes "monkey trial" and the banning in
Boston of Sinclair Lewis's novel about a thoroughly corrupt minister,
Elmer Gantry. The year 1925 was the much-ballyhooed four-hundredth
birthday of the Tyndale Bible, the first printed translation of the New
Testament into English, and the Church of England spent much of
the decade embroiled in well-publicized controversy over a new *Book of
Common Prayer*. Mass-market magazines like *Pictorial Review*, *Woman's
Home Companion*, and *Ladies' Home Journal* ran religious texts as their lead-
ing serials. The number of religious books published increased dramati-
cally, and religious titles—Henrik Van Loon's *The Story of the Bible* (1923),
Giovanni Papini's *Life of Christ* (trans. Dorothy Canfield Fisher, 1923),

and Bruce Barton's *The Man Nobody Knows* (1925) and *The Book Nobody Knows* (1926)—held top spots on the nonfiction best-seller lists, even outselling most popular novels.[3] In 1927 two trade publishing houses (Harper's and Winston & Co.) added religion departments. The same year, amid this surge of activity in the world of religious print culture, the Religious Book Club was founded.[4]

A mail-order book club modeled after the Book-of-the-Month Club, the Religious Book Club (RBC) was created to take advantage of the burgeoning interest of lay men and women in religious topics and to serve as a reading service for clergy and church workers. The RBC redefined "religious books" in extraordinarily broad terms—those "in which moral and spiritual ideals find effective expression."[5] Possible subjects included philosophy, history, contemporary domestic and international problems, psychology, fiction and poetry, some of which lacked an obvious connection to religion. For example, a number of manuals such as *Love and Marriage, Problems of the Family,* and *Sex and Youth* appeared as alternate selections. Occasionally, RBC editorial board members would point out the usefulness of such (secular) guides for ministers counseling young people or troubled congregants, or offer reassurance: "An atmosphere of religious and social idealism surrounds the book."[6] The RBC further muddied the sacred/secular distinction by experimenting with general interest ("wholesome," "idealistic") alternate selections.[7]

Shortly after the founding of the Club in November 1927, Dr. S. Parkes Cadman, the chair of the editorial board, explained its purpose in a *Publishers' Weekly* article: "The Religious Book Club is one more indication of the extraordinary interest in religion today. The undertaking was born in the conviction that hosts of men and women all over the United States are hungrily seeking for light on the great problems of religious life and thought. Such people are eager to avail themselves of the opportunity to keep abreast of the best insight and scholarship in the realm of religion. And it is a great mistake to assume that they are found only among clergymen and professional religious workers. The man in the street, who often seems concerned only with the stock market and the World Series, is really immensely interested in religion."[8] The RBC was the brainchild of Samuel McCrea Cavert, editor of *Federal Council Bulletin,* and his friend, Maxwell Geffen, president of Select Printing Company. Cavert and Geffen were inspired by a letter from a California pastor asking if the Federal Council of Churches (an umbrella organization of twenty-eight Protestant denominations) would start a reading service for ministers that would inform them of new developments in religious literature and make available the best such books. The Council declined the proposition, but Cavert and Geffen formed their own company modeled on the Book-of-the-Month Club (founded in 1926), which would "create a wider interest in religious literature" by each month sending members "the best new book in the religious field as selected by an editorial committee of five outstanding religious leaders of the country."[9]

The five original judges were distinguished leaders with significant ties to large, liberal Protestant churches and/or institutions of higher learning, and most were popular writers/speakers in their own right. They included Dr. S. Parkes Cadman (minister of Central Congregational Church, Brooklyn, and president of the Federal Council of Churches), Episcopal Bishop Charles H. Brent (formerly chief of chaplains in the American Expeditionary Forces during World War I and chairman of the World Conference on Faith and Order at Lausanne), Dr. Harry Emerson Fosdick (pastor of Park Avenue Baptist Church, New York, professor of practical theology at Union Theological Seminary, popular writer and radio personality), Bishop Francis J. McConnell of the Methodist Church (former president of DePauw University and president of the Religious Education Association), and Mary E. Woolley (president of Mount Holyoke College, president of the American Association of University Women, former head of the biblical history and literature department at Wellesley, and a member of the National Board of the YWCA). Each brought his or her prominence and experience in education and the popular media to bear on the endeavor of getting more religious books into the hands and minds of readers. Although overwhelmingly liberal and Protestant, the editorial panel made an effort to present the best religious books from many different faith traditions and viewpoints.

What can we learn about religion and print culture in the 1920s from the book reviews and reader letters in the *Religious Book Club Bulletin* and a decade's worth of book advertising and editorial coverage related to religion in the industry journal, *Publishers' Weekly?* What kinds of readers belonged to the Club? What concerns and preoccupations shaped their reading? What kinds of communities—real and imagined—did it foster? What kind of religion did it sell to readers? With the exception of quotations from reader letters published in the *RBC Bulletin*, direct testimony about how religious texts functioned in the lives of readers is lacking.

However, as Robert Darnton reminds us, information about the production, marketing, and distribution of texts can—in part—compensate
for a lack of knowledge about readers and reception.[10]

What Kinds of Religious Books
Did 1920s Americans Want to Read?

In 1928, Gilbert Loveland of Henry Holt and Company surveyed over
one hundred laymen about what kinds of religious books they wanted to
read. Loveland summarized their responses in six questions, with over
60 percent of respondents concentrating on the first two issues:

1. What kind of God can a man believe, in this scientific day?
2. How should a man think of Jesus?
3. What is left of the Bible, after criticism has done its worst?
4. Is prayer anything more than auto-suggestion?
5. Why is Christianity supposed to be superior to other religions?
   And what right has one religion to wage a campaign of religious
   imperialism?
6. What is the function of the church in modern society?[11]

Holt noted that the best sellers of 1928 were those that addressed
these very questions. More important for my purposes, however, are the
particular ways in which Loveland phrased these questions. Lay readers
presumably felt defensive about, and embattled in, their religious belief.
They asked not what prayer was good for, but whether it might be good
for anything at all. They did not ask for help reading the Bible, but
asked instead whether there were any point in reading the Bible, once
modern criticism had done its worst. These are not so much questions
about *kinds* of religious belief and practices as they are questions about
whether it is possible to *have* religious belief in a modern, scientific society. Could one be religious without being a gullible, unintelligent fool?

That thousands of readers wanted the answer to be "yes" is evidenced by the offerings of the RBC, which presented book after book to
readers that promised to reconcile their religious faith with evolution
and the other physical sciences, with modern psychology, and with
people of other faiths at home and abroad. These books were so popular because they assuaged a profoundly felt contradiction at the center of liberal, Protestant life.[12] One could be modern, rational, well

educated and also be a person of faith, and the RBC's offerings compulsively explained how—in accessible, lively prose.

The brief description of A. Maude Royden's *I Believe in God* in the *RBC Bulletin* made clear the sense of being embattled that was characteristic of RBC readers: "The volume is not written for the theological or philosophical scholar but for the many men and women and young people who find themselves wondering whether religion is still intellectually respectable. In simple, non-technical language, replete with concrete illustrations, a woman of rare insight reveals the dynamic quality that Christian faith brings into human life and sums up the practical reasons which have sustained belief in God across the centuries."[13] The review promises that this volume will give believers back their self-respect, and that it will do so not in theoretical or abstract terms but in ways that resonate powerfully with readers' everyday lives.

"Living at the same time in two separate worlds": The RBC and Modern Life

The majority of the RBC selections clustered around a few issues— religion and science, religion and psychology, the church in the world (including missions and relations with those of other faiths), and ecumenism.[14] The most important of these, by number of offerings, was clearly religion and science.[15] The particular selection that received the most attention was the August 1928 selection, *Science in Search of God*, by Kirtley F. Mather. Chairman of the geology department at Harvard, Mather was a celebrity of sorts, having served as an expert witness for the defense at the Scopes trial in Tennessee.[16] Like many of the expert witnesses, he expanded his deposition in defense of evolution into a book of general interest. It had the lowest return rate of any of the RBC's offerings—around 3 percent. Return rates for other selections, particularly those that were written in a scholarly way, approached 30 percent.[17] Loveland, whose company, Henry Holt, published the volume, explained *Science in Search of God*'s commercial success both in terms of its timeliness ("a subject of front-page interest") and its accessible style ("simple, vivid language without scholarly formulas"). It could be read in less than three hours.[18] In addition, the message of the book was reassuring to believers, reconciling science and religion—widely held to be in fundamental conflict—by asserting that the conflict existed only between *bad* science and *bad* religion, disappearing once one looked at both intelligently.[19]

Mather's was only the most successful of a sizable class of texts that resolved the tension between science and religion in one of several (sometimes conflicting) ways: (1) that each was valid in its own, distinct realm; (2) that science only offered partial truth; (3) that *real* religion had nothing to do with outmoded scientific theories. The *Bulletin* favorably reviewed two books that took diametrically opposed positions. Dwight Bradley's *The Recovery of Religion* argued that science needed to be "shoved back to its proper field," but Edwin A. Burtt's *Religion in an Age of Science* argued that science belonged everywhere in modern life, and that "religion must adopt the more radical procedure of regarding every conviction as tentative and as always open to fresh inquiry."[20] The sameness underneath the differing views becomes more apparent in the short blurbs the RBC used to remind readers that former selections could be purchased as an alternative to the current month's selection. Under the "On Religion and Science" heading were these representative titles:

> *The Nature of the Physical World* . . . A. S. Eddington $3.75
> A world-famous astronomer discusses "the new physics" and suggests that religious values are in no sense ruled out.
>
> *Old Faith and New Knowledge* . . . James H. Snowden $2.50
> A plea for the constant restudy and restatement of religious convictions, insisting that Christian faith and scientific knowledge are harmonious and supplementary.
>
> *Science and Human Progress* . . . Sir Oliver Lodge $2.00
> The universe is found to be the scene of purpose and reason, with nothing to invalidate belief in God, Christ, prayer and immortality.
>
> *The New Reformation* . . . Michael Pupin $2.50
> An American scientist reviews the advance of physical science and ends in an affirmation of spiritual realities.[21]

However these authors get there, they all conclude that the religion/science conflict is no conflict at all. Readers are given lessons in the tricky art of inhabiting two worlds at once—at being rational, scientific inhabitants of the modern world but also faithful believers in traditional doctrines that give meaning to their lives. The work of these selections was to keep the contradictions in suspension, to structure and restructure people's imaginations so as to avoid painful cognitive dissonance.

The descriptions of these books sound remarkably old-fashioned, and there was a great deal of nostalgia in them for the nineteenth-century unity of science and religion taken for granted by the grandparents and great-grandparents of RBC readers. The field of natural theology was deeply respected until after the Civil War. In it, the laws of nature were elegant illustrations of religious truths, and naturalists describing and classifying the natural world were also explicating the mind of God. These RBC selections hearken back to an era before the specialization of knowledge, when colleges trained gentlemen in the liberal arts and sciences and the opinion of an educated generalist still held sway over those with narrower, specialized expertise.[22] This nostalgia connects the RBC with middlebrow culture, which, Joan Shelley Rubin argues, was the remnant/reinvention of the nineteenth-century genteel tradition. The genteel tradition urged the cultivation of character through exposure to culture in the Arnoldian sense ("classic" texts held to contain the best ideas that had been thought and written in the world). Its survival in a "chastened and redirected form" as middlebrow culture in the 1920s and 1930s testified to the ascendancy in modern America of experts with specialized training.[23]

Similar kinds of arguments were made reconciling religion with psychology or psychoanalysis, areas also widely perceived to be in conflict. RBC offerings insisted that modern psychology was not hostile to religion; that it was a useful tool for counseling troubled congregants; and that religion was—in fact—essential to mental health. For example, the July 1932 main selection, *Psychology for Religious Workers*, promised readers that psychology was no enemy; it could be made to do "yeoman service to the Christian cause."[24] Clifford E. Barbour's *Sin and the New Psychology*, an alternate selection, argued that psychoanalysis "confirms the fundamental truths of the Christian religion." Moreover, psychologists curing neuroses and ministers redeeming sinners were engaged in the same process. Psychoanalytic categories like repression, transference, and sublimation were merely new names for Christian categories like temptation, sin, forgiveness, and sanctification.[25]

Like the selections addressing religion and science, those concerned with psychology and religion promised to reconcile for readers the deeply felt contradictions between traditional faith and modern thought. As Cadman, the chairman of the editorial committee, told *Publishers' Weekly*, the RBC was intended to facilitate the reimagining of faith necessitated by modern living: "The sweeping developments in science and world affairs today make it necessary for all thoughtful people to be re-thinking constantly the meaning of religion for human life. Unless one does this he is in danger of finding himself swept loose from his old moorings and not knowing how to anchor himself to any spiritual real-ities."[26] The RBC offered readers an anchor in the stormy seas of con-temporary life by demonstrating again and again that modernity and tradition were—all appearances to the contrary—not in conflict. Faith and modern thought were either parallel sets of ideas in separate realms, complementary ideas that could render each other great service, or the same ideas expressed in different language. The rapprochement allowed readers to comfortably imagine themselves inhabiting two worlds at once.

Imagined Communities, Ecumenism, and the Nation: The RBC and the World

The RBC was also deeply concerned with religion in the world, partic-ularly how to negotiate encounters with other faiths—in daily life, as part of missionary work, or in finding common cause to act for social justice. Most of the reviews in this category are characterized by a pat-tern of sympathetically exploring other faiths and then reaffirming the superiority of one's own. In this way, doubting Christians are reassured. Even people who have spent many years studying other faiths and who deeply appreciate their nobility *choose* to be Christians. The short blurb for Oscar MacMillan Buck's *"Our Asiatic Christ"* concisely makes this logical maneuver: "An admirable illustration of the attempt to ap-proach other religions in a spirit of warm appreciation of all which they have of value to the human spirit. Professor Buck studies the best in Hindu aspiration and points out how this is beginning to find fulfillment in Jesus Christ."[27]

In this, as in almost every other case, looking at others leads us back to ourselves. In this review, Hindu aspirations are noble and valuable, but only because Hindus are reframed as people embarked (unknow-ingly) on an incomplete Christian journey.[28]

Most of the books about other religions were, in fact, alternate selec-tions. However, in October 1928 the primary selection was *The Pilgrimage of Buddhism,* whose goal was "to discover the actual conditions of the reli-gion as it is believed and lived today." Judges assumed that what readers desired was a kind of empathy: "Many books on the subject leave the reader wondering how any intelligent or spiritually minded person could adhere to such a religion. In contrast, Professor Pratt helps his readers to understand 'how it feels to be a Buddhist,' to catch the 'emotional undertone' of this alien faith, and to enter sympathetically into its symbols, its cult and its art."[29] The judges were clearly nervous about this volume, although they did choose it as the primary selection. "For those who may feel that Buddhism, however competently and fascinatingly treated, is a subject too remote from their daily experience," the judges recommended an alternate volume focused on Christian theism, John Wright Buckham's *The Humanity of God*. Although members were always free to select an alternate rather than the featured book, the RBC editorial board only rarely suggested a specific alternative on the front page.[30]

Like Hindus and Buddhists abroad, Jews and Catholics at home appeared in the RBC's offerings, but only as tokens. For example, the front page of the June 1932 *Bulletin* trumpeted: "This is the first time in the history of the Religious Book Club when a primary selection has come from the pen of a Roman Catholic Author."[31] Similarly, the April 1929 primary selection, Ernest R. Trattner's *Unraveling the Book of Books*, a popularization of historical biblical scholarship, was marked as the first primary selection by a Jewish writer. In addition, these writers were assumed to speak for and to represent all Catholic or Jewish writers. Trattner's book, for example, was interesting "as indicative of liberal Hebrew scholarship today."[32] Further, like the Hindus abroad, the Catholics at home merely affirmed the universal validity of one's own faith: "The volume has a further significance as a disclosure of how much Protestants and Catholics have in common when they get down to the basic elements of the faith that both live by. Many Protestant readers will find themselves gaining a new sense of spiritual fellowship with Catholics as a result of this book."[33] Once again, the book has as its goal a sense of spiritual fellowship, of appreciation of other faith traditions, but again these others are mostly interesting as mirrors of ourselves. Catholic faith is most engaging at the level of "basic elements"— which differ very little from those of Protestant Americans. They are important in that they affirm our own sense of universality or superiority (i.e., they are really just like us, or given time and enlightenment, they will be just like us).

Selections aside, not many Catholics thought the RBC was for them. Less than a year after the RBC's founding, the Catholic Book Club (initially called the Catholic Literary Guild of America) was chartered. Funded by donations from lay people, its purpose was twofold. First, it was designed to select for Catholics the books they should read and those they should not. Second, recognizing that not a single Catholic author appeared on the current best-seller list (although many books the Catholic Church opposed did), the Catholic Book Club wished to recognize and promote Catholic writers of merit.[34]

The RBC did, however, have an inclusive, ecumenical philosophy about most Protestants, offering many selections addressing interdenominational cooperation.[35] Again and again, readers were offered books that documented what was going on at the great ecumenical conferences of the day or that affirmed a central "core" Christianity and criticized the denominational squabbles that separated them from each other. H. R. L. Sheppard's *The Impatience of a Parson* is a case in point. Its brief summary called it: "'A plea for the recovery of vital Christianity'— and for a church that makes more of the things that were central in the experience of Jesus, and less of ecclesiastical and creedal forms, worldly prestige and the things that divide Christians into separate groups."[36]

In some ways, the RBC was engaged in creating an imagined community that intersected, and at times conflicted, with other identities based on religion, race, gender, class, and nation. The "we" hailed by the Club's *Bulletin* needed to have Catholicism and Judaism made comprehensible in terms of liberal Protestantism. Conservative Christians who wished to avoid certain offensive liberal doctrines were given fair warning by the Club and could custom-tailor their selections to meet their more traditional tastes. Hinduism and Buddhism, although interesting if considered in comparative perspective, were suspected of being so far off the beaten path as to lack interest. Perhaps the only foreigners who counted as "us" were the British—whose volumes filled the pages of the *RBC Bulletin* and seamlessly melded with the concerns of their New World brothers.

Although there were a few offerings by women authors, most were by men, usually ministers or professors at divinity schools. Two alternate offerings were noteworthy as the exceptions that proved the rule; they made gender visible. Charles E. Raven's *Women and the Ministry* presented statistics about women in the church and argued for their ordination on the grounds that churches needed them. G. A. Studdert Kennedy's *The Warrior, the Woman, and the Christ* argued that Christ merged the best qualities of manhood and womanhood.[37] These selections were striking, however, precisely because most other texts just assumed an unmarked, universal human subject who was implicitly male. Similarly, the presence of a token woman, Mary Woolley, on the founding editorial committee, does not appear to have challenged the implicit equation of humanity with men. Although some of the offerings explicitly addressed the "race question," it, too, was usually absent from the discourse, assuming an unmarked, universal reading subject who was white. For example, Edwin Smith's *The Golden Stool* examined the relationships between white and black people in Africa. The editors urged its relevance to religious life by linking these concerns to missionary work and asserting that it illuminated "the problem of race relationships as one of the most pressing issues confronting the Church today."[38]

In this way, the assumed RBC readership resembled what Michael Warner calls the "republic of letters," the imagined community of white, male, propertied citizens who constituted the public sphere and the new nation in eighteenth-century America. These citizens were held to be rational, disinterested, and capable of governing for the public good, unlike those whose humanity (and capacity for reason or self-governance) was compromised by their gender, race/ethnicity, or lack of literacy or property.[39] If the RBC was a free marketplace of religious ideas, it was nonetheless one to which not everyone had equal access.

The RBC and the Middlebrow

RBC readers clearly wanted books that reconciled faith and modern science, religious pluralism and Protestant superiority, but they only wanted books that achieved this reconciliation in particular—*middlebrow*—ways. Middlebrow institutions aimed to make high culture and all the benefits it promised accessible to a broader public. It typically involved wedding the machinery of mass production and mass distribution to culturally esteemed texts—literature, art, classical music, et cetera. Janice Radway has argued in her discussion of the Book-of-the-Month Club that the term "middlebrow" names not just a set of institutions or cultural texts but also a distinct aesthetic and way of reading.[40] I will discuss here three specific ways in which the RBC engaged the middlebrow: (1) the promise to combine rigorous scholarship with lively accessibility; (2) the embrace of a pluralistic, conditional aesthetic; and (3) the opportunity for readers to engage affectively with characters, authors, and judges in ways that seemed intimate and personal.

First, much of the space in the *RBC Bulletin* was given over to reassuring readers that selected books were accessibly written and not overly abstract and theoretical—not what Cavert derisively described as "dog-eared tomes of out-of-date theology" and "goody-goody treatises on piety."[41] This lively, pleasurable presentation was not to be understood as a "dumbing down" of scholarship, however. The *RBC Bulletin* reviews always highlight *both* the writers' expertise and the accessibility of their prose. Clement F. Rogers's *The Case for Christianity* is a case in point: "The author, well known in British church circles as professor of pastoral theology in King's College, University of London, has for eight years spoken on Christian themes to heterogeneous audiences in Hyde Park on Sunday afternoons and undergone the blunt cross-examination for which the Park is notable. As a result, the author has the happy faculty of dealing with questions of Christian belief in a concrete and pungent manner."[42] As in many other reviews, oral and written language are seamlessly connected here. For example, the RBC prominently featured printed sermons and collections of addresses from religious symposia. Many reviews emphasized the distinctive "voice" of the author one "heard" in the (written) work. Presumably, one who regularly spoke to masses of ordinary people knew how to explain difficult theological concepts in accessible, lively language in print as well.

Besides learned language, the other bugbear the RBC editorial committee sought to avoid was overly abstract or theoretical works—works that readers could not make resonate with their everyday lives. In describing *Present-Day Dilemmas in Religion* by Charles W. Gilkey, for example, the editors insisted: "Dr. Gilkey possesses the rare faculty of presenting a profound subject in such a wealth of concrete illustrations and revealing incidents as to remove it far from the realm of the abstract or the academic. This it is which makes him listened to so eagerly both by student groups and by popular audiences."[43] Amy Johnson Frykholm describes a similar "life-application method" of reading characteristic of contemporary evangelicals. As when reading scripture, readers look for a take-home message in religious books to immediately apply to their own lives.[44] The boundary between books and readers' lives here is purposely porous, unlike the distanced, "pure" aesthetic ways of reading required by literary modernism in the same era.[45]

Second, the pluralistic and conditional aesthetic of the Book-of-the-Month Club was readily apparent in the RBC, its religious knock-off. Radway argues that BOMC judges did not rank books along a continuum from good to bad but insisted instead that there were different *kinds* of books that were good for different kinds of readers.[46] Comparing a trashy mystery to the work of Henry James was like comparing apples and oranges. Henry James's work was good for certain kinds of pleasure; the mystery, for certain others. The BOMC's goal was to pick the best book for each particular kind of reading experience.

Again and again, the editors of the *RBC Bulletin* made clear that certain kinds of books were good for certain kinds of readers, recognizing (for example) that a practical exposition of new Sunday school techniques that might be riveting to a Sunday school teacher might bore an amateur philosopher to death. A discussion of fund-raising for the church might be very useful to the chair of the stewardship committee but lack general appeal.[47] The effort to match particular readers with the right kinds of books sometimes required warning readers away from a primary selection. For example, Canon B. H. Streeter's *The Primitive Church* was the February 1928 main selection, but judges made clear that the book was perhaps a bad fit for nonspecialist readers: "The Editorial Committee desires to make it clear that this book is not written from the standpoint of general popularity and does not yield its treasure to casual skimming; it is rather a volume of most careful scholarship, the kind which will long be referred to as an authoritative work. Those (especially laymen) who prefer a volume for easy reading, or one dealing with less historical detail, should select as an alternative one of the important supplementary recommendations described on the following pages."[48]

The RBC recognized that people bought and read even the Bible for different (though equally valid) purposes. In the late 1920s and early 1930s, the RBC made two editions of the Bible available to Club members. First was the quintessential middlebrow Bible, *The Living Bible,* christened "the whole Bible in the fewest words." It was shorter, not because important material had been removed, but because "repetitions, ceremonial details, land boundaries, genealogies of kings and other matters of less general interest" were omitted. To make the presentation more accessible, chapter numbers were moved to the margins and descriptive titles put in their place. Second was *The Oxford Bible,* as important as a beautiful artifact as it was a text to be read. The King James

Version, "printed in its entirety," this volume was notable for the quality of its binding and printing rather than the qualities of its text: "Bound in blue buckram, with red leather label stamped in gold, with a gilt top and untrimmed edges, and beautifully printed in large type with wide margins, it is a volume the appearance of which at once suggests a literary treasure."[49] Some books are clearly understood to be valued for their otherworldly aura, whereas others are meant to communicate efficiently information we require for daily living. Neither kind of book is privileged as superior, but every effort is made to bring each book to the appropriate reader, to successfully match consumer desires with consumer goods without judging the social or cultural consequences of those desires.

Finally, the Religious Book Club promised readers what Janice Radway has called "middlebrow personalism"—the sense of communion with authors or characters as real, idiosyncratic individuals with distinctive personal voices.[50] The sense of intimate, meaningful dialogue was particularly appealing in the 1920s, since large numbers of readers were struggling with the transition from traditional rural and small-town communities characterized by face-to-face communication to large, bustling, anonymous cities. This personalism is most obvious in the *Bulletin*'s discussion of biographies of saints and religious leaders from the past. Robert Norwood's *The Heresy of Antioch*, for example, presented the life of the Apostle Paul. The *Bulletin* promised, "Under Dr. Norwood's brush the outlines of the Apostle Paul stand out so clearly as to make him seem no longer a dim figure of the first century but a vital force in the modern world." The *Bulletin* explained to readers what Norwood's biography would do, in part, by telling them what it would not do. "The volume is not so much an attempt to set forth the historic facts of Paul's life," it explained, "as to interpret his meaning for today." Moreover, those interested in theology and dogma should look elsewhere: "The Great Apostle is portrayed, not as a theologian, but as a great human. His letters are described, not as the effort to formulate a doctrinal system, but rather as the outpouring of the heart of a great poet and mystic, throbbing with love for Jesus Christ, in whom he had seen God revealed as Love."[51] We are concerned less with Paul's thought, then, than we are with Paul, hearing him as if he were a personal friend confiding his feelings to us. The institution he spent his lifetime building pales in importance beside his individual experience of the divine; the Christian church he built impresses us less than his mysticism.

Tracy D. Mygatt and Frances Witherspoon's *Armor of Light* appeared on the RBC list of alternate selections. Although it was fiction, the RBC editorial committee claimed it possessed what they called "emotional realism," or an essential truth: "To be transported in imagination across the chasm of nearly nineteen centuries and to live vividly in the world of the first century Christians is the experience of the readers of this beautiful narrative."[52] It is noteworthy that the RBC did not initially distinguish fiction from nonfiction. They were run together in reviews and descriptions. Even the list of former selections, which were broken down into thematic categories (On Jesus Christ, On Religion and Science, On Psychology, Religious Education, etc.) did not list "fiction" as a separate category until the late 1930s. Novels about Jesus, for example, appeared alongside nonfiction in "On Jesus Christ." A historical account of the Bible in English promised "the charm and glamour of fiction while recording historic fact."[53] The truth/fiction distinction was simply not useful, when one's purpose for reading was a deep, emotional identification rather than a scholarly, contemplative distance.

Middlebrow personalism named not only a way of identifying with vividly drawn characters but also a kind of dialogue a reader experienced with the author through the act of reading. Comparing his popularizing work to what H. G. Wells did for secular history in his *Outline of History*, the RBC describes Gaius Glenn Atkins's *Procession of the Gods*, the primary selection for October 1930, as follows: "Dr. Atkins takes the detailed data gathered by the researches of the specialists—the scholars in the fields of comparative religion, psychology, anthropology and archaeology—and lets this vast mass of material pass through his own reflection and imagination till it comes forth, no longer abstract and technical, but intensely human, rich in color and palpitating with life."[54] In short, Atkins is not only a scholar and a popularizer of the first order, but his book also gives us a sense of his own rich imagination. We as readers are educated, entertained, and feel as though we have made meaningful contact with a single, distinctive mind. The objective voice of science is not what makes Atkins's book so appealing; it is, instead, his personal voice. The "conversation" with him is part of the book's appeal.

Letters from Club members published periodically in the *Bulletin* testify further that some readers felt that reading the RBC's primary selections not only gave them communion with authors and characters, but also with the judges. "I know the arrival of your choice will be an event looked for in each month," wrote one minister. "It is like being taken into the study of each of the members of your committee and given a share of an intimacy of which ministers in small towns are sorely in need."[55]

The imagined community of the RBC was not only the communion of readers with the judges, authors, or characters. Readers were also asked to recommend the Club to their friends in exchange for free books or a free six-month or year subscription. Some readers did actually form real communities to read the offerings together. In Lorain, Ohio, a group of readers, many of whom were members of the RBC, met to discuss one of its offerings at their regular meeting after hearing a review from one of the members.[56] In this way, the Club *Bulletin* was a resource for readers who were forming their own reading and writing communities.

The RBC and the Marketplace

Reader letters make clear that the Club made the literary marketplace knowable to readers overwhelmed by its size and complexity—in other words, the Club responded to deeply felt needs of subjects of a consumer capitalist state. Many readers were overwhelmed by the number of books in print and appreciated the help selecting which ones might be the best for them to read. "In this day of mass production of books such a service is a real one which will be taken advantage of by thousands of church people," editorialized one religious newspaper. "There are so many books coming from the press that your service makes our book dollars do double duty," wrote a minister from Cincinnati.[57]

Several letters made specific reference to book distribution difficulties that membership in the RBC alleviated. "I am very glad to have the opportunity of having my books selected by master minds, especially since I am much shut in during the winter," testified one letter. "I am greatly enjoying this service which you offer, especially since we live in the interior and are unable to secure selected new books when we desire them," wrote another from Huchow, China—undoubtedly a missionary.[58]

Whatever else could be said of the RBC's offerings, they hailed readers as individuals—usually liberal, Protestant, white, male individuals. Although the offerings were uniformly critical of individualism and the therapeutic ethos that T. J. Jackson Lears claims came with it,[59] all were deeply complicit. The therapeutic ethos is a way of being in the world that focuses exclusively on improving and perfecting one's own physical and mental health to the exclusion of more traditional religious practices such as service to others or obedience to holy scriptures. Lears argues that around the turn of the century, there was a shift of emphasis in psychological and religious discourses from salvation through self-denial to self-realization as manifested in this obsessive concern with individual psychological and physical health. This increasing focus on improving and perfecting the self elided larger social, moral, and institutional structures, preparing the way for consumption as a way of being in the world.

The RBC participated in this reimagining of models of the self. Described as "a popular interpretation, for the general reader, of the views held by the principal groups of thinkers in the churches," Gerald Birney Smith's *Current Christian Thinking* appeared to be about social institutions and the beliefs shared by faith communities. The review explained: "The earlier chapters describe the viewpoint of the Roman Catholic, the Protestant, the 'Modernist' and the 'Fundamentalist,' and try to define, clearly and simply, the positions for which each of these groups is contending. The issues that are discussed are highly controversial, but the author handles them, in the main, in an objective manner. Other chapters are concerned with the present-day emphasis on Christian experience, the appeal to Christ, the controversy over evolution, and the various ways in which modern men are pursuing the quest for God."[60] The last chapter, however, holds the author's own position—which presumably interested those seeking middlebrow personalism more. He is a proponent of the "Evangelical Movement," not because of its superior doctrine ("which he shows to have been largely taken over from Catholicism") but because of its emphasis on "a genuine, first-hand, personal experience of salvation."[61] Institutions and ideas are of little importance (in spite of the careful, comparative discussion earlier in the text); what really matters is individual experience of the divine—which need not involve a community or a coherent set of beliefs at all. Rufus Jones's *New Studies in Mystical Religion* addressed religion specifically "as direct personal awareness of God," an alternative selection that—like many—focused more on mysticism than on institutions.[62] Some offerings even seemed to offer an anti-institutional bias. *Shoddy*, for example, a novel about how the spirituality and moral leadership of one minister are corrupted by the politics of the Church, suggests that "pure" religion occurs outside the pew.[63]

In addition to its individualism, the RBC was implicated with the logic of consumer capitalism in its agnosticism on controversial questions of theology. The RBC took no stand on doctrinal issues and frequently offered books taking diametrically opposed positions. The RBC did not care what you believed (within a vaguely Christian framework) as long as you believed something that required you to do some reading. For example, the April 1929 main selection was Ernest R. Trattner's *Unravelling the Book of Books*, a popularization of historical biblical scholarship. The editorial committee was enthusiastic about it, arguing that "the results of the foremost technical scholarship are presented to the lay reader in a brisk and captivating style, as readable as a novel and abounding in human interest and dramatic color." Nonetheless, the review was at pains to assuage any anxieties that investigating the *human* origins of the Bible might arouse. "The results of historical and textual criticism are held to be positive rather than negative," the review promises, quoting the author's belief that what the various versions of sacred texts have in common far outweigh their differences.[64]

All the praise and reassurances aside, however, the editorial committee named an alternate selection on the front page of the *Bulletin, The Authority of the Bible* by Charles H. Dodd, "for those who may prefer a volume interpreting the message of the Bible and the nature of its inspiration, rather than the historical processes by which it was produced."[65] Dodd's book seemed the perfect antithesis to the main selection and was offered in part to allay the anxiety that books like *Unravelling the Book of Books* created for some readers. The first paragraph of the review maintains: "The modern revolt against authority and the scientific study of the Bible have so combined to undermine the traditional views about it that a volume which builds up a tenable basis for belief in an authority still unshaken fills a sorely felt need. This is what Professor Dodd's book does. Not from any *a priori* assumption, but from an inductive study of the contents of the Bible and of their spiritual value, he arrives at a doctrine of authority which is certain to be reassuring to many."[66] If you need traditional faith, then the RBC is ready to provide it; if, on the other hand, you require a scientific investigation of the historical origins of those articles of faith, the RBC can provide that, as well. The Club exists not to pursue Truth or truths, but to meet the spiritual needs of consumers, whatever they might be.

In the April 1930 *Bulletin*, the RBC recommended both *The Atonement and the Social Process* by Shailer Matthews (liberal dean of the University of Chicago Divinity School) and *The Virgin Birth of Christ* by J. Gresham Machen (Princeton Seminary's foremost fundamentalist thinker). Reviews clearly marked these products with their (controversial) theological positions and made clear which readers would find them pleasing. Matthews's volume demonstrated that doctrines are not timeless truths but instead reflect the concerns of their specific, historical moment. Matthews did not care which theory of the atonement was "correct"; his purpose was to explain the social worlds from which each theory arose and the intellectual and spiritual needs it met. Two pages later, Machen's book is offered as "an exhaustive statement of the historical evidence supporting belief in the virgin birth of Jesus Christ," and Machen himself is identified as "presenting a thoroughly conservative interpretation of Christianity."[67] In some ways, what the RBC did was to reframe profound and painful differences in theology and worldview as consumer choices. If it did not resolve these contradictions, it at least offered ways of thinking about them that made the intellectual and cultural world of American Protestantism easier to inhabit. Although the presence of books like Machen's *The Virgin Birth of Christ* and Dodd's *The Authority of the Bible* might suggest a significant conservative Christian readership, the context in which these books were offered—as one of many possible sets of beliefs and values rather than as the Truth—participates in a liberal religious logic.

The highly ambivalent nature of the resolution between conflicting theologies was readily apparent in the review of the July 1928 main selection, Daniel Johnson Fleming's *Attitudes Toward Other Faiths*. As in reviews of most books of this ilk, the RBC praised both Fleming's real reverence and respect for other faiths and his affirmation of "the unique place of Christ as the fulfillment of all the best aspirations of mankind." Fleming and the review sidestep the contradictions implicit in celebrating diverse religions and maintaining the ultimate superiority of one's own by invoking a common enemy—the materialistic, secular world: "the greatest rival of Christ today is not Confucius or Buddha or Mohammed, but the spirit of rampant materialism and sheer irreligion."[68] The logic of the marketplace deeply permeates this condemnation of the marketplace. It does not matter which God you choose to worship, which set of rituals and traditions you choose to embrace, as long as you choose one (and buy some books about it).

The Religious Book Club participated in the remaking of relationships between religious institutions, individual believers, and the literary marketplace. The RBC solved persistent problems with book distribution and provided expert guidance to readers in negotiating the overwhelming literary marketplace. The adamantly ecumenical RBC called into being an imagined faith community that was implicitly white, male, and Protestant, although it engaged with Catholics, Jews, Buddhists, and Hindus in a spirit of (albeit limited) empathy and tolerance. Its offerings reassured anxious readers that traditional faith and modern thought were easily reconciled, that one could be both a person of faith and a rational, scientific thinker. The RBC promised further that the best of religious scholarship was available in lively, accessible prose that offered readers something that felt like authentic fellowship with characters, authors, and judges. The RBC was selling a religious (and a literary) way of being in the world, but not necessarily a particular set of beliefs or doctrines. Readers were hailed as individual believers (even mystics) rather than as members of particular faith traditions or congregations. The RBC constructed a highly contradictory world in which faith is held up as the enemy of a materialistic, consumption-driven world, while participating in the remaking of faith to fit a liberal, consumerist logic.

Many contemporary religious trends—the growth in mysticism and declining importance of denominational affiliations, the texts and print culture institutions catering to individual "seekers," the felt conflict between modernity and traditional faith—echo concerns at the center of RBC readers' lives. My hope is that studying the commodification of religion and the popular tastes of ordinary readers in the 1920s "religious renaissance" might better equip us to think about and talk about our own.

Notes

1. "New Interest in Religious Books," *Publishers' Weekly*, 23 February 1924, 596. (After mid-century, the *Weekly* dropped the apostrophe in its title.)

2. See, for example, "The Religious Renaissance," *Publishers' Weekly*, 19 February 1927, 684. See also "New Interest in Religious Books," *Publishers' Weekly*, 23 February 1924, 596; "The Religious Book Season," *Publishers' Weekly*, 18 February 1928, 666–68; "Bibles and Best Sellers," *Publishers' Weekly*, 6 October 1923, 1219; J. F. Newton, "Religious Books," *Publishers' Weekly*, 21 May 1927, 2002–3.

3. Most in the industry believed that sales of religious books were dramatically increased (see, for example, "New Interest in Religious Books," "Religious Renaissance," and "Religious Books as Best Sellers," [*Publishers' Weekly*, 3 April 1926, 1194]), but there were those who disagreed. Grant Overton argued in "Twentieth Century [*sic*] Book Buying Habits: Some Notes on Non-fiction, 1900–1920" (*Publishers' Weekly*, 26 January 1924), 237–39, that large, steady sales of religious books dated back at least as far as 1900.

4. "Two New Religious Departments," *Publishers' Weekly*, 15 January 1927, 195; "Why Harper's Have Entered the Field of Religious Books," *Publishers' Weekly*, 19 February 1927, 695; and "Religious Books of the Month," *Publishers' Weekly*, 29 October 1927, 1641. The RBC was founded in November of 1927 with 980 members. Fifteen months later, it had 7,500 members in all fifty states and thirty-two foreign countries (Samuel McCrea Cavert, "What Religious Books Are Read," *Publishers' Weekly*, 16 February 1929, 752). In 1930 it merged with the Christian Century Book Service conducted by the periodical *Christian Century* when its editor, Dr. Charles Clayton Morrison, joined the Editorial Committee (*Religious Book Club Bulletin* [hereafter *RBC Bulletin*], July 1929). It was subsequently owned by Book Club Associates, Meredith Corporation, Iverson-Norman Associates, and (since 1988) by Crossroad/Continuum Publishing Group, where it continues to function as a separate operating unit ("Crossroad Acquires Two Religious Book Clubs," *Publishers Weekly*, 11 November 1988, 14). In 1988, it had 6,000 members, mostly mainline Protestant clergy ("Religious Book Clubs 1988," *Publishers Weekly*, 4 March 1988, 46–47).

5. "Religious Books of the Month," *Publishers' Weekly*, 29 October 1927, 1641.

6. See the review of *Love and Marriage*, by Winfield Scott Hall, *RBC Bulletin*, December 1929, 5.

7. See, for example, *RBC Bulletin*, February 1929, 4. Selections included Robert S. Lynd and Helen Merrell Lynd's *Middletown: A Study in Modern American Culture*, Stephen Vincent Benet's "John Brown's Body," Mark Van Doren's *Anthology of World Poetry*, Franz Boas's *Anthropology and Modern Life*, Charles and Mary Beard's *Rise of American Civilization*, and Countee Cullen's "The Black Christ," among others. These "general interest" books appeared irregularly and disappeared from the *Bulletin* soon after, suggesting the experiment was a failure.

8. "Religious Books of the Month," *Publishers' Weekly*, 29 October 1927, 1641. At least 80 percent of the correspondence published from readers in the *RBC Bulletin* came from ministers, and in the 1940s, helpful reminders appeared around tax time that those volumes purchased for professional improvement could be written off one's taxes (*RBC Bulletin*, March 1947, 6).

9. "Religious Books of the Month," *Publishers' Weekly*, 29 October 1927, 1641. See also John Tebbel, *A History of Book Publishing in the United States*, vol. 3, *The Golden Age between Two Wars, 1920–1940* (New York: Bowker, 1978), 299.

10. Robert Darnton, *The Forbidden Bestsellers of Pre-Revolutionary France* (New York: Norton, 1995), 184.

11. Gilbert Loveland, "Laymen's Interest in Religious Books," *Publishers' Weekly*, 16 February 1929, 755.

12. This deeply felt conflict is apparent not only in the *RBC Bulletin* copy but also in the writings of both ordinary laypeople and religious intellectuals. Letters written to Bruce Barton, author of the best-selling 1925 life of Christ, *The Man Nobody Knows*, testify to this painful contradiction (see Erin A. Smith, "'Jesus, My Pal': Reading and Religion in Middlebrow America," *Canadian Review of American Studies* 37, no. 2 (2007): 147–81). Quaker mystic and best-selling author Rufus Jones explained this early twentieth-century conflict (which the Quakers experienced earlier than most other religious communities) as follows: "There are few crises to compare with that which appears when the simple, childhood religion, imbibed at mother's knee and absorbed from early home and church environment, comes into collision with a scientific, solidly reasoned system." Rufus M. Jones, *Social Law in the Spiritual World: Studies in Human and Divine Inter-Relationships* (Philadelphia: John C. Winston Co., 1904), 9–10.

13. *RBC Bulletin*, December 1927, 3.

14. The title of this section, "Living at the same time in two separate worlds," comes from a review of Dwight Bradley's *The Recovery of Religion*, which sought to reconcile science and religion through a "separate realms" argument: "'Science and religion are sovereign each in its own realm, the realm of the former being that of objective research, the realm of the latter being that of subjective experience.' A keen appreciation of this dilemma of living at the same time in two separate worlds, the objective and the subjective, is felt to be necessary to the recovery of vital religion" (*RBC Bulletin*, December 1929, 5).

15. See Samuel McCrea Cavert, "A Year's Additions to the Church Library," *Publishers' Weekly*, 18 February 1928, 663; and Cavert, "What Religious Books Are Read," *Publishers' Weekly*, 16 February 1929, 752.

16. Mather also helped Clarence Darrow prepare his famous interrogation of William Jennings Bryan by pretending to be Bryan during a weekend rehearsal before the final day of the trial.

17. Members could return a selection for full credit within ten days of receipt, if they were not satisfied with it. They automatically received the main selection, unless they returned a form requesting one of the month's alternate selections or a past selection in its place. Members could also purchase alternates or past selections in addition to a month's main selection.

18. Loveland, "Laymen's Interest in Religious Books," *Publishers' Weekly*, 16 February 1929, 755.

19. Mather was uniquely qualified to offer RBC readers this kind of reassurance. As a Harvard geologist, he was "unhesitatingly accepted as an authority in his field," and he wrote this book for laymen not in order to debunk

religion but as "interpreter of the spiritual meaning of the universe" and as "champion of religious faith." See *RBC Bulletin*, August 1928, 1. Born into a devout family of Baptists, Mather was deeply influenced by Social Gospel thinkers, who focused attention on bringing about a just order here on earth by transforming social institutions according to Christian principles. See Kennard Baker Bork, *Cracking Rocks and Defending Democracy: Kirtley Fletcher Mather, Scientist, Teacher, Social Activist, 1888–1978* (San Francisco: Pacific Division AAAS, 1994), chap. 16.

20. *RBC Bulletin*, December 1929, 5; *RBC Bulletin*, August 1929, 4.

21. All brief reviews from *RBC Bulletin*, May 1929, 6.

22. Howard Schweber calls this approach to the natural sciences "Protestant Baconianism," which he describes as the marriage of Bacon's inductive scientific method and the theology/epistemology of Scottish Common Sense. Protestant Baconianism had four core tenets: (1) commitment to natural theology (i.e., the study of nature proved religious truths); (2) an understanding of science as an exercise in taxonomy; (3) belief in a grand synthesis of all knowledge into a single system; and (4) an understanding of science as public endeavor that would yield moral and civic uplift. See Howard Schweber, "The 'Science' of Legal Science: The Model of the Natural Sciences in Nineteenth-Century American Legal Education," *Law and History Review* 17, no. 3 (Fall 1999): 421–66. On nineteenth- and twentieth-century beliefs about the relationship between religion and science, see Jon H. Roberts, *Darwinism and the Divine in America: Protestant Intellectuals and Organic Evolution, 1859–1900* (Madison: University of Wisconsin Press, 1988); and John Durant, ed., *Darwinism and Divinity: Essays on Evolution and Religious Belief* (New York: Blackwell, 1985). Roberts argues that evolution did not significantly disturb theology until the last quarter of the nineteenth century, when intellectuals were forced to either reject Darwin's theories or achieve some kind of rapprochement between biblical truths and modern science.

23. See Joan Shelley Rubin, *The Making of Middlebrow Culture* (Chapel Hill: University of North Carolina Press, 1992), xvii, xvi–xviii, 10–15.

24. *RBC Bulletin*, July 1932, 1. See also the review of *The Bearing of Psychology Upon Religion* by Harrison Sacket Elliott (*RBC Bulletin*, February 1928, 3–4); and the review of *Psychology and Religious Experience* by W. Fearson Halliday (*RBC Bulletin*, April 1930, 4).

25. *RBC Bulletin*, October 1930, 3.

26. "Religious Books of the Month," *Publishers' Weekly*, 29 October 1927, 1641.

27. *RBC Bulletin*, February 1928, 6.

28. See also the review of *The Gospel for Asia: A Study of Three Religious Masterpieces: Gita, Lotus, and Fourth Gospel*, by Kenneth Saunders (*RBC Bulletin*, April 1928, 4). Saunders's book is characterized as "breathing appreciation more

than criticism" for other faiths, but the review is quick to affirm that the author is "an ardent Christian himself," however much he might admire these other faiths. The November 1928 *RBC Bulletin* featured a review of the alternate title, *The Christian Life and Message in Relation to Non-Christian Systems of Life and Thought.* It reads: "The Relation of Christianity to each of the major non-Christian religions is briefly and lucidly surveyed, with special reference to the best elements in those religions. . . . The argument of Archbishop Temple is a masterful setting forth of the claim of Christianity to uniqueness and universality" (4–5).

29. *RBC Bulletin,* October 1928, 2.

30. *RBC Bulletin,* October 1928, 1. The review of *The Pilgrimage of Buddhism* additionally described Pratt's conclusion that Christian missionaries must not seek to destroy or supersede Buddhism as "the point at which there is most room for differing with some of the author's conclusions" (2).

31. Review of *What We Live By,* by Abbe Ernest Dimnet (*RBC Bulletin,* June 1932, 1).

32. *RBC Bulletin,* April 1929, 2. See also review of *How the Reformation Happened,* by Hillaire Belloc (*RBC Bulletin,* May 1928, 3): "it may doubtless be taken as representative of the view of many liberal-minded members of the Roman Church."

33. *RBC Bulletin,* June 1932, 2.

34. See "Another Book Club," *Publishers' Weekly,* 14 April 1928, 1624; "Catholic Book Club Names Directors," *Publishers' Weekly,* 5 May 1928, 1856. At the same time, the Catholic Book Club was careful to assert that it was *not* a sectarian organization. Any author, regardless of his or her faith tradition, could be featured if the work had adequate literary merit and did not violate Catholic teachings.

35. See, for example, review of *Lausanne: The Will to Understand,* by Edmund Davison Soper (*RBC Bulletin,* March 1928, 3); review of *The Scandal of Christianity,* by Peter Ainsle (*RBC Bulletin,* April 1929, 5); and the review of *Christian Unity,* by Gaius Jackson Slosser (*RBC Bulletin,* May 1929, 4), which provided an historical overview of movements for Christian unity in order to provide context for contemporary debates.

36. *RBC Bulletin,* February 1928, 5.

37. See *RBC Bulletin,* April 1929, 4; *RBC Bulletin,* May 1929, 3.

38. *RBC Bulletin,* February 1928, 4–5.

39. Michael Warner, *The Letters of the Republic: Publication and the Public Sphere in Eighteenth-Century America* (Cambridge, MA: Harvard University Press, 1990).

40. Janice Radway, *A Feeling for Books: The Book-of-the-Month Club and American Literary Taste* (Chapel Hill: University of North Carolina Press, 1997), 284–85.

41. Cavert, "What Religious Books Are Read," 752.

42. *RBC Bulletin*, August 1928, 3. This double reassurance about the soundness of scholarship and accessibility of presentation was characteristic of the *Bulletin*. C. S. Woodward's *Christ in the Common Ways of Life*, for example, was described as "written on the level of the layman" "from the first page to the last," but "this never means any sacrifice of depth or solidity" (*RBC Bulletin*, July 1928, 3).

43. *RBC Bulletin*, February 1928, 2–3. See also the review of *The Dilemma of Protestantism*, by William E. Hammond *(RBC Bulletin*, August 1929, 4–5). Hammond's discussion is praised particularly for its focus on local, specific, concrete, everyday problems. He takes the viewpoint of a practicing pastor versus a theoretical or abstract approach.

44. Amy Johnson Frykholm, *Rapture Culture:* Left Behind *in Evangelical America* (New York: Oxford University Press, 2004), 111.

45. On the pure aesthetic versus the popular ethos, see Pierre Bourdieu, *Distinction: A Cultural Critique of the Judgment of Taste*, trans. Richard Nice (Cambridge, MA: Harvard University Press, 1984), 28–44.

46. Radway, *Feeling for Books*, chap. 8.

47. William H. Leach's *Church Finance* was introduced as "a book full of practical suggestiveness for the minister and officers who are charged with responsibility for the financial administration of the local church" (*RBC Bulletin*, February 1929, 4).

48. *RBC Bulletin*, February 1928, 1.

49. *RBC Bulletin*, March 1928, 5.

50. Radway, *Feeling for Books*, 284–85.

51. *RBC Bulletin*, February 1928, 3.

52. *RBC Bulletin*, April 1930, 4.

53. See the review of *The Romance of the English Bible*, by Laura H. Wild (*RBC Bulletin*, August 1929, 5).

54. *RBC Bulletin*, October 1930, 2.

55. *RBC Bulletin*, June 1928, 8. Others described the Club as a strict tutor that kept them reading the best books on religion, whether they wanted to or not. "A man who is free to read what he will does not always read what he should," wrote one subscriber, explaining the service the RBC rendered to him (ibid.). Another reinstated his subscription after canceling it, because he discovered that "buying and reading books without the monthly recommendation of the Religious Book Club is like trying to worship God in the great out of doors instead of going to church—you can, but you don't" (*RBC Bulletin*, March 1929, 8).

56. *RBC Bulletin*, March 1928, 7.

57. Quoted in *RBC Bulletin*, December 1927, 6; *RBC Bulletin*, October 1928, 5.

58. *RBC Bulletin*, December 1927, 6; ibid., October 1928, 5.

59. T. J. Jackson Lears, "From Salvation to Self-Realization: Advertising and the Therapeutic Roots of the Consumer Culture, 1880–1930," in *The Culture of Consumption: Critical Essays in American History, 1880–1980*, ed. Richard Wightman Fox and T. J. Jackson Lears (New York: Pantheon, 1983), 3–38.

60. *RBC Bulletin*, March 1928, 3–4.

61. Ibid.

62. Ibid., 7.

63. *RBC Bulletin*, April 1928, 3–4.

64. *RBC Bulletin*, April 1929, 1.

65. Ibid.

66. Ibid, 3.

67. *RBC Bulletin*, April 1930, 2, 4.

68. *RBC Bulletin*, July 1928, 2.

Psychology and Mysticism in 1940s Religion

Reading the Readers of Fosdick, Liebman, and Merton

MATTHEW S. HEDSTROM

"I can't help but feel that we are on the brink of a great spiritual renaissance," wrote reader Marian Grassley[1] to Harry Emerson Fosdick in 1956. Grassley had recently come across Fosdick's 1932 best seller *As I See Religion* in her local public library in Columbia, South Carolina. Having read with frustration other popular religious books of the day, she praised Fosdick for "telling us what we want and need to hear. . . . Your essays and books written in the twenties, thirties, and forties are even more apropos now then [*sic*] they were then." Ms. Grassley—or as she signed her letter, Mrs. John Grassley—was not only an admirer but also an astute cultural observer. She made note of a widespread, growing realization that materialism and social striving do not bring greater happiness, then added: "World War II had something to do with bringing this realization about. I know that there are many more people like myself who are searching in current religious books for the answers."[2]

Ms. Grassley was indeed right that Americans were consuming religious books more than ever after the war. After a lull during the Depression, sales of religious books, in both absolute and percentage terms,

increased dramatically in the postwar period.[3] Professor Halford Luc-
cock of Yale, a frequent commenter on religious publishing, went so far
as to declare the trend in 1953 "one of the most striking changes in feeling, mood, and taste which has occurred in centuries . . . telescoped into
a very few years."[4] But more importantly, Grassley was also right that
the culture was on the verge of a great spiritual transformation—a
transformation commonly referred to as, simply, "the Sixties." The seis-
mic social and cultural forces of the era—the civil rights movements; the
antiwar movement; the sexual, pharmaceutical, musical, and social experimentation of the counterculture; and the 1965 immigration reform
act—all shaped the spiritual revolution of this watershed decade. Ms.
Grassley, in her letter, recognized a key turning point in World War II;
the war, indeed, set in motion many of the trends that would culminate
in "the Sixties." But she also hinted at another, less often examined,
cause of this spiritual renaissance—the print culture of liberal religion
itself, especially in the immediate postwar years.

To fully develop that thesis would require a thorough investigation
of the changing business practices and agendas of mass-market religious
publishing in this era and the impact of the major best sellers—and that
is beyond the scope of this essay. However, three texts, each representing a different tradition of faith, stand out from among the religious best
sellers of the mid-1940s for their combination of immense national popularity, intellectual sophistication, and practical applicability. An examination of the print history, readership, and reception of these books, all
number-one best sellers, illuminates the emergence of psychology and
mysticism in popular American religion, the place of religious reading
in American spiritual practice, and the way in which the national experience of war shaped these developments. The first two books, *On Being
a Real Person* (1943) by Harry Emerson Fosdick, a leading liberal Protestant, and *Peace of Mind* (1946), by Joshua Loth Liebman, a Reform rabbi,
helped bring depth psychology into the religious mainstream. They did
so by placing psychological concepts into a liberal religious framework,
couched in a religious idiom. The history of psychology in America has
too often been dominated by scholarly studies of atheistic Freudianism,
masking the complicated ways in which millions of Americans made use
of psychology—as a complement to, and not a substitute for, religious
faith. The third book, *The Seven Storey Mountain* (1948) by Thomas Merton,
a Roman Catholic convert and Trappist monk, is "an autobiography of

faith," unlike the other two books, which are how-tos. Merton's story popularized and humanized the otherwise esoteric matters of mystical experience and practice. Together, these three books presented to the reading public ideas that greatly influenced the new spiritual culture that began to emerge after the war and flowered in the 1960s. The dynamic interplay of the new psychology and ancient mysticism accelerated trends in American religious culture already moving toward an experience-based, instrumental, subject-focused spirituality.[5] Modern psychology and mysticism were hardly new in the 1940s, but their presentation in best-selling books, marketed with the techniques of modern consumer culture, proved especially potent in speaking to, and in turn shaping, the spiritual needs of millions of postwar American readers.

Since the beginning of the century, American clergymen had attempted to incorporate concepts from the new academic psychology into their pastoral work, but the effort did not gain wide acceptance until the 1920s and 1930s.[6] The first sustained effort was the Emmanuel Movement, begun in 1905 by Elwood Worcester, rector of Emmanuel Episcopal Church in Boston, and his colleague Samuel McComb. Disciples of the Harvard psychologist William James, Worcester and McComb developed a style of group therapy aimed at healing mind and body, with loose similarities to Christian Science and New Thought. The movement quickly spread through the urban centers of the Northeast, especially among middle- and upper-middle-class women, and retained a sizeable following into the 1920s.[7] The Emmanuel Movement "helped introduce the new psychology into the church at a time when it was barely understood within the hospital," and before long, sophisticated ministers, along with other literate Americans, were caught up in a psychology craze.[8] Fosdick was among an avant-garde of liberal Protestant leaders in the 1920s who turned to the new psychology to aid in pastoral counseling; this trend eventually resulted in the work of Anton Boisen, Richard Cabot, and others who instituted clinical pastoral training as a routine component of seminary education. These spiritual pioneers revolutionized the practice of liberal religious pastoral care, and their influence was eventually felt far beyond the churches and seminaries, as the leading historian of the field has noted. "The pastoral theologians of the 1930s did a considerable amount of stumbling around," E. Brooks Holifield remarks, "but they laid the foundations for a postwar renaissance that would have surprised even them."[9] Through their best-selling books, Reverend Fosdick and Rabbi Liebman—two key religious figures of this postwar psychological renaissance—brought the new pastoral counseling to the readers of a needy nation.

The Second World War had prepared Americans to accept a psychological message from their religious leaders; without the experience
of war, Fosdick and Liebman would most likely never have commanded
the audiences they did. Depth psychology had been slowly gaining acceptance among cultural elites since just after the turn of the century,
but not until midcentury did psychological conceptions of the self gain
wide currency. Psychological analysis had been utilized in the First
World War—most famously, for the one hundred thousand soldiers
who were treated for "shell shock"—but in the Second World War psychology truly became a mass endeavor. During the latter war, Army
hospitals saw one million psychiatric admissions, and yet the reach of
the psychological and psychiatric professions extended even beyond the
treatment of war trauma. Military officials used psychological assessment as a vital tool in the induction and training of new recruits. By
war's end, fifteen million draftees—more than 10 percent of the national
population—had undergone some form of psychological testing, "most
of them encountering psychological logic for the first time."[10] Throughout the war, civilians back home read reports from the front thick with
psychological analysis, such as a *Newsweek* story from the Pacific describing "Guadalcanal Neurosis." In a nation gripped by war and enamored
of scientific expertise, the psychologist had ascended to an unprecedented cultural status by 1945. "It is hard to believe that a few hundred
professionals could change the culture of a nation," notes historian Andrew Heinze, "but that is what happened in the United States after the
Second World War."[11]

The dramatic conclusions of the war in Europe and the Pacific only
heightened its psychological impact. The advance of Allied forces into
Nazi death camps, in April and May of 1945, forced the American public to confront unfathomable brutality in the heart of Western civilization. Stories of Nazi atrocities had circulated widely in the United States
since 1942, but "the liberations made horrified believers out of the skeptics and brought a new and hideous sense of reality even to those who
never doubted the worst."[12] Images from photographers such as Margaret Bourke-White—including those displayed by Joseph Pulitzer to
throngs in Saint Louis—and graphic newsreels shown nationwide made
intimate to millions of Americans the worst in human nature. Though

most Americans were intellectually able to grapple with these new realities—84 percent believed the reports about Nazi death camps, according to a Gallup poll in May 1945, up from 76 percent in November 1944—many experienced psychological and emotional strains.[13] "Like the soldiers at the camps," writes historian Robert H. Abzug, "those who came upon Belsen and Buchenwald in a newsreel or picture magazine experienced a potent mixture of shock, anger, shame, guilt, and fear. And like the soldiers, they felt a great need for distance and disconnection."[14] This shock, fear, and need for disconnection grew exponentially in August 1945, when the atomic bombings of Hiroshima and Nagasaki demonstrated a new means of mass extermination that might one day visit American soil. The threat of atomic annihilation meant "that no sentient man or woman can really find peace of mind or body," declared the psychiatrist Jules H. Masserman in an address delivered a year after Liebman's book made the phrase famous, while the columnist Dorothy Thompson remarked in October 1945 that atomic terror was leading to "a world-wide nervous breakdown."[15] Such was the psychological climate for these literary pastoral counselors.

Mysticism, like psychology, was a critical component of the postwar spiritual renaissance, and as with psychology, American interest in mystical experience steadily grew in the early twentieth century and spiked after the experience of total war in the 1940s. William James's *Varieties of Religious Experience* (1902) provided the conceptual categories for a generation of American intellectuals to describe "the ineffable," and his ideas found their way to the wider reading public through fellow students of mysticism, foremost among them the Quaker Rufus Jones.[16] In *Social Law in the Spiritual World* (1904), Jones had placed psychological understanding at the center of mystical practice, recognizing that all experience of the divine is mediated through consciousness. Throughout his long and prolific career, Jones argued in a steady stream of popular books and magazine articles that mystical experience is not the province of a spiritual elite but is open to all.[17] In 1942, toward the end of his life, Jones saw that from the horrors of war might come a revitalized concern for direct contact with the divine. He opened yet another *Atlantic Monthly* essay on mystical experience by remarking: "While I am writing this, the world seems to be collapsing into a primitive chaos of revolution and destruction."[18] Yet, Jones continued, "it is now if ever that we need the voice of those who, 'listening to the inner flow of things, speak to the age out of Eternity.'"[19] A vast readership of Americans, both

Protestant and Catholic, soon found such a voice in Thomas Merton
and his personal tale of the contemplative life.

We must look beyond this cultural and intellectual history of psychology and mysticism, however, to grasp the full significance of Fosdick's, Liebman's, and Merton's best sellers. An analysis of these books'
readers and their reading practices provides a clearer window into the
absorption of psychological thinking and mystical practice into American popular religion, as well as a glimpse at the importance of reading
as a spiritual practice in postwar America. All three texts participated in
a thriving midcentury "religious middlebrow" culture, a rubric that describes the relationship of readers to texts, encompassing the medium,
the marketplace, and matters of authority and agency. Scholars such as
Joan Shelly Rubin in *The Making of Middlebrow Culture* have begun to examine the emergence of a "middlebrow culture" in the United States in
the second quarter of the twentieth century, but they have not yet fully
attended to the religious dimensions of this new cultural space. While
the middlebrow Rubin describes brought "refinement" to the socially
anxious, the religious middlebrow sought to provide "peace of mind" to
the existentially anxious during the decades of Depression, World War,
and Cold War. Rubin quotes a 1930s critic who defined the middlebrow
as "the men and women, fairly civilized, fairly literate, who support the
critics and lecturers and publishers by purchasing their wares." Neither
"the tabloid addict class" nor "a tiny group of intellectuals," this critic
continued, they are simply "the majority reader."[20] Such a characterization aptly describes the readers of Fosdick, Liebman, and Merton.

Religious leaders of the era encouraged the reading of religious
books as a critical means of spiritual self-improvement, often giving advice not only on *what* to read but *how*. Rufus Jones, for example, in a
memorable piece written to promote Religious Book Week in 1921, told
readers that they needed to buy, not borrow, their books, so they could
underline and reread. His advice not only situated religious reading
squarely in the consumer marketplace but also, by advocating reading
"with a pencil in hand," as he put it, exemplified the earnest quest for
self-improvement of the middlebrow reading posture.[21] The consequences of this new religious middlebrow culture were far-reaching—it
provided millions of Americans with access to academic theology, psychology, and mysticism and tied American religious culture evermore
tightly to the consumer marketplace. This nexus of print culture and

consumerism brought previously esoteric and academic ideas into the mainstream, with implications for private spirituality and institutional religion.

The Authors and Their Audiences

Rabbi Joshua Loth Liebman's secretaries were very busy in 1947. His book, *Peace of Mind*, had burst onto the publishing scene in the spring of 1946 and would soon pass the one million mark in sales and become the best-selling nonfiction religious book of the twentieth century to that point.[22] Only thirty-nine years old when the book appeared, handsome, with a silky baritone voice, an engaging prose style, and an agile and retentive mind, Liebman was on his way to celebrity; his sudden death in 1948, at age forty-one, is all that kept him from lasting fame. Before *Peace of Mind* he was already known across New England for his weekly radio sermons. Now, with the astonishing commercial success of this book, his office at Boston's Temple Israel was inundated with letters, mostly from women. Liebman would quickly scan each of the thousands of letters—many heartbreaking, others shockingly confessional—and scribble a brief but personal response in the margin. His staff carefully typed and mailed each of these responses, often with a relevant sermon enclosed.

A Jewish woman from Big Wells, Texas, wrote Rabbi Liebman for help. She was forty-two years old, a college-educated high school teacher, a wife and mother. She had been married for fifteen years to a man whom she "respected very much" but found, as she put it, "the sexual relation almost unbearable." Recently, she had fallen in love with one of her students, a high school senior soon to join the Marines. "I have tried to find something in religion to help me, and I have prayed for guidance and understanding thousands of times, but that has failed," she wrote. "If you cannot help me I do not know where to turn."[23] A man from Tampa, Florida, wrote to Rabbi Liebman of "an entity from another life or existence" that spoke with him. He had not yet finished reading *Peace of Mind*, but when he had, he assured the rabbi, he would write again to let Liebman know what the entity thought of the book.[24] One wonders, indeed, just what the entity made of this curious best seller, the first religious book from a non-Christian author to reach a mass audience in the United States.[25] For despite its title, the book that inspired so many letter writers was no inspirational pabulum. Rather, Liebman presented an account of human nature based on a sophisticated rendition of Freudian psychology. The insights of Freud, Liebman argued, when coupled with personal faith and the wisdom of the Jewish prophetic tradition, offered the best hope for survival, and perhaps, one might dare hope, even happiness, in the troubled modern world. Based on the flood of letters streaming into Liebman's office, it seems many troubled, modern souls in postwar America dared hope right along with him.

Simon and Schuster, Liebman's publisher, advertised *Peace of Mind* widely, but the book's sales, and Liebman's flood of fan mail, probably stemmed more from enthusiastic coverage in newspapers and popular magazines such as *Life, Look, The Ladies' Home Journal,* and *Cosmopolitan.* These pieces cemented the book's status as a postwar spiritual guide. The *Look* piece focused on Liebman the man, his Midwestern roots, his own experience with psychoanalysis, and his daily professional and personal routines. Carrying the subtitle "Joshua Loth Liebman's best-seller has guided thousands to serenity," the article also included a digest of Liebman's chapter on grief, perhaps the most directly relevant portion to a postwar audience.[26] The *Boston Post* ran a story on Liebman under the banner headline "Writer of Clean Best-Seller Presents His Views," in which Liebman answered critics and offered his take on the success of his book. Naturally, he pointed to the role of the war in opening American readers to a psychological message, but more personally, he remarked on his place as a Jewish counselor to a largely Christian nation. Liebman told the *Post* reporter of the survivors of a deadly fire in Georgia who requested autographed copies of his book. As the reporter recounted: "His eyes moistened, his shoulders sagged a little, as he told about it the other day. 'They are Christian men and women,' he stated softly. 'Here I am, a rabbi and a Jew.'"[27]

Liberal Protestants, by 1946, were already warming to psychological insight, and now, in the wake of the Holocaust of European Jewry, American readers for the first time embraced the spiritual counsel of a rabbi. As early as 1942, book industry insiders had noticed increased sales of Jewish books to both Jews and non-Jews, "largely because of the Nazi persecutions in Europe."[28] The war, as we have seen, also exposed the American public to modern psychology in massive numbers, and the horrors of Nazi crimes and atomic weapons made the promise of psychology seem all the more compelling. Psychology's emergence as liberal religion's *lingua franca* provided a vocabulary for a non-Christian to speak to the spiritual needs of ordinary Americans. Andrew Heinze terms the emerging climate "a spiritual democracy" and contends "as a result, for the first time in nearly two millennia, a rabbi had a solid platform from which to preach spiritual answers to an interfaith audience."[29] The unique credibility bestowed on Liebman as a Jew in the postwar climate only deepened his mass appeal. "By virtue of both his Jewishness and his Freudianism," continues Heinze, "Liebman was taken as an authority on wartime suffering and prejudice."[30] Liberal religious institutions in the United States had been moving toward a greater ecumenism for decades, as exemplified by the Federal Council of Churches and the National Conference of Christians and Jews. Now, in the wake of the war, the time was ripe for this ecumenism to bear spiritual fruit in rabbi Liebman's literary ministry.

Liebman's work closely resembled another national best seller, a book that preceded it by only three years, Harry Emerson Fosdick's *On Being a Real Person*. Fosdick, too, had offered Americans an unusually learned mix of psychology and liberal religion and, like Liebman, was rewarded with a number-one spot on national best-seller lists. While Liebman was a fresh face on the scene of liberal religion in 1946, Fosdick was liberalism's best-known clergyman.[31] Author of many popular books since the 1910s, Fosdick had gained the national spotlight with his 1922 sermon "Shall the Fundamentalists Win?" which directly challenged what he perceived as the growing threat of fundamentalism to progressive religion. Fosdick's passionate and articulate defense of a modern, liberal faith won him the support of liberal Protestantism's greatest champion in 1920s America, John D. Rockefeller Jr.[32] Rockefeller actively supported Fosdick for the remainder of his career, most especially by building for him the grand Protestant cathedral on Manhattan's Morningside Heights, the Riverside Church. Since 1927, Fosdick had been America's preacher, due to his hugely successful "National Vespers" show on WJZ, a New York radio station that was carried nationally on the NBC network. Through his Sunday evening radio addresses (never called sermons)—which ran until his retirement in 1946—and through his books, Fosdick brought theological modernism and modern psychology into the homes of millions of Americans. *Time* magazine estimated upon Fosdick's retirement that his books and radio addresses brought him 125,000 letters a year, a number that would have overwhelmed Liebman's staff of two.[33]

As soon as Liebman's book appeared in 1946, he and Fosdick were linked in the public mind. Liebman had been somewhat dismayed when Fosdick's book first appeared, fearing the eminent churchman's efforts would overshadow his own planned work. Yet he delivered a very favorable sermon called "On Being a Real Person" in April 1943, in which he tied the main themes of Fosdick's work to those he was developing. "Now, if we are ever to be real persons, if we are ever to have genuine peace of mind," he declared, drawing a parallel between the title of Fosdick's book and his own, yet to be published, "we must learn how to believe again—to believe in friendship and human love and social causes and an undergirding, universal mind."[34] He complimented Fosdick for renouncing Puritan notions of the body and original sin, and even his criticisms of Fosdick, for failing to show his readers how to become the real persons he so ably described, were polite. Fosdick, in turn, warmly welcomed Liebman's publication, writing the young rabbi: "It is very gratifying and encouraging to know that a book like this is sustaining this preeminent position, and I congratulate you on behalf of the whole religious community. . . ."[35] What most likely sealed the association between the two books in the public's mind was their simultaneous appearance in the 1948 hardbound volume *14 Reader's Digest Books*.[36] *Reader's Digest* offered the largest possible audience a chance to read critical portions of each book side by side.

In the fall of 1948, while *Reader's Digest* was promoting the therapeutic gospels of Fosdick and Liebman, Thomas Merton's autobiography hit the best-seller lists.[37] Merton, like Fosdick and Liebman, transcended the category "religious author" to become a national media phenomenon. Sydney Ahlstrom described Merton as "the American who brought the mystical tradition to full expression," and certainly to its widest American audience yet.[38] The success of Merton's autobiography, which shocked its publisher by remaining at or near the top of the *New York Times* best-seller list for the fall of 1948 and much of 1949, was due as well, no doubt, in large degree to the Second World War, and to many Americans' longing for security, meaning, and spiritual solace in the face of the horrors of war and the potentially greater horrors of the next war.[39] Reviewers frequently referred to Merton as an "atomic age Augustine," and in such troubled times, what better symbol of security and serenity than the monastery? Thomas Merton's book reached these soul-weary Americans with the story of his life transformed by a mystical faith. A *Life* magazine article on the *Seven Storey* phenomenon attested to Merton's broad appeal, noting that in many cities more Protestants than Catholics were reading the book.[40] The appeal across tradition was undoubtedly true for Liebman's book as well, as indicated both by its huge sales and by the many letters from non-Jewish readers.

For all the apparent foreignness of this monk's Roman Catholic mysticism to a still predominantly Protestant America, the interest in *The Seven Storey Mountain* among many Protestants does not, on closer inspection, come as a total surprise. As noted earlier, liberal Protestants such as Rufus Jones had been writing of mystical experience in popular books and magazines for decades, and Fosdick himself, influenced by Jones, often argued that for a liberal faith to remain living, it must make room for personal connection with the divine. Gary Dorrien has labeled Fosdick's brand of theological liberalism "personalism," a term that nicely reflects Fosdick's attention to both mystical experience and the study of the consciousness that mediates that experience.[41] Fosdick himself, in fact, may aptly be described as a mystic, as evidenced by his theology of "personalism," his indebtedness to Rufus Jones, and his membership in the Wider Quaker Fellowship, a body founded by Jones in 1936 and open to all "persons who believe in direct and immediate relation between the human soul and God, who are eager for refreshment and inspiration through times of silent communion with God and who [have] faith that there are divine possibilities in all persons."[42] So, with pioneers like Jones and Fosdick, liberal Protestant America was prepared for the message of Thomas Merton.

All three of these texts exhibit a remarkable degree of sophistication and depth for a genre, the inspirational best seller, so often demeaned as "popular." If one were to read *On Being a Real Person*, with its chapters on "The Principle of Self-Acceptance," "Mastering Depression," and "Handling Our Mischievous Consciences," or Liebman's treatment of conscience, self-love, grief, and faith in *Peace of Mind*, one would find two literate, compassionate, and insightful preachers and pastors. Merton's autobiography, the story of a young bohemian's gradual spiritual awakening—though written from the often highly critical perspective of his new self, remade as Father Louis, Trappist monk—retains an overarching hopefulness, evident in the lyrical accounts of the joy Merton ultimately found in Catholic spiritual discipline. Each of these books merits a close read, but more useful in reconstructing the place of these texts in liberal religious print culture is identifying their readers and understanding how and why these books were read. Part of the answer to these "who," "how," and "why" questions can be found in the hundreds of letters from readers in the Liebman and Fosdick archives and in the small collection of letters Merton sent to associates in which he discusses his readership.

As already noted, most of the letters in the Liebman archive are from women, and while this hardly represents a scientific survey, it does provide one clue into the gender composition of his readership. Andrew Heinze has likewise speculated that Liebman's book reached a largely female audience, in part because "it spoke to a more 'feminine' interest in the psyche for its own sake" rather than preach a turn to inner power for material gain. One thinks, in contrast, of popular positive thinkers Napoleon Hill and Norman Vincent Peale, each of whom applied his theories to success in the male-dominated business world.[43] Heinze's notion of the "feminine" draws on prevailing cultural notions, dating at least to the nineteenth century, which coded any deep examination of the inner life, whether emotional or spiritual, as feminine.[44] Heinze also notes that the book's thoughtful and sensitive treatment of the subject of grief undoubtedly appealed to the women whose sons and fathers, husbands and lovers, had been lost in the war. Tellingly, both the *Look* article and the *Reader's Digest* condensation chose to focus on Liebman's discussion of grief, and many of the advertisements for the book depicted it open to the beginning of the grief chapter. The feature stories on Liebman, already mentioned, in women's magazines such as *Cosmopolitan* and *Ladies Home Journal* further attest to the likelihood of a predominately female readership.

Journalists and editors may have seen grieving as the emotional work of women in the year after the war's conclusion, but three years earlier, still in the midst of war, Fosdick's book entered a more ambiguously gendered emotional context. The Council on Books in Wartime, a consortium of the major publishing houses that produced over one hundred million cheap paperbacks for servicemen under the slogan "Books Are Weapons in the War of Ideas," chose *On Being a Real Person* for an Armed Services Edition. Thousands of copies were mailed to servicemen throughout the fall of 1943, straining limited resources. Demand, both military and civilian, remained so high that Fosdick's publisher, Eugene Exman of Harper & Brothers, wrote repeatedly to the War Production Board to request increases in the book's paper allotment. Additional paper was warranted, Exman claimed, because the book "is speaking to the spiritual, mental, and morale needs of the

American people."[45] In a later letter, Exman further pleaded: "We respectfully request additional paper so that we may not be forced to curtail sales of Dr. Fosdick's book which is doing so much to add spiritual strength to people's lives today."[46] The War Production Board denied the request, and despite Harper's efforts at printing the book on lighter stock, ultimately the paper rationing necessitated a reduced production. Some reviewers of Fosdick's book understood these wartime pressures and associated its call for "real personhood" with the wartime struggle against Nazism; these reviewers, therefore, gave the book a masculine spin. The review in the Champaign, Illinois, *News-Gazette,* for example, which appeared on Easter Sunday 1943, a day "when we pause to evaluate our religious—even our patriotic—faith," argued that "high on your reading list, if you would become a real person, a real American, [should be] Fosdick's 'On Being a Real Person.'"[47]

Men in the service were among the throngs who deluged Fosdick with correspondence. One soldier wrote him in 1949: "On Being a Real Person was the set of ideas about religion and God that made sense to my somewhat skeptical mind. It was the key inspiration . . . the foundation that began a complete reorientation of my value system . . . and my life. . . . I carried it for 22 months in the Pacific Theater of Operations. I'm certain that I've read it 15 times through while I was in the army."[48] Another wrote of reading the book in an internment camp in the Philippines.[49] A third, Captain William Graber, wrote directly from the Pacific in November 1944: "After 1500 miles in the air our C-47 dropped in on Henderson Field, Guadalcanal. While having a quick cup of coffee at the Red Cross hut there on a reading table was a copy of *On Being a Real Person.* 'Stolen sweets are sweetest.' That's what I did. Now for the first time in ages a crime was committed and I'm not sorry. After that for another 1500 miles at an altitude of over 10,000 feet your book was greatly enjoyed."[50]

Yet this appeal to patriotic machismo does not by any means tell the whole story of Fosdick's readership. Women, too, served in the Second World War, and many encountered Fosdick's book in the military as well. A private, Janet Royce, from the Second Signal Company of Virginia, wrote Fosdick, "The book is making the rounds of the barracks and in our next all night session it will probably be torn to pieces and chewed back and forth between us."[51] Many more readers, of course, encountered *On Being a Real Person* as civilians, and it seems that, as with Liebman, the majority of Fosdick's stateside readers were women on the home front, who almost certainly turned to Fosdick's book for the same reasons they would read Liebman's a few years later. Fosdick, as noted, had been a pioneer in the field of pastoral counseling, and in the introduction to *On Being a Real Person,* he wrote of his book's intended audience: "I have pictured its readers in terms of the many, diverse individuals who have come to me for help."[52] The Fosdick archive contains records of many hundreds of such counseling sessions, and from this evidence it seems that the majority were white, middle-class women.

The marketing of the book provides further clues about its readership. It was excerpted in women's magazines such as *Yours* and advertised in venues likely to attract the notice of middle-class women. As just one example, Marshall Field's, the large downtown Chicago department store, took out a full-page advertisement in the *Chicago Tribune* to promote its sale of *On Being a Real Person.* "Out of his 20 years' experience as a personal counselor," the ad ran, "Dr. Fosdick now writes to all those who need inner security in these trying times. Out of all he has learned . . . he has chosen the most important things to set down for you."[53] Alongside shoes for the kids and a tie for the husband, the advertisement seems to imply, come and get inner security for *you.* The likelihood of a female majority among Fosdick's and Liebman's readership takes on added significance when one considers the central role that women, and feminism, played in the spiritual transformations that were to come. At a time when men dominated the leadership of church and synagogue, religious middlebrow reading—both the medium and the message—freed women to construct their own worlds of meaning from the raw materials provided by mass-market books.

At least as important as *who* read Fosdick's and Liebman's books are the questions of *why* readers turned to these books and *how* they read them. Interestingly, as far back as 1931, Fosdick had published a series of articles aptly entitled "Building a Personality" in the popular fitness-and-beauty magazine *Physical Culture,* a venue that certainly underscores the intended middle-class audience and utilitarian purpose of his message. A reviewer of Fosdick's book also connected the wartime strains to reading habits: "The terrible pressures of the times are such that great numbers of people who have not manifested any interest in religion previously are now turning to spiritual sources for help in the time of their trouble." He continued with a comment on the potentially wider impact of commodified religion: "But turning to religion does not mean, necessarily, a turning to Church. Indeed, hundreds of thousands of people are reading religious books who will never darken the door of any house of worship."[54] Again, though, the servicemen and women who wrote to Fosdick offer direct testimony, testimony that gives witness to a middlebrow hunger for spiritual self-improvement. We have already heard from the soldier who read *On Being a Real Person* fifteen times, and the private in the signal company who commented that her buddies would tear the book to pieces in an "all-night session." Another Fosdick writer, a veteran recovering in a Miami hospital, wrote on Red Cross stationery, "[I am] now days deep in your book. The main fault with you is that it is too full of wisdom I have read each chapter twice and then I am afraid I am missing something. Often I wonder why I hadn't thought of it before. What I like best about it is that it is all down right horse sense!"[55] This rereading of a book that is both "horse sense" and "too full of wisdom" perfectly describes a reader hoping to glean life lessons from a book that bridges the high and the low.

The letters to Rabbi Liebman also illuminate habits of religious middlebrow reading. The middle-aged high school teacher who wrote Liebman of her love for a student noted elsewhere in her letter, "I have read all of your book twice, and some parts of it several times. I found much help in it," but then added, "although some of it is too deep for me to understand."[56] Her relationship to the text—reading and rereading, probing despite it being "too deep"—sounds much like the veteran in Miami who read and reread Fosdick's book. "My husband works 18 hrs a day," wrote another woman, named Lillian, after reading *Peace of Mind*. With only four years of education, married at age twenty, now a housewife and mother, she confided to Rabbi Liebman: "Therefore, I am a very lonely woman, and since I have 2 children and have to do my own babysitting, I have resorted to reading. Dear Rabbi, words just couldn't express what reading has done for me. It has given me insight into the world around me." Contrary to stereotype, she then adds, "Of late it seems fiction doesn't seem to interest me. I can benefit from non-fiction so much more."[57] The word choice here, "resort to reading" and "benefit from non-fiction," testifies to the potency of the religious middlebrow endeavor.

Lillian's plight as a "lonely woman" trapped with small children perfectly mirrors the "Problem That Has No Name" so famously described by Betty Friedan more than a decade later in *The Feminine Mystique*. Though Lillian was less well educated than Friedan's Smith College classmates, many of the other readers of postwar religious best sellers were very likely college-educated women seeking to understand how to cope with the stifling demands of wartime and, later, Cold War family life. As the nation shifted from fighting Fascism to fighting Communism, Congress passed the National Mental Health Act, which, recognizing the need for a psychologically healthy population to win the twilight struggle to come, established the National Institutes of Mental Health in 1946. In this battle, the family itself was on the front lines, as "the home came to be viewed as a bulwark against Communism."[58] Popular movies such as *The Snake Pit* (1948), the increasingly therapeutic-minded women's magazines, and even socially conservative authors such as Marynia Farnham all acknowledged the strains of Cold War family life on American women.[59]

Though Friedan's assessment of postwar gender relations has become a commonplace, in the 1940s and 1950s, as Elaine Tyler May observes, "critical observers of middle-class life considered homemakers to be emancipated and men to be oppressed."[60] Women such as those who wrote to Liebman and Fosdick were hard pressed to find public advocates, especially among religious writers. By the mid-1950s, a few women's voices, such as Anne Morrow Lindbergh's and Catherine Marshall's, were heard.[61] In a more elite cultural vein, Georgia Harkness published commercially successful books on prayer in the late 1940s.[62] Yet in spite of these few women writers, men dominated public religion—institutional leadership, broadcast media, and print—in 1940s and 1950s America as perhaps never before or since, producing a generation of what Martin Marty has called "seething women." Their letters, written out of this silent suffering to distant, male authors, reveal previously obscured layers of the social history of American religion.

Indeed, the Fosdick and Liebman reader letters, ripe with phrases such as "resort to reading" and "benefiting from non-fiction," demonstrate the complex interplay of reading practice and spirituality. More than anything, these readers' accounts indicate the practical utility of reading as a spiritual act and the felt need for religion to solve real-world problems. A member of the Riverside congregation who had served in the European theater wrote to Fosdick in August 1945, "I feel that one constructive result of the war will be a realization of the need for 'faith in belief' since we have put religion to work, and found that it worked!"[63] The missionary who wrote of reading *On Being a Real Person* in an internment camp in the Philippines noted: "But even there I kept insisting that life in a camp is also life and an opportunity. What use would religion be if it could not help us in a situation like that?"[64] And we recall the lonely housewife and the sexually conflicted schoolteacher who turned to Liebman's *Peace of Mind* for specific help.

Of course, Liebman's and Fosdick's books were how-tos, and so an instrumental take on spirituality makes sense for their readers. The readership of Merton's autobiography, therefore, provides an instructive comparison. While Merton's personal example in 1948 was as an apparently world-renouncing cloistered monk, his appeal for his readers was the same as Liebman's and Fosdick's—the book offered a faith of personal and social utility in everyday life. The 11 October 1948 issue of *Time* carried a short article in the "Religion" section with the intriguing title "Mystics Among Us," which profiled Merton, declaring "the world still has millions of mystics, and the most mystical human beings are often among the most practical as well."[65] The British novelist Graham Greene, in his dust-jacket blurb, indicated that Merton's book might inspire readers to follow Rufus Jones's book-reading advice: "*The Seven Storey Mountain*," declared Greene, "is a book one reads with a pencil so as to make it one's own." One can hardly conjure a better image of the middlebrow reader.

The Seven Storey Mountain proved so immensely popular that many of these readers apparently took their pencils and wrote directly to Merton. Merton was so inundated with mail from readers that, as he joked to a friend, "I have a secretary who mails out the "Trappist-no-write-letters" card to the fans."[66] (Merton did, of course, maintain a lively correspondence with friends and colleagues.) Merton revealed much about who these readers were and how and why they read his book in letters to friends and colleagues. He confided to Sister Therese Lentfoehr: "Letters come in from everywhere, Park Avenue and San Quentin Prison, the sanctuary and the studio,"[67] but, he wrote elsewhere, "more of them are usually sensible married women who want to find out how you can lead the contemplative life and take care of the children at the same time."[68] This was the practical faith that Fosdick and Liebman had each advocated, and that Merton's readers, the "sensible married women," evidently sought as well.

Conclusion: Re-Thinking Will Herberg's
Protestant, Catholic, Jew

With the rise of religious middlebrow culture in the second quarter of the twentieth century, we can see that mass-marketed books brought significant changes to American religious life. Harry Emerson Fosdick, Thomas Merton, and Joshua Loth Liebman—one Protestant, one Catholic, one Jew—produced widely successful texts, each read by large numbers of readers from other faiths. This fact alone points to an accelerating ecumenism, described most influentially by Will Herberg in 1955 as an emerging Judeo-Christian "American Way of Life."[69] Herberg feared that the so-called "triple melting pot" was leading to insipid theology and the loss of integrity for each faith tradition. Inasmuch as the letters to all three authors reveal shared, pragmatic concerns for the everyday utility of spirituality, while indicating very little interest in formal theology or creeds, Herberg's fears seem realized in these texts.

Yet these books refute as much as they confirm Herberg's famous thesis. Liebman and Merton, each in his own way, were fiercely partisan, often criticizing Protestant religious culture, especially traditional orthodoxies. In his chapter in *Peace of Mind* on conscience, for example, Liebman criticized Paul, Augustine, Luther, and Calvin as unhealthily obsessed with human beings' natural wickedness—and with repression and atonement as responses—rather than advocating a more psychologically sound focus on growth; in numerous instances throughout the book, such as in his reference to sitting *shiva* in his chapter on grief, Liebman used Jewish practices and teachings as the basis for what he considered a healthier approach to life.[70] "Liebman thrilled to the idea that Judaism's insights into human nature matched those of dynamic psychology," writes Heinze; "That idea fueled the Jewish polemic in *Peace of Mind*."[71] Merton, likewise, was not shy in his attacks on the prevailing values in Protestant America, a sharp contrast with many of his Catholic contemporaries, who sought to downplay Catholic distinctiveness in an effort to further interfaith dialogue and, in turn, the social standing of Catholic Americans.[72] In a passage on virtue that echoes Liebman's on conscience, Merton declared that the term's enduring currency in Catholic countries "is a testimony to the fact that it suffered [in the United States and Protestant Europe] mostly from the mangling it underwent at the hands of Calvinists and Puritans."[73] Ecumenism certainly contributed to the commercial success of *Peace of Mind* and *The Seven Storey Mountain,* but these are not thoroughly ecumenical books. Liebman and Merton shared with Fosdick a deep, modern distrust of conservative Protestant notions of sin, self, and emotional well-being. Part of what makes Liebman's and Merton's broad successes remarkable, in particular in an age of ecumenism, is their appeal precisely because of the polemical qualities of their books. Here we see the depth of longing in the postwar period for meaningful spiritual alternatives to conservative Protestantism.

More than some bland, totalizing Judeo-Christian religious center, then, these three books, and the letters from their readers, point to a dynamism in liberal religion, especially in the increasingly psychological and mystical cast to liberal American spirituality. These developments, beyond anything Herberg identified, suggest a new American way. Religious middlebrow books introduced millions of Americans to ways of understanding the self that seamlessly blended modern psychology, mysticism, and liberal religion. Critics have asserted that liberal Protestantism's embrace of psychology was a critical factor in the secularization of American religion in the twentieth century.[74] Rather than disappearing or retreating further into the private sphere, as various theories of secularization predict, however, liberal religion incorporated psychology as part of a process of renewal. Moreover, much of the vitality that remained in liberal religion stemmed from its embrace of the mystical alongside the psychological, a pairing whose importance Rufus Jones and Harry Emerson Fosdick well understood, and whose roots date back in American culture at least to the nineteenth-century Transcendentalists.[75]

Religious middlebrow culture, with its embrace of psychology and a faith mediated through mass-market commodities, did contribute to a rift in American religious life between personal spirituality and religious institutions, a rift captured in the often-heard phrase "spiritual but not religious." Sociologists and historians of American religion have developed an entire subfield devoted to exploring the changes in American religious life since the 1960s, employing terms such as "postmodern" and "seeker" to describe the changing spiritual landscape.[76] The endeavor of seeking, of finding spiritual sustenance beyond the bounds of formal institutions, though with deep roots in American culture, gained new tools and expanded possibilities with the explosion of mass-market religious publishing in the mid-twentieth century. From the point of view of both reader and writer, the middlebrow enterprise was an eclectic one. Religious consumers, as they became more dependent on the commercial marketplace, were freer to pick and choose among various takes on the spiritual life. Not coincidentally, the psychological orientation aimed at self-realization, such as that promoted by Fosdick and Liebman, fit better with such a consumer model of faith than with older models of the self aimed at otherworldly salvation.[77] Examining the print culture of postwar liberal religion helps explain the psychological and mystical turns of the 1940s—and how, eventually, "the Sixties" happened.

In addition to presenting an accessible religious psychology, the mass marketing of books also brought the mysticism of Harry Emerson Fosdick and Thomas Merton to the vast reading public. In doing so, it reinforced trends already evident in liberal Protestantism toward spiritual individualism and eclecticism. Mystical religion, in fact, helped lower the walls dividing Protestant and Catholic, black and white, and later, East and West. Leigh Eric Schmidt contends that mysticism in midcentury "was a means of interreligious engagement—a sympathetic meeting point in an increasingly global encounter of religions."[78] These trends reached their fullest expression in the spiritual renaissance of the 1960s, the renaissance predicted by Marian Grassley in her 1956 letter to Harry Emerson Fosdick. "Understanding how *mysticism* took on such a wide sense," Schmidt writes, "is an important step in fathoming how *spirituality* itself has now become such an expansive term in the religious vernacular of the twenty-first century."[79] Indeed, the very language we use to define this newly expansive spirituality is rooted in the discourses of mysticism and psychology, discourses popularized by the reading culture of the mid-twentieth century.

Notes

1. Pseudonyms are used, in the text as well as the endnotes, when referring to individual readers of Fosdick and Liebman.

2. Marian Grassley to Harry Emerson Fosdick, 29 November 1956, Series 2b, Box 1, Folder 10, Harry Emerson Fosdick Papers, the Burke Library archives at Union Theological Seminary in the City of New York.

3. Quoted in Eugene Exman, "Reading, Writing, and Religion," *Harper's Magazine* 206, no. 1236 (May 1953): 84.

4. Exman, "Reading, Writing, and Religion," 84.

5. See, for example, Harold Bloom, *The American Religion: The Emergence of the Post-Christian Nation* (New York: Simon and Schuster, 1992); Christopher Lasch, *The Culture of Narcissism: American Life in an Age of Diminishing Expectations* (New York: Norton, 1979); Philip Rieff, *The Triumph of the Therapeutic: Uses of Faith after Freud* (New York: Harper and Row, 1966).

6. For a useful overview of the relationship between psychoanalysis in particular and Protestantism in early twentieth-century America, see Jon H. Roberts, "Psychoanalysis and American Christianity, 1900–1945," in *When Science and Christianity Meet*, ed. David C. Lindberg and Ronald L. Numbers (Chicago: University of Chicago Press, 2003), 225–44.

7. E. Brooks Holifield, *A History of Pastoral Care in America: From Salvation to Self-Realization* (Nashville, TN: Abingdon Press, 1983). On women in New Thought, see Beryl Satter, *Each Mind a Kingdom: American Women, Sexual Purity, and the New Thought Movement, 1875–1920* (Berkeley: University of California Press, 1999).

8. Holifield, *History of Pastoral Care in America*, 207.

9. Holifield, *History of Pastoral Care in America*, 221.

10. Eva S. Moskowitz, *In Therapy We Trust: America's Obsession with Self-Fulfillment* (Baltimore: Johns Hopkins University Press, 2001), 102, 105.

11. Andrew R. Heinze, *Jews and the American Soul: Human Nature in the Twentieth Century* (Princeton, NJ: Princeton University Press, 2004), 202.

12. Robert H. Abzug, *Inside the Vicious Heart: Americans and the Liberation of Nazi Concentration Camps* (New York: Oxford University Press, 1985), 19.

13. Abzug, *Inside the Vicious Heart*, 10, 39.

14. Abzug, *Inside the Vicious Heart*, 170–71.

15. Quoted in Paul Boyer, *By the Bomb's Early Light: American Thought and Culture at the Dawn of the Atomic Age* (Chapel Hill: University of North Carolina Press, 1994), 277, 281.

16. Other key scholars of mysticism of the era included Dean W. R. Inge, Evelyn Underhill, Baron Friedrich von Hügel, and a bit later, Rudolf Otto. See Leigh Eric Schmidt, "The Making of Modern 'Mysticism,'" *Journal of the American Academy of Religion* 71, no. 2 (June 2003): 273–302.

17. I make this argument at greater length in "Rufus Jones and Mysticism for the Masses," *CrossCurrents* 54, no. 2 (Summer 2004): 31–44.

18. Rufus M. Jones, "Mystical Experience," *The Atlantic Monthly* 169 (May 1942): 634.

19. Jones, "Mystical Experience," 635.

20. Joan Shelley Rubin, *The Making of Middlebrow Culture* (Chapel Hill: University of North Carolina Press, 1992), xii–xiii.

21. Rufus M. Jones, "The Habit of Reading," *The Watchword*, 13 March 1921.

22. The authority on Liebman is Heinze, *Jews and the American Soul*.

23. Mrs. Edith Fischman to Joshua Loth Liebman, 23 June 1947, Joshua Loth Liebman Collection, The Howard Gotlieb Archival Research Center at Boston University (henceforth Liebman Collection), Box 28, Folder "Fo Misc."

24. Charles Edmonds to Joshua Loth Liebman, 27 August 1947, Liebman Collection, Box 28, Folder "E—Misc."

25. Excluding, of course, the sacred texts of various traditions, most especially the Bible.

26. Harold B. Clemenko, "The Man Behind 'Peace of Mind'," *Look* 12 (6 January 1948): 15–17.

27. Mark Hatch, "Writer of Clean Best-Seller Presents His Views," *Boston Post*, 22 June 1947.

28. "Publishers of Jewish Books Find Increased Market," *Publishers' Weekly*, 21 February 1942, 859.

29. Heinze, *Jews and the American Soul*, 238.

30. Heinze, *Jews and the American Soul*, 215.

31. On Fosdick, see Robert Moats Miller, *Harry Emerson Fosdick: Pastor, Preacher, Prophet* (New York: Oxford University Press, 1985).

32. On Rockefeller's religious philanthropy, see Albert F. Schenkel, *The Rich Man and the Kingdom: John D. Rockefeller, Jr., and the Protestant Establishment* (Minneapolis: Fortress Press, 1995).

33. "Fosdick's Last Year," *Time* 47 (18 June 1946): 56.

34. Joshua Loth Liebman, "On Being a Real Person: A Discussion of Harry Emerson Fosdick's New Book," sermon delivered Friday, 2 April 1943, typescript in Liebman Collection, Box 66 (no folders in box).

35. Harry Emerson Fosdick to Joshua Loth Liebman, 9 April 1947, Liebman Collection, Box 3, Folder "letters."

36. *14 Reader's Digest Books* (Pleasantville, NY: Reader's Digest Association, 1948).

37. On Merton, the biographical literature is extensive, but most comprehensive is Michael Mott, *The Seven Mountains of Thomas Merton* (Boston: Houghton Mifflin, 1984).

38. Sydney Ahlstrom, *A Religious History of the American People* (New Haven, CT: Yale University Press, 1972), 1035.

39. The cultural impact of the bomb was immediate. Paul Boyer quotes a critic from the *New York Times* who wrote on 8 August 1945 that the dropping of the atomic bomb was "an explosion in men's minds." See *By the Bomb's Early Light*, xxi.

40. *Life* 26 (23 May 1949): 85.

41. Gary J. Dorrien, *The Making of American Liberal Theology: Idealism, Realism, and Modernity, 1900–1950* (Louisville, KY: Westminster John Knox Press, 2003).

42. Quoted in Elizabeth Gray Vining, *Friend of Life: The Biography of Rufus M. Jones* (Philadelphia: J. B. Lippincott Company, 1958), 268.

43. Andrew R. Heinze, "*Peace of Mind* (1946): Judaism and the Therapeutic Polemic of Postwar America," *Religion and American Culture* 12, no. 1 (Winter 2002): 40. On Hill and Peale see Napoleon Hill, *Think and Grow Rich* (Meriden, CT: The Ralston Society, 1937), and Norman Vincent Peale, *The Power of Positive Thinking* (New York: Prentice-Hall, 1952).

44. The literature here is extensive, but see especially Anne Braude, "Women's History *Is* American Religious History," in *Retelling U.S. Religious History*, ed. Thomas A. Tweed (Berkeley: University of California Press, 1997).

45. Eugene Exman to Harry West, 30 July 1943, Harper & Brothers Papers, Rare Book and Manuscript Library, Columbia University, Box 99, Folder "Harry Emerson Fosdick."

46. Eugene Exman to Harry West, 4 August 1943, Harper & Brothers Papers, Box 99, Folder "Harry Emerson Fosdick."

47. C. C. Burford, untitled review, *Champaign News-Gazette*, 25 April 1943.

48. Frederick Gorman to Harry Emerson Fosdick, 29 April 1949 (first two ellipses in the original), Series 2b, Box 3, Folder 3, Harry Emerson Fosdick Papers, Burke Library archives at Union Theological Seminary in the City of New York (henceforth Fosdick Papers).

49. Benjamin Berry to Harry Emerson Fosdick, 26 April 1945, Series 2b, Box 4, Folder 11, Fosdick Papers.

50. Capt. William Graber to Harry Emerson Fosdick, 28 November 1944, Series 2b, Box 4, Folder 12, Fosdick Papers.

51. Pvt. Janet Royce to Harry Emerson Fosdick, n.d., Series 2b, Box 3, Folder 2, Fosdick Papers.

52. Harry Emerson Fosdick, *On Being a Real Person* (New York: Harper & Brothers, 1943), ix.

53. *Chicago Tribune*, 12 March 1943, 9.

54. Unsigned review, *The Christian Advocate* 118, no. 17 (29 April 1943): 516–17.

55. Walter Blankenship to Harry Emerson Fosdick, 10 April 1943, Series 2b, Box 4, Folder 11, Fosdick Papers.

56. Mrs. Edith Fischman to Joshua Loth Liebman, 23 June 1947, Liebman Collection.

57. Lillian to Joshua Loth Liebman, 15 March 1948, Liebman Collection.

58. Moskowitz, *In Therapy We Trust*, 169.

59. A point made by Moskowitz in *In Therapy We Trust*, 165. See Ferdinand Lundberg and Marynia F. Farnham, M.D., *The Modern Woman: The Lost Sex* (New York: Harper & Brothers, 1947). As Lundberg and Farnham wrote: "Women are the pivot around which much of the unhappiness of our day revolves, like a captive planet. To a significant extent they are responsible for it. . . . Women as a whole (with exceptions) are maladjusted, much more so than men. For men have appropriate means to social adjustment: economic and political power, scientific power and athletic prowess" (24).

60. Elaine Tyler May, *Homeward Bound: American Families in the Cold War Era* (New York: Basic Books, 1988), 20.

61. See Catherine Marshall, *A Man Called Peter* (New York: McGraw-Hill Book Co., 1951), and Anne Morrow Lindbergh, *Gift from the Sea* (New York: Pantheon, 1955).

62. See, most notably, Georgia Harkness, *Prayer and the Common Life* (New York: Abingdon-Cokesbury, 1948).

63. Lt. Kenneth Booth to Harry Emerson Fosdick, 31 August 1945, Series 2b, Box 4, Folder 11, Fosdick Papers.

64. Benjamin Berry to Harry Emerson Fosdick, 26 April 1945, Series 2b, Box 4, Folder 11, Fosdick Papers.

65. Religion Section, *Time* 52 (11 October 1948): 87–89.

66. Thomas Merton to Sister Therese Lentfoehr, 25 February 1950, Thomas Merton Papers, Rare Books and Manuscript Library, Columbia University (henceforth Merton Papers). All quotations from this collection are used by permission of the Merton Legacy Trust.

67. Thomas Merton to Sister Therese Lentfoehr, 27 December 1948, Merton Papers.

68. Thomas Merton to Robert Lax, 24 November 1948, Merton Papers.

69. Will Herberg, *Protestant, Catholic, Jew: An Essay in American Religious Sociology* (Garden City, NY: Doubleday, 1955).

70. Joshua Loth Liebman, *Peace of Mind* (New York: Simon and Schuster, 1946), 24, 123.

71. Heinze, *Jews and the American Soul*, 220.

72. Merton's biographer, Michael Mott, writes rather simply, "His autobiography was neither ecumenical nor restrained." See Mott, *The Seven Mountains of Thomas Merton*, 247. And Robert Inchausti, seemingly in direct response to Herberg, argues, "With one honest book, *The Seven Storey Mountain,* Merton had boldly refuted both the soulless instrumentalism of the postwar technocrats and the insipid religious bromides offered by their positive-thinking preacher cohorts." See Robert Inchausti, *Thomas Merton's American Prophecy* (Albany, NY: SUNY Press, 1998), 141.

73. Thomas Merton, *The Seven Storey Mountain: An Autobiography of Faith* (New York: Harcourt Brace, 1999), 223.

74. Kevin G. Meador, "'My Own Salvation': The *Christian Century* and Psychology's Secularizing of American Protestantism," in *The Secular Revolution: Power, Interests, and Conflict in the Secularization of American Public Life,* ed. Christian Smith (Berkeley: University of California Press, 2003), 269–309.

75. Leigh Eric Schmidt makes a very compelling form of this argument in *Restless Souls: The Making of American Spirituality from Emerson to Oprah* (San Francisco: HarperSanFrancisco, 2005).

76. The literature here is extensive, but certain landmark texts along the way include Wade Clark Roof, *A Generation of Seekers: The Spiritual Journeys of the Baby-Boom Generation* (San Francisco: HarperSanFrancisco, 1993), and *Spiritual Marketplace: Baby Boomers and the Remaking of American Religion* (Princeton, NJ: Princeton University Press, 1999); Robert Wuthnow, *After Heaven: Spirituality in America since the 1950s* (Berkeley: University of California Press, 1998); and Robert

C. Fuller, *Spiritual, But Not Religious: Understanding Unchurched America* (New York: Oxford University Press, 2001). In a different vein, see also Dean Kelley's seminal *Why Conservative Churches Are Growing: A Study in the Sociology of Religion* (New York: Harper & Row, 1972).

77. See Donald Meyer's classic *The Positive Thinkers: Religion as Pop Psychology from Mary Baker Eddy to Oral Roberts* (New York: Pantheon Books, 1980), in addition to Holifield, *A History of Pastoral Care in America*. Scholars have, for some time, fruitfully applied economic models to early American religion, yet the insightfulness of these studies need not mitigate the argument that American religious life has become *even more* amenable to consumerist approaches with the psychological turn of the twentieth century. See especially Roger Finke and Rodney Stark, *The Churching of America, 1776–1990: Winners and Losers in Our Religious Economy* (New Brunswick, NJ: Rutgers University Press, 1992), and R. Laurence Moore, *Selling God: American Religion in the Marketplace of Culture* (New York: Oxford University Press, 1994).

78. Schmidt, "Making of Modern 'Mysticism,'" 290.

79. Schmidt, "Making of Modern 'Mysticism,'" 276 (emphasis in original).

6

Religion and Print Culture in Contemporary America

Healing Words

Narratives of Spiritual Healing and Kathryn Kuhlman's Uses of Print Culture, 1947–76

CANDY GUNTHER BROWN

Kathryn Kuhlman (1907–76) was an obscure itinerant evangelist with a questionable past until one fateful day in 1947 when the forty-year-old redhead stood before a small audience in Franklin, Pennsylvania. A woman interrupted Kuhlman's sermon to announce that a tumor had disappeared from her body the previous evening while Kuhlman had been preaching and that her doctor had just confirmed the healing. Kuhlman had not prayed for the woman and had not been preaching on the subject of spiritual healing. Soon, other people began to report spontaneous healing during Kuhlman's services, especially when she preached on the Holy Spirit. From such humble beginnings, Kuhlman became an internationally prominent healing evangelist who, by the mid-1960s, was holding regular services for overflow crowds of thousands in Pittsburgh, Los Angeles, and other cities across the United States and Canada. The daughter of Baptist and Methodist parents, Kuhlman captivated ecumenical audiences who sometimes traveled thousands of miles to attend her services. Kathryn Kuhlman became a household name throughout much of churchgoing America. Pope Paul VI invited her for a visit, and the municipal governments of Los Angeles, Pittsburgh,

and St. Louis bestowed on her civic awards. The meteoric rise in Kuhlman's profile resulted from the publicity that print, radio, and television
gave to the dramatic stories of those who reported healing during her
miracle services. Hearing about the alleged healings, the crowds came,
and Kuhlman developed more formalized strategies to maintain decorum in her services and to manage the publicity that they generated.[1]

Following a lineage of controversial female healing evangelists in the
Holiness and Pentecostal traditions, such as Maria Woodworth-Etter
(1844–1924) and Aimee Semple McPherson (1890–1944), Kuhlman used
her winsome style to usher new expectation of spiritual healing and
other charisma, or gifts of the Holy Spirit, into Protestant and Roman
Catholic churches previously resistant to presumed Pentecostal fanaticism. Kuhlman's success in crossing once rigid boundaries between religious communities suggests a major cultural shift—which Kuhlman's
career reflects and to which it also contributed—from the traditional
Protestant-Catholic divide toward a new polarity between those who
subscribed to supernatural and naturalistic worldviews.[2] Kuhlman rose
to prominence in an era when more and more Americans, including ec-
onomically mobile intellectual sophisticates, were beginning to question
the functionally naturalistic assumptions that had dominated much of
medical as well as evangelical and liberal Protestant discourse during
the first half of the twentieth century. The charismatic movement that
Kuhlman represented blossomed even while non-Christian healing alternatives such as New Age crystal, yoga, and psychic healing also flourished.[3] Kuhlman's teaching on spiritual healing, popularized through
modern communication media, exemplified and encouraged widespread disillusionment with a naturalistic worldview that denied either
the existence or relevance of an unseen higher power to everyday life.[4]
At the turn of the twenty-first century, in part because of Kuhlman's
legacy, public opinion polls suggest that 70 to 80 percent of Americans
believe that God supernaturally heals people in answer to prayer.[5]

Narratives of spiritual healing published by Kuhlman offer a rich approach to debates over the supernatural because of their implications for
fields of discourse rarely treated together, including religion and science,
the history of medicine, gender studies, the history of the body, theology,
narrative theory, and print culture. Kuhlman deployed healing narratives as a direct challenge to the controlling assumption of scientific naturalism: that permanent natural laws account for every phenomenon. In

response to issues raised by Kuhlman and others, strange new alliances formed, with scientific naturalists and functionally naturalistic evangelical and liberal Protestants positioned across a philosophical chasm from neo-Pentecostal Protestants, Catholics, and New Age practitioners who expected supernatural healing of hurting physical bodies.[6]

In this essay, I analyze Kuhlman's trilogy, *I Believe in Miracles* (1962), *God Can Do It Again* (1969), and *Nothing Is Impossible with God* (1974), as strategically crafted apologetics for spiritual healing.[7] By presenting empirical evidence acceptable within a naturalistic paradigm and reinterpreting that evidence through the lens of personal testimony, Kuhlman questioned the adequacy of dominant scientific and religious constructions of the human body and of the meanings of health, illness, and healing. Kuhlman defied her critics either to present an interpretation of the evidence at least as plausible as hers or to acknowledge that God both exists and acts supernaturally in the phenomenal world.[8]

Spiritual Healing and Print Culture

National media coverage of Kuhlman by the secular press convinced her of the usefulness of wielding medical evidence to argue for spiritual healing. *Redbook* magazine commissioned an avowedly skeptical reporter, Emily Gardiner Neal, to write an article on Kuhlman in 1950, entitled "Can Faith in God Heal the Sick?"[9] After her investigation, Neal—sufficiently convinced to become Kuhlman's ghostwriter and begin her own healing ministry—wrote a positive article.[10] *Redbook*'s editors appended a forward endorsing Neal's findings with the claim that "this magazine has in its custody the following confidential documents": medical and X-ray records, workmen's compensation reports, letters from clergy and public officials, and testimonials from eight people who insisted that God had healed them supernaturally.[11] A 1970 *Time* magazine article similarly concluded: "miraculous cures seem to occur" and termed Kuhlman a "veritable one-woman shrine of Lourdes."[12] Media attention by *People, Christianity Today,* and *U.S. Catholic* magazines and the television talk shows of Johnny Carson, Mike Douglas, Merv Griffin, and Dinah Shore suggested that many Americans were open to spiritual healing—that they wanted to believe in it—but that they also wanted medical verification.[13]

Kuhlman's decision to rely upon medical evidence in her own publications contrasted with the strategies undertaken by many other proponents of spiritual healing, who rejected the medical gaze as irrelevant. Unlike evangelists who urged the sick to "claim" healing by faith, regardless of physical symptoms, or who discouraged the sick from seeking medical attention, Kuhlman insisted that medical evidence back every healing report.[14] Unlike most of her contemporary healing evangelists, such as the Oklahoma-based Oral Roberts, Kuhlman did not publicize healing through a regularly issued periodical, lest printing deadlines interfere with the systematic collection and presentation of evidence.[15] Kuhlman did produce a total of four thousand radio and five hundred television broadcasts, many of which included healing testimonials. Her nationally syndicated weekly telecast *I Believe in Miracles,* produced by Dick Ross between 1966 and 1976, was the longest running thirty-minute program filmed in CBS studios.[16]

The first and most widely circulated of Kuhlman's major books, *I Believe in Miracles,* sold more than two million copies between the 1960s and the 1990s.[17] Despite the advice of supporters to generate greater interest in her ministry by publishing sequels in quick succession, Kuhlman's perfectionism led her to proceed slowly, lest a failed new project undermine the favorable publicity she had already achieved.[18] Alongside the personal satisfaction that drawing large audiences of service attendees, readers, and radio and television listeners doubtless gave her, Kuhlman stated her apologetic goal in *I Believe in Miracles:* "My purpose is to save souls, and my particular calling is to offer proof of the power of God."[19] In publishing carefully selected and edited narratives of miraculous healing, Kuhlman pursued the agenda of making credible the central miracle claim of Christianity, the resurrection of Jesus of Nazareth.

In order to attract secular as well as religious readers, Kuhlman worked with a trade press, Prentice-Hall, that specialized in academic, business, and professional books, issuing a relatively small percentage of religious titles.[20] As Prentice-Hall moved further away from religious publishing in the 1990s, the Kathryn Kuhlman Foundation turned to a major Christian publishing house, Bridge-Logos, to issue reprint editions of all three volumes. Marketing the books through mainstream retailers such as Barnes & Noble as well as Christian bookstores, Bridge-Logos continued to list *I Believe in Miracles* as one of its "best sellers" in 2007.[21]

Kuhlman crafted her publications to instill faith for healing by suggesting that anyone could be healed of any condition by trusting God. With the aid of professional ghostwriters Emily Gardiner Neal and Jamie Buckingham, Kuhlman produced three best sellers, all of which remained in print in 2007. Introductory and concluding chapters in Kuhlman's voice frame the trilogy, the body of which consists of sixty different individuals' narratives, each approximately ten pages in length. A straightforward, matter-of-fact prose style portrays Kuhlman as an objective reporter of healing claims. Interviews with those claiming healing form the basis of third-person narratives in volume 1, the only book ghostwritten by Neal. Perhaps because of Buckingham's differing stylistic preferences, and perhaps because of criticisms that her first book generated, volumes 2 and 3 invite more personal identification between readers and narrators by presenting first-person accounts, written in collaboration between the individuals, Kuhlman, and Buckingham.[22]

The question of what role each participant played in constructing the narratives is both significant and difficult to answer. Buckingham, in his biography of Kuhlman, described the large number of letters that individuals wrote to Kuhlman to ask for prayer or testify to healing; he and Kuhlman conducted more than two hundred follow-up interviews of those whose testimonies seemed promising.[23] Most of the narratives published in the trilogy also formed the basis of radio and/or television broadcasts. Some of these interviews aired before publication of the narratives, some after. In several particularly revealing cases, a broadcast preceded a narrative's publication and was succeeded by a follow-up broadcast months or years later.[24] In comparing the various versions of each narrative, what stands out are similarities, rather than differences, in the structure of the accounts, the details selected, and the overall tone and message conveyed. This is not to say that Kuhlman and/or Buckingham exerted a negligible influence on the printed version of the testimonies, only that this influence is difficult to trace. Even in the radio and television interviews, Kuhlman frequently asked leading questions, responded most enthusiastically to comments that supported her own views, and rerecorded any interview with which she did not feel fully satisfied.[25] Apart from Kuhlman's direct influence, the individuals who contributed their stories for public consumption participated in a long-standing cultural tradition, governed by unspoken narrative conventions, of the Christian healing testimonial.[26] Rather than seek to separate out the relative contributions of each participant in this cultural matrix, this essay seeks to understand the cultural strategies and uses of such narratives as exemplified by Kuhlman's publications.

The trilogy emphasizes the narrators' truth claims by supplying the actual names and other identifying information for each individual in biographical introductions. Only in a single instance, a young girl from a prominent family who recovered from drug addiction, did the text supply the pseudonym "Rose."[27] Half the testimonies in the second and third volumes refer to the act of reading Kuhlman's earlier book(s), often in addition to the Bible and other religious texts, as a critical preparation for receiving healing. Several individuals whose narratives appear in the second and third volumes also describe their face-to-face conversations with the people whose stories they had previously read as confirming the accuracy of the printed testimonies. The plot of a typical narrative is that a friend gives a copy of one of Kuhlman's books to a sick acquaintance who has never considered modern-day spiritual healing. The acquaintance listens to Kuhlman's radio or television broadcasts, eventually attends one or more miracle services, receives physical healing, and grows spiritually closer to God. One such individual, Kenneth May, was apparently dying from Hodgkin's disease when he read a copy of *I Believe in Miracles* loaned by a neighbor. "Can it be," May wondered, "that God can heal someone in the advanced stages of terminal cancer? Can it happen to me?"[28] Implicitly, readers of May's narrative are invited to ask whether healing is available for them.

In constructing her volumes to maximize their apologetic value, Kuhlman selected narrators who represented a range of occupational, ethnic, and religious backgrounds. She included five medical doctors, one nurse, two pastors, two news reporters, five individuals connected with the Hollywood film industry, a chemical engineer, two veterans, a police captain, a professional drummer, a public accountant, a congressional aide, as well as homemakers and factory workers. Several narrators were recent immigrants from Mexico, Nigeria, Bulgaria, Hungary, Germany, Finland, Switzerland, Greece, Russia, and other countries. Kuhlman's choices suggested to readers that the people healed were much like themselves or people they knew and that many were intellectually sophisticated or socially prominent.

By not privileging any particular tradition within orthodox Christianity, the trilogy attracted a diverse audience of Protestants, Catholics, and secular readers. Marketing her books through a trade press, Kuhlman did not hesitate to circumvent hostile religious authority structures to appeal directly to individual members of mainstream denominations. Of the sixty testimonials, Roman Catholics wrote eight. Seventeen narrators considered themselves religious skeptics. More than half belonged to mainstream denominations such as Methodist, Baptist, Presbyterian, Episcopalian, Lutheran, Greek Orthodox, or the United Church of Canada, or identified themselves simply as Christians. Of these the overwhelming majority attested that they believed in biblical miracles but that prior to their introduction to Kuhlman, they had not believed in contemporary miracles. "As a Bible-believing Baptist," explained Walter Bennett, "I believed that God could heal sick bodies. The difference was that I had never believed that God actually did it today. Healing today is done by the doctors and hospitals, I had thought."[29] Only one narrator grew up in a denomination that emphasized spiritual healing, the Church of God (Anderson, Indiana), but he had drifted from the church, and he no longer considered himself very religious.[30] Conspicuously absent from Kuhlman's volumes are narrators from Pentecostal denominations whom readers might dismiss as predisposed to believe in spiritual healing.

The testimonials included in the trilogy represented a range of diseases and disabilities, with disproportionate emphasis given to serious conditions difficult to explain in terms of misdiagnosis or psychosomatic factors. Twelve narrators reported dramatic recoveries from cancer diagnosed by their doctors as terminal. Steel-factory worker Harry Stephenson was sent home to die with cancer of the bowels and stomach, given a month to live by his doctors. Stephenson claimed that he had been unable to eat for thirty days and that he could no longer even keep water down. He was listening to Kuhlman's radio broadcast at home when, by his account, he felt the power of the Holy Spirit, and all pain left his body. That day, thirteen years before the publication of his testimony, Stephenson recalled eating fried eggs and hot dogs with onions, and reportedly experienced no adverse symptoms from that time forward.[31] Mary Schmidt testified that she had suffered from a goiter for thirty-six years, which had grown to sixteen and one-half inches in diameter. After attending Kuhlman's miracle services for several months, Schmidt recalled that during one particular service, she felt a sudden pain in the top of her head and a pull at her neck. Feeling for her goiter, she could not find it. Thirteen years later, she was goiter free.[32] Not only did narrators report the disappearance of unwanted growths, but some also insisted on the reappearance of decayed bones and tissues. James

McCutcheon's doctor reportedly exclaimed "This is truly a miracle" when X-rays showed that a piece of bone had mysteriously grown over a broken hip that five operations had failed to restore.[33] Injured by molten iron in an industrial accident, World War I veteran George Orr had been blind in his right eye for over twenty-one years when he claimed to regain his sight during a miracle service. The same doctor who had diagnosed his disability attested that Orr's left eye, which had deteriorated from the strain of overuse, was perfectly restored and that his right eye was 85 percent functional. Seventeen years later, an investigator interviewed Orr and claimed that he still enjoyed good vision.[34]

Kuhlman selected each case with the potential responses of critics in mind. She included seven testimonials of the healing of infants or young children, of such maladies as congenital bone deformities, epilepsy, blood diseases, eczema, and hydrocephalus. One such healing reportedly came to a four-month-old baby who had been born with a dislocated hip, the daughter of Richard Owellen, M.D., Ph.D., a cancer researcher, professor, and staff doctor at Johns Hopkins University. After watching his baby's leg straighten, Dr. Owellen announced: "I had often wondered if many of the healings I had seen weren't psychosomatic. . . . But a four-month-old baby doesn't know enough to have a psychosomatic healing."[35] Owellen deployed his medical qualifications and former avowed skepticism to bolster the credibility of his personal testimony. Of the remaining narratives, three individuals unexpectedly recovered from paralysis secondary to injury or disease; five experienced the discontinuance of the symptoms of multiple sclerosis. Five attested to instantaneous deliverance from drug or alcohol addiction. Other ailments apparently healed included emphysema, asthma, arthritis, heart conditions, diabetes, myasthenia gravis, stroke, and curvature of the spine.

Rather than directly attacking physicians who viewed patients as objects from whom disease must be excised, Kuhlman's principles of selection acknowledged the authority of medical doctors to referee claims of illness and healing on the basis of objective evidence rather than subjective symptoms.[36] Kuhlman selected a panel of supportive physicians to assess the healing claims that came to her attention, based upon a set of criteria similar to those that the Roman Catholic Church had employed for more than a century. First, the disease or injury had to have been medically diagnosed as resulting from an organic or structural problem, involving more than the unexplained failure of a body part to function.

Second, the healing had to have occurred rapidly, involving changes that could not be explained as psychosomatic. Third, the patient's primary physician had to verify the healing. Fourth, the healing had to have occurred long enough in the past that it could not be diagnosed as remission.[37] The rigid application of these four criteria preempted, although it did not succeed in silencing, the most common naturalistic explanations of spiritual healing claims.

Medical and Religious Critiques

At every stage of her public career and for decades after her death, Kuhlman drew thousands of admirers and scores of impassioned and vocal critics from the medical and religious professions. Refutations of Kuhlman's healing claims fall into four major categories: scientific and religious commentators advanced two criticisms from a shared naturalistic paradigm and religious opponents launched two additional attacks from a theological paradigm. Rather than evaluating the validity of any of these critiques, or of Kuhlman's responses to them, the purpose of this essay is to suggest some of the issues at stake in debates between Kuhlman and her critics and to explore the role of print culture in shaping these debates.

First, critics denied that people received any healing during Kuhlman's services, through her broadcasts, or through reading her books. Possibly Kuhlman committed outright deception, they suggested. Alternatively, a related line of criticism posited that basically healthy but naive people who failed to get proper medical diagnoses did not have the ailments they thought they did. Or, genuinely sick or disabled people became overly excited under the influence of emotional singing and temporarily believed themselves cured when in fact they were not. Regardless of the explanation for Kuhlman's unwarranted claims, these critics insisted, her exhortations were worse than benignly ineffectual: she did more harm than good by raising and then dashing the hopes of the desperately ill or, worse, convincing them to postpone or refuse medical treatment while chasing a phantom remedy.[38]

Second, critics suggested that if people did regain function of certain body parts, no organic or structural changes occurred. Drawing upon psychological theory and physiological understandings of the connections between mind and body, critics proposed the mechanisms of suggestion, hypnotism, and mass hysteria to account for psychosomatic healing. When the symptoms of organic diseases, such as cancer, apparently disappeared, critics argued that these recoveries would have occurred with or without Kuhlman as a result of medical treatment, the body's natural healing processes, or through the natural, although inexplicable, phenomenon of spontaneous remission.[39]

Kuhlman's most vocal medical critic, William A. Nolen, M.D., used the medium of print to challenge Kuhlman, writing a widely heralded exposé, *Healing: A Doctor in Search of a Miracle* (1974). Nolen practiced surgery in the five-thousand-person town of Litchfield, Minnesota, while pursuing a dual career as an author for the popular press. He wrote a monthly syndicated medical advice column for *McCall's* magazine and, within a span of fourteen years, published eight semi-autobiographical trade books, one of which, *The Making of a Surgeon* (1970), became an international best seller. In *Healing,* Nolen described his travels to the Philippines to make a personal investigation of Filipino psychic surgery as a parallel to Kuhlman's miracle services. After attending a Kuhlman service in Minneapolis in 1973, Nolen interviewed twenty-three people who believed themselves healed, and reported on five presumably typical cases: multiple sclerosis, migraine headaches, bursitis, acne, and varicose veins. All five narrators affirmed that they had kept their healings, but Nolen explained each as psychosomatic or trivial, rather than miraculous. Nolen also followed up with five cancer patients who initially claimed healing but later found they were mistaken, two of whom died shortly thereafter.[40]

Not every medical doctor shared Nolen's starkly negative assessment of Kuhlman's miracle claims. Indeed, the degree to which Kuhlman's career generated heated debates within the medical profession suggests just how much was at stake for medical epistemology and how powerfully trade publications shaped scientific and popular evaluations of supernatural healing claims. One of Kuhlman's medical supporters, H. Richard Casdorph, M.D., Ph.D., wrote *The Miracles* (1976) as a direct rebuttal to Nolen's best seller in an effort to provide irrefutable medical documentation for ten healing claims.[41] Although employed as a faculty member at the University of California, Los Angeles, Medical School and the University of California Medical School, Irvine, following his training in cardiovascular diseases at the Mayo Clinic, Casdorph's publishing record has compromised his reputation within the medical profession.[42] In addition to endorsing spiritual healing, the majority of

Casdorph's scientific publications, including the book *Toxic Metal Syndrome* (1995), promote chelation therapy—a medical "alternative," the efficacy of which is questioned in the standard medical literature. In *The Miracles*, Casdorph published before-and-after photographs of X-rays, laboratory films, and medical reports of ten individuals, whose real names and other identifying information he provided—noting that Nolen had not provided similar means of authentication. Casdorph selected diseases that were both more serious than the healing claims Nolen highlighted and, in most cases, more difficult to class as psychosomatic: bone cancer, kidney cancer, two cancerous brain tumors, two instances of rheumatoid and/or osteoarthritis, osteoporosis, multiple sclerosis, a massive gastrointestinal hemorrhage, and heart disease.[43] Casdorph's book generated sufficient notice that the *Mike Douglas Show* invited him and Nolen to debate on national television in 1975. Casdorph brought with him one of his book's case studies—teenager Lisa Larios, whose testimony of being healed from terminal bone cancer at age twelve had earlier appeared in Kuhlman's book, *Nothing Is Impossible with God*.[44] Neither Nolen nor Casdorph changed opinions as a result of their debate, but the televised encounter suggests how Kuhlman polarized medical and lay onlookers eager to evaluate supernatural healing claims.

In a third line of disputation, religious critics raised theological objections to the idea that God healed anyone supernaturally in the post-biblical age. Indeed, Kuhlman's most adamant critics emerged from the religious, rather than the medical, establishment. Christians who opposed Kuhlman generally reacted strongly against the wider charismatic movement that she represented, using a variety of print outlets to publicize their concerns including secular newspapers and magazines, Christian publishing houses, vanity presses, seminary theses, and, more recently, the Internet. In 1952, shortly after Kuhlman began to attract national attention, a well-known Baptist minister named Dallas Billington used Akron, Ohio, newspapers to challenge her. From 1953 to 1954, a secular magazine, *The Pittsburgher*, published a yearlong series of critical articles, "Kathryn Kuhlman, Good or Bad for Our People?" written by an anonymous "defender of orthodox Christianity."[45] A Christian publisher issued an English translation of Kurt Koch's *Occult ABC* in 1978, excerpts of which relating to Kuhlman circulated as recently as 2007 on an Internet site sponsored by the group "Deception in the Church," which is critical of the charismatic movement.[46] A stream of

theses and books opposing Kuhlman and other advocates of spiritual
healing have appeared for decades following her death, such as Patrick
Geracie's Baptist seminary thesis, "A Biblical and Historical Examination of the Positive Confession Movement" (1993); Yves Brault's vanity-
published *Behind the Scenes: The True Face of the Fake Faith Healers* (1997);
and Hank Hanegraaff's widely circulated trade book, *Christianity in Crisis* (1993), published by Harvest House, one of the largest Christian
presses in America.[47]

Christian theology, which has historically depended upon miracle
claims—most notably Jesus's healings and exorcisms of others and his
own resurrection—has had to grapple with whether ongoing supernatural interventions should be expected.[48] During the Reformation, the
Roman Catholic Church challenged Protestants to produce miracles in
defense of their theology. John Calvin insisted that the Reformers did
not need miracles since theirs was not a new gospel. Calvin developed
the doctrine of cessationism to argue for a limited age of miracles. After
the formation of the biblical canon, healings, miracles, prophecy, speaking in tongues, and other gifts of the Holy Spirit had ceased because
they had only been necessary to validate the Word. Roman Catholics
continued to affirm miracles, particularly as credentials for sainthood,
but cessationist assumptions predominated among Protestants between
the Reformation and the mid-nineteenth century, persisting in many
evangelical churches at the time of Kuhlman's writing.[49] The most influential modern spokesperson of the cessationist position, Reformed
theologian Benjamin B. Warfield, published *Counterfeit Miracles* in 1918.
The text, regularly cited by cessationist theologians throughout the
twentieth century, was reissued by Banner of Truth Trust for a popular
religious audience in 1972, at a moment when Kuhlman's popularity
was at its zenith, and again in 1996, during the height of the charismatic
revivals dubbed the "Toronto Blessing."[50]

Both Kuhlman and her religious critics drew upon a Baconian philosophical tradition that placed a high value on empirical evidence.[51]
Yet Kuhlman's critics found themselves in the position of denying the
evidentiary value of medical records and personal testimony, arguing
that one book, the Bible, not experience, is the standard by which all
truth claims must be measured.[52] Cessationist theologians saw no in-
consistency, however, in arguing from experience that godly people
failed to receive healing or from the absence of experience that miracles
had ceased in the postapostolic age.[53] Experience taught, moreover,

that since theologically marginal groups, such as Christian Science, New Thought, Unity, and Religious Science, also published testimonies of miraculous healings, Kuhlman's similar claims cast doubt upon her religious orthodoxy. Since all such modern-day miracles failed the theological test of measuring up in quantity or quality to biblical miracles, cessationists found it more credible to attribute modern miracles to Satan than to God.[54] When Kuhlman countered that she based her belief in healing on biblical promises, critics rejoined that she gave a "hyperliteral" reading to figurative or spiritual promises that at most foreshadowed physical blessings deferred until the afterlife.[55]

Fourth, Kuhlman's religious critics called attention to character flaws, often without denying—or even while affirming—that healing took place in her services. Kuhlman was "not worthy of ministerial emulation" because of her marriage in 1938 to Burroughs Waltrip, an itinerant evangelist who had divorced his wife and left his children to marry her.[56] Further, Kuhlman had separated from Waltrip in 1944, leading him to divorce her. In addition to her moral failings, Kuhlman's critics charged, she flaunted her wealth and, as a woman—"more given to emotion" and "easily deceived"—had no biblical authority to preach or pray for the sick, even if healings could be shown to result from these practices.[57]

Kuhlman's trilogy emerged in the context of widespread criticism of her healing claims publicized through a variety of print outlets. She in turn used print to refute her medical and religious critics.

Medical Constructions of the Body

Kuhlman selected and structured the testimonials included in her publications to deny implicitly each of the charges directed against her, while never directly addressing any of her critics. In an apparently conciliatory gesture to modern medicine, Kuhlman affirmed that God often worked through doctors and medicine to heal. She liberally quoted medical opinions and solicited testimonials from physicians, whose professional qualifications she described in detail. At the same time, Kuhlman insisted, God also had the "power to heal instantly without the material tools of scientific medicine."[58] The proliferation of supernatural healing narratives in effect demoted the medical profession to one of many potential tools in God's sovereign hands.

By conceding limited ground to the medical profession, Kuhlman subverted the authority of physicians to construct the human body as a biological organism subject to scientific scrutiny and management.[59] While acknowledging medical professionals' expertise in diagnosis, she denied that they were uniquely qualified to prescribe treatment or determine prognosis. The status of the medical profession rested upon the popular perception that doctors were best equipped to help people when they were at their weakest. In selecting testimonials, Kuhlman privileged cases in which doctors had acknowledged that there was nothing more that they could do to help. At the very point where doctors admitted that they had reached their limits, Kuhlman promised recourse to a higher authority and power to heal. By encouraging people to return to their doctors to verify their healings, Kuhlman aimed to force doctors to admit their inability to explain recoveries that they had previously told their patients not to expect.

One narrative after another suggested that people who had suffered not only from their illnesses but also from their doctors' pessimistic prognoses had regained control over their bodies and felt a newfound power to confront the future with hope. Freda Longstaff, for example, described her experience suffering from congenital dislocation of the hips and curvature of the spine, which caused her left hip to stick out and her left knee to turn inward, making walking awkward. After Longstaff's doctors performed surgery when she was seven years old, they purportedly told her parents: "She will always be deformed." Longstaff married and had two children, but her doctors warned her against having a third child because her hips and pelvis could not bear the strain. One night, after attending a Kuhlman miracle service, Longstaff was kneeling on her bedroom floor praying when, as she reported, "I felt a strange, tingling sensation in my hips—then a grinding noise. . . . I could feel my body moving and shifting as a powerful, yet so gentle, force put it into perfect alignment." When she arose from her knees, her legs were, as she described them, perfectly straight. A year later, Longstaff gave birth to a daughter without complication, and "as though to add frosting on the cake," seven years later she bore twin sons.[60]

Religious Constructions of the Body

Kuhlman's publications represented an alternative not only to medical constructions of the body as biologically determined but also to a religious dualism that constructed the body as inferior to the spirit.[61] If the body is inherently evil and passive, the prison of the soul, it follows that God sends sickness as a loving, fatherly chastisement to benefit the Christian through the spiritual sanctification that physical suffering produces.[62] In this religious model, God himself ordained sickness and death as penalties for sin, part of the "curse of the fall." Although some sicknesses resulted directly from moral failure, even faithful Christians should not expect immunity from sickness while living in a sinful world.[63] Christians in the Holiness and Pentecostal movements had embraced a contrasting theology of sanctification as early as the mid-nineteenth century, which, taken to its logical conclusion, implied that God could free the sanctified body of disease as easily as cleanse the spirit from sin. Satan authored sin and sickness, while God provided forgiveness for the spirit and healing for the body.[64] In contrast to Christian Scientists, who denied the reality of physical sickness, Kuhlman claimed that the healing of physically real diseases resulted in even more significant spiritual healing.[65]

Kuhlman's trilogy portrayed a harmonious connection between the body and the spirit. The typical testimonial described a spiritual transformation that accompanied physical healing, drawing not only the person healed, but also family and friends into a deeper relationship with God. Gilbert Strackbein had long felt antagonistic toward Christianity before his wife, Arlene, was diagnosed with multiple sclerosis. Gilbert began searching for God as Arlene's condition worsened: "In the beginning I was thinking only of Arlene's healing. But the more I read the Bible I realized that it also contained the answer to my own personal needs." After months of such spiritual searching, Gilbert reported, his wife was physically healed during a Kuhlman meeting. "It would seem that Arlene's healing should have been the climax of our lives," reported Gilbert, "but instead, it has been only the beginning." After being "baptized" in the Holy Spirit, Gilbert began leading his family in nightly devotions and, together with Arlene, taught a Sunday school class at their Methodist church.[66]

Kuhlman's narrative selections undercut essentialist gender assumptions that not only cast the body as inferior to the spirit, but also women's bodies as inferior to men's bodies. Aware of the charge that women predominated among the ranks of the sick and the healed because of their alleged hysterical tendencies, she conveyed the impression that gender was inconsequential to receiving healing by publishing exactly thirty testimonials from men and thirty from women.[67] She emphasized the educational attainments and unemotional reasoning of female narrators such as Dolly Graham, who claimed to have been healed of a heart condition. "After graduating from college," Graham recounted, "I just considered myself too intelligent and too 'intellectual' to believe" in spiritual healing.[68] Only Kuhlman's scriptural exegesis convinced Graham. Graham's narrative challenged a religious paradigm that associated women with emotional experience and men with reasoned theology.[69]

Never far in the background of her publications was Kuhlman's effort to justify her right, as a woman, to preach and pray for the sick. Kuhlman framed her volumes as a "reasonable" and "logical" argument: since in the Bible God promised resurrection of physical bodies in the future, God could and would also provide healing for the physical body today.[70] Kuhlman conceded to men titles such as pastor or preacher by encouraging people to refer to her simply as "Miss Kuhlman," a form of address that also deflected attention away from her past marriage and divorce.[71] Seven of the trilogy's narrators, three men and four women, overcame theological objections to a woman praying for the sick before receiving healing. Charles Wood had resisted listening to Kuhlman's radio broadcasts because, as a Baptist, "women preachers just did not fit" into his theology.[72] Roman Catholic Rita Romanowsky reacted even more strongly against Kuhlman: "This is blasphemy, I thought. How can this woman claim that God is speaking through her? She is no priest. She is not even a nun."[73] Wood, Romanowsky, and others avowedly changed their minds about Kuhlman after reasoned investigation, removing a barrier to healing by setting aside gendered presuppositions.

Narrative Uses

The narratives at the heart of Kuhlman's trilogy ordered and interpreted the experiences of illness and healing, deconstructing dominant naturalistic narratives and replacing them with a supernatural explanation of bodily healing.[74] Kuhlman structured her volumes to document medically unexpected healings using empirical evidence acceptable within a naturalistic frame of reference, while simultaneously deploying personal testimony as a tool to interpret the causes and meanings of healings in terms of supernaturalism. The authority of personal experience functioned to subvert the theoretical presuppositions of a worldview that *a priori* excluded the category of the supernatural and wrested power from medical and religious elites who had constructed and controlled narrators' bodies, illnesses, and hopes for healing.[75] Narratives served the private, therapeutic functions of allowing individuals who had emerged from major life crises to tell their stories, relate their experiences to larger narratives of the meanings of human life, and identify with extended belief communities that insulated them from ridicule for subscribing to unconventional views on healing.[76] The narratives also served the public, testimonial functions of affirming God's goodness and encouraging other people to seek spiritual healing.[77] Many of Kuhlman's critics remained skeptical of the proof value of the narratives, since, by definition, no quantity or quality of testimonial evidence can prove the existence of the supernatural within a paradigm that makes such causal factors a logical impossibility or explains them on naturalistic grounds.[78]

The mere fact that a person recovers from a bodily affliction may not validate any particular interpretation of how or why the recovery took place, nor does it explain why the healing should be meaningful to anyone besides the person healed. When disease disappears, scientists typically bracket questions of miraculous causation while conducting their investigations, focusing more narrowly on the study of "present and reproducible phenomena."[79] Capitalizing on the refusal of many medical practitioners to generalize from observable phenomena to ultimate meanings, Kuhlman used testimonials to suggest supernatural causation for healings that doctors could not attribute to medical or surgical interventions or the body's natural healing processes, as currently understood.

Denoting an unexpected healing as "miraculous" is a public interpretive act that argues for the existence of a supernatural realm that directly affects the phenomenal world. Healings subjectively determined by the disappearance of symptoms or credited to medical intervention directly benefit one afflicted individual. A healing that is apparently documented by objective medical evidence and attributed to divine agency is meaningful to a larger interpretive community in that it claims to give evidence for the existence and character of God. Because miracles purportedly demonstrate God's supernatural power, rejection or acceptance of miracles implies a choice between naturalistic and supernatural worldviews. As Christianity's detractors have noted at least since David Hume's *Inquiry Concerning Human Understanding* (1748), disproof of modern miracles is a strong argument against the probability of biblical miracles.[80]

Framing miracles in terms of empirical inquiry, Kuhlman set out to demonstrate by a proliferation of examples that miracles conform to the higher, regularly operating spiritual laws of faith, love, and mercy, rather than being rare aberrations in an otherwise perfect natural order.[81] Faith for healing led to predictable action patterns: removing a brace contrary to doctors' orders, kneeling or lifting hands in worship regardless of what other people thought, fasting in defiance of the body's appetites, praying for others instead of focusing on oneself, undertaking a lengthy pilgrimage to attend a miracle service in spite of discomfort or expense, or praying persistently rather than abandoning hope if healing was delayed.[82] The circumstances of healing varied, suggesting that readers must place their faith in God alone, rather than thinking healing depended on Kuhlman or participation in a miracle service. Several narrators claimed to have been healed before reaching a service: while sleeping on a chartered bus, standing outside the auditorium, lying in a hospital room bed, or sitting alone at home.[83] Some believed themselves healed during their first service, while others went to services for months before reporting healing.

By foregrounding delayed healings, Kuhlman responded indirectly to the charge, levied by critics like Dr. Nolen who had observed only a single miracle service, that people left meetings unhealed. Narrators who reported healings after attending multiple services framed their accounts to erase any feelings of bitterness or disappointment at the delay, claiming instead to have felt drawn to meetings repeatedly by their sense of the presence and power of the Holy Spirit.[84] Dolly Graham interpreted the delay in her healing of a heart condition from the perspective of looking back on the event seven years later. From this vantage, Graham insisted that when she first attended a miracle service, "I wasn't ready yet for my healing. I was still too ignorant of spiritual matters." After the service, she began to read her Bible "for the first time in many years" and began attending church. "Had I received my healing immediately," Graham hypothesized, "I don't believe I would have felt the need, or been so eager to go deeper into the ways of God."[85] At the time of her narrative's composition, Graham remembered the delay in her physical healing as necessary to her spiritual transformation.

Kuhlman provided circumstantial evidence for supernatural causation by including several testimonials in which narrators reported feeling unusual physical sensations at the precise moment when they believed themselves healed. These feelings, which narrators interpreted as the power of the Holy Spirit, include intense heat, uncontrollable shaking or crying, waves of electricity, falling, rising, a soft breeze, or a feather-light tickle.[86] Paul Gunn, a night watchman afflicted with terminal lung cancer, considered himself instantaneously healed in 1949 at the fourth Kuhlman service that he had attended, thirteen years before the publication of his narrative: "Suddenly the power of God came down. It hit me and just for an instant the sensation of burning fire in my lung was more intense than it had ever been before. I thought I couldn't stand it. . . . From that moment on there was no more burning, no more pain, no more ache. And there hasn't been from that day to this."[87] Sara Hopkins, a Hollywood actress and cofounder of International Orphans, Inc., claimed to have been healed of metastatic cancer during a Kuhlman service. She reported that she knew she was healed when she saw a "pink mist or cloud" engulf her and felt as if she had "grabbed an electrical hot line." Hopkins recalled that "needles of fire surged through my body—like I was being charged with a thousand volts of electricity. I felt intense heat through my chest and midsection, and my body began to shake so hard I was afraid I would fall out of my seat."[88] The proliferation of such examples argued against the naturalistic explanation of spontaneous remission, a rare occurrence in which a person unexpectedly recovers for no clear reason. Dr. Nolen estimated that in treating fifty-six hundred patients, he had witnessed one spontaneous remission.[89] Kuhlman implied the improbability of so many spontaneous remissions occurring coincidentally with physical sensations that narrators attributed to the power of God.

At least some of Kuhlman's narrators interpreted their sensations within a framework provided by previous healing narratives. Richard Kichline described his recovery from paralysis secondary to acute transverse myelitis thirteen years after the event, at which time he had been sixteen years old. Kichline remembered listening to Kuhlman's radio broadcast in his hospital room bed, while his mother and friends knelt in prayer and fasting. At exactly 10:55 a.m., recalled Richard, "I felt the power of God go through my whole body. . . . I began to shake violently and uncontrollably. I suppose this lasted for four or five minutes. Then it stopped, and almost immediately I began to have sensation in my legs." Kichline acknowledged that he had borrowed language to describe his experience from other people's testimonies. "I didn't *really* know what had happened. You see, I had never been to a healing service, and it was not until I started to regularly attend Miss Kuhlman's meetings after my healing, that I realized I had experienced the power of God in my own body."[90] Healing testimonials transmitted orally or through print instructed subsequent narrators how to frame their experiences, even retrospectively, in terms calculated to combat naturalistic explanations of healing.

Because written in the third person with scattered first-person quotations, narratives like Richard Kichline's in Kuhlman's first volume provided a skeletal paradigm for readers to flesh out in explaining their related, yet distinctive experiences. Perhaps because Kuhlman and Buckingham sensed that readers wanted models for use in formulating their own narratives, volumes 2 and 3 are written entirely in the first person. The later books have in common more personal language and more extended attention to telling the story of receiving healing, yet there is no clear developmental sequence between the volumes in terms of content or style. Testimonies in all three books share certain narrative conventions and plot sequences yet differ in significant details that suggest the individuality of each person's experiences. None of the narrators in the first two volumes described sensations that corresponded to those of volume 3's Arlene Strackbein, who felt "a soft, caressing breeze all over my body," as she claimed healing from multiple sclerosis.[91] Nor did any of the earlier narrators report phenomena comparable to volume 3's Evelyn Allen, who experienced "a light tickle, like the tips of a feather, that started behind my left ear and with a faint brushing feeling swept down the left side of my body," as she declared herself free from myasthenia gravis.[92] Readers of Kuhlman's books who subsequently reported healing borrowed from the earlier accounts, but where these testimonials failed to provide useful models, each narrator, likely with the help of Kuhlman and Buckingham, struggled to find adequate language to frame new bodily experiences.

Kuhlman herself, ironically, suffered from an enlarged heart for years, but never experienced a spiritual, or any other kind, of healing for her own body. Throughout her career, Kuhlman frequently denied knowing why God healed some people but not others, perhaps thinking of her own case as well as many other instances in which healing did not seem to correlate with faith. Kuhlman sought medical treatment, which she had often endorsed publicly as one of the means that God used to heal, but she did this discreetly lest critics ridicule her failure to receive supernatural healing. She underwent open-heart surgery a few weeks before her death, at age sixty-eight. Oral and Evelyn Roberts, who had expressed admiration of Kuhlman for years, offered to pray for healing in her hospital room, but she refused. According to her supporters, Kuhlman, who had never claimed to be the one responsible for anybody's healing, was tired from arduous years of conducting miracle services and wanted to die.[93]

By interpreting medical evidence through the lens of personal testimony, Kuhlman's publications presented what to many readers seemed an attractive alternative to naturalistic ways of rendering reality. Published narratives helped their writers and readers to explain experiences of illness and to find hope for healing from a God who cared about their bodies as well as their spirits. Unpacking the narrative conventions and editorial strategies at play in Kuhlman's trilogy illustrates the power of print culture to shape religious and medical discourse about health, illness, and healing. The publications of Kuhlman and her critics clarify the differences in assumptions between supernatural and naturalistic worldviews, forcing readers to choose sides and perhaps find themselves in unexpected company.

Notes

1. Jamie Buckingham, *Daughter of Destiny: Kathryn Kuhlman . . . Her Story* (Plainfield, NJ: Logos, 1976), 12, 14, 24, 25, 158, 208; Wayne Warner, *Kathryn Kuhlman: The Woman Behind the Miracles* (Ann Arbor, MI: Servant, 1993), 61, 131, 172; Kuhlman retained her childhood Baptist membership; the interdenominational Evangelical Church Alliance ordained her in 1968.

2. Robert Bruce Mullin, in *Miracles and the Modern Religious Imagination* (New Haven, CT: Yale University Press, 1996), 3, 101, "tentatively" proposes that debates over the supernatural have become more significant than Protestant-Catholic divisions.

3. For a discussion of how these practices relate to healing, see Robert C. Fuller, *Alternative Medicine and American Religious Life* (New York: Oxford University Press, 1989), 10.

4. Harvey Cox, *Fire from Heaven: The Rise of Pentecostal Spirituality and the Reshaping of Religion in the Twenty-First Century* (Reading, MA: Addison-Wesley, 1995), 104.

5. A 2003 *Newsweek* poll found 72 percent of Americans believing that "praying to God can cure someone—even if science says the person doesn't

stand a chance"; Claudia Kalb et al., "Faith and Healing," *Newsweek* 10, November 2003. A 1996 Gallup Poll showed 82 percent believing "in the healing power of personal prayer" and 77 percent agreeing that "God sometimes intervenes to cure people who have a serious illness"; John Cole, "Gallup Poll Again Shows Confusion," *NCSE Reports* (Spring 1996): 9; and Claudia Wallis, "Faith and Healing," *Time* (24 June 1996): 63, quoted in Ronald L. Numbers, "Science without God: Natural Laws and Christian Beliefs," in *When Science and Christianity Meet*, ed. David C. Lindberg and Robert L. Numbers (Chicago: University of Chicago Press, 2003), 284. Other polls suggest that 61 to 80 percent believe in miracles. Mullin, *Miracles*, 262; Stephen J. Pullum, *"Foul Demons, Come Out!": The Rhetoric of Twentieth-Century American Faith Healing* (Westport, CT: Praeger, 1999), 150.

6. Mullin, *Miracles*, 186, 212, 264.

7. Kathryn Kuhlman, *I Believe in Miracles: Streams of Healing from the Heart of a Woman of Faith* (Englewood Cliffs, NJ: Prentice-Hall, 1962; rev. ed., Gainesville, FL: Bridge-Logos, 1992); Kuhlman, *God Can Do It Again: Amazing Testimonies Wrought by God's Extraordinary Servant* (Englewood Cliffs, NJ: Prentice-Hall, 1969; rev. ed., Gainesville, FL: Bridge-Logos, 1993); Kuhlman, *Nothing Is Impossible with God: Modern-Day Miracles in the Ministry of a Daughter of Destiny* (Englewood Cliffs, NJ: Prentice-Hall, 1974; rev. ed., Gainesville, FL: Bridge-Logos, 1999).

8. Kuhlman, *I Believe in Miracles*, 204.

9. Warner, *Kathryn Kuhlman*, 20.

10. Neal, *A Reporter Finds God Through Spiritual Healing* (New York: Morehouse-Gorham, 1956), 185.

11. Buckingham, *Daughter of Destiny*, 122.

12. Warner, *Kathryn Kuhlman*, 203.

13. Buckingham, *Daughter of Destiny*, 250; Roberts Liardon, *God's Generals: Why They Succeeded and Why Some Failed* (Tulsa, OK: Albury, 1996), 303.

14. Kuhlman, *I Believe in Miracles*, xiv. Some contemporaries did print before-and-after X-rays. David Edwin Harrell, Jr., *All Things Are Possible: The Healing and Charismatic Revivals in Modern America* (Bloomington: Indiana University Press, 1975), 90.

15. Kuhlman issued a periodical, *The Eye-Opener*, in the 1940s to attack theological liberals. Warner, *Kathryn Kuhlman*, 161.

16. Kuhlman began to use television in the 1950s, with the broadcast *Your Faith & Mine;* Warner, *Kathryn Kuhlman*, 193; Buckingham, *Daughter of Destiny*, 208.

17. Frederick W. Jordan, "At Arm's Length: The First Presbyterian Church, Pittsburgh, and Kathryn Kuhlman," in *Pentecostal Currents in American Protestantism*, ed. Edith L. Blumhofer, Russell P. Spittler, and Grant A. Wacker (Urbana: University of Illinois Press, 1999), 189. Kuhlman had years earlier written a booklet, *The Lord's Healing Touch* (Pittsburgh, PA: Kathryn Kuhlman, n.d.). Warner, *Kathryn Kuhlman*, 135.

18. Buckingham, *Daughter of Destiny*, 158–59.

19. Kuhlman, *I Believe in Miracles*, xiv, 4.

20. "About Pearson Prentice Hall," http://www.phschool.com/about_ph/ (accessed 27 April 2005).

21. "Best Sellers," http://www.bridgelogos.com/bestsellers.html (accessed 14 August 2007).

22. Buckingham ghostwrote *God Can Do It Again*, *Nothing Is Impossible with God*, and six single-testimony booklets: *Captain LeVrier Believes in Miracles* (Minneapolis: Bethany House, 1973); *10,000 Miles for a Miracle* (Minneapolis: Bethany House, 1974); *How Big Is God?* (Minneapolis: Bethany House, 1974); *Never Too Late* (South Plainfield, NJ: Bridge, 1975); *Standing Tall* (Minneapolis: Bethany House, 1975); and *Twilight and Dawn* (Minneapolis: Bethany House, 1976). Buckingham, *Daughter of Destiny*, vii, 122.

23. Buckingham, *Daughter of Destiny*, 142, 212.

24. The archives at the Billy Graham Center at Wheaton College, Wheaton, Illinois, house a large collection of Kuhlman's radio and television broadcasts. Examples of narratives available in multiple versions are Paul Gunn's testimony of being healed of lung cancer in 1949, aired on radio in 1960, published in *I Believe in Miracles*, 147–55, in 1962 and aired on television in 1966; and Freda Longstaff's testimony of being healed of congenital dislocation of the hips and curvature of the spine in 1950, aired on television (*Your Faith & Mine*) in 1952, aired on radio and television (*I Believe in Miracles*) in 1968, and finally printed in *God Can Do It Again*, 195–205, in 1969.

25. Buckingham, *Daughter of Destiny*, 158.

26. Grant Wacker, *Heaven Below: Early Pentecostals and American Culture* (Cambridge, MA: Harvard University Press, 2001), 58.

27. Kuhlman, *I Believe in Miracles*, 91.

28. Kuhlman, *God Can Do It Again*, 57.

29. Ibid., 227.

30. Ibid., 196.

31. Kuhlman, *I Believe in Miracles*, 197.

32. Ibid., 101.

33. Ibid., 177.

34. Ibid., 38; Warner, *Kathryn Kuhlman*, 269.

35. Kuhlman, *Nothing Is Impossible with God*, 71.

36. Michel Foucault, *The Birth of the Clinic: An Archaeology of Medical Perception* (New York: Pantheon Books, 1973); Roy Porter, "Western Medicine and Pain: Historical Perspectives," in *Religion, Health and Suffering*, ed. John R. Hinnells and Roy Porter (New York: Kegan Paul, 1999), 368.

37. Paul Gale Chappell, "The Divine Healing Movement in America" (Ph.D. dissertation, Drew University, 1983), 144; Buckingham, *Daughter of Destiny*, 179.

38. For an example of these charges, see Yves Brault, *Behind the Scenes: The True Face of the Fake Faith Healers* (Pittsburgh, PA: Dorrance, 1997), 39.

39. For an example of such claims, see Wade H. Boggs, Jr., *Faith Healing and the Christian Faith* (Richmond, VA: John Knox, 1956), 64.

40. William A. Nolen, *Healing: A Doctor in Search of a Miracle* (New York: Random House, 1974), 42, 75, 101, 301; Nolen wrote *The Making of a Surgeon* (New York: Random House, 1970); *Spare Parts for the Human Body* (New York: Random House, 1971); *A Surgeon's World* (New York: Random House, 1972); *Surgeon under the Knife* (New York: Coward, McCann & Geoghegan, 1976); *The Baby in the Bottle: An Investigative Review of the Edelin Case and Its Larger Meanings for the Controversy over Abortion Reform* (New York: Coward, McCann & Geoghegan, 1978); *A Surgeon's Book of Hope* (New York: Coward, McCann & Geoghegan, 1980); and *Crisis Time!: Love, Marriage, and the Male at Mid-Life* (New York: Dodd, Mead, 1984).

41. H. Richard Casdorph, *The Miracles* (Plainfield, NJ: Logos International, 1976), 16.

42. A generally respected Internet site, "Quackwatch," provides a revealing window onto the close association between spiritual healing and alternative medicine in the view of many conventional medical practitioners. See Saul Green, Ph.D., "Chelation Therapy: Unproven Claims and Unsound Theories," http://www.quackwatch.org/01QuackeryRelatedTopics/chelation.html (accessed 29 April 2005), and Stephen Barrett, M.D., "Some Thoughts about Faith Healing," http://www.quackwatch.org/01QuackeryRelated Topics/faith.html (accessed 29 April 2005).

43. In addition to his scientific articles, Casdorph wrote *Treatment of the Hyperlipidemic States* (Springfield, IL: Thomas, 1971); *Dream Journey* (Long Beach, CA: Sword, 1978); *Toxic Metal Syndrome: How Metal Poisonings Can Affect Your Brain*, by Casdorph and Morton Walker (Garden City Park, NY: Avery, 1995); and *Real Miracles: Indisputable Evidence That God Heals* (Gainesville, FL: Bridge-Logos, 2003).

44. Kuhlman, *Nothing Is Impossible with God,* 39; Buckingham, *Daughter of Destiny,* 212.

45. Warner, *Kathryn Kuhlman,* 174–76.

46. Kurt Koch, *Occult ABC,* translated by Michael Freeman (Grand Rapids, MI: Grand Rapids International Publications, 1978); "'Kathryn Kuhlman' from 'Occult ABC' by Kurt Koch, 1978," http://www.deceptioninthechurch.com/kuhlman.htm (accessed 14 August 2007).

47. Patrick Geracie, "A Biblical and Historical Examination of the Positive Confession Movement" (M.A. thesis, Western Seminary, 1993); Brault printed *Behind the Scenes* with the subscription publisher Dorrance; Hank Hanegraaff, *Christianity in Crisis* (Eugene, OR: Harvest House, 1993).

48. Amanda Porterfield, *Healing in the History of Christianity* (New York: Oxford University Press, 2005), 21–22.

49. Mullin, *Miracles*, 1, 16.

50. Warfield, *Counterfeit Miracles* (New York: C. Scribner's, 1918; London: Banner of Truth Trust, 1972; Carlisle, PA: Banner of Truth Trust, 1996); subscribing to the Westminster Confession, Banner of Truth Trust formed in London in 1957 to recover from "oblivion" the "best literature of historic Christianity"; Iain H. Murray, "The Story of the Banner of Truth," http://www.banneroftruth.org/pages/about/about.html (accessed 27 April 2005).

51. Mullin, *Miracles*, 98.

52. For an example of this argument, see Bruce Barron, *The Health and Wealth Gospel: What's Going on Today in a Movement That Has Shaped the Faith of Millions?* (Downers Grove, IL: InterVarsity, 1987), 155.

53. Gary B. Ferngren, "Evangelical-Fundamentalist Tradition," in *Caring and Curing: Health and Medicine in the Western Religious Traditions*, ed. Ronald L. Numbers and Darrel W. Amundsen (New York: Macmillan, 1986), 497.

54. For an example of this claim, see D. R. McConnell, *A Different Gospel*, updated ed. (Peabody, MA: Hendrickson, 1995), 148.

55. Such arguments can be seen in Hank Hanegraaff, *What's Wrong with the Faith Movement* (Pensacola, FL: Chapel Library, 1993), 24; Gordon D. Fee, *The Disease of the Health and Wealth Gospels* (Beverly, MA: Frontline, 1985), 14.

56. For an example of this argument, see Justin Davis Peters, "Examination and Critique of the Life, Ministry, and Theology of Healing Evangelist Benny Hinn" (M.A. thesis, Southwestern Baptist Theological Seminary, 2002), 8. Kuhlman insisted that the Holy Spirit led her to separate from Waltrip as a condition for regaining the ministry that her admittedly "sinful" marriage had nearly aborted (Warner, *Kathryn Kuhlman*, 109).

57. Even Kuhlman's ghostwriter, Jamie Buckingham, *Daughter of Destiny*, 152–53, 208, criticized her expensive tastes in antiques, although he also notes that her appeals for funds were always "low-key" and that she gave away large sums to charities. Curtis I. Crenshaw, in *Man as God: The Word of Faith Movement: An Evangelical Analysis of the Beliefs with the Christian Alternative Also Presented* (Memphis: Footstool, 1994), 43, 62, denies Kuhlman's biblical authority (citing 1 Tim. 2:12–14), as a woman, to preach or pray for the sick, but he does not question whether healings occurred in her services, instead noting that Kuhlman insisted upon medical verification for healings included in her books.

58. Kuhlman, *I Believe in Miracles*, 3.

59. James William Opp, *The Lord for the Body: Religion, Medicine, and Protestant Faith Healing in Canada, 1880–1930* (Ithaca, NY: McGill-Queen's University Press, 2005), 6.

60. Kuhlman, *God Can Do It Again*, 200, 205.

61. See, in Numbers and Amundsen, *Caring and Curing:* Darrel W. Amundsen and Gary B. Ferngren, "The Early Christian Tradition," 46; Marvin R. O'Connell, "Roman Catholic Tradition," 121; and Timothy P. Weber, "Baptist Tradition," 292.

62. David J. Melling, "Suffering and Sanctification in Christianity," in Hinnells and Porter, *Religion, Health and Suffering,* 47.

63. For an example of this argument, see J. Sidlow Baxter, *Divine Healing of the Body* (Grand Rapids, MI: Zondervan, 1979), 14.

64. Grant Wacker, "The Pentecostal Tradition," in Numbers and Amundsen, *Caring and Curing,* 517.

65. See, for instance, Kuhlman's comments in *I Believe in Miracles,* 79, 154, that "God never inflicts disease," but heals body and spirit simultaneously since Jesus "paid" for sickness as well as sin "on Calvary"; advocates of divine healing, like Kuhlman, typically supported this interpretation of the "atonement" by referring to Isaiah 53:5 (AV): "But he was wounded for our transgressions, he was bruised for our iniquities: the chastisement of our peace was upon him; and with his stripes we are healed."

66. Kuhlman, *Nothing Is Impossible with God,* 84, 99.

67. For an early religious articulation of the charge that women interested in healing tended to hysteria, see J. M. Buckley, *Faith-Healing, Christian Science and Kindred Phenomena* (New York: Century, 1887), 7. Scholars have often noted the predominance of women at religious services, and Opp, *Lord for the Body,* 39, observed this pattern in his study of the campaigns of healing-evangelist Charles Price (1880–1947); no comparable study has indicated the ratio of those who attended Kuhlman meetings, although photographs and film footage reveal the presence of large numbers of both women and men.

68. Kuhlman, *I Believe in Miracles,* 131.

69. For an example of this argument, see Crenshaw, *Man as God,* 43.

70. Kuhlman, *I Believe in Miracles,* 5.

71. Warner, *Kathryn Kuhlman,* 162, 200.

72. Kuhlman, *God Can Do It Again,* 135.

73. Ibid., 74.

74. Stanley Hauerwas and L. Gregory Jones, eds., *Why Narrative?: Readings in Narrative Theology* (Grand Rapids, MI: Eerdmans, 1989), 14.

75. Louis O. Mink, "Narrative Form as a Cognitive Instrument," in *The Writing of History: Literary Form and Historical Understanding,* ed. Robert H. Canary and Henry Kozicki (Madison: University of Wisconsin Press, 1978), 131.

76. Nicholas Lash, "Ideology, Metaphor, and Analogy," in Hauerwas and Jones, *Why Narrative?* 120; Opp, *Lord for the Body,* 37.

77. Chappell, "Divine Healing Movement in America," 84.

78. Mullin, *Miracles,* 139.

79. Numbers, "Science without God," 282.

80. Mullin, *Miracles*, 99, 115.

81. Kuhlman, *God Can Do It Again*, 44; philosophers and theologians, including Immanuel Kant and William James, had long debated the relationship between natural and spiritual laws; Mullin, *Miracles*, 192.

82. Kuhlman, *I Believe in Miracles*, 27, 43, 69; Kuhlman, *God Can Do It Again*, 89, 158; Kuhlman, *Nothing Is Impossible with God*, 187.

83. Kuhlman, *I Believe in Miracles*, 53, 77; Kuhlman, *God Can Do It Again*, 200; Kuhlman, *Nothing Is Impossible with God*, 132.

84. Kuhlman, *I Believe in Miracles*, 27.

85. Ibid., 132, 134.

86. Ibid., 163; Kuhlman, *God Can Do It Again*, 91; Kuhlman, *Nothing Is Impossible with God*, 286.

87. Kuhlman, *I Believe in Miracles*, 150.

88. Kuhlman, *Nothing Is Impossible with God*, 273, 274.

89. Nolen, *Healing*, 301.

90. Kuhlman, *I Believe in Miracles*, 163.

91. Kuhlman, *Nothing Is Impossible with God*, 95.

92. Ibid., 286.

93. Liardon, *God's Generals*, 302, 305; for examples of Kuhlman's statements on failures to receive healing, the legitimacy of medical treatment, and her inability to heal anyone, consult her radio sermon, "Why Aren't Some Healed?" (Pittsburgh: Kathryn Kuhlman Foundation, 1969), and her interview, "Healing in the Spirit," *Christianity Today* 20 (July 1973): 1, 6.

New Age Feminism?

*Reading the Woman's "New Age" Nonfiction
Best Seller in the United States*

KARLYN CROWLEY

About a decade ago, my mother began a "Women Who Run with the Wolves" group. She promptly bought a drum and jokingly howled at me while playing it, but I knew that this groundswell of female bonding, brought on by the huge success of Clarissa Pinkola Estes's book by the same name, was nothing to laugh at.[1] Estes's book, which peaked at number seven on the 1993 *Publishers Weekly* nonfiction best-seller list, became an urtext for my mother's group, which longed for feminist revisions of fairytales and myths. While Estes's book is more Jungian than feminist, and more spiritual than political, it was one among a number of New Age best sellers in the United States that appealed to women from the 1970s to the 1990s.[2] These female New Age authors—Ruth Montgomery, Shirley MacLaine, Marianne Williamson, Louise Hay, Rosemary Altea, Sarah Ban Breathnach, Caroline Myss, Betty Eade, to name only a few—often spoke to their audiences by fusing metaphysical power with women's power.[3] Though rarely self-defined as feminist or recognized by critics as such, many of these authors drew on the language of women's power in complicated ways that have been ignored by scholars, largely out of abhorrence of the New Age generally.

"New Age culture," an umbrella term for diverse spiritual, social, and political beliefs and practices that promote personal and societal change through spiritual transformation, rose in the 1970s, but was seen by many as a manifestation of everything wrong with post-1960s American culture. Some critics argued that New Age culture was antireligious, anti-Christian, antimodern, essentialist, racist, antipolitical, lowbrow cant. Was there anything worth redeeming, let alone studying? As critics dismissed this body of literature, however, authors and readers went on to create a formidable array of spiritual works. Though a number of men produced foundational texts of New Age culture, female New Age authors, in particular, took on the added challenge of coming to terms with the burgeoning women's movement and its political aims.[4] Were female New Age authors political even as most critics argued they were not? Or did their politics amount to nothing more than the wildly ecstatic "running with wolves"? The answer is complicated and contradictory. By investigating the print culture of New Age women's texts, focusing, in particular, on best-selling authors Louise Hay and Marianne Williamson, it will become clear exactly how feminism and New Age spirituality have catalyzed and criticized each other.[5] Hay and Williamson are particularly interesting because they have written popular best sellers specifically about women's issues directed to a New Age audience. As we shall see, these female-centered New Age texts are contradictory: while they often reject feminism, they also embrace it more than their critics have imagined. Feminism may have an alternative manifestation in women's New Age culture.

A Short History of the New Age Movement

The New Age. The dawning of Aquarius. The Harmonic Convergence. Although the New Age movement has its roots in the early 1970s, by the early twenty-first century its followers had taken it far past the fringe and into the boardroom and bedroom. From the *Tao of Leadership* and other New Age practices aiming to "humanize" business, to relationship books like *Mars and Venus in the Bedroom*, New-Age-speak is common parlance in elite seminars and popular talk shows. Some say the United States is in the midst of a "spiritual revival" or another "Great Awakening," as religious historians call periods of extensive spiritual crisis and reorientation.[6] The contemporary Great Awakening is marked by a turn toward spiritual individualism and a desire to seek multiple religious alternatives, rather than to commit more deeply to one faith.[7] In other words, though mainline church and synagogue attendance may currently be down in the United States, spiritual belief is high. Studies show that "more than 90 percent of Americans profess a belief in God," and a surprising number believe in the supernatural generally.[8] As Sarah Pike argues, the New Age has added to the "rise of alternate ritual spaces in which people find religious community."[9] In *Spiritual but Not Religious: Understanding Unchurched America,* Robert Fuller suggests that "the United States is arguably the most religious nation on earth."[10] However, Fuller notes that we can grasp this fact only if we expand traditional notions of organized religion and "look well beyond the boundaries of the nation's churches."[11] By expanding the definition of the spiritual, it might also include not only those who identify themselves by their New Age beliefs but also those who subscribe to some New Age beliefs but do not claim them as the basis for an identity. Given that belief in the supernatural is so prevalent, what in particular constitutes the New Age?

Generally, the "New Age" is an umbrella term for varying practices, beliefs, and lifestyles of those seeking alternative spiritual truths in the late twentieth century. Though the New Age is particularly popular in the United States, it is increasingly a global phenomenon. While it is difficult to synthesize this vast and amorphous "umbrella," many cite Ram Dass as an early spokesperson for the New Age as well as Marilyn Ferguson's *The Aquarian Conspiracy* (1980) as a "commonly accepted statement of the movement's ideals and goals."[12] Robert Wuthnow suggests that New Age culture marks a shift from spiritual "dwelling to seeking," a shift from being firmly rooted within *one* religious tradition to exploring *multiple* practices from many traditions.[13] New Age practices range from the specific to the general: some New Agers engage in particular practices like channeling, Wicca, shamanism, and self-help, while others hold certain beliefs like acknowledging that the earth is our "Mother" and her resources are limited, or sensing that a larger societal turn toward technology and materialistic consumption ends in spiritual decline. According to Wouter Hanegraaff, New Agers hold four foundational beliefs: (1) there is a thin line between the material world and the world beyond (which is why such practices as channeling or past life regression are so popular); (2) there is an interrelatedness to all things—one action can affect the whole; (3) there is an "evolution of consciousness": we are evolving toward a higher consciousness that can be accelerated by seeking out psychological, spiritual, or physical healing; and (4) there is a "psychologization of religion and sacralization of psychology."[14]

It is commonly agreed upon that such New Age beliefs in the United States are historically based in five traditions, which Michael York highlights as: (1) the "alternative religious tradition in the West (Swedenborgianism, Kabbalah, gnosticism, mystical traditions, etc.); (2) Eastern religious concepts (karma, auras, chakras, etc.); (3) the American metaphysical movement (Spiritualism, Theosophy, the Arcane School, etc.); (4) the occult (goddess cults, witchcraft and paganism, Satanism, magic, astrology, etc.); and (5) the Transcendentalists (Emerson, Thoreau, Alcott, Margaret Fuller, etc.)."[15] J. Gordon Melton cites the combination of Eastern religion and transpersonal psychology as the "key elements needed to create the distinctive synthesis" of the New Age.[16] Clearly, the New Age is not so "new" but rather a recirculation of older movements already present in the United States. Because New Age culture pulls from various traditions, religious scholars in particular are wary of giving credence to a movement seemingly comprised of spiritual dilettantes.[17] Huston Smith calls the New Age a "cafeteria approach to spirituality."[18] Though Smith and others look down on such practices, New Agers' ability to consume multiple spiritual practices creates a spirituality tailored to their needs.

Although New Age draws on historically disparate sources—from Transcendentalism to countercultural movements in the 1970s—it was really the 1960s that birthed the American New Age movement as we now know it. First, the leftist political and drug counterculture of the 1960s provided a springboard for many to experiment with spirituality. Second, the repeal of the Asian Immigration Act in 1965 caused an influx of Asian religious practitioners who made Eastern practices more accessible.[19] Even as the New Age was emerging, however, political critiques were already being levied against it for being passive, apolitical navel gazing. The New Age movement in the sixties was not associated with overt political action or with any of the many political countercultures of the time and was already splintering off from what was perceived to be "activism in the world."[20] Walter Anderson notes that it was soon generally accepted that "the youth movement a la Reich [his *The Greening of America* that called for a revolution], the human potential movement a la Esalen [the "mother church" of the New Age movement], and the humanistic psychology movement were all of a piece—euphoric, naive, and depoliticized visions of a hastening upper middle class millennium."[21] In the midst of the many flourishing civil rights movements—racial equality, gay pride, women's rights—New Age culture seemed willfully and woefully unaware of broader power imbalances. Rather than organize protesters, New Agers declared a coming shift in consciousness. Rather than work for structural change, New Agers declared that structures were outmoded and new paradigms would hasten this New Age of consciousness. As activist Abbie Hoffman said, "If I close my eyes and think of New Age consciousness, I see yuppies."[22] This critique that New Agers are apolitical still dogs New Age culture today.

If the political movements of the left found the New Age too tame and apolitical, mainstream and fundamentalist religions, in turn, found it too liberal and individualistic. As New Age culture grew, it created fissures in American religion between religious pluralism and the "one voice" of the Protestant mainstream.[23] Catherine Albanese has argued that New Age spirituality was an "expansive" philosophy that attracted Eastern and countercultural movements and believed in pooling ideas from many movements, while fundamentalists were "contractive," and sought to shore up their movement by implementing a "pro-America" philosophy that encouraged people to "return" to "American" principles like "family values," "buy American," and the inclusion of school prayer into classrooms.[24] For mainstream religion, New Age culture was associated with the counterculture and became polarized against God-fearing, family values citizenship. For many fundamentalists, the New Age was not just countercultural but evil. As fundamentalist Christian writer Wanda Marrs argues, "the seduction of women is top priority on Satan's hidden New Age agenda."[25]

Regardless of how it was viewed, New Age had become a movement in its own right. In 1987 the Harmonic Convergence, a worldwide spiritual event held at sacred sites to usher in a new era, had thousands of attendees.[26] After the turn of the century, the numbers continued to rise, though people self-defining as "spiritual" rather than "New Age" came more into vogue. Robert Fuller notes that in 2002, "about 20 percent of the population can be said to be sympathetic with the New Age movement."[27] Scholar Paul Heelas argues further in *The Spiritual Revolution: Why Religion Is Giving Way to Spirituality* that this turn toward the spiritual, one so influenced by New Age culture, marks a "tectonic shift" and may "prove even more significant than the Protestant Reformation of the sixteenth century."[28]

Women and the New Age Movement

Women, in particular, have been drawn to New Age culture. The sociological data has suggested that women are "more likely than men to believe in and participate in New Age movements," and a *Body Mind Spirit* magazine questionnaire found that 73 percent of those who self-defined as New Age adherents were female.[29] At the Omega Institute, one of the biggest New Age centers in the United States, co-founder Elizabeth Lesser says that "we do 300 to 400 workshops a year, and 75 percent of our students are women."[30] In his study on channeling, or communicating with spirits in the past or future, Michael Brown notes that at channeling sessions "women often outnumber men by a factor of three to one or more."[31] This overwhelming participation of women in New Age culture is not just restricted to the United States. In a recent study in Kendal, England, scholars discovered that "80 per cent of those active in the holistic milieu of Kendal and environs are female; 78 per cent of groups are led or facilitated by women; 80 per cent of one-to-one practitioners are women."[32]

While men have also participated greatly in New Age culture, particularly in creating the equally controversial "men's movement" that was influenced by Robert Bly's *Iron John,* New Age culture as a whole has remained overwhelmingly female. Interestingly, women account not only for the majority of participants but for the majority of leaders as well. As Stuart Rose points out, "the number of influential female teachers in the New Age movement appears to be on the ascendancy, increasing sevenfold between 1977 and 1994."[33] Though it is not exceptional to find co-ed subcultures in which women are statistically dominant in the United States, it is still unusual to find women occupying the primary positions of leadership in co-ed subcultures. In virtually every New Age practice, for every famous man, like channeler Jack Purcell, there are two equally famous women, like channelers Jane Roberts or J. Z. Knight. Women in New Age culture have not been relegated to one subscribed position, but have occupied multiple positions from producer to consumer.[34] The New Age movement gave many women the opportunity to figure publicly as spiritual authorities in a way that has not been seen since the nineteenth-century fin de siècle, when women were practicing actively alternative spiritualities like spiritualism and theosophy.

Furthermore, the 1960s and '70s found increasing numbers of women critiquing patriarchal religious institutions and seeking spiritual solace outside those institutions. In the '80s a wave of spiritually oriented New Age books, workshops, and seminars burst forth to meet that demand. Best-selling books, films, television shows, and corporate workshops all reflected New Age sensibilities. By the 1990s not only was the New Age already "so visible that it is invisible," but it had also become strongly associated with women.[35] Nina Wisniewski, a New Age workshop leader and teacher, says that "a lot of women who come [to New Age workshops] have a longing to connect with an inner self."[36] In fact, female New Age authors topped the best-seller lists from the 1970s to the 1990s, often by writing books as well as other print materials dealing with New Age spirituality and women's issues.[37]

By the 1990s all things New Age, from books to crystals to American Indian crafts to Gregorian chants, became a multi-billion-dollar industry, one particularly supported by women. When New Age products range from a $13 book to a $500 angel workshop, many practitioners can afford some product on that spectrum. In 1996 *Forbes* estimated that "close to $2 billion goes every year to thousands of aromatherapists, channelers, macrobiotic-food vendors and assorted massagers of mind and body."[38] The "typical profile" of a New Age customer "is a white, upscale female, age 35–65, who may have been raised within a Judeo-Christian tradition who is in search of more spirituality or alternative spirituality and a continuum of mind, body, and spirit," states Jerry Clow, owner of a large, independent New Age publishing house.[39] Furthermore, New Age consumption patterns seem to be largely middle to upper-middle class, as sociologists Daniel Mears and Christopher Ellison suggest: "New Age beliefs and materials may be most appealing to persons who are well-educated, perhaps members of the so-called 'knowledge class' (or cultural producers), for whom the pursuit of new and heterodox forms of spirituality may be attractive and fashionable. New Age consumption may also be the province of more affluent persons, who may have more time and resources than others to engage in religious or spiritual experimentation."[40] In their study of New Age culture in Kendal, England, Paul Heelas and Linda Woodhead suggest that sales of "holistic spirituality" products rose at least 15 percent from 2001 to 2003.[41] In fact, the "purchasing-culture" of these products has also depended on "the veritable explosion of interest in books to do with holistic spiritualities of life."[42]

Indeed, the print culture of the New Age has expanded exponentially in the past thirty years. As Douglas McDonald, editor at Amazon .com, says, "Religion and spirituality is one of the top categories at

Amazon.com in unit sales."[43] And in the moment of larger monopoly bookstores and presses, independent New Age presses continue to do well. At Louise Hay's press, Hay House, publicity director Jacqui Clark notes that "New Age titles are still the cash cow."[44] Such "cash cow" items include tarot and meditation cards, bumper stickers, calendars, workbooks and journals, audio CDs including lectures and meditations, and DVDs of inspirational speeches. Many of these items are best sellers, as publicist Jody Winters of Bear & Co., notes: "Medicine Cards," based on American Indian animal folklore, are the "hottest product in our line," with worldwide sales of over one million copies.[45] And as three New Age book buyers note, it is overwhelmingly women who buy New Age books and products. "Seventy percent of our customer base is female," says Jason Smith of Transitions, a large New Age bookstore in Chicago.[46]

Not only are women the largest consumers of New Age products, as workshop and book sales indicate, but their consumption patterns have also spread beyond a particular niche and into the mainstream. New Age products have become so ubiquitous that, as one New Age entrepreneur says, "It's so mainstream . . . you can see [these products] in a mall."[47] Even mainstream commercials include yoga, and major beverage companies use New Age "health" marketing to increase sales. According to Amy Hertz, an editor at Harpers San Francisco's "spiritual division," one has only to "open up any women's magazine—and they're all kind of closet New Age magazines."[48] At *O*, Oprah's magazine, which had the "most successful launch in the history of magazine publishing," editors say that "women are looking for meaning in their lives. . . . It's the right message at the right time."[49] It is no coincidence that *O*, whose motto is "about looking inside yourself," sold out its initial newsstand issue.[50]

Many critics predicted—perhaps wishfully—the death or decline of New Age culture by the end of the decade. However, it seemed as if the spiritual renaissance in the United States was just getting bigger and more mainstream. Even the "material girl's" turn away from the material proved to be another marker that spiritual seeking was hitting a new high. In 1998 Madonna, the pop cultural style and music icon for many women, moved from selling sex to touting spiritual nirvana on her album *Ray of Light*. In a typical New Age quest, Madonna pieced together practices from several religious traditions (yoga, the study of Sanskrit, and the Kabbalah) and combined them with American self-help to finally, as she put it, "become aware of people's divine nature."[51] While her new album may be less overtly spiritual than the last, not only does it still contain songs about Kabbalah but Madonna has also become one of the biggest and most famous practitioners of New Age Jewish mysticism.[52] When Madonna said, "I am slowly revealing who I am," she verbalized many women's description of their spiritual autobiography.[53] For Madonna, her quest was a *self* quest of spiritual discovery, which still held power for many women.

Oil and Water? The New Age Movement Meets the Feminist Movement

From Madonna to health-food advertisements to alternative medicine, the New Age had become its own buzzword: natural. "Everyone appears to be convinced of the virtues of eating 'naturally,' of living as 'natural' a life style as possible, of following 'natural' principles," suggests feminist scholar Rosalind Coward in her critique of health fads.[54] However, while New Agers tout the benefits of all things "natural," feminists have fought to "denaturalize" the very same term: from its insurgency, the New Age movement has run chronologically alongside the feminist movement and its followers, who have struggled to define womanhood as more than "nature," especially when man represents "culture." For a variety of reasons, the connection between these two movements has been ignored. While feminists disassociate themselves from a movement perceived as irrational and apolitical, New Agers do not want to solve spiritual problems with material politics, and often turn to a language of individualism instead. Furthermore, since academics dismiss the New Age as lowbrow and regressive, most academic work on the New Age that does exist usually has "the normative bias of an apologist, an opponent, or an apostate."[55] Thus, the gender politics of the New Age movement and the spiritual politics of the feminist movement have gone unnoticed.

In the most simplistic analyses of the New Age, even though women represent the New Age's most prominent leaders and practitioners, politics simply vanish, to be usurped entirely by the personal. The myth is that nothing political happens within New Age culture, and the New Age is critiqued for its feminizing influences, without studying, complicating, and attributing these influences to the powerful female voices of the movement. If the personal and political remain polarized, then the complicated practices of New Age women, who may not self-define as feminist, drop out.

However, there are several key features of New Age women's literature that can be understood to not only complement but also intersect with central feminist claims: (1) the awareness that gender matters and plays a significant role in shaping identity; (2) that personal power and agency are important for women; and (3) that women want control over their bodies. Since so many New Age women are focused on creating personal power—usually in the metaphysical or personal realm first—the primary mode of expression of these basic tenets that the two movements and ideologies have in common is articulated through essentialist ideas about women. New Age women tend to describe gender in essentialist terms, that is, as an "essence" or biological "difference," one that often makes them particular or special in their own right, sometimes even superior to men. Yet while "essentialism" is still popular outside the academy, feminist critics have dismissed it for some time. This tension between debates about gender identity does not erase the importance of discussing exactly how New Age women authors articulate their central concern: women's relationship to power.

There are a number of avenues for pursuing power in New Age culture. One of the most foundational beliefs and schools is that of Metaphysics, a contemporary form of the New Thought movement. In New Age culture, Metaphysics, a more extreme version of "self-help" philosophies, believes that what one thinks has ultimate control over what one feels or does. In short, Metaphysics is about gaining personal power: it uses the mind to control the body, even one's destiny. In her excellent work on the New Thought movement, Beryl Satter notes: "Throughout the twentieth century, New Thought's central premise—the power of thought to alter circumstances—had a strong allure for millions of Americans."[56] Satter documents how New Thought changed from the Victorian period to the twentieth century and how that change helped many women create a more powerful gender identity. New Thought texts, Satter argues, "show how late-nineteenth-century women struggled to create a new kind of white woman's self or ego in the midst of a culture that was rapidly changing the ground rules of gender."[57] In other words, New Thought helped women have what they long have not had—control.

Having control over one's life is a familiar goal in the feminist movement: from "taking back the night" to eliminate sexual violence to "freedom of choice" to support a woman's right to an abortion, women have sought control over their lives for decades. It goes without saying that second-wave feminism has far from eliminated sexism. While many

women suffer from poor self-esteem and disempowerment, some Metaphysical philosophies assert power and control in ways that would make
feminists blush. While these "power of positive thought" practices promote power over internal mental limits, many feminist practices promote power over external problems in the world: while the former
movement is woefully weak in cultural analysis, the latter struggles with
making the political powerful, sometimes at the cost of the personal.
When Gloria Steinem turns her attention to the "revolution within"
to examine how her political actions make her ignore her own self-
actualization, she provides a clear signal that the feminist movement
still has much to learn about internalized oppression.[58] Conversely, the
powerful women in the Metaphysical movement have no language for
parts of their struggle, and thus simplify certain problems. It seems
naive at best, for example, that so many New Age women imagine that
global problems can be addressed solely on an individual basis. It is
clear that the mass political struggles of the 1960s have brought many
gains to women, but it's increasingly clear that spiritual movements
have made a contribution too: it remains to find a language to enable
the two to speak with each other.

Though New Age women imagine that the mind can control anything, second-wave feminists made it possible for women to use their
minds, in higher education in particular. Feminists fought for better
educational opportunities for women, and as universities and colleges
went co-ed in the 1970s, and as students simultaneously protested for
the right to have a voice in their education, reforms became a reality.
Experts in the 1950s said that "every year a girl spent developing her
mind 'reduced the probability of a woman marrying.'"[59] By the 1970s
"a revolution in knowledge [had] occurred" as "feminist scholars began
challenging the established lists—canons—of literature, art, music."[60]
Women began going to school and entering professions (blue and white
collar) in record numbers.[61] Feminists reformed education and started
women's studies programs. Feminists reformed the workplace and challenged pay inequity. These reforms, now often taken for granted, made
it possible for intellectual work on women's issues to be done at the same
time that political organizing took place; in tandem, they helped to produce an active feminist movement.

As the feminist movement was fighting to change the worlds of education and work, women in the New Age movement were testifying to
the power of their minds to create a new world. While feminists most

often understand the "mind" as something to be developed through equal opportunity education, New Age women understand the "mind" as a way to exceed one's gender limitations, though they do not articulate it in those terms. This New Age belief, that one can manifest in physical reality whatever one desires, is actually a form of "agency," a central tenet of the women's movement. In Metaphysics, New Thought, and "self-help," women are assumed to be equal to men in the mental realm, that is, they can take charge of their own lives through intention and will. This belief is central to the print culture of the New Age, in which hundreds of texts, often autobiographical, narrate a path of spiritual progress. Female New Age authors speaking to a spiritually hungry female audience frequently use their life stories as a model of spiritual progress to inspire their largely female readership.

If New Age authors transition from being victims to realizing their potential through spirituality, then they hope their readers can do the same. For example, Rosemary Altea, an Indian spirit guide channeler, chronicles how she found the strength to leave her abusive relationship with a man after discovering her psychic powers. Caroline Myss tells her life story as a model of moving from being victimized and reveling in "woundology" to discovering her powers as a "medical intuitive," someone who can diagnose the diseases of others telepathically. "We are not meant to stay wounded," says Myss, and her book instructs readers on how to gain personal and physical power.[62] With so many spiritual "makeover stories," it is easy to see why struggling women found them so appealing. Furthermore, these texts often addressed women's issues such as self-esteem, body image, health, relationships, financial success, and empowerment. New Age authors Louise Hay and Marianne Williamson both draw on this autobiographical mode to highlight the mind's ability to manifest any desire or goal. By more carefully analyzing their work, we can better grasp the nature of the power they articulate, a power that appeals to many women.

The Privatization of Power: The Metaphysical World of Louise Hay

In order to understand Louise Hay, one must understand not only the nature of her New Age empire but also that creating and maintaining such an empire is common to most popular female New Age authors.

Hay is so savvy in marketing her products that she has established a kind of one-woman dynasty. Not only does she sell almost every conceivable companion product to her books—nearly two hundred items for sale—she publishes most of them herself through Hay House, her own company.[63] One can purchase her monthly newsletter through her Web site and also buy her companion workbooks; lectures; audio CDs including songs, chants, and affirmations; CDs with subliminal messages; "Affirmation Journals"; and "page-a-day calendars." Her most famous work, *You Can Heal Your Life* (1982), can be purchased in a "gift edition" and as part of a "gift set," or with a "study course" or "affirmation kit." Hay sells at least five different kinds of affirmation card decks, ranging from "I Can Do It Cards: Affirmations for Self-Esteem" to "Wisdom" cards. While Hay focuses on affirmations and healing, she also has books on women (*Empowering Women: Every Woman's Guide to Successful Living,* 1997); on accumulating wealth (*Receiving Prosperity,* Audio CD, 2005); and three children's books that include coloring books and audio. Having worked with the AIDS community in Southern California (*The AIDS Book: Creating a Positive Approach,* 1988), Hay has now branched out to work on other illnesses with her audio CD entitled *Cancer* (2004).

Hay began preaching at an alternative healing church in New York about twenty years ago (she calls herself a "Science of Mind" minister) and soon after became a guru in the AIDS community. She believes not only in the power of the mind but also that the mind has control over emotions, which is a particularly important point for women, who have been stereotyped as too emotional. Essentially, Hay believes that one can fulfill any desire by visualizing and affirming it, that one can turn disease to health by visualizing it, and that subconsciously held negative beliefs may cause disease. With the publication of her first book, *You Can Heal Your Life* (1982), Hay soon became an underground phenomenon: gay men flocked to her to find out how to visualize and release toxins from their bodies in order to be healed from AIDS and to recognize how they might have played a role in causing their disease in the first place. While criticism from others has caused Hay to temper her belief that we cause our own diseases, her work states repeatedly: "Every thought we think is creating our future."[64] Hay believes that we choose our thoughts, and that whatever we believe is our destiny. She also says, "I believe that we choose our parents" and that we "look around for the particular set of parents who will mirror the pattern we are bringing in to work on in this lifetime."[65] Hay has publicly come out as an incest and rape survivor. Rather than talk about anger or her legal rights for retribution against her attackers, she still feels that she "chose" her parents to learn a lesson and that that lesson is to "love herself" and her sexuality. It is not difficult to understand why feminists and some gay activists have taken Hay to task for this profoundly naive orientation to healing, which looks only at the personal, not at how larger systems are at work.

But Hay is not so easy to pin down. Many New Age texts appear apolitical, and Hay appears to have no political agenda. Her message is solely personal. At other moments, Hay articulates a politics that is largely about female power and how to access it. In *Empowering Women: Every Woman's Guide to Successful Living* (1997), Hay states that "from the level of emotional maturity, women are at the highest point in the evolution of this lifetime."[66] Initially, Hay seemed only interested in the "pure mind" to achieve its goals; she now articulates a strong "difference feminism" of women's superiority. Women's superiority, however, is hampered by external circumstances, and Hay argues that women must rewrite the laws so that they are "equally favorable to both men and women."[67] Notably, Hay does recognize that women cannot express their full spiritual potential if they are unequal on the material level.

But if Hay is willing to grant that current laws are sexist, she argues that women should reclaim power not through feminist action but by not "being victims." She notes: "I know that when the feminist movement first came about, women were so angry at the injustices that were levied upon them that they blamed men for everything."[68] Though Hay recognizes that women might be angry at sexist injustice, her solution is not to act on it but to get over it. As she urges, "The best thing we can do for the men in our world is to stop being victims and get our own acts together."[69] Here she is strangely in accord with the many critics who suggest that women should stop being victims, such as antifeminist or "backlash" critics like Katie Roiphe, Camille Paglia, and Christina Hoff Sommers.[70] Further, Hay says that women need to stop being victims "for the men." This focus on men signals a contradiction: on the one hand, women are "at the highest point" of emotional maturity, but on the other hand, they are still chastised to get their "acts together" for *men*.

Thus, while Hay uses gender as a lens to diagnose problems, she is ambivalent about women's power. For example, Hay includes an entire chapter on sexual harassment and describes how she struggled with an employee whom she later found out had harassed a number of people, including her friends and other staff in her home. Hay discusses at length the ways in which women are cowed into remaining silent and how no one had revealed to her their own experiences of harassment by this man. Hay eventually fires him, but part of her final conclusion is "that there must still be a part of me that attracts this behavior. . . . I will do whatever it takes to clear the rest of the pattern within me."[71] That Hay "attracts" sexual harassment on an unconscious level is just another version of the psychology that victims are responsible for their illness or whatever other harm comes to them. Hay misses the irony: if she tells women to stop being victims but then blames them and herself for attracting certain gendered problems, she perpetuates the very cycle of victimization.

Admittedly, many of Hay's claims about how to harness the power of the mind are retrograde. She claims that "one of the things we are capable of doing with our minds" is to control pregnancy: "I look forward to the time when we have learned to mentally accept or reject pregnancy."[72] Rather than demand that pharmaceutical companies and the government create birth control alternatives for men and women, Hay wants women to control it themselves. She even suggests that "sending love to your breasts combined with positive affirmations has increased bust sizes for some women."[73] Hay ignores systemic pressures that might cause women to want larger breasts and focuses only on a simplistic optimism about the power of the mind. It is easy here to see the split between feminists, who critique systems of oppression, and Hay, who critiques individuals. At the same time, Hay rightly asserts that healing oneself may sometimes be more effective than depending on a failing and inadequate system of health care. Many of Hay's claims for the power of the mind are being embraced by the mainstream medical profession as more and more hospitals use programs in visualization to help their patients heal. Feminists have also critiqued the modern health care system. They have argued that the sexism of Western medicine and health care generally has at best ignored and at worst harmed women's health.[74] Feminist critics and Louise Hay critique the same system, though somewhat differently.

As much as many critics might like to denounce Hay as prescribing individualistic responses to systemic problems, these critics would be inaccurate if they say she only turns inward. Not only does she address the sexual harassment incident above, but when documenting the negative effects of advertising on women, she urges women to write a postcard to sexist organizations saying, "How dare you try to exploit me. I will never buy your product again!"[75] Furthermore, she concludes *Empowering Women* by inviting women to create a kind of feminist "consciousness raising" group that she calls an "Empowering Women" support group. Perhaps to the dismay of some critics, Hay grasps feminist issues, whether it is sexual violence or oppressive beauty standards. Power has indeed become more private but has not disappeared from the public sphere altogether.

Emotional Affect, Female Agency, and Marianne Williamson

Like Louise Hay, Marianne Williamson stresses the power of the mind to focus and visualize women's agency and strength. But Williamson also emphasizes the presence of love through God as well as the agency of the individual in democracy, which makes her more interested in direct political action than Hay. Williamson is best known for her work *A Return to Love: Reflections on the Principles of "A Course in Miracles"* (1996). "A Course in Miracles" is a channeled text that came through Dr. Helen Schucman, a Columbia psychologist, and was published in 1975.[76] The "Course" is ecumenical and focuses on banishing fear and emphasizing love and miracles in one's life. It has been published in a number of languages and has had a popular following in New Age culture. Williamson is its most famous translator or "face."

Williamson, like Hay, also has numerous products for sale, though she has published more books on a wider range of subject matters such as race (*Beyond Fear: Twelve Spiritual Keys to Racial Healing*, 1999); democracy and citizenship (*Healing the Soul of America: Reclaiming Our Voices as Spiritual Citizens*, 2000); prayer (*Illuminata: A Return to Prayer*, 1995); and women's issues (*A Woman's Worth*, 1994). She has an audio series entitled "Marianne Williamson on . . ." where she discusses topics like abundance, anger, intimacy, emotional healing, relationships, simplicity, success, commitment, work, communication, and death. Williamson also has "gift sets," audio "workshops," calendars, "miracle cards," audio CDs featuring "music, meditation, and prayer," and a children's book, *Emma and Mommy Talk to God* (1996). This multiplicity of products is part of New Age culture's emphasis on individual spirituality and transformation — at any moment, New Age practitioners can individually participate in their own religious service by playing music or reading books suited to their own spiritual tastes.

In *A Woman's Worth*, Williamson draws on Jungian archetypal language that emphasizes both the "divine feminine" and innate differences between women and men. Williamson's essentialist or "difference" feminism allows her to recuperate and celebrate "woman" with little qualification of difference among them such as race, class, and sexual orientation. Similarly to Hay, she notes that simply inserting women into patriarchal power structures, like putting a woman in political office, is no guarantee of more peaceful, equitable policies. While she is willing to admit that women may not always be true to their essential good nature, her foundational belief is that they must try. For example, throughout her text she wants to celebrate women's singular ability to give birth to such an extent that "birthing" and "mothering" become central metaphors. She discusses how women need to birth and mother themselves to reach their full potential. She notes how women should reclaim historic and religious women as mother figures and fecund goddesses to squelch patriarchy and embrace the "divine feminine." Williamson has clearly been influenced by the belief that women once ruled the world before patriarchal domination, an archeological and spiritual hypothesis that many academics find faulty but that has had enormous popularity in New Age and Wiccan culture. Chapter titles like "Glorious Queens and Slave Girls," "The Castle Walls," and "Embracing the Goddess" signal her interest in fairy tales, archetypes, and prepatriarchal religion. Rather than note all of the interlocking systems of oppression that disable women, Williamson is focused on celebrating women's difference from men and avoiding anger toward them. Rebellion is celebration. Her definition of feminist "honors the role of the feminine — nurturing, care giving, compassionate, loving."[77]

Ironically, the example she gives for her definition of feminism involves Hillary Rodham Clinton. In the well-known furor over her strong presence in Bill Clinton's first presidential election, Rodham Clinton was punished by the media for playing one of the most public first-lady roles in a presidency since perhaps Eleanor Roosevelt. While Williamson does acknowledge that Rodham Clinton was "attacked," she suggests that her most important role was to nurture Bill. Williamson states: "There was a time when I would have found that an unliberated answer. Today, I find it sublime, sane, and feminist."[78] Williamson believes that if "the purpose of life as a woman is to ascend to the throne and rule with heart," she must do so through positive "feminine" emotional qualities.[79] How can Rodham Clinton claim equal status as a policy maker and leader if her most significant role is to nurture Bill? This dilemma is a classic case of what feminist scholar Marilyn Frye calls the "double bind."[80] Any choice Rodham Clinton makes is unacceptable and is not a real choice: if she strives to be equal she is considered uppity and presumptuous, and if she strives to be supportive she neglects her rightful power and talent.

At the very moment when her work seems reducible to a popular essentialist feminism that is naive and inadequate to account for the complexity of gender and power, however, Williamson, like Hay, makes systematic political critiques that cannot be solved solely through spiritual power and a change in consciousness. She notes that "the world treats us [women] as second-class citizens as a means of control over us," and that government is "not our boss. We are its boss. Big distinction, and one too easily forgotten by disempowered people."[81] Not only does Williamson recognize systematic power imbalances and oppression, she cites sexism as part of the problem. When discussing the political ramifications of what are often considered "women's issues"—abortion, beauty culture, mothering, sexual abuse—she does not ignore them or provide antifeminist responses but rather addresses them with some gender analysis. For example, when considering beauty issues, Williamson agrees that we should recognize cultural differences because "in other cultures the range of what is considered beautiful is much wider than ours."[82] Abortion "can be an overwhelming loss. That doesn't mean it shouldn't be legal—I think it should—but that still doesn't mean it's not a terrible emotional pain."[83] This analysis is not entirely devoid of political awareness, but merges the political and personal. Williamson never resolves the real tension at the heart of her analysis, which is reconciling how to name, fight for, and gain specific political change and yet simultaneously turn away from agitation for that change and focus on love.

Toward the end of her text, after she has articulated some of the specific issues confronting women, Williamson focuses on how "women have more power than we know," again encouraging women to attend to already being powerful, rather than name the powerlessness. In most New Age philosophies like Metaphysics, Science of Mind, and New Thought, practitioners focus on the positive because the mind's thoughts determine the outcome of an event. Further, these New Age philosophies, along with *The Course in Miracles,* focus more on how humans are good rather than sinful. These beliefs in the power of the mind and the power of the good lead Williamson to suggest naively that "the regime of oppression is almost over; its life force is waning, and only its ghost remains."[84] She says, "As we change our minds, we will change the world."[85] Political activists and feminists have certainly drawn on inspirational moments to envision the future, but can the revolution be achieved through positive visualization? The fact that Hay and Williamson fantasize about a utopian future rather than a difficult present is often satisfying to readers who long for something more hopeful. Williamson notes that "female power transcends what are known politically as 'women's issues.'"[86] In other words, "women's issues" are as much about daily, subtle oppression, and "not speaking up" as Williamson argues, as the larger issues she mentions. In the same way, for some time, feminists have highlighted how "the personal is political," or how daily, personal experiences shape and affect political reality. Thus even as she continues to appear naive about real equality, Williamson is savvier about the complexities of power than her critics give her credit for.

New Age Feminism and the Politics of Recognition

Perhaps to the surprise of many critics, feminism is being actively figured out in New Age culture, though often with different terms and names. In *The Culture of Recovery: Making Sense of the Self-Help Movement in Women's Lives,* Elayne Rapping suggests that at least parts of the New Age movement stem from feminism. She argues that the roots of the "recovery movement" (twelve-step programs, confessional talk shows, and self-help books) "are planted deep in the history of feminism itself."[87] For example, in early feminist consciousness-raising groups, women were encouraged to express themselves by speaking up and finding their voice, a practice that became a central tenet of the women's movement and one also encouraged in twelve-step programs for addiction recovery. Feminism also resides within New Age practices; as Michael Brown found, "most women involved in channeling hold feminist positions on grassroots issues: equal pay, child care, sex discrimination, and abortion rights. As a group, they are precisely the sort of self-confident, forceful women one might expect to identify with a feminist agenda."[88] However, both Brown and Rapping conclude that few New

Age women will claim the "F-word." Indeed, this is a common trend generally, notes Kristin Rowe-Finkbeiner: "It's so taboo that even some women's magazines jokingly use 'the f-word' when referring to feminism, and the word is often hurled in insults on talk radio—think feminazi. That's a lot of flack for a word that simply means the belief in the social, political, and economic equality of the sexes."[89] Given that so many women do not identify as feminists, what gender satisfactions does spirituality offer that feminism does not?

While feminist and New Age women have one thing in common— they do not like patriarchal institutions—they do not protest them in the same way. Many feminists fear that Hay represents a "therapeutic feminism," which has taken the place of political feminism. Ruth Rosen defines "therapeutic feminism" as "programs of self-help that ignored the economic or sociological obstacles women faced, and instead emphasized the way in which each individual woman, if she only thought positively about herself, could achieve some form of self-realization and emancipation."[90] Jillian Sandell explains that the rise of therapeutic feminism risks "confusing individual coping strategies with collective social change."[91] Rosen goes one step further, claiming that "therapeutic feminism" helped to end *the* women's movement, for which she and many other feminists are nostalgic.

But if, as feminist scholar Jennifer Wicke has suggested, "a singular feminist movement no longer exists" and "academic feminism is itself splintered into many domains, as is feminism in the supposedly real world outside the academy," then it is possible to understand New Age women's culture as one kind of feminism among many, however fraught that feminism might be.[92] Indeed, claiming power is something feminists can understand, even if it comes in guises that may be unappealing, including certain theories that many feminists hoped were dead. Still, by continuing to look back with nostalgia on second-wave feminism, as so much feminist theory has done, what is missed are all of the viable and fascinating, though troubling, offshoots of feminism, like New Age culture.[93]

It is in the best interest of feminists and other critics to understand the complicated ideological and aesthetic appeal of New Age culture, which infiltrates almost every aspect of American life. If critics continue to ignore New Age appeal, they may be further alienated from the large number of Americans who in some way subscribe to New Age tenets. Feminists in particular must look closely at the ever-increasing move toward the "personal" at this juncture in American culture; to ignore the New Age as one of America's most prominent answers to spirituality is to ignore an all-too-large portion of twenty-first-century America. As Beryl Satter suggests: "Today's New Age and self-help authors represent not a national wallowing in self-indulgence, but an eerily accurate barometer of the nation's most pressing personal and political concerns."[94]

In 1848 the Fox sisters heard rappings from the dead, and in the same year Elizabeth Cady Stanton and Susan B. Anthony organized the Seneca Falls convention to lobby for women's right to vote. In the nineteenth century these movements comingled, but in the twenty-first century there is barely a conversation between them. Not only has feminism profoundly influenced New Age culture, but New Age culture has also profoundly influenced the public conversation about women's power, even if it has not influenced feminism directly. It is not that New Age culture could liberate all women, but that its all-pervasive rhetorical platforms need to be understood as very real and legitimate ways that some women navigate power. As New Age author Lynn Andrews says: "Power is female. That's always the first lesson of shamanistic training."[95] And feminism has yet to reckon with that power, however troubling it might be.

Notes

I want to thank John Pennington at Saint Norbert College for helpful support and criticism on this piece.

1. Clarissa Pinkola Estes, *Women Who Run with the Wolves: Myths and Stories of the Wild Woman Archetype* (New York: Ballantine Books, 1992). For a listing of *Publishers Weekly* best-sellers lists, see Michael Korda, *Making the List: A Cultural History of the American Bestseller, 1900–1999* (New York: Barnes & Noble Books, 2001), 207.

2. Both fictional and nonfictional books on religion have long been a staple of best-seller lists. "Best seller" traditionally means that the book has appeared on best-seller lists in *Publishers Weekly*, a trade publication documenting sales, and/or the *New York Times Book Review*, which compiles sales data from bookstores and other outlets around the United States. See Karen Hinckley and Barbara Hinckley, *American Best Sellers: A Reader's Guide to Popular Fiction* (Bloomington: Indiana University Press, 1989); and Alice Payne Hackett and James Henry Burke, *80 Years of Best Sellers, 1895–1975* (New York: R. R. Bowker, 1977).

For works specifically on religious best sellers, see Ralph Carey, "Best Selling Religion: A History of Popular Religious Thought in America as Reflected in Religious Best Sellers, 1850–1960" (Ph.D. dissertation, Michigan State University, 1971).

3. For a sample of late twentieth-century women's New Age best sellers according to *Publishers Weekly* year-end best-seller lists, see Korda, *Making the List, 1900–1999:*

Ruth Montgomery, *A Gift of Prophecy,* #2, 1965, Nonfiction
Ruth Montgomery, *A World Beyond,* #8, 1972, Nonfiction
Shirley MacLaine, *Dancing in the Light,* #6, 1985, Nonfiction
Shirley MacLaine, *It's All in the Playing,* #7, 1987, Nonfiction
Marianne Williamson, *A Return to Love,* #5, 1992, Nonfiction
Betty Eadie, *Embraced by the Light,* #4, 1993, Nonfiction
Sarah Ban Breathnach, *Simple Abundance,* #4, 1996, and #2, 1997, Nonfiction
Iyanla Vanzant, *In the Meantime,* #8, 1998, Nonfiction

And according to the *New York Times Book Review* best-seller lists by date:

Louise Hay, *You Can Heal Your Life,* 12 June 1988, 8 weeks
Marianne Williamson, *A Woman's Worth,* 29 August 1993, 18 weeks
Rosemary Altea, *The Eagle and the Rose,* 27 August 1995, 8 weeks
Caroline Myss, *Anatomy of the Spirit,* 11 July 1999, 29 weeks

4. For a sample of late twentieth-century men's New Age best sellers according to *Publishers Weekly* year-end best-seller lists, see Korda, *Making the List, 1900–1999:*

Richard Bach, *Jonathan Livingston Seagull,* #1, 1972 and 1973, Fiction
Richard Bach, *Illusions: The Adventures of a Reluctant Messiah,* #3, 1977, Fiction
Richard Bach, *One: A Novel,* #9, 1988, Fiction
Carlos Castaneda, *Journey to Ixtlan,* #9, 1972, Nonfiction
Carlos Castaneda, *Tales of Power,* #6, 1974, Nonfiction
Carlos Castaneda, *The Second Ring of Power,* #8, 1976, Nonfiction
Deepak Chopra, *Ageless Body, Timeless Mind,* #5, 1993, Nonfiction
James Redfield, *The Celestine Prophecy,* #3, 1994, and #6, 1995, Fiction
Neale Donald Walsch, *Conversations with God, Book 1,* #8, 1997, Nonfiction
James Van Praagh, *Talking to Heaven,* #6, 1998, Nonfiction

5. While there has been some critical attention on women and best sellers and women's best sellers, so far none of it has addressed the New Age phenomenon. For more information on women and best sellers, see Resa L. Dudovitz, *The Myth of Superwoman: Women's Bestsellers in France and the United States* (New York:

Routledge, 1990); Madonne Miner, *Insatiable Appetites: Twentieth-Century American Women's Bestsellers* (Westport, CT: Greenwood, 1984); and Ruth Miller Elson, *Myths and Mores in American Best Sellers, 1865–1965* (New York: Garland, 1985).

6. The first and second American Great Awakenings, dated from 1730–60 and 1800–30, respectively, were times when religious experimentation rose and tent revival meetings and preaching proliferated. Catherine Albanese, *American Religions and Religion* (Belmont, CA: Wadsworth, 1992), 154.

7. Ibid., 155. For further identification of current spiritual seeking as a "Great Awakening," see Jennifer Harrison, "Advertising Joins the Journey of the Soul," *American Demographics* 19, no. 6 (June 1997): 22; David Klinghoffer, "Ghost Story: New Age Spirituality in the United States," *National Review* 50, no. 6 (6 April 1998): 32; and Ruth Clifford Engs, *Clean Living Movements: American Cycles of Health Reform* (Westport, CT: Praeger, 2000), 3. Engs marks the historical movements differently as "Great Awakenings of the Jacksonian (1830–60), the progressive (1890–1920), and the current millennial (1970–2000) reform eras."

8. Kenneth L. Woodward, "The Rites of Americans," *Newsweek* 122, no. 22 (29 November 1993): 80. See also George Gallup, Jr., and Frank Newport, "Normal and Paranormal . . . What Americans Believe," *St. Louis Post-Dispatch*, 5 August 1990, 1D. According to a *Time* magazine poll, "69 percent of people polled believe in angels, and 46 percent believe they have their own guardian angel." See Nancy Gibbs, "Angels Among Us," *Time*, 27 December 1993, 56; and William L. MacDonald, "The Popularity of Paranormal Experiences in the United States," *Journal of American Culture* 17, no. 3 (Fall 1994): 35.

9. Sarah M. Pike, *New Age and Neopagan Religions in America* (New York: Columbia University Press, 2004), 172.

10. Robert Fuller, *Spiritual but Not Religious: Understanding Unchurched America* (New York: Oxford University Press, 2001), 1.

11. Ibid., 1.

12. J. Gordon Melton and James Lewis, eds., *Perspectives on the New Age* (Albany: SUNY University Press, 1992), 44.

13. Robert Wuthnow, *After Heaven: Spirituality in America Since the 1950s* (Berkeley: University of California Press, 1998), 6.

14. Wouter J. Hanegraaff, *New Age Religion and Western Culture: Esotericism in the Mirror of Secular Thought* (New York: E. J. Brill, 1996), 114, 115.

15. Michael York, *The Emerging Network: A Sociology of the New Age and Neo-Pagan Movements* (London: Rowman & Littlefield Press, 1995), 33.

16. Robert Basil, ed., *Not Necessarily the New Age: Critical Essays* (Buffalo, NY: Prometheus Books, 1988), 36.

17. New Age culture has also been critiqued, documented, or promoted by five diverse communities: popular journalism, fundamentalist Christians, "skeptical" literature, sociological theories, and "literature written from New

Age perspectives." See Hanegraaff, *New Age Religion and Western Culture*, 3. Of these five communities, the first three—popular journalism, fundamentalist Christians, and "skeptical" literature—are largely negative about the New Age; sociological theories attempt to be evenhanded and offer more description of the New Age than analysis or critique; other academic studies range from considering the New Age as worthy of study to dismissing it as corrupting rational discourse; and finally, "literature written from New Age perspectives" is overwhelmingly positive about New Age philosophies, with the exception of a few practitioners who critique elements of the New Age while still self-identifying with the culture.

18. Marilyn Snell, "The World of Religion According to Huston Smith," *Mother Jones* 22, no. 6 (November–December 1997): 40.

19. Eastern philosophies were particularly appealing to leftists: "Many who felt that racism, exploitation, oppression and other basic ills characterized American society turned to the Oriental philosophies and religions that form so much a part of New Age thinking," notes scholar Mitchell Pacwa, quoted in Robert Di Veroli, "New Age Adherents Labeled as Products of Counterculture," *San Diego Union-Tribune*, 4 August 1990, B4.

20. Hanegraaff, *New Age Religion and Western Culture*, 11.

21. Walter Truett Anderson, *The Upstart Spring: Esalen and the American Awakening* (Reading, MA: Addison-Wesley, 1983).

22. Marion Long, "In Search of a Definition: New Age Theory," *Omni* 10 (October 1987): 80.

23. Albanese, *American Religions and Religion*, 384.

24. Ibid., 388. Even while the New Age and Christian fundamentalism seem polarized, several polls indicate otherwise. A Princeton Religion Research Center study showed that "a surprisingly high number of Christians identify beliefs generally described as New Age. At the same time, however, many have doubts that New Age spirituality is compatible with Christianity. Among Catholics, 59 percent said they consider New Age beliefs to be compatible with Christianity, compared with 23 percent of Protestants." See Randall Balmer, "New Age Beliefs Are Really Quite Old," *Los Angeles Times*, 11 January 1992, F15.

25. Wanda Marrs, *New Age Lies to Women* (Austin, TX: Living Truth Publishers, 1989), ix.

26. Religious scholar Erling Jorstad argues that "the decade coheres into a meaningful pattern when its religious expression is seen in a threefold design: (1) mainline [religion] moves into frontline; (2) evangelicalism moves toward popular religion; and (3) privatization moves into New Age religion." See Erling Jorstad, *Holding Fast/Pressing On: Religion in America in the 1980s* (New York: Praeger, 1990), x. Critic Harold Bloom has suggested that the New Age "may have achieved its greatest prominence throughout the 1980s." See Harold

Bloom, *The American Religion: The Emergence of a Post-Christian Nation* (New York: Simon & Schuster, 1992), 183.

27. Felix Hoover, "Spiritual Seekers Often Shun Churches," *The Columbus Dispatch*, 20 September 2002, 01D.

28. Paul Heelas and Linda Woodhead, *The Spiritual Revolution: Why Religion Is Giving Way to Spirituality* (London: Blackwell, 2005), 2.

29. Daniel P. Mears and Christopher G. Ellison, "Who Buys New Age Materials?: Exploring Sociodemographic, Religious, Network, and Contextual Correlates of New Age Consumption," *Sociology of Religion* 61 (Fall 2000): 292; Jorstad, *Holding Fast/Pressing On*, 175. Statistical and anecdotal evidence also suggest that women make up the largest consumer base of New Age culture. "Middle-aged women make up the majority of their large New Age bookstore's customers," notes Bridget Kinsella, "Gayle & Howard Mandel," *Publishers Weekly*, 14 June 1999, 42. It is clear, as one critic said, that "one can get a feeling for the subculture . . . by spending an hour browsing in a New Age bookshop" (Robert Balch, "The Evolution of a New Age Cult: From Total Overcomers Anonymous to Death at Heaven's Gate," in *Sects, Cults & Spiritual Communities: A Sociological Analysi*s, ed. William W. Zellner and Marc Petrowsky [Westport, CT: Praeger, 1998], 4); and at a channeling workshop featuring J. Z. Knight: "Most are middle-aged women" (see Katherine Lowry, "Channelers," *Omni* 10 [October 1987]: 47).

30. Karin Evans, "Journeys of the Spirit," *Health* 15, no. 3 (April 2001): 123.

31. Michael F. Brown, *The Channeling Zone: American Spirituality in an Anxious Age* (Cambridge, MA: Harvard University Press, 1997), 95.

32. Heelas and Woodhead, *Spiritual Revolution*, 94.

33. Stuart Rose, "New Age Women: Spearheading the Movement?" *Women's Studies* 30 (2001): 330.

34. There are certainly exceptions to the access to power women have felt in New Age culture. At the Esalen Institute in the 1970s, a major conference was conceived that featured no women as panelists. Although feminists protested, such institutions were quite androcentric until confronted by the women's movement in the 1970s. See Anderson, *Upstart*, 263.

35. Margaret Jones, "Publishing for 'Spiritual Seekers,'" *Publishers Weekly*, 6 December 1993, 48.

36. Evans, "Journeys of the Spirit," 178.

37. See Korda, *Making the List*, 196–219.

38. Josephine Lee and Tom Ferguson, "Coin of the New Age," *Forbes*, 9 September 1996, 86.

39. Jones, "Publishing for 'Spiritual Seekers,'" 45.

40. Notably, Mears and Ellison go on to say that "one might suspect that New Age materials in fact are more popular among less affluent and/or less educated persons, or among un(der)employed persons. These groups may view

New Age materials as leading to insight and self-empowerment (e.g., a central goal of many New Age books, journals, tapes, and so forth) that in turn might facilitate, if indirectly, upward mobility." See Mears and Ellison, "Who Buys New Age Materials?" 290.

41. Heelas and Woodhead, *Spiritual Revolution*, 68.

42. Ibid., 69.

43. Martin E. Marty, "Not-so-new age," *Christian Century*, 8 September 1999, 879.

44. Judith Rosen, "Casting a Wider Spell: 'Mainstream' Is Definitely the Word for This Flourishing Category," *Publishers Weekly*, 1 September 2003, 38. After 9/11 and into the twenty-first century, the next expanding market is teens, and publishers have started various lines ranging from Wicca to Buddhist-inspired punk. See Angie Kiesling, "God, Sex, and Rock-n-Roll: Spirituality, Relationships, and Popular Culture Dominate the Teen and 20-Something Market," *Publishers Weekly*, 11 August 2003, 130.

45. Lynn Garrett, "New Age Is All the Rage," *Publishers Weekly*, 10 March 1997, 39.

46. Margaret Langstaff, "Mind+Body+Spirit=New Age," *Publishers Weekly*, 15 May 2000, 65.

47. Debra Phillips, "Coming of Age," *Entrepreneur*, July 1996, 99.

48. Jones, "Publishing for 'Spiritual Seekers,'" 47.

49. Sarah Gonser, "O, the Incredible, Sellable," *Folio: The Magazine for Magazine Management*, February 2001, 26.

50. Noreen O'Leary, "O Positive—O, *The Oprah Magazine*, profile," *Brandweek*, March 2001, 2.

51. Quoted in Ann Powers, "New Tune for the Material Girl: I'm Neither," *New York Times*, 1 March 1998, 34.

52. Steven Kotler, "God's Hip Language," *Salon*, 29 July 2003.

53. Powers, "New Tune for the Material Girl," 34.

54. Rosalind Coward, *The Whole Truth: The Myth of Alternative Health* (London: Faber and Faber, 1989), 17.

55. Mary Farrell Bednarowski, *New Religions and the Theological Imagination in America* (Bloomington: Indiana University Press, 1989), vii.

56. Beryl Satter, *Each Mind a Kingdom: American Women, Sexual Purity, and the New Thought Movement, 1870–1920* (Berkeley: University of California Press, 1999), 6.

57. Ibid., 17.

58. Gloria Steinem, *Revolution from Within: A Book of Self-Esteem* (New York: Little, Brown; reprint edition, 1993).

59. Ruth Rosen, *The World Split Open: How the Modern Women's Movement Changed America* (New York: Viking, 2000), 40.

60. Ibid., 40.

61. Ibid., 266.

62. Caroline Myss, *Why People Do Not Heal and How They Can* (New York: Harmony Books, 1997), 15.

63. As of August 2005, Amazon.com book sales carried 183 Louise Hay items, most of them still in print and in a variety of languages.

64. Louise Hay, *You Can Heal Your Life* (Santa Monica, CA: Hay House, 1987), 7.

65. Ibid., 10.

66. Louise Hay, *Empowering Women: Every Woman's Guide to Successful Living* (Carlsbad, CA: Hay House, 1997), 4.

67. Ibid., 8.

68. Ibid., 6.

69. Ibid., 4.

70. Katie Roiphe, *The Morning After: Sex, Fear, and Feminism* (New York: Back Bay Books, 1994); Camille Paglia, *Sex, Art, and American Culture: Essays* (New York: Vintage, 1992); Christina Hoff Sommers, *Who Stole Feminism? How Women Have Betrayed Women* (New York: Simon & Schuster, 1995).

71. Hay, *Empowering Women*, 98.

72. Ibid., 61.

73. Ibid., 82.

74. See Barbara Ehrenreich and Deirdre English, *For Her Own Good: Two Centuries of the Experts' Advice to Women* (New York: Anchor, 2005); Paul Starr, *The Social Transformation of American Medicine* (New York: Basic Books, 1984).

75. Ibid., 14.

76. Eileen Campbell and J. H. Brennan, *Body, Mind & Spirit: A Dictionary of New Age Ideas, People, Places, and Terms* (Boston: Charles E. Tuttle Company, 1994).

77. Marianne Williamson, *A Woman's Worth* (New York: Ballantine, 1993), 108.

78. Ibid., 108.

79. Ibid., 11.

80. Marilyn Frye, *The Politics of Reality* (Berkeley, CA: The Crossing Press, 1983), 5.

81. Williamson, *A Woman's Worth*, 34, 115.

82. Ibid., 35.

83. Ibid., 106.

84. Ibid., 137.

85. Ibid., 137.

86. Ibid., 69.

87. Elayne Rapping, *The Culture of Recovery: Making Sense of the Self-Help Movement in Women's Lives* (Boston: Beacon Press, 1996), 11.

88. Brown, *The Channeling Zone*, 99.

89. Kristin Rowe-Finkbeiner, *The F-Word: Feminism In Jeopardy—Women, Politics and the Future* (Boston: Seal Press, 2004). Earlier, a 20 February 1990 Time/CNN poll reported that 63 percent of women say that they do not identify as feminists.

90. Rosen, *The World Split Open,* 316.

91. Jillian Sandell, "Adjusting to Oppression: The Rise of Therapeutic Feminism in the United States," in *"Bad Girls"/"Good Girls": Women, Sex, and Power in the Nineties,* ed. Nan Bauer Maglin and Donna Perry (New Brunswick, NJ: Rutgers University Press, 1994).

92. Jennifer Wicke and Margaret Ferguson, eds., *Feminism and Postmodernism* (Durham, NC: Duke University Press, 1994), 33.

93. For one of the better examples of nostalgia for second-wave feminism, see Gayle Greene and Coppelia Kahn, eds., *Changing Subjects: The Making of Feminist Literary Criticism* (New York: Routledge, 1993).

94. Satter, *Each Mind a Kingdom,* 254.

95. Rose Marie Staubs, "Andrews's Sisters," *Omni* 10 (October 1987): 28.

The Bible-zine *Revolve* and the Evolution of the Culturally Relevant Bible in America

PAUL C. GUTJAHR

"The world's largest publisher of religious material is selling the sizzle along with the solemn in a line of Bible-zines."[1] So began a Reuters news service story on Thomas Nelson Publishers and a new trend of selling the Bible packaged as a magazine. This hybrid form, half magazine/half Bible, was not completely new to American Bible publishing, but its success in the American marketplace in the opening years of the twenty-first century was. *Revolve*, Thomas Nelson's Bible-zine for teenage women, was released to wide media exposure and magnificent sales in the summer of 2003. Whereas most Bible editions at the time sold an average of forty thousand copies a year, that many copies of *Revolve* flew off bookstore shelves in the first eight weeks after its release.[2] *Revolve*'s editorial team was focused on making a Bible edition that would reach a generation of young American women, a generation that their market research told them had little or no interest in reading the traditional Bible.[3] They wished to engage this demographic by giving them the Bible in a style that fell well within their "comfort zone," an edition of the Christian sacred scriptures that would look cool to their peer group, be accessible in its content, and enable these ancient writings to speak to their twenty-first century lives.[4]

Fusing the Bible with the magazine, however, is not without certain interpretive consequences. One need only take a moment to examine *Revolve* to see how important a type of media can be to the message it conveys. A study of *Revolve* not only enables one to catch a glimpse of the changing nature of Bible publishing in the United States but also how the quest to make the sacred Christian scriptures culturally relevant may, in this instance, work against the very goal of making Americans pay closer attention to the Christian Gospel.

The American Quest for the Culturally Relevant Bible

Attempting to make the Christian Bible more intellectually engaging and accessible is nothing new. In fact, there is a centuries-old tradition of creating Bible editions that seek to bridge the gap between the historical nature of the biblical text and the more contemporary setting into which that text is inserted. Such Bible editions might be called "culturally relevant," as they are designed with the goal of making these ancient writings meaningful to modern readers.

Most frequently, culturally relevant Bible editions have focused on changing the language of the Bible's core text to make it more understandable. Saint Jerome made the most famous early attempt at revising the Christian scriptures in this regard when Pope Damasus commissioned him in 382 to produce a Latin version of the scriptures meant to be the standard, accessible text for Christians of the day. Saint Jerome's efforts produced the *editio vulgata* or "common version." Both the German reformer Martin Luther and the Englishman William Tyndale followed in the spirit of Jerome's "common version" twelve centuries later when they produced their own translations of the Christian scriptures from the Greek in the opening decades of the sixteenth century. Both were momentous translations, but it was ultimately Tyndale's translation work that changed forever the way English-speaking people encountered the Bible. His translation set the standard for providing the Christian scriptures to the ordinary English-speaking reader for the next four centuries.[5]

Americans joined in these efforts to make the Bible's core text more accessible in a number of translations that began to appear in the early nineteenth century. Charles Thomson, the former long-serving secretary of the First Continental Congress, produced the first American translation of the Christian scriptures into English in 1808. He concerned himself not only with making an accurate and academically credible translation of the Greek Septuagint text but also with producing a version that would use a common idiom familiar to educated Americans of the time. In the four decades that followed the appearance of Thomson's translation, just shy of twenty other Americans would turn their attention to publishing new translations of the Christian scriptures.[6] Many of these American translators joined Thomson in the quest of making the language of this formidable book less intimidating to the common reader.

The most successful of this American wave of translators was Alexander Campbell, who released his own revision of the New Testament, *The Sacred Writings of the Apostles and Evangelists of Jesus Christ,* in 1826. Campbell's revision of the New Testament is noteworthy for two reasons. First, he was thoroughly committed to making the language of the Bible contemporary for his antebellum American readers. He wished to remake phrases that had become "awkward and obsolete" into passages that would capture and convey the original meaning of the sacred text to his readers.[7] For example, Campbell changed 1 Thessalonians 4:15 to use the word *anticipate* rather than the word *prevent* (a word that had meant "anticipate" in the 1600s but in the 1820s held only the meaning of "hindering" or "obstructing").[8] Campbell also dropped all the *eth* endings off the verbs and changed words like *doeth* to *does* and *keepeth* to *keeps*. Campbell knew that his fellow Americans did not speak like Shakespeare in everyday discourse, and he wanted his version of the New Testament to be used every day.

Second, Campbell paid significant attention to the format of the Bible itself. He moved beyond the words of the actual text to how those words were presented. Rather than replicate the standard, imposing double column format found in Bible editions of the time, Campbell presented his new, contemporary-idiom translation in a single column without the conventional verse and chapter markings in an attempt to encourage the narrative flow of the text. What is instructive about *The Sacred Writings* is just how sensitive Campbell was to the fact that content and format worked together to convey God's message to humanity.

THE
TESTIMONY
OF
JOHN,
THE APOSTLE.

FIRST PUBLISHED IN EPHESUS, A. D. 68.

JOHN'S PREFACE.

I. IN the beginning was the Word, and the Word was with God, and the Word was God. This was in the beginning with God. All things were made by it, and without it not a single creature was made. In it was life, and the life was the light of men. And the light shone in darkness; but the darkness admitted it not.

SECTION I.

The Testimony of John the Immerser.

6. A man named John was sent from God. This man came as a witness to testify concerning the light, that through him all might believe. He was not himself the light, but came to testify concerning the light. The true light was he who, coming into the world, enlighteneth every man.

He was in the world, and the world was made by him; yet the world knew him not. He came to his own land, and his own people* did not receive him; but to as many

* App. No. XXVIII.

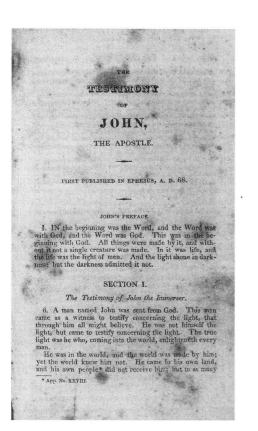

Figure 14.1. First page of the Gospel of John from Alexander Campbell's 1826 edition of *The Sacred Writings*. Note the single-column page without conventional verse and chapter markings, changes that encourage easy reading and narrative flow. (Courtesy of the American Bible Society Library.)

Chriſt transfigured. CHAP. XVIII. *Chriſt teacheth to be humble.*

thou art an offence unto me: for thou
ſavoureſt not the things that be of
God, but thoſe that be of men.
24 ¶ Then ſaid Jeſus unto his diſciples, If any *man* will come after me,
let him deny himſelf, and take up his
croſs, and follow me.
25 For whoſoever will ſave his life
ſhall loſe it: and whoſoever will loſe
his life for my ſake ſhall find it.
26 For what is a man profited, if he
ſhall gain the whole world, and loſe
his own ſoul? or what ſhall a man
give in exchange for his ſoul?
27 For the Son of man ſhall come in
the glory of his Father with his angels;
and then he ſhall reward every man
according to his works.
28 Verily I ſay unto you, There be
ſome ſtanding here, which ſhall not
taſte of death, till they ſee the Son of
man coming in his kingdom.
CHAP. XVII.
AND after ſix days Jeſus taketh
Peter, James, and John his brother, and bringeth them up into an
high mountain apart,
2 And was transfigured before them:
and his face did ſhine as the ſun, and
his raiment was white as the light.
3 And, behold, there appeared unto
them Moſes and Elias talking with
him.
4 Then anſwered Peter, and ſaid
unto Jeſus, Lord, it is good for us to
be here: if thou wilt, let us make
here three tabernacles; one for thee,
and one for Moſes, and one for Elias.
5 While he yet ſpake, behold, a
bright cloud overſhadowed them: and
behold a voice out of the cloud, which
ſaid, This is my beloved Son, in whom
I am well pleaſed; hear ye him.
6 And when the diſciples heard *it*,
they fell on their face, and were ſore
afraid.
7 And Jeſus came and touched them,
and ſaid, Ariſe, and be not afraid.
8 And when they had lifted up their
eyes, they ſaw no man, ſave Jeſus
only.
9 And as they came down from the
mountain, Jeſus charged them, ſaying, Tell the viſion to no man, until
the Son of man be riſen again from
the dead.
10 ¶ And his diſciples aſked him,
ſaying, Why then ſay the ſcribes that
Elias muſt firſt come?
11 And Jeſus anſwered and ſaid unto
them, Elias truly ſhall firſt come, and
reſtore all things.
12 But I ſay unto you, That Elias is
come already, and they knew him
not, but have done unto him what-
ſoever they liſted. Likewiſe ſhall alſo
the Son of man ſuffer of them.
13 Then the diſciples underſtood
that he ſpake unto them of John the
Baptiſt.
14 ¶ And when they were come to
the multitude, there came to him a
certain man, kneeling down to him,
and ſaying,
15 Lord, have mercy on my ſon:
for he is lunatick, and ſore vexed:
for oft-times he falleth into the fire,
and oft into the water.
16 And I brought him to thy diſciples, and they could not cure him.
17 Then Jeſus anſwered and ſaid, O
faithleſs and perverſe generation, how
long ſhall I be with you? how long
ſhall I ſuffer you? bring him hither
to me.
18 And Jeſus rebuked the devil; and
he departed out of him: and the child
was cured from that very hour.
19 Then came the diſciples to Jeſus
apart, and ſaid, Why could not we caſt
him out?
20 And Jeſus ſaid unto them, Be-
cauſe of your unbelief: for verily I
ſay unto you, If ye have faith as a
grain of muſtard-ſeed, ye ſhall ſay
unto this mountain, Remove hence to
yonder place; and it ſhall remove; and
nothing ſhall be impoſſible unto you.
21 Howbeit this kind goeth not out
but by prayer and faſting.
22 ¶ And while they abode in Galilee, Jeſus ſaid unto them, The Son of
man ſhall be betrayed into the hands of
men:
23 And they ſhall kill him, and the
third day he ſhall be raiſed again.
And they were exceeding ſorry.
24 ¶ And when they were come to
Capernaum, they that received tribute
money came to Peter, and ſaid, Doth
not your maſter pay tribute?
25 He ſaith, Yes. And when he was
come into the houſe, Jeſus prevented
him, ſaying, What thinkeſt thou, Simon? Of whom do the kings of the
earth take cuſtom or tribute? of their
own children, or of ſtrangers?
26 Peter ſaith unto him, Of ſtrangers.
Jeſus ſaith unto him, Then are the
children free.
27 Notwithſtanding, leſt we ſhould
offend them, go thou to the ſea, and
caſt an hook, and take up the fiſh
that firſt cometh up; and when thou
haſt opened his mouth, thou ſhalt
find a piece of money: that take, and
give unto them for me and thee.
CHAP. XVIII.
AT the ſame time came the diſciples unto Jeſus, ſaying, Who is
the greateſt in the kingdom of heaven?
2 And Jeſus called a little child unto
him, and ſet him in the midſt of
them,
3 And ſaid, Verily I ſay unto you,
Except ye be converted, and become
as little children, ye ſhall not enter
into the kingdom of heaven.
4 Whoſoever therefore ſhall humble himſelf as this little child, the
ſame is greateſt in the kingdom of
heaven.
5 And whoſo ſhall receive one ſuch
little child in my name receiveth me.
6 But whoſo ſhall offend one of
theſe little ones which believe in
me, it were better for him that a mill-
ſtone were hanged about his neck,
and *that* he were drowned in the depth
of the ſea.
B2

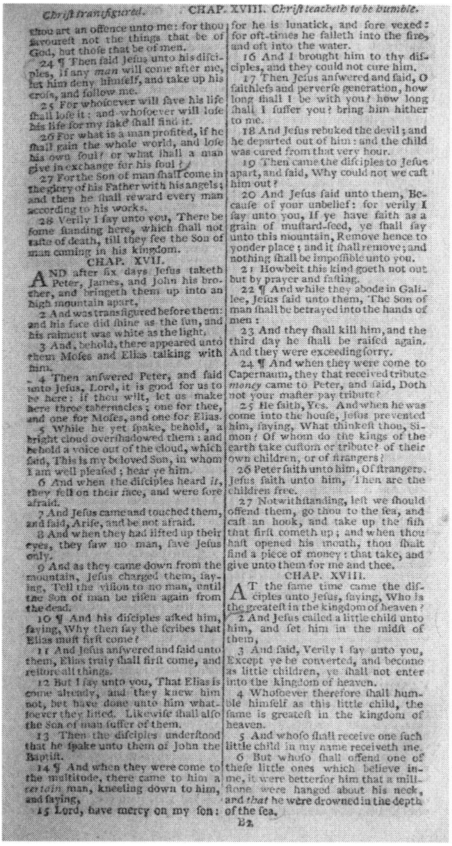

Figure 14.2. Standard double-column format found in Bibles throughout the nineteenth and early twentieth centuries. This example is from a small, 1810 pocket New Testament printed by William Woodward in Philadelphia. (Library of the Author.)

This sensitivity paid rich dividends. By the time he died in 1866, his New Testament had sold over forty thousand copies, making it the second best-selling translation of the Christian scriptures in the United States next to the ubiquitous King James Version.[9]

The quest for making the Bible culturally relevant for Americans would continue in the years following the appearance of Campbell's *The Sacred Writings,* but it would not be until nearly one hundred and fifty years later that it would reach a sort of critical mass in the early 1980s as literally hundreds of specialty Bibles poured forth from American presses beginning in an attempt to reach out to specific American audiences with the Christian scriptures. Beginning in the 1980s, American Bible publishers turned their energies to an unprecedented degree toward producing and marketing specialty Bibles targeted with almost surgical precision toward markets such as dieters, newlyweds, mothers, fathers, parents, single parents, adolescents, and those who suffered from drug and alcohol addictions. All these different Bible editions have sought to make the word of God relevant to a specific audience with a defined set of perceived needs.[10] Through this tremendous growth in niche Bible production and marketing, the universal message of Christian salvation has become increasingly particularized in the last twenty-five years.

New capitalization and distribution practices adopted by Christian publishing houses coupled with new publishing technologies established the early 1980s as a watershed moment in specialty Bible production in the United States.[11] Of particular importance are these new publishing technologies. Christian publishers followed the rest of the publishing industry during this decade as they moved away from traditional methods of offset printing and moved instead toward the use of computers and digital printing processes.[12] These technologies made the formerly imposing and immensely complex nature of typesetting Bibles and formatting them with special accompaniments such as pictures and sidebars immeasurably easier. They allowed publishers to manipulate texts and modes of presentation quickly and efficiently. New computer software revolutionized the work of formatting pages as the former time-intensive and cumbersome tools of tape, glue, rulers, and scissors became obsolete. Thus, publishers were able to easily place a wide range of English Bible translations into a variety of mutable formats with specialized study aids and concordances. Such technology provided publishers with the means to produce both large and small, highly targeted press runs of specific Bible editions. The age of the specialized study and niche Bible had arrived in American print culture to a degree never before witnessed.

Perhaps no publishing firm was more influential in this trend toward Bible edition specialization and multiplication than Thomas Nelson, the largest publisher of Bibles in the United States in the closing decades of the twentieth century. Thomas Nelson Publishers, a firm that dates its publishing activities to 1798, has had a long and distinguished history of Bible production in the United States. In 1946 it was the debut publisher in America for the immensely popular Revised Standard Version, a revision of the important, but less popular, Revised Version of 1881. Thirty years later the firm would begin work on the New King James Version, another hugely popular revision of a well-loved biblical translation, the time-honored King James Version of 1611. Thomas Nelson, therefore, already enjoyed a significant tradition of providing the religious marketplace with innovative Bibles when it launched *Revolve* in the summer of 2003. *Revolve* was destined to add another chapter to the story of Nelson's dominance in the American Bible marketplace.

A Not So Daring Idea

At first glance, *Revolve* might seem like a singularly daring idea. After all, Christian publishing had practically no history of trying a Bible/magazine hybrid. The one notable exception appeared in the 1950s when the American Bible Society (ABS) began serially to publish *The Good News, The New Testament With Over 500 Illustrations and Maps*. *The Good News* used both the King James and Revised Standard Versions of the biblical text ensconced in a magazine format intended to imitate the highly popular photo news magazines of the day, such as *Time, Life* and *Look*.

The Good News was the idea of Reverend Gilbert Darlington, the long-time treasurer of the ABS and, more importantly, the head of the society's publication department. Through force of personality and the fact that he held a key publication post in the society, Darlington almost single-handedly conceptualized and then pushed *The Good News* to completion. His was an idea born not of market research, but of personal passion and conviction. He held the unwavering belief that the Bible created in the image of a photo magazine would enjoy wide popularity among American Bible readers. So committed was he to the idea, that he personally financed the production of the first installment on the Sermon on the Mount. Only after this initial installment did the ABS decide to undertake this edition.[13]

Darlington sold the idea to the ABS, which had a long tradition of producing the scriptures "without note or comment," by showing that the Bible would be not only contemporary in design but also academically credible.[14] He hired a number of prominent biblical scholars to check through the accompanying photos and sidebar information for biblical and historical accuracy.[15] *The Good News* was modern in its formatting but staunchly traditional in the material that accompanied the actual biblical text. A board of experts carefully vetted hundreds of drawings, photographs, and informative captions so that every illustration of the biblical text was both edifying and accurate.

With *The Good News*, the American hybrid magazine/Bible was born. But even though the ABS distributed millions of copies of this Biblezine, it proved more a novelty than a trendsetter.[16] The vast majority of American Bible readers wanted a more traditional Bible for their devotional and study purposes.

In *Revolve*, Thomas Nelson Publishers took a slightly different tack from the ABS. Instead of fusing widely used Bible translations with a general interest magazine, Nelson used its newly created New Century Version (a specialized, contemporary and ultra-reader-friendly translation completed in 1991) and packaged it in the guise of a young woman's magazine. Unlike the ABS's intention to produce a broad audience Bible with *The Good News*, Thomas Nelson targeted *Revolve* for a narrow, tightly defined audience, namely, teenage American girls. *Revolve*'s editorial staff even took the Bible edition's name from ideas given them by teenage girls through online surveys. The name foregrounded change and newness, an accurate reflection of the constant change and motion inherent in the life of American teenagers.[17]

Thomas Nelson Publishers also departed from the traditional path of Bible design by not using any of its in-house graphics personnel to design *Revolve*. Instead, *Revolve*'s editorial team gave the design commission for its Bible edition to the Irish graphic design firm Four5One (named after Ray Bradbury's famous novel *Fahrenheit 451*). *Revolve*'s editors chose Four5One because it was outside the "Christian Ghetto of Bible design" found in Nelson's own ranks.[18] It was a firm that had made a name for itself doing album covers for such highly popular rock 'n' roll acts as U2 and Elvis Costello. Nelson wanted *Revolve* to have the freshest possible

Figure 14.3. Front Cover of the Bible-zine *Revolve*, first printing, 2003. (Courtesy of Thomas Nelson, Inc. Library of the Author.)

look and felt that hiring a firm that had an established track record for doing graphic projects largely targeted at the contemporary youth culture would accomplish this.[19]

Consequently, Four5One created a hip-looking Bible that deeply echoed the look and feel of any number of thick magazines a young girl might pick up at a newsstand. It was printed on glossy paper, and its cover could easily make one at first glance mistake it for *Cosmo-Girl* or *Seventeen*. Once opened, *Revolve*'s contents also clearly echoed this female teenage magazine culture. *Revolve* contains calendars, quizzes, beauty and dating tips, and countless lists that young readers can peruse as they read through this highly stylized version of the New Testament. In making such format decisions, the editors of *Revolve* clearly set their edition within the "culturally relevant" Bible tradition by fusing it with the vibrant, contemporary print culture of the American women's magazine.

Considering the impressive and long-standing popularity of women's magazines in American print culture, *Revolve* was not as risky an enterprise as it might have at first appeared. Recent studies have shown that even in the midst of ever-growing and competing forms of media, there exists a profound and extensive female magazine culture in the United States. It is a culture that reaches all the way back to the 1790s when the first periodicals targeted specifically at women began to appear in America.[20] Not until the 1840s and 1850s, however, with antebellum periodicals such as *Godey's Lady's Book, Graham's,* and *Peterson's* did American women's magazines gain the popularity and prominence they still enjoy.

Since the prominence of magazines among women readers first gained a foothold in the decades leading up to the Civil War, American women's interest in, and commitment to, magazine reading has not wavered. Even today, it can be argued, women read more magazines than any other single genre of printed material. Evidence for just how popular magazines are among women readers can be found in a study completed in 2001 by Rob Frydlewicz, an advertising company vice president. Frydlewicz drove home the astounding popularity and market penetration of women's magazines in contemporary American print culture by documenting that the top twenty-five women's magazines command larger audiences than the top twenty-five female-targeted television shows.[21] Magazines "such as *Cosmopolitan, Glamour* or *Vogue* had a 73 percent larger audience among women age 18 to 49 than TV shows such as Friends, Ally McBeal and ER."[22] While other magazines and other areas of print have felt the pinch of competing media, women buy magazines at such a rate that advertising prices in women's magazines have continued to rise even while the ad revenues of many non-women's magazines are fading.[23]

Revolve became a part of the magazine culture that American women already knew and to which they were firmly committed. Such a Bible-zine combined two of the most popular printed genres in American culture: the woman's magazine and the Bible. While American women had long enjoyed the magazine as a periodical that had a distinctive format and look, they also had an equally long engagement with the Bible as a book that had a distinctive mode of presentation. The radical nature of this Bible-zine hybrid needs to be understood not only in the context of American women and their magazine culture but also in the context of American women and their Bibles.

Breaking with Tradition

To appreciate fully the importance of *Revolve* not only as a magazine but also as a Bible edition, it is important to point out that *Revolve*'s main editor and visionary, Kate Etue, initially found it extremely difficult to sell this hybrid concept to her superiors at Thomas Nelson.[24] Ms. Etue edited Nelson's teenage line of books called "Extreme for Jesus" when she first began to contemplate the idea of a Bible-zine for American teenage women. Extreme for Jesus was a department with Thomas Nelson specifically empowered to produce Bible study guides and other material focused on engaging an American teenage audience. As Ms. Etue and her staff did regular focus groups and online surveys with teenage readers, they continually came across the fact that girls were often readers, but not Bible readers. They found the book too long and too intimidating in terms of its language. At the same time, the Extreme for Jesus staffers also discovered that girls were regular and devoted magazine readers, a fact that reached into even the preteen age of the girls they surveyed.

Ms. Etue and her staff made the natural conceptual leap that if American teenage girls were reading more magazines than any other form of printed material, they might perhaps be coaxed into reading the Bible if it appeared in a magazine format. After all, the New Testament was a brief book. The Extreme for Jesus staffers reasoned that it would take no longer to read the New Testament than it would to finish the typical magazine.[25]

At first, the idea impressed few at Nelson's Bible division. The firm had a rich tradition of successful Bible publishing, but it was based on the bedrock belief that the Bible was like no other book and thus should be produced in a format that echoed the volume's uniqueness. While Thomas Nelson was more than willing to innovate when it came to more modern language translations of the biblical text, the concept of *Revolve* showed that it was far less eager to innovate in the area of biblical format and presentation.

In considering the substantial opposition Kate Etue and her creative team faced in pushing forward with their idea of a Bible-zine, it is critical to note that while American Bible publishers have had a long tradition of producing and marketing culturally relevant Bible editions, these editions have always been only a small sliver of the American Bible marketplace. American Bible publishers have almost entirely sought to produce and market their Bible editions with an eye to its unique status as a book and religious icon. After all, the Bible was like no other book, and this singularity was often carefully choreographed into its presentation.

Until the closing decades of the twentieth century, American Bible publishers produced Bibles meant to look expensive, important, well made, and unique. Such publishers predominantly bound them in leather with frequently thin, high-quality, gilt-edged pages. Such leather-covered volumes still make up a significant percentage of American Bibles produced today. The choice of expensive binding and special paper was intended to reflect the importance of the text the book contained. Even today, Bibles are among the few leather-bound, gilded books to be found in Barnes & Noble or Borders bookstores. A Bible remains a recognizable book even at a distance. The distinctive binding and paper helps reinforce the unique nature of the book and the timeless nature of the message it contains. Christians believe that the word of God is the same yesterday, today, and tomorrow, and for decades American Bible publishers reinforced this sentiment in the ways they produced and presented the volume to their customers.

American women, long numerically dominant over men when it comes to American church membership and involvement, partook fully in this more traditional view of American Bible production.[26] Because of their rising literacy rates and their commitment to religious and moral education, beginning in the early nineteenth century women became important and influential buyers of American Bibles. Aside from smaller, more mobile Bibles that came into wide use in the 1820s and after, antebellum women began to use Bibles as key markers of religious devotion and social refinement in their houses. These house Bibles were much larger than volumes that women carried to their churches and Bible studies. They were imposing volumes displayed prominently, most often in parlors. That women loved to use Bibles as a distinctive form of decorative furniture was not lost on American Bible publishers, who produced ever more elaborately illustrated and bound Bible volumes for home use and display. Such Bible editions often contained the words "Family Bible" and were filled with illustrations that favored female biblical figures over male, indicating just how important women were to the Bible industry throughout the nineteenth and early twentieth centuries.[27] Such ornate family Bibles fell out of use by the middle of the twentieth century, but women continued to buy smaller Bible versions that were still bound in high-quality leather.

Although *Revolve* was a Bible edition deeply interested in the female Bible buyer market, it was also a significant step away from the traditional and easily recognized leather-bound Bibles found throughout American female religious print culture. It was a step that the leaders at Nelson were not sure American women would easily take. History had shown that women had long bought Bibles that highlighted the special nature of the book and were clearly identifiable as Bibles. *Revolve* wanted to be something entirely different. Instead of its binding showing it as an expensive, well-made, and attractive book, *Revolve* was targeted to partake of the more ephemeral and disposable magazine culture. Such a change was radically different from the past, and initially, a bit too radical for the Bible editors at Nelson.

More recent Bible production and marketing should have reassured these editors to some degree. *Revolve* was in many ways groundbreaking for the teenage market, but it was not without precedent as a culturally relevant Bible edition. *Revolve* partook of a strain of Bible publishing that moved away from the traditional totemic Bible packaging in favor of a more contemporary look. The single most important Bible edition in this more contemporary strain appeared in the mid-1960s when the ABS produced a small paperback New Testament entitled *Good News for Modern Man*.

In 1966 the ABS released a new modern language Bible translation that it called "Today's English Version" (TEV). The Society had become convinced that there was a need to provide Americans with a new, fresh translation of the Bible that used "strictly modern speech forms and a vocabulary of commonly recognized words" that could be understood regardless of a reader's "level of formal education."[28] Coupled with the desire to provide a new, accessible modern language translation was a desire to make the book inviting through its packaging. Thus, the ABS produced the TEV from the outset in a format that looked like your typical mass-market paperback book. The paperback book market in the United States had exploded in the 1940s and 1950s, and the ABS felt that a new translation would reach readers in part by imitating the friendly look and low cost of a paperback book.[29] Upon its release, *Good News for Modern Man* sold for only a quarter, about half of what paperback novels cost—and one-eighth the cost of traditional Bibles—at the time.

In no way did *Good News for Modern Man* look like a traditional Bible. Instead, it perfectly mimicked the look of a paperback novel. Rather than a plain brown leather cover with gold embossing, *Good News for Modern Man*'s cover encapsulated its goal to be culturally relevant and universal in its application by displaying headlines from across the world. Even the volume's cover signaled that this Bible spoke to the most contemporary events. Further, the ABS gave it the title *Good News for Modern Man* because it wanted readers to know that its new translation was a message applicable to their contemporary lives. Just how radical *Good News for Modern Man* was can be seen in the fact that it was the first-ever American Bible translation presented simultaneously with illustrations developed specifically for the translation by the Swiss artist Amy Vallotton. This new visual element was just one more way that the designers of the *Good News* hoped this Bible would engage a wider range of readers with the biblical text.[30]

Good News for Modern Man proved astronomically popular. The ABS's initial printing of 150,000 copies sold out almost immediately. Within one year, 5 million copies were in print, and in the next twenty-five years, 75 million copies would be in circulation.[31] The culturally relevant Bible edition had arrived with a vengeance, and *Good News for Modern Man* had almost single-handedly inaugurated a trend that coupled relevant language with a new, more contemporary format.

Other, similar culturally relevant Bible editions soon followed, most noticeably *The Way* (1971), an edition targeted to high-school and college-age readers. *The Way* was yet another new modern-language translation Bible edition (this time *The Living Bible* paraphrase) masterminded by Kenneth Taylor, the founder of Tyndale House Publishers.

LUKE 5   163

saw Jesus, he threw himself down and begged him, "Sir, if you want to, you can make me clean!"*
13 Jesus reached out and touched him. "I do want to," he answered. "Be clean!" At once the disease left the man. 14 Jesus ordered him, "Don't tell anyone, but go straight to the priest and let him examine you; then to prove to everyone that you are cured, offer the sacrifice as Moses ordered."
15 But the news about Jesus spread all the more widely, and crowds of people came to hear him and be healed from their diseases. 16 But he would go away to lonely places, where he prayed.

Let him down on his bed into the middle of the group. (Lk 5.19)

Jesus Heals a Paralyzed Man
(Matthew 9.1–8; Mark 2.1–12)

17 One day when Jesus was teaching, some Pharisees and teachers of the Law were sitting there who had come from every town in Galilee and Judea and from Jerusalem. The power of the Lord was present for Jesus to heal the sick. 18 Some men came carrying a paralyzed

MAKE ME CLEAN: This disease was considered to make a person ritually unclean.

Figure 14.4. Front Cover, *Good News for Modern Man*, 1966. Note the newspaper titles in the background of the cover art, signaling the contemporary relevance of the message inside. (Courtesy of the American Bible Society. Library of the Author.)

Figure 14.5. Illustration from Luke, chapter 5, *Good News for Modern Man*, 1966. Note the famous stick figure illustrations created by the Swiss artist Amy Vallotton to accompany the American Bible Society's new translation. (Courtesy of the American Bible Society. Library of the Author.)

Taylor was deeply disturbed by the unrest and distrust of authority felt by much of the nation's youth in the wake of the Vietnam War and the Civil Rights Movement, and he sought to capitalize on the spiritual hunger these societal cataclysms had caused by providing young Americans with a Bible edition that highlighted the social activism of Jesus and the relevance of his message as a catalyst for cultural as well as spiritual change.[32]

Within five years, *The Way* had sold almost five million copies as young readers were drawn to its contemporary illustrations and a format that sought to address their world.[33] *The Way* is filled with dozens of photographs of young people placed next to scripture passages in such a way as to link the contemporary setting to the biblical message. For example, activists are shown addressing groups of teenagers concerning topics such as "Protest: a Right and a Responsibility."[34] The opening page of the Gospel of Mark contains a short essay entitled "Be a Rebel with a Cause," which tells readers that Christ was "the greatest spiritual Activist who ever lived." By positioning Christ as a meaningful example of protest and cultural engagement, *The Way* sought to appeal to the cause-oriented American youth of the late 1960s and early 1970s.[35]

Thus, *Revolve* was not a new concept in its desire to speak to a contemporary audience through its modern language translation and formatting choices. It was clearly rooted in the culturally relevant Bible tradition pioneered by *The Good News, Good News for Modern Man* and *The Way*. It is a Bible edition bent on taking the traditional Bible message and placing it before readers in a nontraditional, culturally relevant format. Thus hundreds of double-columned pages with small print are replaced with a presentation that is more inviting to the ordinary reader. Making such changes to the Bible's formatting, however, is not without its consequences, and some of these consequences can be seen as standing at cross-purposes with the message that format is meant to convey.

Revolve and Its Interpretive Consequences

While a "culturally relevant" Bible might engage new or hesitant readers with the biblical text, the interpretative consequences of its formatting choices are profound. In the end, one must question whether or not the new form really delivers what it promises. Are readers attracted and moved to engage the text through such formatting strategies, or is the very text they are supposed to be drawn to simply overwhelmed and deemphasized through the editorial choices made in presenting the Gospel message to modern-day readers? Such a question moves center stage when considering *Revolve*. In order for *Revolve* to be part and parcel of the teenage girls' magazine culture, the volume's editors included a number of extras such as "Guys Speak Out," "TOPten" lists, "Beauty Secrets," "Blabs" (which deal with such issues as kissing and having sex in a friendly question-and-answer format), short biographical snippets of Bible characters, calendars, and numerous quizzes on everything from whether you are dating a "Godly guy" to what your spiritual gifts might be. Placing such sidebar items in juxtaposition with the biblical text on every page continually distracts the reader's attention from the scriptural content.

Even the most casual reader will notice that on page after page, the actual biblical text in *Revolve* is crowded out by the apparatus that surrounds it. It becomes just one text among many. Here, it may be helpful to think of what one might call a reader's interpretative energy when he or she tries to makes sense of a page of text. If a page contains only a single column of words, the vast majority of the reader's interpretative energy will be spent on reading the words on that page. If a picture appears with those words, the reader's interpretative energy is divided and redirected by the presence of words and illustration in such close proximity. The reader's view of the picture will be informed by the accompanying words, and the interpretation of the words will be influenced by the presence of the picture. If several pictures, sidebars, or other formatting inclusions accompany a text, a reader's interpretative energy is again redirected to attempt to make sense of the various texts both singularly and then in combination. Such a combination of textual elements works both to create new texts by combining the many different texts and meanings on a page, and it also serves to diffuse the attention and importance placed on any single given textual element found on a page.[36]

Such diffusion has particular importance when it comes to sacred texts. Sacred texts position themselves as more than simply words on a page. For believers, they are words that are divine in origin and have meanings that claim far more importance than the words one encounters in a best-selling novel or a morning newspaper. For Christians, this view is summarized well in the core sentiment of Matthew 24:35: heaven and earth may pass away, but the word of God will not. The claim is toward total importance, and the call of those words is for unmitigated

allegiance. Both this importance and allegiance are potentially undercut by the way in which culturally relevant Bibles such as *Revolve* present
the sacred words of a divine scripture to the reader.

The choice to offer readers the biblical text in a format similar to a
grocery store checkout line magazine downplays the significance of these
sacred words. No longer are they offered in a format that underlines
their transcendent importance. They are presented like so many other
words that teenage girls daily encounter in their magazine reading. Far
from underlining the text's importance, the ephemeral nature of the
magazine format can easily signal to a reader that the words they present are of a temporal and transient nature.

Bible editions that strive for cultural relevance can undercut the significance of their text in yet another way: offering material alongside the
text that does not match the content or help explain the meaning of
the sacred text in the volume. In this regard, it is instructive to consider the pictures that help illustrate *Revolve*. The briefest examination of
this Bible-zine's photographic illustrations shows that these illustrations
are almost completely dominated by pictures of young people—mostly
women, mostly white, and almost entirely good-looking and smiling.

Two aspects of the volume's illustrations are particularly worthy of
notice. First, any kind of diversity one might find in the text concentrating on features such as economic income, status in society, occupation,
race, or even age is completely left out in such pictures. For example,
that the Gospel of Luke is deeply concerned with society's poor, elderly,
and the socially disenfranchised is in no way reflected in the pictures
that accompany this particular gospel in *Revolve*. Some fifty-eight faces
of young people serve as the sole photographic illustrations to the forty-
seven pages of text. The message of these illustrations is relentlessly
young and upbeat, while the tone and message of the Gospel is much
more sober and varied. Juxtaposed to the text of Jesus's crucifixion is a
picture of five smiling white girls. The biblical message is one of tragedy
and sadness at this point in Christ's life; the parallel picture is one of
convivial mirth and camaraderie.

Such a vivid juxtaposition suggests a second noteworthy attribute of
Revolve's formatting strategy. American Bible publishers have long used
illustrations to contextualize a given passage with historical material or
pictures that represent the action of the text. Passages on the crucifixion
would often have accompanying pictures of Jesus on the cross. What is

more, Bibles often became quasi-encyclopedias of biblical knowledge, presenting to their readers extended excursuses and pictures on biblical flora and fauna, biblical customs and occupations, ancient cities, and historical events such as battles or celebrations. *Revolve*'s strategy, and the strategy of culturally relevant Bibles more generally, is to use pictures to draw the reader into the text by echoing the present, not the past. They offer the already familiar rather than seeking to make the strangeness of the biblical text and its context more familiar through illustrative pictures and essays. Culturally relevant Bibles seek to give readers illustrations that invite comfort and imitation. Beautiful smiling women are subjects that many readers would like to be or associate with. Disconcerting scenes involving people who are seriously ill, demon possessed, poor, persecuted, and suffering thus fall out of the text. As a consequence, *Revolve* deemphasizes many of the core attributes of Jesus's ministry.

Also missing from many culturally relevant Bibles such as *Revolve* is what one might term more educative material focused on explaining various biblical passages. Such exposition, found most often in footnotes, marginal commentary, maps, and pictures, is a staple of nineteenth- and twentieth-century editions. The educative glosses found in *Revolve* are of an entirely different nature. Readers are still guided by sidebars and illustrations, but they rarely focus on the historical context, or even the content, of the accompanying text. In *Revolve*, when Jesus is prophesying about the fall of Jerusalem with such dire warnings as: "How terrible it will be for women who are pregnant or have nursing babies! Great trouble will come upon this land, and God will be angry with these people" (Luke 21:23), the accompanying illustration shows a smiling young man in a graduation robe defining his ideal girl as someone who is: "Cute, adventurous, athletic, and [has] a great personality."[37] The sidebar about the young's man preference concerning women can certainly be engaging and even help guide the reader's own thoughts on what a perfect young lady might be like, but they have little to do with Jesus's dire predictions about the future of Jerusalem.

The formatting and illustration strategy of *Revolve* is targeted in directions different from historical or biblical exposition of the text. *Revolve*'s apparatus seeks to speak to its readers in a given cultural moment by being contemporary, inviting, and relevant. In attempting to be so reader centered, these Bible editions risk becoming quickly outdated.

They need to constantly evolve and be reissued to stay contemporary with their readership. For example, Tyndale's 1971 *The Way* was tremendously popular at the end of the Vietnam War era, with its stress on social activism and the relevance of Jesus as a rebel determined to change society, but everything about this Bible edition, from the socially active emphasis to the dated hairstyles and clothing in its illustrations, ensured that it would have a brief shelf life. As social activism gave way to the hedonism and consumerism of the late 1970s, *The Way* became sorely dated and its sales slumped.

Yet another consequence of the emphasis on cultural relevance and of modifying the biblical format to match the contemporary moment is that the biblical text itself can come to be seen as just as dated as the accompanying images and words. Are the designers of culturally relevant Bibles such as *Revolve* sending the message that the Word of God can become similarly dated and out of step with an ever-changing society?

Finally, the publishers of culturally relevant Bibles such as *Revolve* have become increasingly dependent on market research to formulate their content and presentation. Focus groups are employed and editors carefully solicit reader feedback as to what they find appealing and useful and what they do not. *Revolve* has taken such market-sensitive formatting to a whole new level as changes in publishing technology enable the editors to jiggle content from printing to printing, enabling *Revolve* to change with each printing iteration. Thanks to reader feedback, the *Revolve* that was released in July 2003 differed from printings released only a few months later. One example of this market sensitivity can be seen in how *Revolve*'s editors have quickly removed sections that proved unpopular among their readers. In early printings of *Revolve*, for example, young women were told that it is not proper to telephone guys. Guys should do the calling. The uproar over this rather conservative stance was such that the editors decided to remove it from later editions of the magazine.[38]

Early American publishers were far less likely to have the market dictate the interpretative comments found in their Bibles. Interpretative apparatus was largely directed in early editions by clergy and other ecclesiastical authorities who credentialed Bible editions and made certain that their commentary helped readers toward a specific theological stance. Well-known examples of this practice include Scott's study Bible of the early nineteenth century, which championed a brand of conservative Calvinism, the heavily annotated Catholic Bible editions of the mid-nineteenth century, and Scofield's Study Bible of the early twenti-eth century, which made famous a distinct type of eschatology.[39]

Revolve is driven by no such theological mandate. Instead, its content is dictated by readers to a degree largely unknown until the late decades of the twentieth century. Thus, editorial staff members, design teams, and readers are dictating the content of the material that surrounds a biblical translation to an unprecedented degree. With this latest itera-tion of the culturally relevant Bible, long gone are the days when an ed-ucated or God-ordained elite were the guiding lights behind a certain type of Bible edition that sought to make sense of the biblical message for the masses. Again, the mutability of the message becomes an issue in seeking to meet the needs of a contemporary, selected readership.

Conclusion

Ultimately, the formatting decisions involved in producing a Bible edi-tion such as *Revolve* can be seen as a metaphor for the place of the Bible more generally in contemporary American culture. Just as the words of scripture that believers revere as sacred are crowded out from the central view of the reader when they encounter the biblical words on *Revolve*'s pages, so, too, are the Bible's words crowded from any central role in broader segments of American culture. One can easily miss the reality that an attempt to make the words of scripture more relevant may just as easily be undercutting the importance of those words, mak-ing them less relevant in the lives of readers.

Close examinations of Bible editions such as *Revolve* remind us that the medium is critical to the message itself. An attempt to make a sacred text more "timely" can also work against that very purpose, denying a text its greatest strength—an aura of timeless uniqueness—and con-demning it to cultural obsolescence. The goal of market penetration might lead to an expanded readership in the short term, but it can also lead to various forms of interpretative dilution. In the end, the Bible's message may not be destroyed, but it is inevitably reshaped as the me-dium that carries that message is transformed. How medium and mes-sage interact is something that every reader, publisher, and student of sacred texts must keep in mind to assess whether the form in which a message is presented might, in the end, undercut both that message and its mission.

Notes

1. Pat Harris, "Bible-Zine for Boys Set for Easter Launch," http://story .news.yahoo.com/news?story&cid=572 (accessed 16 March 2004).

2. Agnieszka Tennant, "Ten Things You Should Know About the New Girls' Biblezine," http://www.christianitytoday.com/ct/2003137/21 .ohtml (accessed 16 September 2003).

3. Phone interview with Kate Etue, 2 June 2005.

4. Jim Remsen, "A new spin on the Bible," *The Philadelphia Inquirer,* http:// www.philly.com/mld/inquirer/living/religion/6634674.html (accessed 28 August 2003).

5. For an insightful analysis of William Tyndale and his translation's influence, see David Daniell, *William Tyndale: A Biography* (New Haven, CT: Yale University Press, 2001).

6. Paul C. Gutjahr, *An American Bible: A History of the Good Book in the United States, 1777–1880* (Stanford: Stanford University Press, 1999), 193–94.

7. Alexander Campbell, *The Sacred Writings of the Apostles and Evangelists of Jesus Christ: Commonly Styled the New Testament* (Buffaloe, VA: Printed by Alexander Campbell, 1826), iii.

8. Ibid., iv–v.

9. Cecil K. Thomas, *Alexander Campbell and His New Version* (St. Louis, MO: The Bethany Press, 1958), 62.

10. For brief, yet informative, treatments of the popularity of study and specialty Bibles in the United States, see "A Bible for Everybody: The Niche Phenomenon," *Publishers Weekly,* 9 October 1995, 58ff.; Nick Harrison, "Sacred Texts: It's Still the Good Book," *Publishers Weekly,* 13 October 1997, 32–40; "Niche Bibles: Good News and Bad News," *The Christian,* June 1996, 6; Glenn Paauw, "What's So Special About Specialty Bibles?" *The Banner,* 19 February 1996, 12–15.

11. For a good, although brief, overview of contemporary Christian and Bible publishing in the United States, see Allan Fisher, "Evangelical-Christians Publishing," *Publishing Research Quarterly* 14, no. 3 (Fall 1998): 1–12.

12. For an overview of the technological changes in printing during this period, see Edward Webster, *Print Unchained: Fifty Years of Digital Printing, 1950– 2000 and Beyond—A Saga of Invention and Enterprise (*New Castle, DE: Oak Knoll Press, 2000), 129–81.

13. Informative accounts on the creation and popularity of *The Good News* can be found in William F. Asbury, "A Publication Milestone: The Illustrated New Testament—a five year project—has now been completed," *Bible Society Record* 100, no. 5 (May 1955): 84–85; and Francis C. Stifler, "Illustrated Gospel of St. Luke: A New Departure in the American Bible Society's Production of Gospel Portions," *Bible Society Record* 95, no. 7 (September 1950): 100–101.

14. For a history of the American Bible Society tradition of producing editions of the Bible "without note or comment," see Gutjahr, *American Bible*, 29–30.

15. Margaret Hills, *The English Bible in America* (New York: American Bible Society, 1962), 422.

16. *American Bible Society Annual Report* (New York: American Bible Society, 1954), 138, 31–32.

17. Phone interview with Kate Etue, 2 June 2005.

18. Ibid.

19. Ibid.

20. A succinct overview of early women's magazine culture in the United States can be found in John Tebbel and Mary Ellen Zuckerman, *The Magazine in America, 1741–1990* (New York: Oxford University Press, 1991), 27–38.

21. Alison Stein Wellner, "The Female Persuasion," *American Demographics* 24, no. 2 (February 2002): 24.

22. Ibid. There has been much recent work on American women and their engagement with magazines. Informative studies in this regard include Carolyn Kitch, *The Girl on the Magazine Cover: The Origins of Visual Stereotypes in American Mass Media* (Chapel Hill: University of North Carolina Press, 2001); Amy Erdman Farrell, *Yours in Sisterhood:* Ms. *Magazine and the Promise of Popular Feminism* (Chapel Hill: University of North Carolina Press, 1998); and Mary Ellen Zuckerman, *A History of Popular Women's Magazines in the United States, 1792–1995* (Westport, CT: Greenwood Press, 1998).

23. Wellner, "The Female Persuasion," 24.

24. Phone interview with Kate Etue, 2 June 2005.

25. Ibid.

26. A substantial body of work underscores the numerical dominance of women over men in American Christianity. For a brief overview of this research, see Roger Finke and Rodney Stark, *The Churching of America, 1776–1990* (New Brunswick, NJ: Rutgers University Press, 1992), 35.

27. A more thorough discussion of women and their relationship to the American Bible market can be found in Gutjahr, *American Bible*, 69–88.

28. Folder "Historical Essays TEV—Secondary Material," RG 53, Box 2, Historical Essays, Studies Nos. 1–15, American Bible Society Archives, NY. John D. Erickson, "The Today's English Version: A Bible for Today's Church" (n.d.), 3, American Bible Society Archives, NY.

29. The standard history of the rise of the popularity of the paperback in American print culture is Kenneth C. Davis, *Two-Bit Culture: The Paperbacking of America* (Boston, MA: Houghton Mifflin, 1984).

30. Folder "Historical Essays TEV—Secondary Material," RG 53, Box 2, Historical Essays, Studies Nos. 1–15, American Bible Society Archives, NY, 2.

31. Ibid., 2, 12.

32. Ken Taylor, *My Life: A Guided Tour* (Wheaton, IL: Tyndale House, 1991), 257.

33. Sales statistic taken from *The Way: An Illustrated Edition of The Living Bible* (Wheaton, IL: Tyndale House, July 1976 [17th printing]), title page.

34. *The Way: An Illustrated Edition of The Living Bible* (Wheaton, IL: Tyndale House, 1971), 833.

35. Ibid., 832–33.

36. Helpful scholarly discussions on the interplay between juxtaposed visual and verbal texts include W. J. T. Mitchell, ed., *Iconology: Image, Text, Ideology* (Chicago: University of Chicago Press, 1987), and J. Hillis Miller, *Illustration* (Cambridge, MA: Harvard University Press, 1992).

37. *Revolve: The Complete New Testament* (Nashville, TN: Thomas Nelson, 2003), 121.

38. Jim Remsen, "New Spin on the Bible"; phone interview with Kate Etue, 2 June 2005.

39. Treatments of these popular study Bibles can be found in Gutjahr, *American Bible*, 125–36, and Joseph M. Canfield, *The Incredible Scofield and His Book* (Vallecito, CA: Ross House Books, 1988).

Contributors

PAUL S. BOYER is Merle Curti Professor of History emeritus at the University of Wisconsin–Madison. Among his publications are: *When Time Shall Be No More: Prophecy Belief in Modern American Culture* (1994); *By the Bomb's Early Light: American Thought and Culture at the Dawn of the Atomic Age* (1985); *Urban Masses and Moral Order in America, 1820–1920* (1978); *Purity in Print: Book Censorship in America from the Gilded Age to the Computer Age* (2nd ed. 2002 [orig. 1968]); and with Stephen Nissenbaum, *Salem Possessed: The Social Origins of Witchcraft* (1974), which won the Dunning Prize from the American Historical Association.

CANDY GUNTHER BROWN is associate professor of religious studies at Indiana University. She is the author of *The Word in the World: Evangelical Writing, Publishing, and Reading in America, 1789–1880* (2004) and is writing a cultural history of spiritual healing in America. She has won the Sidney E. Mead Prize from the American Society of Church History, the John Clive Teaching Prize from Harvard University, and an Outstanding Junior Faculty Award from Indiana University.

CHARLES L. COHEN is professor of history and religious studies at the University of Wisconsin–Madison and director of the Lubar Institute for the Study of the Abrahamic Religions. He has recently published articles on Mormonism as well as religion in colonial America. He is currently coediting two books, *Theology and the Soul of the Liberal State* and a volume on religious pluralism in modern America.

KARLYN CROWLEY is assistant professor of English and director of women's and gender studies at Saint Norbert College. Her current project, "When Spirits Take Over: Gender and American New Age Culture," investigates how a decline in certain public feminisms in the United States has led to a rise in a popular and yet more private "female-centered" spirituality. A recent article from this project includes "Gender on a Plate: The Calibration of

Identity in American Macrobiotics," *Gastronomica: The Journal of Food and Culture* (August 2002).

EDWARD B. DAVIS is professor of the history of science at Messiah College (Grantham, PA), where he teaches courses on historical and contemporary aspects of Christianity and science. Mainly known for his work on the scientific revolution of the seventeenth century, Dr. Davis edited (with Michael Hunter) *The Works of Robert Boyle*, 14 vols. (1999–2000). He has also written several articles on the history of religion and science in America, including an essay about the Dover intelligent design trial in *Religion in the News* (Winter 2006).

PAUL C. GUTJAHR is associate professor of English, American studies, and religious studies at Indiana University. Along with numerous articles and book chapters, he is the author of *An American Bible: A History of the Good Book in the United States, 1777–1880* (1999). He has also coedited *Illuminating Letters: Essays on Typography and Literary Interpretation* (2001) and edited an anthology entitled *American Popular Literature of the Nineteenth-Century* (2001).

MATTHEW S. HEDSTROM is a 2007–2008 postdoctoral research associate in the Center for the Study of Religion at Princeton University. He has previously taught American studies, U.S. history, and religious studies at Valparaiso University, where he was a Lilly Fellow in humanities and the arts, and the University of Texas at Austin, where he received his Ph.D. in American studies. Currently, he is finishing a book project on the role of print culture in the shaping of spirituality in the 1920s, 1930s, and 1940s.

GARI-ANNE PATZWALD is a freelance archivist and editor. She is the author of *Waiting for Elijah: A History of the Megiddo Mission* (2002) and associate editor of *The Historical Dictionary of the Holiness Movement* (2001). She divides her time between Hillsboro, Kansas, and Clark County, Wisconsin.

JONATHAN Z. S. POLLACK is instructor of history at Madison Area Technical College. His current project focuses on Madison, Wisconsin, as a site for examining how higher education transformed Jewish communities that had been founded by immigrant entrepreneurs. Previous research on this subject was published as "Jewish Problems: Eastern and Western Jewish Identities in Conflict at the University of Wisconsin, 1919–1941," *American Jewish History* 89:2 (2001). He is a coeditor (with Jonathan Rees) of *The Voice of the People: Primary Sources on the History of American Labor, Industrial Relations, and Working-Class Culture* (2004).

JAMES EMMETT RYAN is associate professor of English at Auburn University. His essays on religion in American literature and culture have appeared recently in *American Literary History, Studies in American Fiction, American Quarterly,* and *Religion and American Culture*. Currently, he is researching early histories of the Religious Society of Friends.

RENNIE B. SCHOEPFLIN is professor of history and chair of the history department at California State University, Los Angeles. He is the author of *Christian Science on Trial: Religious Healing in America* (2003). He is currently writing a monograph that examines changing American understandings of the relationship among natural law, God's providence, and God's goodness as revealed by an examination of their explanations for earthquakes and other natural disasters.

ERIN A. SMITH is associate professor of American studies and literature and associate director of the gender studies program at the University of Texas at Dallas. Her first book, *Hard-Boiled: Working-Class Readers and Pulp Magazines* (2000), examined popular readers of pulp detective stories in the early twentieth century. She is currently working on a study of twentieth-century American religious best sellers and their readers.

WILLIAM VANCE TROLLINGER JR. is associate professor of history and director of graduate programs in religious studies at the University of Dayton, where he has also served as director of the core integrated studies program and humanities fellow. His recent publications include "An Outpouring of 'Faithful' Words: Protestant Publishing in the United States, 1880–1945," in *A History of the Book in America*, vol. 4, *Print in Motion: The Expansion of Publishing and Reading in the United States, 1880–1945*, ed. Carl F. Kaestle and Janice A. Radway (forthcoming); "Protestantism and Fundamentalism," in *The Blackwell Companion to Protestantism*, ed. A. E. McGrath and D. C. Marks (Blackwell, 2003); and "Is There a Center to American Religious History?" *Church History* (June 2002).

DAVID J. WHITTAKER is the curator of nineteenth-century Western and Mormon manuscripts, L. Tom Perry Special Collections, Harold B. Lee Library, and associate professor of history, Brigham Young University, Provo, Utah. He was the William F. Fulbright Senior Fellow, David and Mary Eccles Centre for American Studies, British Library, 1993–94, and is a past president of the Mormon History Association (1995–96). He serves as a member of the Board of Directors of the Society for the History of Authorship, Reading and Publishing (SHARP) and is currently an editor for the forthcoming multivolume series the "Papers of Joseph Smith." His most recent publications include *Studies in Mormon History, 1830–1997: An Indexed Bibliography* (2000), and *Mormon History* (2002), both coauthored with James B. Allen and Ronald W. Walker.

Index